JAPAN

ITS HISTORY AND CULTURE

Frontispiece:

Sword guard (*tsuba*), eighteenth century; copper and other alloys with gold incrustation. Ht., 3$\frac{1}{16}$ in.

A general (left) is bracing his bow against a rock, while a soldier looks on and another soldier holds a standard. The general is probably Minamoto Yoshiiye, who with his father fought in the bitter Nine Years War beginning A.D. 1051 in northern Japan. He was nicknamed by the soldiers Hachiman Taro, Firstborn of the God of War.

Collection of The Newark Museum. Photography by Keith Scott Morton

JAPAN
ITS HISTORY AND CULTURE
FOURTH EDITION

W. SCOTT MORTON
J. KENNETH OLENIK

McGraw-Hill, Inc.

New York   Chicago   San Francisco
Lisbon   London   Madrid   Mexico City
Milan   New Delhi   San Juan   Seoul
Singapore   Sydney   Toronto

16 17 18 19 20 DOC/DOC 1 9 8 7 6 5

ISBN 0-07-141280-8

McGraw-Hill books are available at special quantity discounts to use as premiums and sales promotions, or for use in corporate training programs. For more information, please write to the Director of Special Sales, Professional Publishing, McGraw-Hill, Two Penn Plaza, New York, NY 10121-2298. Or contact your local bookstore.

 This book is printed on recycled, acid-free paper containing a minimum of 50% recycled, de-inked fiber.

Library of Congress Cataloging-in-Publication Data

Morton, W. Scott (William Scott)
  Japan : its history and culture / W. Scott Morton, J. Kenneth Olenik.—4th ed.
    p. cm.
  Includes bibliographical references and index.
  ISBN 0-07-141280-8 (alk. paper)
1. Japan—History.   I. Olenik, J. Kenneth.   II. Title.
  DS835.M64 2005
  952—dc22
                                                        2004012713

CONTENTS

ILLUSTRATIONS

FOREWORD

Japan's history and culture are strikingly individual, but they are no less remarkable for the influence of the cultures of China and the West. Periods of dramatic institutional change have alternated with those of appropriation and domestication of the institutions introduced into Japan, and the end result was usually very different from the import.

In the seventh century Chinese models of government, and especially the figure of the sovereign, were soon modified to fit Japanese realities. The modern monarchy bore even less resemblance to the German pattern on which it had initially been cut. Less strikingly, but no less surely, Japan's Buddhism, Confucianism, art, and literature resonated to emphases different from those of China. Throughout all cultural change a consistent and distinctive sensitivity and selectivity—in views of nature, time, and space and in values of honor, loyalty, and sincerity—distinguished Japan's great tradition of art, letters, and especially poetry.

In modern times the pace of change has quickened and the tide of influence has broadened, but the pattern of selective adaptation of outside example remains visible. The flood of Western influence in the nineteenth century brought a period of tumultuous change. In politics the national resolve to restore autonomy and equality had dramatic influence on the international system. As the first non-Western state to modernize its institutions Japan struggled first to join and then to defeat Western colonialism. It succeeded as it failed, and helped end all colonialisms including its own. Thereafter Japanese leaders and citizens turned to pursue new goals of social justice and economic gain with a vigor that is today transforming the international economic order as thoroughly as the earlier drive to great power status that remade the international political order.

These pendulum swings of enthusiasm should not, however, distract attention from the more important and consistent process of development within Japanese society. The political events that attract the reader's attention illumine, but did not cause, that process. It was one in which Japan moved from an aristocratic, to a feudal, to an urban, and finally to a mass society. Japanese society has been revolutionized without internal revolution in response to modern knowledge and technology, and within a century a society structured on lines of hereditary privilege has been transformed into a mass society with an unusually even income distribution, one in which the prizes are reserved for a meritocracy of talent selected on the basis of educational attainment. As a result Japan's experience of transformation and resilience forces itself upon the attention of the world. It invites a rethinking of theories and explanations of the modern world that have hitherto been based upon the experience of the Atlantic states.

Professor Morton's brisk narrative provides a pleasing entrance into that experience and helps to make its outlines accessible to readers in several lands and several languages. One welcomes this edition and hopes that it will find wide use.

Marius B. Jansen
Professor of History and East Asian Studies
Princeton University

PREFACE TO THE FOURTH EDITION

There is an important change to be noted with the issue of the fourth edition of this book. Professor J. Kenneth Olenik of the history department at Montclair State University, New Jersey, joins me as coauthor. *Japan: Its History and Culture* was originally published in 1970, has been in continuous use as a college text as well as a book for the general reader, and has been updated in new editions in 1984 and 1994. It is quite clear by this time that the book needs the input of someone more familiar with the Japan of 2004 than I. Professor Olenik has kindly agreed to update this history with new material in the last chapters. With a doctorate from Cornell University, long periods of residence and study in both Japan and China, and considerable teaching experience in teaching and writing about East Asia, he is well qualified for giving a close-up picture of present-day Japan.

In previous editions of the book I made the point that my aim was to give approximately equal emphasis to all periods, ancient and modern, in Japanese history. With a lapse of over thirty years since the first edition it is obvious that the addition of new and up-to-date material has made completely equal treatment impossible. We have endeavored, however, in this fourth edition to connect the past with the present, and to trace a continuity in the flow of Japanese cultural history.

The relative order of surname and given name in Japanese presents a slight problem. Traditionally the surname came first, while the present practice is, for the most part, to place the surname last. As in earlier editions, in the interests of simplicity and consistency with historical Japanese practice, surnames have been placed first throughout this text.

I owe a debt of gratitude to several friends who have helped in the preparation of this and earlier editions. I am grateful to the late Dr. John L. Mish, director of the Oriental and Slavonic Divisions of the New York Public Library; Professor H. Paul Varley, Columbia University; Allen Wardwell and Robert D. Mowry of the Asia Society; William H. Gleysteen Jr., president of the Japan Society; Ohtsuka Seiichiro and Idaka Ikuo of the Japanese Consulate General in New York; and officials of the Japan National Tourist Organization.

I should also like to thank Professor Fujioka Nobukatsu of the Faculty of Education of Tokyo University; Professor Kenneth Olenik of Montclair State University, New Jersey; Joan Hartman Goldsmith, director of the Institute for Asian Studies, New York; Professor James Shields, City College, New York; and Trish Foley.

My son, Keith Scott Morton, and his wife, Christine Churchill, provided the frontispiece illustration, with the kind permission of Valrae Reynolds of the Newark Museum. I am also grateful for the generous help of the museums and organizations that have provided me with illustrations.

Special thanks go once again to Professor Ardath W. Burks of Rutgers University for introductions which he has given me, for kindly reading and commenting on the new text, and for his friendship over many years. Responsibility for what is in the text rests upon the author alone.

W. Scott Morton
New York

JAPAN

ITS HISTORY AND CULTURE

JAPAN

Oki

MAEDA

ECHIGO

KANAZAWA

Tsushima Islands

Iki

Hakata
Bay

CHOSHU

HIROSHIMA

IKEDA

ECHIZEN

HONSHU

HIRADO

SHIMONOSEKI

DAN-NO-URA

ASANO

IKEDA

Mt. Hiei

Lake Biwa

SEKIGAHARA

HIZEN

KOBE

KYOTO

OTSU

AZUCHI

OWARI

NAGASAKI

Inland Sea

YASHIMA

ICHI-NO-TANI

OSAKA

NARA

NAGOYA

Mt. Fuji

KOFU

KYUSHU

SHIKOKU

SAKAI

SHIZUOKA

HAKONE

Shimabara
Peninsula

HOSOKAWA

TOSA

Awaji
Is.

YOSHINO

KII

KAMAKURA

SATSUMA

Ise
Peninsula

KAGOSHIMA

Tanegashima Islands

HOKKAIDO

SAPPORO

HAKODATE

AOMORI

DATE

NIIGATA   SENDAI

MITO

MITO

TOKYO
KAWASAKI
YOKOHAMA

Names of main islands and city names in Roman capitals
Han or fief names in italic capitals
Other geographical features in upper and lower case type

0   100   200   300
KILOMETERS

INTRODUCTION

According to Japanese legends the people of Japan are descended from the Sun Goddess. Not only so, but the land itself is characterized as divine. Looking down from a pine-clad promontory onto the glinting waters and clustered islands of the Inland Sea, or up to the snow-capped cone of Mount Fuji rising out of swirling mist and surrounded at its base by the vivid green of fertile rice fields, it is easy to understand how the early Japanese might have come to feel this sense of immanent divinity. For natural beauty of scenery, Japan has few equals. Its people are a distinctive group, conscious of their heritage, having some ties with the mainland but living their separate life as an island people.

The main elements of Japanese higher culture are derived from China. But the Japanese are not alone in this. China has for long been the dominant power all over East Asia, not merely by virtue of its size or its large population, but because of its superior culture. Tibet, Mongolia, Korea, and parts of Southeast Asia, as well as Japan, have been accustomed to look to China as a source of leadership and inspiration, a cultural stimulus, and a cultural storehouse.

Japanese culture is nevertheless distinctive. One of the most intriguing features of the Japanese people is their capacity to borrow and adapt and yet to retain their own individuality and their own style. Thus though they are heavily indebted to China for the shape of their culture, what emerges is distinctively Japanese. They have always shown great powers of converting borrowed material to their special purposes, purposes conceived deep within their own national consciousness, and so of molding a culture that no one could think was anything but Japanese.

These purposes, this style and stamp, do not yield themselves up to superficial inquiry. Students of Japan must submit themselves to a soaking pro-

1

cess. They must steep themselves in all aspects of Japanese history, language, and life, and this is not easy to do, especially if it must be done without the benefit of residence in Japan. The process of assimilating the spirit of an alien culture is always difficult, but special difficulties attend those who want to understand Japan. To the blunt Westerner the Japanese seem to exhibit at every turn a preference for the indirect—indirectness of statement in the language, indirectness in social life for politeness's sake, and indirect rule in politics, exercised through an anonymous group ruling in the name of a figurehead. Nevertheless there is every incentive to study Japan, for rich rewards in the form of the beautiful, the intriguing, the terrible, and the exotic are scattered profusely along the uphill path.

The history of Japan is like its language, apparently simple in the first stages of acquaintance but growing rapidly more complex and subtle the further one penetrates the mysterious regions of idiom and thought process. So it is also true to say that Japanese history has at first a simplicity of outline but on deeper analysis presents a Sphinx face of stubborn mystery. It seems simple at first because the country is smaller and the span of recorded history shorter than those of the vast neighbor, China. But the intentional indirectness already referred to in the Japanese character and the gulf fixed between Western and Japanese categories of what is important and valuable make it unusually hard for Western scientific history to lay bare the real character of the chain of Japanese historical experience.

However, by a curious and fortunate process of compensation, it seems possible to make a few valid generalizations. Two characteristics of the Japanese that may be mentioned at the very beginning, to reemerge frequently in the course of this story, are their military, feudal qualities and their natural artistic gifts. It may be because Shinto enshrines and fosters both these characteristics that it has, in spite of its primitive nature, remained strong as a religion down the Japanese centuries.

In an attempt to present the history of Japan to those generally unfamiliar with it, some use will be made in this book of Japanese terms. The process of explaining and filling out the meaning of these terms will serve to illuminate much that would otherwise remain obscure. An author writing about another culture tends instinctively to introduce those terms in the native language which least lend themselves to direct translation and which most typically illustrate the views that the people of the country hold about their own culture. When the subject is an Asian country, this practice may be of more than ordinary value since Asian history can best be approached in terms of the unity of history, language, and culture.

The scholars of both China and Japan, unaware of the division of disciplines customary in the West, were at one and the same time scholars, philosophers, artists, poets, calligraphers, essayists, and often historians. They did not so much conceive of their culture as a unity as never imagine it could be anything else. And this feeling of theirs, though not all their concepts, percolated down to the common people. Their culture must therefore, even in outline form, be studied through all avenues of art, religion, and economic and social life as well as through the avenues more classic in the West, such as political and military history. By trying to recount the outward events of Japanese history always with an eye to the attitude and stance of the chief actors and of the common folk, we may be able to obtain a truer and more rounded view of the whole. We may be able to arrive at some understanding of that remarkable élan which impelled the vigorous Japanese through their long history and projected them suddenly, by their design but perhaps to their surprise, into the forefront of the twentieth-century world.

1

THE ORIGINS AND EARLY HISTORY
OF THE JAPANESE

The origins of the Japanese people are mixed and obscure. One thing is certain: there were other races, of a non-Japanese character, living on the islands of Japan before the arrival of the Japanese themselves. One of these races, the Ainu, has survived, though precariously, to the present day. The Ainu are of Caucasian type, with white skin and profuse beards. Their totem is the bear, and their way of life that of hunters and fishers. For centuries they dominated the northern section of the islands, but they are now reduced to a small group living in Hokkaido.

The Japanese, on the other hand, are of Mongolian race, smaller in stature, with the typical Mongolian features of the fold in the eyelid, a yellow tinge in pigmentation, black hair, faces on the whole flatter than the Caucasian type, high cheekbones, and limbs proportionately short in relation to the trunk. This last feature helps to conserve body heat, which would otherwise be dissipated by long extremities. This, along with the eye fold, which may offer protection against snow glare, is thought by some to point to a reservoir of Mongolian peoples living in prehistoric times in the Siberian north.

But within the Mongolian family at least two more exact areas of origin may be distinguished for those peoples who mingled to form the Japanese race. The first is central Asia. The evidence for this is to be found not only in the physical type already mentioned but also in the language. Japanese in its syllabary (consonant followed by vowel) and in certain roots shows some similarities to Hungarian-Magyar and to Finnish. All three probably stem from a common central Asian source. The second area of origin for one of the Japanese strains is the South China region. This is indicated by certain physical features, such as the comparatively small size, yellower skin, and delicate bone structure of the Japanese, which correspond more closely to the

4

people of South China than to those of North China. Certain items of diet, notably the use of wet rice, also point to a South China origin. There is a third possible strain in the Japanese people, namely one stemming from Southeast Asia and the Pacific islands; but this is controversial. The main argument for it is found in the form of architecture used in old Japanese farmhouses and in the Shinto shrine buildings, for example at Ise. In all these, and in the huts of the dwellers in Malaysia and Polynesia, the main roof beams at the gable ends are not sawed off but allowed to project at the top for a considerable distance in the form of an X. One objection to this theory is that the islanders could never have covered the distance from the South Pacific islands to Japan in open boats and without navigational aids. But the use of a simple coconut shell device for a sextant, with a water level within it to maintain the artificial horizon, might well have allowed adventurous mariners to complete the journey to Japan successfully. Present-day Polynesians in outrigger canoes with similar navigational devices are known to be able to sail immense distances with remarkable accuracy.

What of the land itself in which these people mingled and established themselves? Japan consists of four large islands, running from north to south and then bending in a curve to the west, as follows: Hokkaido, Honshu (the main island), Shikoku, and Kyushu, as well as innumerable small islands. Their total area is about the size of the state of California. If superimposed on the east coast area of the United States, Japan would extend as a narrow sickle curve from the Canadian border to the northern edge of Florida. Honshu greatly exceeds the other three main islands in size, so much so that on the superimposed map it alone would run from the latitude of New York to that of Atlanta, Georgia. The climate exhibits differences corresponding to this long north-south range, from deep winter snows in Hokkaido to semitropical vegetation in Kyushu.

A large proportion of the country is mountainous, leaving only 17 percent of the surface area available for agriculture, with a small extra margin to be squeezed out of the hill slopes by terracing. The three chief agricultural plains of Japan are the Kanto Plain around Tokyo, about 5,000 square miles in extent, the Nobi Plain around Nagoya, and the Kansai Plain around Nara, Kyoto, and Osaka at the eastern end of the Inland Sea. The last two are each only about one-tenth the area of the Kanto Plain.

Abundant rainfall and assiduous industry have enabled the Japanese to survive on the products of their farming, but these have always had to be supplemented by the produce of the sea—fish, shellfish, and edible seaweeds. A study carried out by Japanese scientists during World War II demonstrated that seafood and a small amount of meat, rice, and vegetables, especially the vitamin-rich *daikon* or giant radish, would provide an adequate diet at extremely low cost.

It has been noted that the island situation of Japan is similar to that of Great Britain and that, as a consequence, there are certain parallels to be found in the history of each. Both are islands near enough to a great continent to receive cultural stimuli but just sufficiently isolated to evolve their own ways of life, tolerably free from hostile invasion. Both have developed strong navies, doubtless from reservoirs of skill gained in fishing and trading. Finally, both in modern times have had to make strenuous efforts in manufacture and export trade in order to feed their island populations.

In one respect Japan differs geographically from Britain; her islands with mountains two miles high are perched on the edge of a cleft in the ocean floor five miles in depth known as the Tuscarora Deep. Stresses appear to be thus set up which make Japan extremely liable to earthquakes, some of great severity. There are also a number of active volcanoes on the islands. The perfect cone of Mount Fuji is that of an extinct volcano (the last eruption occurred in 1707); but Mount Asama, for instance, is still active, and alarming sulfurous jets of steam pour out of many fissures in the mountains of central Japan.

In mineral resources Japan is comparatively poor. It has very little iron or oil. Coal is scarce and not of superior quality; only copper is fairly abundant. Premodern Japan was, however, amply supplied from the forest slopes with the woods of various kinds it needed for the construction of houses, temples, and the mansions of the great, in addition to boats and implements of all kinds. Its short, fast-flowing rivers give little help in transportation but provide modern Japan with ample sources of hydroelectric power.

Japan is a comparative latecomer in the development of civilization, since cultural movements reached her after passing eastward from central Asia and China. There are three sources of information about ancient Japan, namely, archaeological evidence; Chinese written records, which are reliable but scanty; and Japanese mythology, which is voluminous but difficult to interpret, since the undoubted historical traces within it are hard to disentangle from the legendary material.

There are only a few evidences of Old Stone Age remains in Japan. The first major culture is dated as mesolithic or Middle Stone Age in its earlier stages, beginning around 3000 B.C. This culture is known as the Jomon, from the Japanese word for "cord pattern" which distinguishes its hand-thrown pottery—that is, pottery not made on a wheel. The Jomon people used stone weapons and lived in sunken-pit dwellings of a kind that are also reported to have existed in early China. They did not practice agriculture but lived by gathering roots, nuts, and small game from the forests and shellfish from the shore. Large mounds of discarded shells are associated with their sites. These sites are most plentiful in the east and north of Japan, a probable indication that the Jomon people survived longer in these regions.

The next culture group appears much later, between 300 and 100 B.C., and is known as the Yayoi, from a site in Tokyo where the early discoveries were made, although in fact this culture was strongest in west Japan. They produced wheel-made pots and certainly practiced agriculture of quite an advanced type, in irrigated rice fields after the Chinese manner. They apparently used both bronze and iron together, and thus Japan cannot be said to have gone through a separate Bronze Age. Presumably Japan, being on the edge of the Asian civilized area, received bronze metal techniques slowly and late, while iron, with its immense technical advantages for weapons and tools, moved more rapidly and caught up with bronze in Japan. Among the Yayoi archaeological remains are mirrors, bells, swords, and spears of bronze, the last being ceremonial weapons; but a few tools and actual weapons made of iron have also been found.

The Yayoi people still used pit dwellings and left shell mounds behind them; but in two respects they showed a remarkable affinity with historical Japan, namely in their method of agriculture and in the thatched roofs over the primitive dwellings. These thatched roofs are clearly depicted in the designs on the large, ornamental bronze bells that are a distinctive feature of Yayoi culture.

About the middle of the third century A.D. the Tomb culture was superimposed upon, though it did not altogether replace, the Yayoi culture. The Tomb culture is marked by the building of stone burial chambers and huge earthen mounds, reaching 1,500 feet in length and 120 feet in height. These tombs and tumuli are similar to burial places in Korea and Northeast Asia and indicate further continental influence in addition to what must have come over to Japan in the earlier periods. The tombs are also indicative of a powerful aristocracy able to command large numbers of workers in their construction. Associated with these tombs are the well-known *haniwa* pottery figures of very hard light-brown or reddish clay representing men, houses, and animals, especially horses. Many of the men are depicted wearing elaborate armor and helmets, and carrying swords whose actual counterparts are known to have been of iron. The greatest number of these tombs is found in the Yamato area, and some of the richest of these were almost certainly tombs of the early emperors of the historic imperial line. But the Yamato people do not begin in Yamato but farther west, and their movement is the first decisive episode traceable, though but faintly, in Japanese history.

The Chinese of the Han dynasty, in their confident phase of military expansion, established a colony in Korea in 108 B.C., conquering a native dynasty that had already absorbed considerable Chinese influence. The Han Chinese thus became more closely aware of Japan, and the visit of a Japanese envoy to the Han court is recorded in A.D. 57. But it is in the Chinese records of the Wei dynasty, a smaller state subsequent to the Han, that we first find some concrete details about Japan, which confirm the other sources and add facts not otherwise known. The *Wei chih* of about A.D. 292 (about the time when the Yayoi and Tomb cultures were overlapping) speaks of the Wa (dwarf) people of regions easily identified as Kyushu and West Japan. These people are said to have lived in one hundred "countries" or tribes, of whom thirty had contact with the Wei court. They are portrayed as having respect for law and as being careful to observe social differences, traits that have persisted in Japanese society. Some social distinctions were indicated by tattooing and other body marks. The Wa are described, moreover, as being fond of liquor and as practicing agriculture, spinning, weaving, and fishing.

Haniwa figure representing a man with a miter-shaped hat.

Ibaraki Prefecture; burial figure, late Tomb period, sixth to seventh century. Reddish buff earthenware. Ht., 56 in. The hilt of a sword that hung from his waist marks his elite profession.

The Asia Society, New York: Mr. and Mrs. John D. Rockefeller 3rd Collection. Photography by Otto E. Nelson

The Chinese records state that the rulers are sometimes male and sometimes female, one powerful sovereign being a certain Queen Himeko or Pimiko, meaning "Daughter of the Sun." This alternation between female and male rulers may indicate a change from matriarchal to patriarchal society. Early Japan shows a number of instances of female rulers. Shamanism, or contact with the spirit world through mediums subject to trances, is known to have been a feature of ancient Japanese religion, and indeed of the early religion of East Asia as a whole. Notions that women are peculiarly subject to emotional states leading to trance may, in addition to a general matriarchal tradition, have made them seem especially desirable as priestess-sovereigns in Japan. Among these queens the Himeko mentioned in the Wei records seems to have been a particularly notable ruler toward the end of the third century.

The Shinto legends, the third source of information about early Japan, represent a primal pair, Izanagi, the male god, and Izanami, his consort, standing on the rainbow bridge of Heaven and dipping a spear into the ocean beneath. Drops of water falling from the tip of the spear congealed to form the sacred islands of Japan. In another version the islands were produced from the union in marriage of the god and goddess. In any case they descended to live on the islands, and they had children who were the gods and goddesses of the land. The last god to be born was the Fire God, and his birth caused the death of Izanami. Izanagi went to seek her in the underworld but found that her body had already decayed. When he returned to the light of day, it was at the "Even-Pass-of-Hades" in Izumo, in the west part of Honshu, the main island, opposite Korea. He purified himself from the pollution of death by washing in a river in Kyushu, and various deities were then born from his person, Amaterasu the Sun Goddess from his left eye, Tsukiyomi the Moon Deity from his right eye, and Susanowo the Storm God from his nose. The Moon Deity plays no prominent role in the subsequent story, but the Sun Goddess and the Storm God, her brother and later her consort, become the most important figures in the Japanese pantheon.

The legends represent Susanowo as an unruly fellow, constantly making trouble. For instance, he broke the boundaries of his sister's rice paddies, a heinous crime in any agricultural community, especially one employing irrigation. He slew the piebald colt of Heaven, flayed it, and insolently threw its skin into the Weaving Hall where the Sun Goddess was working with her maidens. For these deliberate acts of lawlessness and ritual defilement (the blood on the horse skin was defiling), he was banished, some accounts say to the nether regions, others say to Izumo. In Izumo Susanowo, "His Swift Impetuous Male Augustness," rescued a maiden by slaying an eight-tailed dragon, having first made it drunk by providing it with eight vats of wine. In one of its tails he discovered a sword, which became part of the jewel-mirror-sword regalia of Japan. Meantime the Sun Goddess, having been mortally offended by her brother's actions, shut herself up in a cave. Men and gods, distressed by the sun's absence, tried to persuade her to come out, but in vain. At length one of the goddesses uncovered herself and performed an obscene dance on an upturned tub, and all the denizens of Heaven laughed uproariously. The Sun Goddess, overcome with a woman's curiosity, put her head out of the cave to see what was happening. The sight of a mirror further intrigued her, and she was seized and brought out so that once again all the world could rejoice in her light.

These tales reflect the primitive nature worship of a people with some humor and strong feelings, and they have many elements—such as the importance attached to sunshine (Amaterasu), storms and rainfall (Susanowo), eclipses (Amaterasu hiding in a cave), and fertility rites (the dance on the tub)—in common with similar cults all over the world.

Some Shinto legends, in addition to referring to such specific geographical locations as Izumo and Kyushu, also contain references to actual political and military events, thus giving valuable clues to history. Kyushu, an island lying to the south and west of the rest of Japan and also near Korea, would be the first place encountered by incomers from South China and Korea. Archaeological research in fact points to Kyushu as an early site of Japanese civilization; and this is confirmed in the legend which relates that the divine grandson of Amaterasu, Ninigi-no-mikoto, came down from Heaven onto a mountaintop in Kyushu. His great-grandson, in turn, Jimmu-tenno,

Shrine at Ise, early and most revered center of the national religion of Shinto.

This, the inner shrine, in archaic Japanese style, is dedicated to Amaterasu, the Sun Goddess.

Japan Information Center

led an expedition eastward along the south coast of the main island. This expedition slowly worked its way up the Inland Sea, and its members established a domain in the Yamato region, which includes the Ise peninsula, today the site of the most sacred and revered shrines of Shinto.

Section XLIV of the *Kojiki* (the "Record of Ancient Things"), the earliest written collection of the legends and dating from A.D. 712, represents this move as being the result of a definite decision.

> The Emperor Jimmu and his elder brother took counsel saying, "By dwelling in what place shall we most quietly carry on the government of the Empire? It were probably best to go east."

But the advance was not an undisputed one.

> When His Augustness Jimmu-tenno made his progress and reached the great cave of Osaka [not the modern Osaka], earth-spiders with tails, [namely]

eighty braves or robber-chiefs were in the cave awaiting him. . . . He commanded that a banquet be bestowed on the eighty braves.[1]

Eighty butlers, each armed with a sword, were appointed to wait on the braves, and when Jimmu-tenno gave the signal by starting to sing, the butlers set upon the braves and slew them.

This picturesque account may be transposed into something like history by reasonable conjecture as follows: warlike clans, headed by what ultimately became the imperial Yamato clan, deliberately decided to leave Kyushu about the first century A.D., in all probability in search of better agricultural land, and they made their way gradually along the coast of the Inland Sea. This journey probably took more than one generation in time, for they met with resistance from the original inhabitants (earth-spiders equal pit dwellers). The ancient records call Jimmu-tenno (Divine-Warrior Emperor) the first *human* emperor of Japan, descended from divine emperor ancestors. This may be taken as a signal that "historical," individually recognizable events, such as a migration or invasion, have now begun to occur.

Dating in this whole early period is highly conjectural and does not become even moderately reliable until after A.D. 400. The traditional date in the *Kojiki* for the establishment of the throne in Yamato by Jimmu-tenno, at the end of the migration from Kyushu, is 660 B.C.; but this probably antedates the events by some seven to eight hundred years. The migration, it is conjectured, started in the first century A.D., and the imperial clan may have been established as rulers in the Yamato region by the third century or possibly the fourth. The consensus of historians today is that more than a dozen of Japan's reputed earliest emperors are later inventions. Most likely the imperial line began in the fifth or sixth centuries. There is also a strong possibility that Korean blood flows in Japan's imperial veins, as in these early times Koreans were highly respected as nobles and one of the early empresses was Korean.

When the position of the imperial clan was sufficiently stable, its members began promulgating a version of the early legends which exalted the place of the Yamato ancestress, the Sun Goddess, over the Storm God ancestor of the Izumo clan or clans. For instance, Onamuji, an Izumo monarch or god, agreed to serve the Yamato dynasty if a palace or temple were built for him and he were suitably worshipped. His son, Kotoshironushi, supported the claims of Yamato and was greatly honored in Ise as a result. However, traces of the early importance of the Izumo region, geographically opposite the source of immigration and higher civilization in Korea, could not be effaced altogether, even from the slanted Yamato records; witness the entitlement of Susanowo, the Izumo Storm God, to the regalia sword by his prowess, and the elaborate care taken in the records to prove him unworthy of leadership by recounting all his misdeeds and consequent banishment.

---

[1] *Kojiki*, Sections XLIV and XLVIII, both passages in B. H. Chamberlain translation.

Notwithstanding the importance of Yamato, there is evidence that Izumo had a higher level of culture, for a hundred skilled workers in clay are said to have been brought from Izumo to Yamato by one Nomi-no-Sukune. He was the reputed inventor of the *haniwa* clay figures used to take the place of human sacrifices previously buried alive in a standing position at the funerals of the great.

The Yamato-Izumo rivalry may also be the reflection of a transition from matriarchy to patriarchy. If this is so, the interpretation would be somewhat as follows: patriarchy, as represented by the male god of Izumo, was becoming dominant in society over the whole country, but matriarchy (the female divinity of Yamato) was the older tradition and its followers were able to assert its seniority in the field of religion and sacred sovereignty. Heads of families were male figures; yet the headship of the nation was still entrusted from time to time to empresses up to the end of the Asuka period in A.D. 710, but only rarely thereafter.

The whole process of recording and editing the legends indicates that long before A.D. 712, the date of publication of the *Kojiki*, and probably before A.D. 300, the approximate date of the Queen Himeko, of the Chinese records, the Yamato clan leader had become the dominant figure in Japan. Starting simply as *primus inter pares*, he reached the point of claiming a paramount role, a position to be dignified by the name of emperor after the Chinese model. It is this family that has provided in an unbroken line the emperors of Japan from the beginning of the Common era to the present day. Even if allowance is made for freedom in marriage rules and recourse to adoption, this is a remarkable record of solidarity and respect for tradition, one that is unmatched in the history of any other modern nation.

The religion of Shinto, although based on quite primitive animism and nature worship, has survived strongly into modern times. Its strength seems to derive from the natural, almost unconscious way it embodies for the Japanese people their deep feelings for nature and their strong love of country.

Shinto has no founder, no inspired scriptures, no moral code. At first it did not even have a name. The word *shinto* means "the way of the gods" and is a term borrowed from the Chinese language long after the legends mentioned above had become a part of the native folk tradition. The same ideographs in Japanese can be read *kami-no-michi*, and the word *kami* can mean "gods" or simply "those above." To understand the term, Westerners must divest their minds of the ideas of holiness and otherness associated with God in Judeo-Christian tradition. *Kami* are of a simpler sort, and their divinity is associated with anything remarkable or extraordinary in nature: a high mountain; an odd, lone tree; a venerable man; even a queer form of insect life— anything, in fact, to which the term *mana* or the Latin *numen* might be applied. An example of the feeling inspired by *kami* would be the sense of awe yet pleasurable thrill experienced by a child who, in climbing up through a sunlit wood, suddenly comes upon a dark cave in a rock overhung with fir trees.

These gods are worshipped before shrines without images in a simple ritual, with hand clapping and bowing. The gods' presence does produce awe in the worshipper, but Shinto on the whole is a sunny rather than a somber religion. Sir George Sansom refers to this fact in discussing the racial origins of the Japanese:

> It may be that, to wayworn tribes from arid regions of Korea and northern China or inhospitable Siberian plains, the genial climate of Japan, with its profusion of trees and flowering shrubs, its fertile soil, and its wealth of running streams, was so pleasing as to make upon them a profound impression, stored up in the racial consciousness as a pervading sentiment of gratitude. Certainly their religion was, as Aston says, a religion of love and gratitude rather than of fear, and the purpose of their religious rites was to praise and thank as much as to placate and mollify their divinities. The very names given in their mythology to their country—the Land of Luxuriant Reed Plains, the Land of Fresh Rice Ears of a Thousand Autumns; and to their gods— the Princess Blossoming-like-the-Flowers-of-the-Trees, and Her Augustness Myriad-Looms-Luxuriant-Dragonfly-Island—testify to their strong sense of the beauty and richness of their environment.[2]

In accordance with the conception of *kami*, the notion of *tsumi*, "crime or sin," in Shinto is connected with ritual impurity rather than with moral guilt. Ritual impurity or pollution is associated with blood, wounds, death, menstruation, sexual intercourse, and childbirth. The word *kega* signifies both "wound" and "defilement." Lustration or symbolic washing, including rinsing the mouth, is necessary before an act of worship can be performed. There are elements of taboo and animal fetishism in early Shinto which are strongly reminiscent of primitive religion in Africa and elsewhere. For example, a goddess in a birth hut thatched with cormorant feathers was spied upon by her husband as, at the moment of giving birth, she turned into her original shape, that of a crocodile. She was vexed at his behavior, but the pair nonetheless remained faithful to each other and exchanged love poems. The god's poem shines with the Japanese poetic pleasure in nature:

His Augustness Fire-subside said, "As for my younger sister, whom I took to sleep [with me] on the island where light the wild-duck, the birds of the offing, I shall not forget her till the end of my life."[3]

Such were the beliefs of the early Japanese. Their political center was firmly established by the third century A.D. or earlier in the fertile land of the Yamato region. The northern part of the main island was still in possession of the Ainu, but the central and western portions of Japan were controlled by that amalgamation of peoples we know as the Japanese. Their society consisted of a number of semi-independent clans, or *uji*, under the general leadership of the Yamato clan. Each *uji* claimed descent from a com-

[2] G. B. Sansom, *Japan, A Short Cultural History* (London: Cresset Press, 1946), pp. 46–47.
[3] *Kojiki*, Section XLII, B. H. Chamberlain translation.

mon ancestor, worshipped the god of the clan, and was united under a clan chief. This aristocracy of chiefs, however, already had distinctions drawn within it. The *Nihongi*, a book of early chronicles dating from 720, or shortly after the *Kojiki*, distinguishes between the Omi of imperial and the Muraji of nonimperial descent. The Muraji in turn were divided into those who spoke of their descent from "heavenly deities" and others descended from "earthly deities." This last distinction is thought to refer in the former case to clans who joined the Yamato in conquest and in the latter to clans who were forced to submit.

There were also corporations, *be* (or *tomo*, "attendants"), which developed within or were attached to certain *uji*. These groups of workers corresponded closely to the corporations of the late Roman Empire, such as the *navicularii* ("seamen") or *pecuarii* ("cattlemen"), being in both instances hereditary in families but not related throughout the corporation by ties of blood. In early Japan there were *be* of carters, seamen, mountain wardens, and others. The heads of the corporations were ennobled and became important enough to rival the clan aristocracy. One reason for their importance was undoubtedly the fact that land was more plentiful than labor in early Japan and skilled workers of all kinds were in demand. Not only did the workers ply their trade, but the corporation as a whole supported itself by working the land granted to it. Some *be* engaged in agriculture only, and the attachment of either an agricultural or an artisan *be* was of great benefit to the *uji* concerned and to its chief.

Several corporations were associated with the imperial clan, and their heads became nobles of high rank. Among these were the great military groups, the Otomo (Great Attendants) and Mononobe (Corporation of Arms). Others attached to the emperor's house had religious functions, such as the Nakatomi (Medium Ministers), Urabe (Corporation of Diviners), and Imibe (Corporation of Abstainers). The original functions of the Imibe, as mentioned in the Chinese records, reveal more about the taboos of early Shinto. "They appoint a man whom they style 'mourning-keeper' [professional abstainer]. He is not allowed to comb his hair, to wash, to eat meat, or to approach women. When they are fortunate, they make him valuable presents; but if they fall ill or meet with disaster, they set it down to the mourning-keeper's failure to observe his vows and together they put him to death."[4]

Workers in certain specialized crafts could be obtained only from China and Korea, among them brocade weavers and scribes. Such skilled men were readily welcomed in Japan, and their leaders, along with refugee aristocrats fleeing the internal troubles of the mainland, seem to have been accepted without question into the ranks of the Japanese nobility. As Reischauer and Fairbank have pointed out,[5] a book of noble genealogies of 815 shows that

[4] James Murdoch, *A History of Japan* (New York: Frederick Ungar, rev. ed. 1964), Vol. I, pt. I, p. 40.
[5] Edwin O. Reischauer and John K. Fairbank, *East Asia, The Great Tradition* (Boston: Houghton Mifflin, 1958), p. 471.

over 33 percent of 1,182 families of the Yamato nobility were of foreign, that is, mainly of Korean, origin.

There are indications both in archaeology and legend of the existence of close ties and a significant two-way traffic between Korea and early Japan. Korean records support the connection, in rather a negative sense, when they mention twenty-five attacks by Japanese on the coasts of the kingdom of Silla from the first to the fifth century A.D. More specifically, the Japanese established a bridgehead on the south tip of the Korean peninsula at Mimana in 369, which they maintained in permanent occupation until 562. From this base a considerable Japanese force moved against the king of Koguryö in 391. The king of Paikche, the third of the kingdoms into which Korea was divided, was grateful for the help of the Japanese, who already had a reputation as warriors, against his Koguryö enemy. Sending gifts of peace in return for aid in war, he dispatched to the Japanese court some scholars trained in the Chinese classics, who brought with them a copy of the *Thousand Character Classic* and possibly also a copy of the *Analects* of Confucius.

Thus the Yamato kingdom by the fifth century or earlier was sufficiently centralized to exercise some control in Japan from the Kanto Plain to Kyushu and was interfering actively in the affairs of Korea, while itself deriving benefit from the Chinese culture that Korea had to offer. China was beginning to exert that strong cultural influence which all the countries on her periphery would sooner or later feel. The next stage of Japanese history was to see an extension of the Chinese influence to Japan to such a marked degree that all subsequent Japanese civilization would be affected by it.

2

THE INTRODUCTION OF CHINESE THOUGHT AND CULTURE

Asuka Period: 552–710

A boat from Korea pulled into the shores of Japan, and the gangplank was arranged with extra care. A large casket shrouded in yellow silk was ceremoniously borne off the boat and placed with reverence on a palanquin carried on the shoulders of the highest retainers of the Soga clan. Accompanied by gongs, banners, ceremonial umbrellas, sutras (scriptures), and chanting priests in saffron robes, the image of Shaka Butsu (Buddha) in gold and copper was solemnly conducted on a long ceremonial progress to the capital of the day. It was in the Yamato region of central Japan, but we do not know exactly where, since it changed with each emperor's reign.

The official date for the introduction of Buddhism to Japan on this occasion is 552, when the image and accompanying cult objects were sent as a gift from the king of Paikche in Korea in the hope of receiving in return military aid against his enemy, at this juncture the king of Silla. Doubtless images, sutras, and priests had arrived via Korea before this date. Certainly Chinese Confucian classical texts and Korean scribes had been introduced into Japan, as we have seen, before 400. As a religion, as a system of thought, and as the bearer of elaborate and artistic ritual, Buddhism was immensely impressive to the Japanese. It came as the revelation of a depth and significance in life and death at which they had not previously guessed, and the spirits of many Japanese responded to the beauty and solemnity of its worship. But it arrived in Japan only after a long pilgrimage from the country of its origin.

Buddhism arose in northern India in the sixth century B.C. through the experiences of a prince, Sakyamuni (or Gautama). According to legend, Sakyamuni was carefully protected by his father and sheltered from the world during his childhood and youth. He was happily married, but as a young man he became suddenly acquainted with suffering. Leaving the palace on four successive days by different gates he met a beggar, then a sick man, then heard

16

the cries of a woman in childbirth, and finally saw a corpse in a funeral procession. Affected by these encounters, he determined to find the cause and solution of suffering in the world. He gave up his former life, bade farewell to his family—an action more readily accepted in India than in the West—and joined a band of Hindu ascetics. Self-inflicted suffering brought him no nearer his goal, and leaving the ascetics he sat down under a bo tree to meditate. In spite of temptations, represented in Buddhist art by seductive maidens dancing around him, he persisted until at length enlightenment came to him and he saw through the *maya,* "illusion," of this world and attained inner harmony. Perceiving that desire is what holds men down, leads them into suffering, and chains them to the constant wheel of rebirth, he obtained release and became Buddha, the Enlightened One.

Buddha then went on to bring the way of enlightenment to any who would listen and gathered round him a group of disciples. His most famous early sermon was preached in the deer park at Benares. In this and subsequent talks he developed the summary of his way in the Four Noble Truths and the Eightfold Path.

Thus Buddhism arose out of Hinduism and was intended in part as a reform of Hinduism. Buddha rejected, for instance, such well-known Hindu tenets as the predominant role of the Brahmins, the caste system, and the value of extreme asceticism (though not of spiritual discipline). Significantly, he neither required nor inculcated belief in a personal god nor indeed in any god at all.

This new faith, with its combination of deep philosophy and practical, ethical appeal, made great progress in India and reached its peak there in the third century B.C. under the great Emperor Asoka (ruled 273–232 B.C.). Asoka as a matter of policy sent missionaries with the trading caravans, which went to other countries and in particular is said to have sent his son to secure the conversion of Ceylon. But a change was taking place, and a new form of Buddhism began to arise which did more to satisfy certain deep religious longings of its adherents. One essential point in this new form was its concept of the Bodhisattva, a merciful being who is ready to pass beyond this life into nirvana, the blessed state of release beyond desire or fear, but who turns back to the world of men vowing not to accept his own release till all have been saved. In the course of time these Bodhisattvas, such as Kuan Yin (Chinese) or Kannon (Japanese), became the hearers of prayer, were paid divine honors, and were virtually turned into gods. All are in essence incarnations of Buddha. It was this form of Buddhism, the Mahayana or Greater Vehicle, which was disseminated over most of East Asia, China, Korea, Japan, Mongolia, and Tibet, as opposed to the form nearer the original, Hinayana, the Lesser Vehicle. Hinayana, or as its followers prefer to call it, Theravada Buddhism (the way of the Elders), has remained strong in Sri Lanka (Ceylon), Myanmar (Burma), and certain parts of Southeast Asia. Both forms have died out in India, the country of their origin.

Buddhism reached China via central Asia and is said to have been introduced in the first century A.D. during the Han dynasty. It did not develop markedly, however, until the fourth century in North China and was at that period also brought to the Korean peninsula. The religion spread rapidly in the sixth century because of the strong support accorded it by the Northern Wei and Liang dynasties in China, and this is the point that corresponds in date to the official introduction of Buddhism into Japan. Throughout China's history the Confucian literati tended to oppose Buddhism, often strongly though rarely violently, as a foreign importation inimical to the Chinese way of life. This may explain why Buddhism, though present, did not develop during the confident, centralized Han dynasty, but did on the other hand burgeon strongly during the succeeding period of divided kingdoms. Then the disturbed conditions weakened the influence of the literati at the same time as they caused the general run of men to look for a source of comfort and strength beyond the present world.

In Japan the new faith was involved in controversy from the start. In the formal account given by the *Nihongi* of the first reception of the image presented by the king of Paikche, the emperor said: "The countenance of this Buddha which has been presented by the western frontier state is of a severe dignity such as we have never at all seen before. Ought it to be worshipped or not?"

The Soga family was for Buddhism; the Mononobe and Nakatomi, both of whom had official duties in the Shinto national cult, were against its introduction. A compromise was reached in which the Soga were given authority to set up Buddhist worship as a kind of religious experiment. A plague broke out, which was attributed to the wrath of the national deities; the new image was thrown into a canal, and its temple burned. After further vicissitudes, Buddhism was strongly supported by the new Emperor Yomei, son of a Soga mother, in 586. Unfortunately he died in the following year, and the Soga were once again faced with a crisis. Their chieftain, Soga Umako, decided to appeal to force and won a definitive victory over the Mononobe at the battle of Shigisen in 587, at which time the Mononobe withdrew their opposition. Buddhism then became somewhat rapidly established among the aristocracy, to the point where there was actual rivalry in the erection of temples. It was to be some time, however, before the new faith was adopted to any marked degree by the mass of the people.

After a series of dynastic quarrels, Soga Umako, now very powerful, placed the Empress Suiko on the throne and arranged that her nephew, also of Soga descent and the second son of the former Emperor Yomei, should become regent. This young man of twenty-one, Prince Shotoku (Shotoku Taishi, 572–622), was on any showing one of the most remarkable figures of Japanese history. He was universally respected for his learning and beloved for his goodness. He was a devout Buddhist and studied under a monk from a region of Korea that had close connections with the strongly Buddhist Sui dynasty in China. When the famous monastery and seminary of Horyuji was founded in 607, Prince Shotoku built within its grounds his residence and

Horyuji Temple, Nara.

This monastery complex, founded in 607, contains some of the oldest wooden buildings in the world. Typical of all Buddhist temples are the main south gate (left), the pagoda, and the principal worship hall (center).

Japan Information Center

chapel, named Yumedono, "The Hall of Dreams." But he also had a Confucian tutor for the Chinese classics, which were becoming highly valued in Japan for their lessons in statecraft.

Prince Shotoku is notable above all for his policy of leading Japan to adopt Chinese models in the spheres of politics, religion, and art. This he accomplished in three ways: the promulgation of a constitution of seventeen articles, the adoption of "cap ranks" at the Japanese court, and the sending of the first official embassy to China in the name of the ruler of a united Japan in 607.

The constitution was not a constitution in the Western sense at all, but rather a collection of maxims to guide and exhort those engaged in government along ethical lines derived mainly from Confucian sources in China. It was a high-level policy directive couched in general terms. There is doubt as to whether Prince Shotoku was actually the author or whether it was written slightly later by some of his followers and piously ascribed to him. It certainly seems to represent his thinking and was probably issued to prepare the way for that reform in government and administration along Chinese lines which is known to have been favored by Prince Shotoku and which actually took place in 645, twenty-three years after his death, under the name of the Taika

Yumedono (the Hall of Dreams), in the Horyuji Temple, Nara, built by Prince Shotoku in 607 for use as a chapel.
The Horyuji is the oldest complete Buddhist monastery complex in Japan.
Japan National Tourist Organization

Reform. The aim of the constitution may be summed up by the words in Article XII: "In a country there are not two lords; the people have not two masters. The sovereign is the master of the people of the whole country."[1] In these parallel phrases so beloved by classical authors, Prince Shotoku's party sought to move away from the traditional Japanese view of the Yamato leader as a paramount chief among chiefs and toward the Chinese bureaucratic pyramid with a sole ruler at the summit.

The institution of ranks at court, designated by different colors and materials in the ceremonial caps, was also intended to strengthen the central government. Apparently minor in itself, the new rule was a first, and perhaps cautious, attempt to substitute for the native Japanese pattern of hereditary aristocracy the Chinese system of officials appointed for merit, and therefore in theory able to be dismissed for demerit. The theory is estimable, but the Japanese reformers were never able to carry it fully into practice.

The third achievement of Prince Shotoku was more successful and indeed of prime importance for the future of Japan. The embassy to China organized in 607 was led by one Ono-no-Imoko, who carried a letter to the Sui emperor at Loyang which began: "The Emperor of the sunrise country

[1] Murdoch, *A History of Japan*, Vol. 1, pt. 1, p. 124.

writes to the Emperor of the sunset country." This phraseology, though impeccable in its style, was scarcely of a tone calculated to win friends at the Chinese court. A second visit, in which the humbler attitude of a vassal was adopted, proved more successful; and the Japanese ambassador returned with the Chinese books which it had been Prince Shotoku's object to secure and, more important, with assurance that an official relationship was now established between the two countries.

These first embassies were succeeded by some fourteen others, extending over two centuries—the last took place in 838—and included their personnel officials, students, Buddhist priests and laypersons, artists, craftsmen, and secretaries. Among the most distinguished of the latter-day visitors to China was Kibi-no-Mabi, who spent seventeen years at Changan, the Tang dynasty capital. He is said to have brought back from China the art of embroidery; the *biwa*, or "four-string lute"; and the game of *go*, or "Chinese chess," favored by Japanese warriors as a means of training in military strategy. He is also supposed to have invented *kana*, the Japanese syllabary of simplified Chinese characters used for phonetic purposes only. Legend to the contrary, however, Japanese court women contributed to the development of *kana*. He was one of the very few in Japanese history who came of common stock and rose to the highest rank by native ability, becoming Minister of the Left (principal minister) in 766.

It is evident that Prince Shotoku was important in his own person as the initiator of a deliberate policy of sinicization, or conforming to Chinese models. But he was also significant as a symbol of certain trends that were to reappear frequently in Japanese history. In the first place, as regent he exercised effective rule but only indirectly, in the name of his aunt, the empress. Later the practice of having a titular ruler and an actual ruler became the common, almost standard, procedure. In many cases indeed the practice of indirect rule was carried further, and the policy of the actual ruler was determined by a small and undefined group of advisers who remained in the background. Though they may have had no known or named leader, their consensus often was too powerful for the ruler to ignore. In the second place, Prince Shotoku led the movement for the conscious introduction of new forms of religion, philosophy, art, and political organization into Japan. This custom of cultural and technological borrowing is recognized as a Japanese trait even by those who have no close acquaintance with Japanese history. But what is not so widely recognized is the distinctive manner in which the Japanese have always been able to assimilate borrowed material and make something of their very own out of it. They frequently succeed in improving upon the original. Buddhism itself provides a major example, for there the leadership in speculative thought and in the creative influence of the religion upon the arts gradually passed from China to Japan. The whole process took centuries because Buddhism was not easily grasped. In modern technology, Japanese mastery and advance have been much more rapid, but the principle of thorough assimilation and intelligent application is the same.

The Japanese who went in search of the new religion and the new arts could not fail to be immensely impressed with the magnificence of Tang China. In A.D. 618 China entered upon a period in which it became the largest, best organized, and culturally most advanced nation in the world. (In Europe, at this time, the western Roman Empire was in ruins; and the eastern half, though still great, was no rival to China. The great Islamic civilization was just about to come to birth.) The Japanese visitors must have been both delighted and overawed by the splendors of the Tang capital at Changan (the modern Xi'an in northwest China). They copied its city planning in the rectangular grid pattern of city streets when they came later to build their new capital at Heian (Kyoto). Nothing in their own experience had prepared them for the sight of the imperial processions, when the Tang emperors made official tours to show the flag, accompanied by the court ladies, officials, army regiments, and wagon trains bearing tent pavilions, tapestries, silk hangings, furniture, porcelain dinner services, golden cups, and the infinite amount of paraphernalia used in Chinese court life. It is said that the retinue took two or three days to pass a given point.

The Japanese were fortunate to be visiting China just before and during the Tang dynasty, for this was the period when China was most hospitable to foreigners and most open to new ideas. Armenians, Jews, Koreans, Arabs, men from central Asia, and Nestorian Christians of the Asian tradition, which traces its spiritual ancestry back to Christ's disciple, Thomas, all were to be found in the streets of Changan. What the Japanese took home with them from this stimulating and enlarging experience were two basic systems of thought, both by now thoroughly Chinese, namely, Confucianism and Buddhism. Japan had earlier received Chinese Buddhism by way of Korea; now she was receiving greater knowledge of the religion and its various sects directly from China. The influence of Confucianism, though less spectacular than that of Buddhism, had a marked and lasting effect upon Japanese political thought and institutions.

These systems of thought did not come alone to Japan, for they brought with them new ways, a new lifestyle, and a degree of sophistication unknown hitherto in Japan. They were accompanied by a number of arts and crafts. Carvers of wood, workers in lacquer, artists skilled in painting on silk and on paper, weavers of brocade, potters, and bronze casters of remarkable proficiency all began to migrate from Korea and China to satisfy the new religious and artistic demands of the Japanese aristocracy. These artists and craftsmen, some prominent, some anonymous and of humble origin, settled down, intermarried with Japanese, and in time contributed an important creative strain to Japanese life. This was eagerly taken up and developed by the Japanese themselves, who were as a people more than usually sensitive to the beauty being created at the centers of Chinese civilization.

But the craftsmen most far-reaching in their influence on the future were the writers and scribes. A religion as developed and as philosophical as Buddhism depended to a much greater degree than the native Shinto upon the

Buddhist *Sutra* (scripture) of the Heian period, c. twelfth century.
The frontispiece and first part of the text, gold ink on deep blue paper.
Arthur M. Sackler Art Museums, Harvard University, Wetzel Bequest

written word for its transmission and propagation. The first scribes were foreigners, but soon the Japanese themselves were copying out the sutras destined for the libraries in the new temples. Before long, even the aristocrats
were toiling over the difficult script, for it became a social hallmark at court
to be able to read and write Chinese. At once the value of a written script became evident in fields other than the religious. The new possibility of keeping accurate and permanent records, particularly tax records, led in turn to
an increase of power and of centralization in the government.

Meanwhile in the political arena the power of the Soga, which had been
instrumental in placing Prince Shotoku in a position to influence affairs, continued unabated. Some twenty years after the prince died in 622, this power
was being exercised in an obnoxious and overbearing manner by Soga Emishi and his son, Soga Iruka. There was more than a suspicion that they were
attempting to arrogate the powers of the emperor to themselves. Opposition
gathered in 644 under the leadership of Prince Naka-no-Oye (later the emperor Tenchi, 661–671), a discontented Soga clansman, and the great Kamatari, the head of the Nakatomi family. Soga Iruka was killed at court, re-
portedly in the very presence of the empress, and Soga Emishi was later
executed. Effective power passed to Prince Naka-no-Oye, although he did

not become emperor until later. He is said to have met Nakatomi Kamatari through an ancient equivalent of the game of soccer, and the two are known to have attended lectures given by the same Confucian teacher and to have plotted the overthrow of the Soga in a garden under cover of discussion of the Confucian classics. Kamatari became the confidential adviser to the prince and actually the chief power in the land. He was known by the sobriquet of Kuromaku, "Black Curtain," a theatrical phrase meaning "stage prompter." Later he was given a new family name, Fujiwara (wisteria), in remembrance of the wisteria garden where the plotting took place. He was thus the founder of the great Fujiwara family, which was to dominate Japanese court life for centuries, without a rival in controlling the national destiny from 857 to 1160, and still influential in the imperial circle right up to the nineteenth century, even though power had passed to the Shogunate.

As soon as the anti-Soga coup had been successfully carried out, Kamatari and Prince Naka-no-Oye proceeded to put through the Taika Reform of 645. The name means "great change" or "great reform," and its provisions were in fact definitive for all subsequent Japanese history. Here a thoroughgoing attempt was made to impose upon Japan a governmental system similar to the bureaucratic administration of China, which the Japanese rightly judged had contributed greatly to China's centralized authority and manifest cultural success. All the land of Japan was declared to belong to the emperor. The great landowning nobles continued to live on their existing territory, but this was technically at the emperor's pleasure. In return they were given court rank and offices as provincial or lesser governors, or as other officials of the emperor, to exercise administrative functions and to receive emoluments corresponding to their rank and office.

The main provisions of the reform edict were four in number:

Article I abolished private holdings of land and of corporations of agricultural workers.

Article II set up the "Inner Provinces" or metropolitan region, with appointment of the necessary officials, and provided for an improved system of communications, roads, and bridges with the outer provinces.

Article III provided for registers of the population for the purpose of allotting rice land to farmers at so much land per "mouth" in the family, for assessment of taxes, and for the appointment of local headmen.

Article IV did away with the old taxes and introduced a new system of taxation. This included taxes on agricultural produce, on textiles, a tax in lieu of corvée or compulsory labor (although in certain instances the corvée was retained), and military service. Those called up for military service were exempt from other taxes, but the soldier went at his own expense and the service was often arduous.

The working of the new tax structure, in common with other features of the reform, was only gradually evolved and was probably not applied fully and equally in all parts of the country. Further regulations and modifications were made at intervals over the next half century, culminating in the Taiho

Code of 702. The Taiho Code provided Japan with what it had never previously possessed, a code of law and a formal system of government administration. The Code of 702 was actually a revision of law codes of a Chinese type issued earlier and an adaptation to Japanese conditions of the Tang administrative system.

The organization of the government under the Taiho Code may be summarized as follows:

1. The central government was in two parts, the Department of Worship (Jingi-kan) taking precedence over the Department of State (Dajo-kan).

2. The Department of Worship took charge of the great national religious ceremonies, the upkeep of shrines, and the recording of oracles. Its sphere was Shinto, not Buddhism.

3. The Department of State was headed by the Great Council of State, presided over by the chancellor (*dajo-daijin*), and consisted of four great councillors (*dainagon*) and three lesser councillors (*shonagon*). The Great Council was the ultimate authority to advise the emperor on all civil and military affairs of state. Routine administration was divided among the various ministries and officials below.

4. Under the chancellor was the minister of the Left (*sadaijin*), the senior minister in charge of all branches of administration.

5. His deputy and junior minister was the minister of the Right (*udaijin*).

6. Four ministries were associated with the office of the Left, namely the Ministry of the Center, the official channel from the Throne to the lower levels of administration; the Ministry of Ceremonial; the Ministry of Civil Affairs; and the Ministry of People's Affairs.

7. The four ministries associated with the office of the Right were the Ministry of Military Affairs, the Ministry of Justice, the Ministry of the Treasury, and the Ministry of the Imperial Household.

The fact that this scheme was closely modeled on the Tang system goes far to explain a circumstance curious to Western eyes, namely, that the ministries of the Right, concerned with war, justice, finance, and the imperial household, were subordinated to the ministries dealing with ceremonial and civil matters. As a matter of record, military and judicial affairs emerged as of paramount importance under the Kamakura Shogunate, in the twelfth and following centuries. In the seventh and eighth centuries, however, neither Japan as a whole nor the imperial house appeared to feel threatened by war, nor was there open military rivalry between the clans. The reformers were therefore able, in their enthusiasm for things Chinese, to institute a system that was surprisingly nonmilitary in its orientation. The Taiho Code also placed much emphasis on the promotion and regulation of court life and comparatively little on the affairs of the common people. Of the eight ministries, only half—namely, the ministries of People's Affairs, Military Affairs, Justice, and the Treasury—were concerned with the nation as a whole. The Ministry of Civil Affairs, which might seem to be concerned with the people, in fact dealt with such miscellaneous and mainly court matters as the marriage and succession of high officials, omens, funerals, reception of foreign envoys, music, and the registration of Buddhist temples and monks. The nature and extent of the government's interest in the life of the common man may be judged from the list of duties of the Ministry of People's Affairs. These included the census, forced labor, and exemption therefrom; relief of the distressed; maintenance of bridges, roads, and harbors; collection of taxes; and management of granaries and land tax in grain. The Treasury had charge of the public accounts, weights and measures, commodity prices, the mint, and the lacquer, weaving, and other industries. It must be borne in mind that this was an ideal scheme; thus when "the maintenance of bridges, roads, and harbors" is mentioned, improvement in communications may in fact have been very limited.

Although Japan was indebted in China for the general shape of its political structure, there were nevertheless some very significant differences between the systems of the two countries. First, the primacy of the Department of Worship was a distinctly Japanese innovation, apparently designed to preserve the sacred functions of the emperor intact. No forfeiting of the "mandate of Heaven" by unworthy rulers and the consequent right of the people to revolt was even envisaged. (An interesting linguistic point preserves clearly early Japanese attitudes regarding the importance of the priest-king nature of the emperor's office: the word for "religious affairs," *matsurigoto,* is also the word for "government.") The second, and greatest, difference lies in the methods of recruitment and appointment of officials. In China the Tang emperors had improved and regularized a system begun under the Han of entrance to the bureaucracy by public, competitive examination, which opened the way for a very gradual but significant infiltration of fresh talent from the nongentry classes into government service. In Japan examinations were of little importance. Exemption from them was granted to sons of noble families, and the whole official system as constituted tended merely to perpetuate the power of the former clan and aristocratic leaders with little change. An edict of 682 openly stated that the considerations in selecting men for office were to be birth, character, and capacity, in that order. Third, the matter of exemption from the taxes set up in the Taika Reform and provided for in the Taiho Code presented peculiar difficulties in Japan and was to have most unfortunate results later on. Stated simply, the problem was that tax exemption was granted to estates held either by government officials or by religious foundations, mainly Buddhist temples and monasteries. Since both these categories were numerous and tended to increase, the effective tax base of the country was constantly being narrowed and the burden of raising revenue tended to fall on fewer and fewer persons. In effect the hardship fell on those least able to pay, since such burdens are always shifted downward onto the peasants.

There is evidence that the census at the time of the Taika Reform was meticulously compiled and the distribution of land at so much per person or "mouth" made with reasonable fairness. But the situation altered, changes in ownership came about, tax exemptions were granted, and the redistribution of land at intervals, as originally planned, proved too difficult to carry through. Even in China little was done to redistribute land to maintain correspondence with family and population changes.

Nevertheless the Taika Reform and Taiho Code marked a clear stage of advance in the Japanese political field. In theory the authority of the emperor was increased, and in practice some centralization and strengthening of governmental power took place. Without this, Japan could not have undertaken its course of future development as effectively as it did.

3

THE STIMULATING EFFECT OF CHINESE CULTURE

Nara Period: 710–794

In 710 the capital of Japan was fixed for the first time and located at Nara in the fertile plain area at the base of the Ise Peninsula and near the east end of the Inland Sea. In the early days of the Yamato kingdom there had been no single capital. Each successive emperor had simply been accustomed to conducting the government from his own residential estate, both for convenience and in order to avoid the ritual pollution attaching to the house of his dead predecessor, according to Shinto belief. Buddhist and Confucian doctrine now rendered the moving of the palace site unnecessary, and the elaboration of court life and religious architecture made it virtually impossible. This settlement of the center of government ushered in the Nara period (710–794).[1] At this time the engrafted shoots of Chinese culture and especially of Buddhism began to flower and soon to bring forth fruit which was truly indigenous and Japanese in nature.

Buddhism continued to grow and to attract to its ranks an increasing number of devotees, mainly from the upper ranks of society. Genuine religious motives were at times mixed with political ambitions, for the fortunes of Buddhism did at first ebb and flow with the fortunes of such families as the Soga. But soon the new religion was so thoroughly established that it was no longer dependent on the favor of one or two clans. The court was generally a staunch supporter of Buddhism, and the Taika reformers, following Prince Shotoku, took the same line. There is no doubt that the profundity, comprehensive orderliness, and moral challenge of this religion, as well as its

---

[1] It should be noted that Japanese chronology differs from that of China and most other countries in being marked not by dynasties (for there is strictly but one dynasty or ruling family) but by periods, whose names are generally the names of the geographical seats of power, e.g., Nara, Kamakura, Edo.

artistic and ritual accompaniments, held an attraction, even a fascination, for the Japanese. In the long run Buddhism exercised a refining and civilizing effect upon the rude warriors of early Japan. It revealed to them the power of gentleness and opened up perspectives on the problems of life, death, and suffering in ways that Shinto was quite incapable of doing.

A concrete example of this kind of influence may be seen in the image of Miroku Bosatsu, the Buddha who is to come, in the Chuguji Nunnery in Nara, dating from the eighth century. This serene figure has a simple, dignified pose—erect but not stiff, calm and self-possessed. His unseeing eyes show him to be absorbed in meditation, yet fully awake and aware. The facial expression, the archaic smile, the middle finger extended to the chin suggesting the formation of an idea, all give an impression of tenderness and gentleness, of quiet inward bliss. When the figure was first seen, the effect on peasants and nobles alike must have been overwhelming.

One obvious measure of the growing influence of Buddhism is the rise in the number of monasteries, monks, and nuns. By 624, two years after the death of Prince Shotoku, and just over seventy years from the official introduction of Buddhism, Japan had 46 monasteries, 816 monks, and 569 nuns. By 692 the 46 monasteries had become 545, and the lavish donations of the court tended to make Buddhism almost the state religion. It never in fact attained that status in any official way; the great Shinto court ceremonies were always maintained, and emperors and nobles supported both Shinto and Buddhist institutions; but the rapid spread and firm hold of Buddhism are well attested.

The sense of exclusiveness and the necessity of deliberate choice that cause Western people to adhere to one religion only are notably absent in East Asia. Neither the Chinese nor the Japanese people have difficulty in regulating their lives by the ideas of more than one faith at the same time. An official might therefore attend a national festival such as the New Year ceremonies, conducted according to Shinto rites, but have a Buddhist service celebrated for the repose of his mother's soul, and apply Confucian canons to his government administration, without the least sense of inner contradiction.

Although the ennobling effect of Buddhism has been mentioned, it is hardly surprising that there is also evidence of the element of superstition in the spread of the new faith. For instance, one of the earliest known examples of printing in the world is to be seen in the distribution by the Empress Suiko of 100,000 copies of a Buddhist charm to ward off disease during an epidemic in the year 770.[2] This incidentally provides an excellent historical example of the kind of emergency circumstances that favored both the expansion of Buddhism and the wider use of the new technology of printing, since

---

[2] The discovery of a still earlier example of printing took place on October 14, 1966, in the stonework of a Buddhist pagoda in the Temple of Pulguksa at Kyongju in South Korea, the ancient capital of the kingdom of Silla. The material was the twenty-foot scroll of a sutra, printed from twelve wood blocks and translated from Sanskrit into Chinese by Mi T'o-hsien, who is known to have lived in the Tang capital of Changan between 680 and 704 A.D. The date of the printing must therefore fall between 680 and 751, the date of the building of the temple.

that was the only conceivable method of reproducing the enormous number of 100,000 examples of a charm in time to counter the disaster of an epidemic.

The art of writing was called to the aid of Shinto as well as of Buddhism. At the very beginning of the Nara period the ancient Shinto legends were written down in the *Kojiki* (712) and the *Nihongi* or *Nihonshoki* ("Chronicles of Japan," 720), to which reference has already been made. These works show clearly the Chinese combined with native elements, the matter being purely Japanese but the form mixed.

The *Kojiki* employs Chinese characters phonetically to represent the sounds of the Japanese language, while the *Nihongi* uses Chinese characters in the Chinese language. The former, it may be imagined, results in a text that is extremely difficult to read. (The simplified *kana* syllabary does not appear until the ninth century.) Painstaking work by the great scholar of late Tokugawa times, Motoori Norinaga (1730–1801), made the text and its meaning more readily available to modern scholars. The language of these works is copied from the rather high-flown style of the Chinese dynastic histories, for they were deliberately written to exalt the prestige of the imperial house. In addition to tracing the descent of the emperors from the Sun Goddess, they supplied elaborate genealogies to strengthen the claims of the landholders of noble families and those who had acquired office under the Taika Reform.

A different type of literature from this same period is represented by the famous collection of poems called the *Manyoshu* ("Collection of a Myriad Leaves"), probably compiled by Tachibana no Moroye (fl. 738–756), a high official who was a protégé of the Fujiwara. The poems, emanating from the court aristocracy from the earliest times to the year 760, deal with many topics such as love of Japan (No. 2), Nature and Man (No. 13), the sadness of banishment (No. 23), and a mallard duck waking (No. 1744). A great number are poems of love, on an absent husband (No. 59), proposal to a maiden (No. 1726), "How can I live alone?" (No. 1728), "to his wife" (No. 1782), and one of the more moving, "She dwells so deep in me" (No. 1792). Already at this early stage there is evident the preference for extremely short, lapidary statements of a theme and the evocation of a mood by a swift parallel from Nature that is to distinguish all subsequent Japanese poetry. Noticeably absent from Japanese, as from Chinese, verse is the grand epic style. Grandeur in language and theme is to be found in the military prose romances such as the *Taiheiki*, but not in poetry, either early or late.

The following examples, quoted in full, will give some idea of the nature of the *Manyoshu* poems.

ON SEEING A MAN DEAD ON MT. TATSUTA DURING HIS TRIP
TO THE WELL OF TAKAHARA

Had he been at home, he would have slept
Upon his dear wife's arm;

Here he lies dead, unhappy man,
On his journey, grass for pillow.[3]
 —Prince Shotoku, sixth/seventh century

YEARNING FOR THE EMPEROR TENJI

While, waiting for you,
My heart is filled with longing,
The autumn wind blows—
As if it were you—
Swaying the bamboo blinds of my door.
 —Princess Nukada,
 latter half of seventh century

The above are poems by famous figures at court, but the two following anonymous poems reflect the simpler life of the people. The first sounds as if it might have come from the *Greek Anthology* or Catullus, but perhaps this is just because the theme is universal.

(UNTITLED)

The vivid smile of my sweetheart
That shone in the bright lamplight,
Ever haunts my eyes.

DIALOGUE POEM

Where others' husbands ride on horseback
Along the Yamashiro road,
You, my husband, trudge on foot.

Every time I see you there I weep,
To think of it my heart aches.

My husband, take on your back
My shining mirror, my mother's keepsake,
Together with the scarf thin as the dragon-fly's wing,
And barter them for a horse,
I pray you, my husband.

ENVOIS

Deep is the ford of the Izumi.
Your travelling clothes, I fear,
Will be drenched, my husband.

---

[3] "Grass for pillow" henceforth is a literary phrase meaning "on a journey away from home."

What worth to me my shining mirror,
When I see you, my husband,
Trudging on your weary way!

BY HER HUSBAND

If I get a horse, my beloved,
You must go on foot;
Though we tread the rocks,
Let's walk, the two of us, together.[4]

The religion of Buddhism is the dominant factor in the history of the whole Nara period, not only in the realms of religion and culture but also in those of economics and politics. The reign of the Emperor Shomu, a zealous supporter of Buddhism, includes the Tempyo period (729–748), famous in art history, when some of the most renowned and graceful of Buddhist statuary in wood and metal were executed. By the time of Shomu's reign the faith was sufficiently established and self-confident to reach some accommodation with the native Shinto belief. The Buddhist monk Gyogi (670–749) taught that the Shinto divinities were avatars or manifestations of Buddha, thus laying the foundation of what was to become in the twelfth century Ryobu Shinto (Dual Shinto). On this theory Amaterasu, the Sun Goddess, was worshipped as Vairocana, the great cosmic Buddhist deity who ruled over a world of light.

Gyogi also devoted himself to collecting alms for the erection of a huge bronze statue of Buddha as Vairocana, the Daibutsu, "Great Buddha," of Nara. This image was erected by the Emperor Shomu with Gyogi's help, in fulfillment of a vow made by the emperor when a severe epidemic of smallpox, which had started in Korea, spread to Japan, seriously threatening the court and the inhabitants of Nara in 735. The casting of the image was an immense and costly effort for a country of Japan's resources, as it was fifty-three feet high, weighed over 500 tons, and was gilded with 500 pounds of gold. The head and neck, over twelve feet high, were cast in one piece. After seven unsuccessful attempts the casting was finally accomplished and the image dedicated in 752 in the vast hall of the Todaiji Temple amid great splendor and enthusiasm. Four years later some of the ritual objects used at the dedication ceremony were laid up in the Shosoin, a treasury made of large wooden logs that still survives with its contents intact. This remarkable treasury containing also personal belongings of the Emperor Shomu was erected and given to the Todaiji by the emperor's widow. Its contents include weapons, pictures, musical instruments, and land and population registers of Japanese origin, as well as pottery and metal work from China, central Asia, and possibly Persia.

---

[4] These translations are taken from *The Manyoshu, The Nippon Gakujutsu Shinkokai Translation of 1,000 Poems* (New York: Columbia University Press, 1965), Nos. 20 (II.415), 29 (IV.488), 944 (XI.2642), and 871–874 (XXIII.3314–3317). The *Manyoshu* reference numbers are in parentheses.

Kofukuji Temple pagoda and
Sarusawa Pond, Nara.

Nara was the oldest capital of Japan,
founded in 710. The Kofukuji dates
from the same period.

Japan National Tourist Organization

It was also during Shomu's reign that the Chinese monk Ganjin arrived in
Nara after five unsuccessful attempts to reach the country and established the
first *kaidan* or "ordination platform" in Japan. His was the Ritsu (Sanskrit,
Vinaya) sect, and this sect with five others formed the group known as the Nara
sects, as distinct from other Buddhist sects introduced at later periods.

Just prior to the Nara period the Horyuji, the temple already mentioned
in connection with Prince Shotoku, was rebuilt (see illustration on page 19).
It had been destroyed by fire and was reconstructed in 708 in the same style
as the original of 607. The Kondo, or Golden Hall, of this temple is a massive but beautifully proportioned structure representing the best of Tang architecture, and is probably the oldest existing wooden building in the world.
The Horyuji, Todaiji, and Kofukuji temples at Nara (the last associated with
the Fujiwara family) and the great temples of Kyoto, founded in the next period, the Heian, all contain a number of common features setting the standards for temple architecture as required by the elaborate cult of Mahayana
Buddhism, features that are impressive still and must at the time have had an
awesome effect upon the Japanese worshippers. These include, first, the great
worship hall with an immense roof expressing majesty and solemnity, high
and spacious within, yet yielding a suitably dim vision of the great image of
the deity. The image combines the remoteness of calm contemplation with
the nearness of compassionate concern in a manner that only the Buddhist

master craftsmen have been able to convey. Leading up to the great hall is the ceremonial gateway with its guardian deities, while to one side or to the rear are the dwellings of the monks. An essential feature is the library, for the scriptures of Buddhism are not one book but many. There are storehouses, such as the Shosoin, for the temple treasures, and many additions made in later years, schoolrooms, offices, gardens, and guest chambers, usually laid out and maintained with order and precision. The arrangements show many similarities to European medieval monasteries. Often but not invariably there is a pagoda, a monument which has no functional use but which serves, with its images in niches and its vertical lines broken by delicate roofs and topped by Buddhist symbols at the peak, to focus the attention of the worshipper on the transcendental or heavenly aspects of the faith.

It is obvious then, on the architectural evidence alone, that the emerging centralized government in the person of the emperor and his court spent large sums of money during the Nara period on the endowment of the Buddhist religion and its priesthood. This fact provoked considerable opposition on the grounds that the Buddhist clergy was becoming too powerful and exercising an altogether excessive influence over the emperors and over what could now begin to be dignified by the name of national policy. At one time, no fewer than 116 priestly exorcists were attached to the court. One Nara temple alone possessed forty-six manors with 5,000 acres of the best land, tax free. The temple domains tended constantly to increase because peasants, to escape taxes, preferred to "commend" their land to a temple and pay rent, since the rent was far less than the taxes.

A reaction against the monasteries was precipitated in the 760s by the misconduct of a Buddhist monk, Dokyo, who managed to ingratiate himself with the Empress Koken by his flattering interpretations of dreams and portents. Despite the efforts of the Fujiwara family to dislodge him, Dokyo became her confidant, her chancellor, and perhaps her lover. He even aspired to be emperor, but the Empress was unwilling to take the ultimate step of legitimating his claims, and at her death in 770 he immediately fell from favor.

The Council of State read the warning signs in this incident. Its members had watched Buddhist power increase at court through the reigns of four empresses, and they now refused to allow another woman to ascend the throne, a precedent followed almost undeviatingly through the remainder of Japanese history. Koken, also known as Shotoku, was thus the last empress with the exception of two unimportant female rulers in the seventeenth century. The succession passed in 781 to Kammu (781–806), who proved to be a strong emperor.

Three years after Kammu's ascent to the throne, the decision was made to move the capital to Nagaoka, a short distance to the north, this time not for reasons of ritual purity but, in part at least, to remove the court from the baleful influence of the great monasteries at Nara. Such a move probably took considerable courage, since it involved braving the unknown dangers of the wrath of the Lord Buddha, which were doubtless stressed by those with vested interests in the old capital. The Emperor Kammu, an able statesman, was well qualified to undertake the task.

The capital remained at Nagaoka for only a decade. The emperor's brother was involved in the murder of the official in charge of the building, was banished, and died of starvation in exile. It was felt that his spirit was haunting the new capital; so Kammu, after careful consultation with the geomancers (experts in the study of the influence of topography on the spirit world), chose a new site, that of modern Kyoto, and settled there in 794. Kyoto was to remain henceforth the seat of the emperor until 1868, when the transfer of the palace to Tokyo coincided with the decision to modernize Japan.

The new capital bore a grand name and had a grand plan. Called Heiankyo, "Capital of Eternal Tranquillity," it was laid out in a grid design, as Nara had been, along the lines of the magnificent contemporary capital of Tang China, Changan. But Japan had nothing like China's resources, and in fact not all the ground within the planned rectangle of the city was taken up or built upon. And yet the very considerable effort made was one more concrete sign that Japan meant seriously to follow in her own way the course of Chinese civilization. She planned to adopt wherever possible a civilian and bureaucratic rather than a military and tribal approach to life and government.

4

THE JAPANESE PATTERN

Early Heian Period: 794–857
Late Heian or Fujiwara Period: 858–1158

In the Heian period Japan clearly came of age. The shorter Early Heian period is distinguished by the reduction of new territory in the east and north to central control and by new developments in Buddhism. The longer Late Heian period is noted for the dominance of the great Fujiwara family and for an unusual elegance of taste in the life of the court, accompanied by achievements in prose literature fit to rank with the best that has been produced anywhere in the world. Yet at the same time, outside court circles, profound changes took place in the Japanese countryside which shifted the basis of power to a new warrior class.

At the outset of the Heian period the Emperor Kammu was compelled to devote attention not only to the founding of two new capitals in succession but also to some distant but pressing problems created by the movement of the Ainu people in the north of Japan. The good rice lands of the Kanto Plain had been gradually settled by the more adventurous Japanese pushing east and then north. They had to farm with one hand and fight with the other, for their advance was disputed by the Ainu, who had held this land since Neolithic times. Kept at a keen edge by constant practice, the prowess of the men of the east was celebrated in early Japan, and they were frequently enlisted for the fourth to sixth century wars in Korea in which Japanese took part. Although there was Ainu resistance, many of these people coexisted peacefully with the incomers. Some of the more warlike Ainu in the far north, aided by Japanese who were not willing to submit to central government control, started a rebellion in 776 and attacked the frontier town of Taga, near the modern Sendai. Raids and counterraids continued, usually ending in ignominious defeat for the government forces. The militia system supplied soldiers from the central rather than the frontier regions, men of little skill and low morale, and the commanders from Heian were more ornamental than useful as generals. The pervading orientation of the Chinese type of government adopted under the Taika Reform did not foster the fighting spirit in either the troops or their officers. In 783 Kammu reprimanded the commanders publicly and instituted a new campaign. At length a fully competent deputy commander, Sakanouye Tamura Maro, was found. He achieved brilliant successes in 795 and again between 800 and 803, when he had full command. Garrison strongholds were built in the extreme north at Izawa and Shiba, and Tamura Maro was rewarded by being granted the title of *sei-i tai-shogun*, "barbarian-subduing generalissimo." He was thus the first holder of a title that was to be the most coveted among military men for the next ten centuries.

At about the same time, in 805 and 806, some twelve years after the establishment of Heian, a twin event occurred which was to be of great significance in the development of Buddhism in Japan, though it was not to free the new capital from the political tensions that religion had brought to the old one at Nara. In those years two prominent scholar-monks, Saicho and Kukai, each at the height of his powers, returned to Japan from a period of study in China.

Saicho (later granted the honorific title of *Dengyo Daishi*) returned to his former settlement on Mount Hiei to the northeast of Heian. His monastery, Enryakuji, founded before Heian was built, enjoyed great prestige because it served to protect the capital from malign influences coming from the Demon Entrance, the unlucky direction of the northeast. Moreover certain Shinto deities were worshipped as mountain gods. Saicho, anxious not to offend the Shinto faith, particularly in the imperial region of Yamato where it was strongest, paid reverence to one of these deities as Sanno, King of the Mountain. Thus Indian Buddhism, Japanese Shinto, and Chinese geomancy all had a part in the spiritual protection his monastery offered the capital. Saicho, on his return from China, brought new doctrine of the Tendai sect to Japan. The word *tendai* means "heavenly platform," and the reference is to a platform for ordination. The new sect gained an important advantage when the emperor granted it the right to ordain Buddhist priests on a par with the older Nara sects. Tendai favored mountain retreats for their value as an aid to the contemplative life. Its doctrine was comprehensive and marked by a certain practical quality congenial to both Chinese and Japanese minds, as opposed to the extreme flights of speculation to be found in the Buddhism native to India. For example, it conceived of the rewards of paradise and the punishments of hell in a definite way, in contrast to the original Buddhist emphasis on the difficult concept of nirvana, release into nonbeing. The sect flourished exceedingly, for in later years there were some 3,000 temples, small chapels, and monasteries scattered over the Mount Hiei range.

The other returning monk, Kukai (or Kobo Daishi), went to Mount Koya in the Yamato region, some distance southeast of the capital, and there introduced the Japanese form of another important sect, the Shingon or True Word. The title implies a gnostic idea of knowledge within knowledge, the

True Word being the special possession of this sect. Later development took place, as might be expected, in two directions: high philosophical refinement of esoteric doctrine and lower popular belief in special charms or mantras. This sect also became powerful, and serious rivalries grew up between the two, often disturbing the peace of the realm. The monasteries on Mount Hiei in particular frequently became a threat to the tranquility of the capital. A division between the Mount Hiei group of monasteries and a branch of the same sect at Miidera on Lake Biwa led in 891 to the recruiting by each side of guards, in reality little more than bullies or strong-arm men, a sinister development in the peaceful religion of Buddhism. A later emperor, Go-Shirakawa, once sadly remarked, "There are three things which I cannot control, the fall of the dice, the flow of the River Kamo, and the turbulent monks of Mount Hiei."

The last of the series of cultural embassies from Japan to China, which had been carried out at irregular intervals for over 200 years, took place in 838. Attached to it was another Japanese scholar-monk, Ennin (793–864). As a young man he was attracted by the famous Saicho and studied under him at Enryakuji Monastery. The embassy made two unsuccessful attempts at the sea crossing. When it did arrive near the mouth of the Yangtze River, Ennin's vessel was wrecked on a shoal, and he reached shore with difficulty. During his nine years of study and travel in China, he kept a careful diary, now an invaluable source for the period.

Ennin was disappointed at not receiving permission to visit Mount Tiantai, the original home of his sect, Tendai. However, he was able to spend time at another important Buddhist site, Mount Wutai. He studied there and at the Tang capital, Changan, under both Chinese and Indian monks. He suffered great anxiety at the time of the major persecution of Buddhism in China (841–845) under the Emperor Wu Zong. He was deported, as indeed he desired to be, and returned to a hero's welcome in Japan, bringing prized scriptures and valuable objects used in the new esoteric worship then spreading in Japan. He received the imperial appointment as Abbot of Enryakuji and the newly created title of *Daishi*, "Great Teacher," which was also given posthumously to Saicho and Kukai. The lives of these three Japanese monks and of the Chinese monk Ganjin illustrate the immense difficulties and hardships involved in the transfer of Buddhism to Japan and the significance of its place in the thought and culture of the country.

Most of the Heian period was dominated by the great Fujiwara family. Its influence began even before the location of the capital at Nara, with Fujiwara Kamatari, founder of the line and architect of the Taika Reform. His son, Fubito, with the aid of a committee, was responsible for the promulgation of the Taiho Code in 702. Fubito's four sons died in 737 in an epidemic of smallpox, but not before they had become the progenitors of the four main branches of the family. In the course of time and not without internal disputes, the Hokke branch from the north emerged as the leaders of the Fujiwara, who now began to rise to a position of supremacy which eclipsed all other clans. They were able to do this first of all by their control of land, the perennial basis of political power in Japan, as more and more small landowners "commended" plots of land to the Fujiwara in order to enjoy their protection. But the primary means used by the Fujiwara to maintain their political dominance was one which the Soga had used to a lesser degree before them, namely, constant intermarriage with the imperial house. The Fujiwara arranged for their daughters, wherever possible, to become the wives or concubines of the successive emperors. Since a Fujiwara was thus usually the father-in-law of the reigning sovereign, he was able, whether officially or unofficially, to exert an enormous influence upon affairs. "The real power of the Fujiwara was attained," in one of Sansom's lapidary phrases, "not by usurping but by protecting the throne."

The point of time generally reckoned as the beginning of the unquestioned supremacy of the Fujiwara is the year 858, when Fujiwara Yoshifusa became *sessho*, "regent," for the nine-year-old Emperor Seiwa. He was the first regent not of imperial blood, and he remained in virtual control of the state until 872. He was succeeded as regent by his nephew, Mototsune, who was first *sessho* and then *kampaku*, an office sometimes translated as "civil dictator." (The *kampaku* continued to act as regent even after an emperor had attained his majority, speaking on behalf of the ruler and issuing commands in his name.) When Mototsune in turn died in 891, his son Tokihira was only twenty-one and no new appointment to the position of *kampaku* was made. The young Emperor Uda, one of the few not born of a Fujiwara mother, preferred to depend for advice on a brilliant official named Sugawara Michizane, formerly a professor of *kambun* or "written Chinese." Michizane rose to high rank and favor, but the Fujiwara were just biding their time. After a brief eclipse until 899 they reasserted themselves and secured the office of minister of the Left, relegating Michizane to second place as minister of the Right. But that was not enough; Michizane was soon given a post in Kyushu, almost equivalent to a sentence of banishment, and died there in 903, it is said of a broken heart. The tale has a curious sequel. Soon after Michizane's death, lightning struck the palace, blinding rainstorms took place over long periods, fires broke out, and important persons died. These dire occurrences were ascribed to the vengeful ghost of the unfortunate Michizane. He was restored posthumously by imperial decree to all his rank and titles. The natural disasters however continued, so a temple was erected for his worship; he was enshrined as the God of Learning and Calligraphy and was given the title of Heavenly Deity in 986.

During his lifetime Michizane was invited to lead one of the long series of embassies to China, but he declined on the grounds of the disorders attending the decline of the Tang dynasty and, further, arranged that such cultural visits be discontinued. The Japanese apparently now felt they had acquired all that China could usefully offer; the next step was to work out in greater fullness their own indigenous culture on the basis of the riches they had already received.

The zenith of Fujiwara glory was reached in the person of Michinaga, who was the most powerful figure at court from the year 995 until his death

Worship of Buddha before the shrine at home.
Japan National Tourist Organization

in 1027. His father and his two brothers had already been regents. He never took the title himself, but he scarcely needed to, for his daughters were consorts to four emperors, though that involved one of the rulers marrying his own aunt. Two emperors were Michinaga's nephews and three were his grandsons. A brilliant man and leader of a brilliant society, he was not without a sense of his own value, for he boasted in a poem that he was "master of his world, like the flawless full moon riding the skies."[1]

Michinaga built a Buddhist monastery, the Hojoji, and dedicated the Golden Hall in it (to the repose of his own soul) on the occasion of his retiring from public life and taking the tonsure. (In the manner of the time he still exercised influence from within the monastery.) There was a dazzling ceremony of dedication and a sumptuous entertainment to follow, attended by the emperor and all the court. Jeweled nets hung down from the branches of plants around the pond on which floated jewel-adorned boats, while peacocks strutted on the island in the center of the pond. The Golden Hall itself had pillars that rested upon masonry supports shaped like huge elephants, a roof ridge of gold and silver, a golden door, and rock crystal foundations.

Michinaga was an adherent of the Jodo or Pure Land sect of Buddhism. The school was brought into prominence in Japan in the tenth century by a

[1] G.B. Sansom, *A History of Japan to 1334* (Stanford, Calif.: Stanford University Press, 1958), p. 174.

learned monk, Eshin. It stressed neither elaborate ritual nor arduous study of abstruse doctrine; repetition of the sacred formula, "*Namu Amida Butsu*," calling upon the Buddha of infinite compassion, was sufficient for salvation and would ensure being reborn in the Western Paradise or Pure Land. It was thus a religion of faith alone and not works, and it made a strong appeal to the common people and the unfortunate. It found a response also among the aristocrats and warriors, for even the educated Japanese were inclined to a faith involving feeling rather than one of abstract speculation. To this day the branches of this sect command the largest following of any in Japan. When Michinaga was dying, he followed the Jodo practice of his day by holding in his hand a thread attached to an image of Amida Buddha, so that he might be drawn into the Western Paradise.

One of the ladies of the court to whom Michinaga at one time paid more than passing attention was the Lady Murasaki Shikibu, lady-in-waiting to the Empress Akiko and author. Girls were not supposed to attempt the study of Chinese, but Murasaki picked up a knowledge of the language when her brother was having his lessons. It was now no longer acceptable for nobles and courtiers to hand over to scribes the task of writing; it was expected that a man of position would be able to write in a calligraphy that was aesthetic and a style that was civilized and elegant. The two systems of writing, one

Buddha, probably Amida, Kama-kura period, c. thirteenth century (wood, *yosegi* or "joined block technique," with polychrome and *kirikane*, "cut gold leaf decoration").

Ht., 47 in. Amida's disciples in the Jodo (Pure Land) sect believe they are saved and received into the Western Paradise by faith alone.

The Asia Society, New York: Mr. and Mrs. John D. Rockefeller 3rd Collection. Photography by Otto E. Nelson

basically Chinese, the other using simplified symbols derived from Chinese to stand for Japanese sounds, had by this time been developed. Murasaki used the latter, *kana*, form of script in writing the famous *Genji Monogatari* (*Tale of Genji*), a novel of remarkable insight that ranks as one of the greatest works in Japanese literature. It was composed in about the year 1008.

This long tale of the loves of the young Prince Genji is filled with a sensitivity, an appreciation of beauty, and a wistful Buddhist melancholy that lent it universal appeal, in spite of the fact that it deals with a small, closed court society with very specialized tastes in a time and an atmosphere remote from our own. In her ability to portray the least vibration of the human heart, Murasaki is the equal of Jane Austen and Charlotte Brontë. Man can write tales of action and intrigue, but perhaps it requires a woman's intuitive discrimination and patience to unravel the timeless motives and responses at the heart of human life. The following passage could well apply to a woman in any century or any land.

> The lady, when no answer came from Genji, thought that he had changed his mind, and though she would have been very angry if he had persisted in his suit, she was not quite prepared to lose him with so little ado.
> But this was a good opportunity once and for all to lock up her heart against him. She thought that she had done so successfully, but found to her surprise that he still occupied an uncommonly large share of her thoughts.[2]

As to the tinge of Buddhist melancholy in the *Tale of Genji*, a Japanese critic in the year 1200 noted the presence of the quality *aware*, which may be translated "sadness," "sensitivity," "that which is emotionally moving." The word *aware* begins as an exclamation of wonder or delight, a reaction to what has been called the "ahness" of things, goes on to mean that peculiar sadness just mentioned, and ends in modern Japanese as plain "wretched," "pitiable." But the high point of the word's significance is in Heian times when "the sadness of things" was very present to men's minds. Virgil's well-known line, *Sunt lacrimae rerum et mentem mortalia tangunt* ("There are tears in everything and the affairs of mortal men touch the heart"), reflects almost the exact feeling of the phrase *aware no mono* and of the spirit of the *Tale of Genji*, in spite of the lightness and frivolity of its topic.

An acquaintance with this novel is essential for the understanding of Heian, and indeed Japanese, aesthetics. The following quotations, from Arthur Waley's incomparable translation,[3] give the flavor of the novel and the feeling of the times. Here is Murasaki's account of Genji's meeting with a mysterious girl, Yugao.

---

[2] *The Tale of Genji*, by Lady Murasaki, tr. Arthur Waley (New York: Doubleday Anchor Books, 1955), p. 58. A new unabridged translation is: Royal Tyler, translator. *The Tale of Genji* (New York: Penguin Books, 2002)
[3] Pp. 68–92 passim.

The Tale of Genji, Lady Murasaki's famous novel, dates from the eleventh century and has been frequently illustrated.

This painting of a scene from the Yugao chapter is of the Tosa school and dates from the eighteenth-nineteenth century.

Arthur M. Sackler Art Museums, Harvard University; Gift of Charles Parker

He had come in a plain coach with no outriders. No one could possibly guess who he was, and feeling quite at his ease, he leant forward and deliberately examined the house. The gate, also made of a kind of trelliswork, stood ajar and he could see enough of the interior to realize that it was a very humble and poorly furnished dwelling. For a moment he pitied those who lived in such a place, but then he remembered the song, "Seek not in the wide world to find a home; but where you chance to rest, call that your house"; and again, "Monarchs may keep their palaces of jade, for in a leafy cottage two can sleep."

There was a wattled fence over which some ivy-like creeper spread its cool green leaves, and among the leaves were white flowers with petals half-unfolded like the lips of people smiling at their own thoughts. "They are called Yugao, Evening Faces," one of his servants told him; "how strange to find so lovely a crowd clustering on this deserted wall!" And indeed it was a most strange and delightful thing to see how on the narrow tenement in a poor quarter of the town they had clambered over rickety eaves and gables and spread wherever there was room for them to grow. He sent one of his servants to pick some. The man entered at the half-opened door, and had begun to pluck the flowers, when a little girl in a long yellow tunic came through a quite genteel sliding door, and holding out towards Genji's servant a white fan heavily perfumed with incense, she said to him, "Would you like something to put them on? I am afraid you have chosen a wretched-looking bunch," and she handed him the fan.

• • •

Having arranged for continual masses to be said on the sick woman's behalf [Genji had been visiting his foster mother, a nun, who was ill, and who lived in the house next door to the mysterious lady], he took his leave, ordering Koremitsu to light him with a candle. As they left the house he looked at the fan upon which the white flowers had been laid. He now saw that there was writing on it, a poem carelessly but elegantly scribbled: "The flower that puzzled you was but the *Yugao*, strange beyond knowing in its dress of shining dew." It was written with a deliberate negligence which seemed to aim at concealing the writer's status and identity. But for all that the hand showed a breeding and distinction which agreeably surprised him. "Who lives in the house on the left?" he asked.

• • •

[Intrigued, Genji replies in verse] "Could I but get a closer view, no longer would they puzzle me,—the flowers that all too dimly in the gathering dusk I saw." [Through arrangements made somewhat unwillingly by Genji's faithful servant, Koremitsu, the couple meets.] Their room was in the front of the house. Genji got up and opened the long sliding shutters. They stood together looking out. In the courtyard near them was a clump of fine Chinese bamboos; dew lay thick on the borders, glittering here no less brightly than in the great gardens to which Genji was better accustomed. There was a confused buzzing of insects. Crickets were chirping in the wall. He had often listened to them, but always at a distance; now, singing so close to him, they made a music which was unfamiliar and indeed seemed far lovelier than that with which he was acquainted. But then, everything in this place where one thing was so much to his liking seemed despite all drawbacks to take on a new tinge of interest and beauty. She was wearing a white bodice with a soft, grey cloak over it. It was a poor dress, but she looked charming and almost distinguished; even so, there was nothing very striking in her appearance—only a certain fragile grace and elegance. . . .

"I am going to take you somewhere not at all far away where we shall be able to pass the rest of the night in peace. We cannot go on like this, parting always at break of day." "Why have you suddenly come to that conclusion?" she asked, but she spoke submissively. He vowed to her that she should be his love in this and in all future lives, and she answered so passionately that she seemed utterly transformed from the listless creature he had known, and it was hard to believe that such vows were no novelty to her.

• • •

[They made the move.] It was now almost daylight. The cocks had stopped crowing. The voice of an old man (a pilgrim preparing for the ascent of the Holy Mountain) sounded somewhere not far away; and as at each prayer he bent forward to touch the ground with his head, they could hear with what pain and difficulty he moved. What could he be asking for in his prayers, this old man whose life seemed fragile as the morning dew? NAMU TORAI NO DOSHI, "Glory be to the Saviour that shall come"; now they could hear the words. "Listen," said Genji tenderly, "is not that an omen that our love shall last through many lives to come?" And he recited the poem: "Do not prove false this omen of the pilgrim's chant; that even in lives to come our love shall last unchanged."

Then unlike the lovers in the "Everlasting Wrong" who prayed that they might be as "twin birds that share a wing" (for they remembered that this story had ended very sadly), they prayed, "May our love last till Maitreya comes as a Buddha into the World." But she, still distrustful, answered his poem with the verse: "Such sorrow have I known in this world that I have small hope of worlds to come." Her versification was still a little tentative.

• • •

[But the story ends tragically. Yugao dies suddenly and mysteriously.] Her breathing had quite stopped. What could he do? To whom could he turn for help? He ought to send for a priest. He tried to control himself but he was very young, and seeing her lying there, all still and pale, he could contain himself no longer and crying, "Come back to me, my own darling, come back to life. Do not look at me so strangely!" he flung his arms about her. But now she was quite cold. Her face was set in a dull, senseless stare.

• • •

[Yugao's body had to be taken away.] A faint light was already showing in the sky when Koremitsu brought the carriage in. Thinking that Genji would not wish to move the body himself, he wrapt it in a rush-mat and carried it towards the carriage. How small she was to hold! Her face was calm and beautiful. He felt no repulsion. He could find no way to secure her hair, and when he began to carry her it overflowed and hung towards the ground. Genji saw and his eyes darkened. A hideous anguish possessed him.

The length of these quotations from the novel of Lady Murasaki is justified not only by the intrinsic beauty of the language but also by the fact that they cast a fascinating light upon the attitudes of the court nobles during that long era when they were the ruling councillors of the Empire of Japan. Here we see them in their casual moments, at play not at work; but it is obvious that these men have moved far from the position of the tribal warriors who were their ancestors. They move in a society with elaborate rules of etiquette and highly refined tastes. Indeed they carry this refinement to the point of preciousness, with a Japanese tendency to exaggeration and extremes. It is surely a little overdone, not to say banal, to end a paragraph of such emotional depth and haunting beauty as the one containing the prayer "May our love last till Maitreya comes as a Buddha into the World" with the sentence "Her versification was still a little tentative." This was scarcely surprising, for Yugao was only nineteen. But the ability to write sophisticated verse was in those days an important social hallmark, and in this as in all else Lady Murasaki faithfully mirrored her times. It almost seems that the primary civilizations of the Greeks and the Chinese had an instinct of restraint and avoidance of extremes that was never quite shared by the derived civilizations of the Romans and the Japanese.

Although the persons reflected in these tales, written, be it noted, sixty years before the Norman Conquest, produced a remarkable indigenous civilization from alien and native elements and set the standard for the future at least in matters of taste, they belonged to the upper crust of society, small in numbers, dwelling mainly in the capital. They were probably even more limited in the range of their contacts within their own nation than the courtiers of the Sun King in seventeenth-century France. And as in Louis XIV's France, the narrow but brilliant civilization of the court was becoming perilously separated from its agricultural base. The continual absence of the landlords in the capital and the heavy tax burdens placed on some manors while so many others were granted tax exemptions for one reason or another (see the end of Chapter 2) created an unstable situation over most of the countryside. Too many *shoen*, or "manors," belonging to officials, nobles, and the Buddhist church were claiming exemption from tax, whether or not they had a valid title to exemption. The very officials who should have enforced the payment of taxes were at the same time the great landowners who gained most from tax exemption, both for themselves and for the smaller farmers who placed land under their protection in return for a fee much less than the tax. With the drying up of tax sources, the organs of the government faded in importance, the scope of their administrative authority shrinking along with their revenues. Thus, the highly centralized government, established on the Chinese model by the Taika Reform, gradually decayed in late Heian times, and the way was prepared for a new military class destined to control the future.

One of the greatest losses in potential tax revenue was from land newly brought under cultivation. New land, particularly in the east and north, had been brought continuously into use by many enterprising lords and Buddhist abbots over a long period of time. Reclamation of land from the wilderness implies at least a rudimentary use of capital. The addition of irrigation canals and the control of water levels in the rice fields required tools and labor along with a high degree of planning and control. Japanese resources apparently were sufficient to meet these needs and were intelligently used. Records of the seventh and eighth centuries show crown gifts of thousands of iron hoes

Peasants winnowing rice in the presence of officials (left), an instance of the strict control of agriculture.

Scroll painting of the Ashikaga (or Muromachi) period (1392–1573).

Arthur M. Sackler Art Museums, Harvard University; Gift of Denman Waldo Ross

and spades to high officers and to monasteries for expansion of the cultivated area. In 722 the court ordered the reclamation of 3 million acres of new land as national policy. But incentives had to be offered, and so the new land was excluded from taxation and reallotment under the Taika Reform. This tended further to invalidate the old reform system and to withdraw from the exchequer the most important source of new revenue.

Considerable change also took place in the legal and administrative system. Developments and early revisions in the Taiho Code had been gathered together in two sections, the *ryo*, or "administrative and civil codes," and the *ritsu*, or "disciplinary and penal regulations." But revisions continued to be made to suit changing conditions, and these were compiled in various collections from 820 onward, ending in 967 with the Engishiki, which aimed at putting administrative procedures into permanent form. Both the Engishiki and the other collections came to have the force of statutory law, in some cases even superseding the original codes. Herein lay a double irony. At the very time that the process of change in law reached its climax in the Engishiki, the whole administrative system was being shunted aside to make way for the personal rule of the Fujiwara. And thus it was the descendants of Fujiwara Kamatari, founder of the Fujiwara family and chief author of the Taika Reform, who served mainly to render that reform defunct.

A curious, though it must be admitted almost inevitable, process set in whereby the *mandokoro*, "the secretariats or estate offices of the great families," and particularly of the Fujiwara, began to assume the functions of government offices and to maintain such administrative liaison as there was between different parts of the country. For example, a letter written by a Fujiwara clerk might affect the tax returns of a whole province owned by the family and would take precedence over a government order through the old channels. This was in a sense bound to happen because the whole Chinese machinery of the Taika Reform and the Taiho Code was alien to the structure of Japanese society, both agrarian and aristocratic. The peasants made the complicated bureaucratic system of periodic reallotment of land completely unworkable by their fierce attachment to their own plots of carefully irrigated rice paddy. Indeed even in China, its country of origin, the full program of periodic redistribution had not been found practicable. The aristocrats nullified the system of public service and promotion by allowing the offices to become hereditary and thus open to no competition on merit. An extreme example was the appointment simply on the basis of pedigree of a young man of seventeen to the office of Commander of the Metropolitan Police Bureau in 1025. The Emperor Toba later gave the qualifications for this same post as good family, good sense, knowledge of precedent, good looks, high court rank, and wealth.

In the end the administrative scheme of government offices became a dead letter, although the titles attached to some of them were retained by court nobles right down to the nineteenth century. Three of the old government offices, however, did remain active. Originally they were of minor importance, but being functionally valuable they grew during the tenth century while the rest declined. They were:

1. The Board of Audit, *Kageyushi*. These "release commissioners" received and audited the accounts of an official leaving office before he was released from his responsibilities. The outgoing official had likewise to submit a report to his successor. In the course of time the whole matter of appointing and dismissing officials, including the creation of new offices and what we would call job descriptions, devolved upon this office. This, however, is not to imply that in appointments they acted independently of the great Fujiwara officers of state. Financial and fiscal affairs continued to be handled through this office as a result of their auditing function.

2. The Bureau of Archivists, *Kurando-dokoro*. This office began as the emperor's private treasury and archives. The officials in it had the responsibility of drawing up the imperial rescripts and edicts and thus had to know something of the emperor's mind. Originally without executive powers, the bureau increased greatly in importance and authority as the Fujiwara found it useful for getting things done without going through channels. For the intelligent and ambitious it offered such good chances of promotion that it became known as *Toryumon*, the Gateway of the Ascending Dragon.

3. The Commissioners of Police, *Kebiishi-cho*. At first a metropolitan po-

lice establishment, its jurisdiction was later extended to the provinces, while its authority covered judicial as well as strictly police matters. The Bureau of Archivists and the family Mandokoro of the Fujiwara may be compared to the private secretariat of the Roman Emperor Augustus, known as *ab epistulis*, and his accountant's office, *a rationibus*, which soon became in effect no longer private household offices but important administrative departments of the government under Augustus and his successors, replacing the official senate machinery.

The successor to the great Fujiwara Michinaga was Fujiwara Yorimichi, who became regent in 1017 and continued in the office for fifty years, during the reigns of three emperors. In spite of this impressive display, however, the power of the Fujiwara was beginning to pass its peak; and when Go-Sanjo became emperor in 1068, it received a check. The new emperor's mother was not a Fujiwara lady, and he himself had been miserably treated by Yorimichi when a youth; he decided he would rule on his own. He established a land record office to try to deal with the problem of the manors and counter the trends so harmful to central administration. He abdicated of his own will in 1072 and intended to continue to rule through his son, Shirakawa, but he unfortunately died in the following year at the early age of thirty-nine.

It was this son, the Emperor Shirakawa, who, in the last decades of the eleventh century, first successfully carried through the curious device known as *insei*, "cloister government." Japanese emperors, and indeed other Japanese dignitaries up to the present day, have a heavy burden of ceremonial duties. The practice, therefore, grew up in the Heian court of early abdication and retirement. The usual way to retire was to take the tonsure and live as a Buddhist monk. This act was not irrevocable, and many government officials and some emperors returned from the monastery to reenter active political life. (The word *in* means a "quiet apartment in a monastery," and by a common Japanese practice the word is transferred from the place to the occupant, Go-Sanjo being known after his abdication as Go-Sanjo In.) Shirakawa, however, seems to have begun the practice of placing on the throne a child emperor, who would give no trouble, and continuing to direct affairs of state from the cloister, with more personal freedom and less obligation to fatiguing ceremonies. He was in this way able to retain his mystic authority as retired emperor but use as his advisers and mouthpieces independent persons of his own choice, outside the official hierarchy. This ingenious device offered the retired emperor several advantages, not least of which was a means to circumvent the Fujiwara, whose whole object for centuries had been to become an indispensable part of the official order, but who had little excuse to interfere in the unofficial arrangements of a retired person who was sheltered by the umbrella of the church, although they continued to serve and usually to direct the titular emperor.

The institution of the *insei* is of sociological and anthropological as well as historical interest, for it is one more move away from matriarchy and toward patriarchy. The installing of empresses had previously been abandoned. Now the emperor was no longer influenced by the men related to his mother and his wife or concubine, the Fujiwara, but by his father, the retired emperor. It seems that sheer biological accident made the shift to the *insei* form easier. After the death of Michinaga, the Fujiwara ladies died young or gave birth to girls almost exclusively or were childless. Divisions within the Fujiwara clan further weakened their position, for Fujiwara Yoshinobu, a dissident clansman, opposed the regent, Fujiwara Yorimichi, and supported Go-Sanjo in his claim to the throne, from which resulted a major check to Fujiwara ambitions.

The *insei* emperors were long-lived. Shirakawa ruled as actual emperor from 1072 to 1086, then abdicated and continued to govern from the cloister for forty-three years more, until his death in 1129. During this long period no fewer than three emperors occupied the throne but ruled in name only. The Emperor Toba ruled for sixteen years in the titular position, and then on the death of Shirakawa six years after his own retirement he held the power of abdicated emperor for twenty-six years. Go-Shirakawa (*Go* in effect means II, "the second") was emperor for three years and then ruled from the cloister for thirty-four years more. Thus the 120 years from 1072 to 1192 are spanned by the rule of only three emperors, and of this period these three ruled as cloistered emperors for 104 years or all but sixteen of the total. Nevertheless it must be made clear that the effective period of *insei* control was in fact limited to seventy years, from 1086, the abdication of Shirakawa, to 1156, the death of Toba. Thereafter the power lay with the warring clans. Go-Shirakawa survived by his cleverness in playing off one side against the other in their rival claims to be the protectors of the Throne, but the real authority no longer lay with him or his advisers. The great period of civilian, and highly civilized, rule by the court nobles was almost over. Armed warriors, cruder and of coarser grain, but more efficient and sometimes wise and far-seeing, were in process of asserting their right to rule in the name of the emperor.

The process was a gradual one, fostered by the continuance of disturbed conditions in the countryside. Skirmishes and revolts broke out as landowners sought, in the absence of a law centrally enforced, to defend their territories or to increase them. As early as 935 a large-scale armed rebellion against the Throne was initiated by Taira Masakado in the eastern region of Japan. During the early tenth century, powerful landowners in the provinces were for all practical purposes supreme in their own domains. They were often given imperial appointments as vice-governors, since the governor was generally an absentee living at the capital, and this gave them virtual control in their own regions. About 935 Taira Masakado began attacking his uncles and other members of the Taira family in order to add to his lands. Encouraged by victories over them and then over government forces sent to subdue him, he secured aid from powerful allies and after some years controlled no fewer than eight of the eastern provinces. In 940 he sent a letter to the chief minister, Fujiwara Tokihira, in which he claimed the title of emperor for himself.

But this was also the year of his nemesis, for he was attacked by powerful forces at the request of the emperor. He expected help from his allies, who had mustered over 8000 troops, but they refused to join him. He was completely defeated and his head put on view in the capital to discourage others.

At the same time in western Japan, Sumitomo, who might be described as a pirate chief, wrought havoc in the Inland Sea with a force of 1,000 small ships until he was defeated in 941.

Nearly a hundred years later in 1028 the vice-governor of Shimosa Province, Taira Tadatsune, overstepped his bounds and attacked two neighboring provinces. After some unsuccessful attempts to crush Tadatsune, the government called on the most famous general of the day, Minamoto Yorinobu, to quell the revolt. Yorinobu had only to move in the direction of the rebel; so great was his prestige that he did not need to attack. Tadatsune gave himself up. The loyal troops of the clans who suppressed these uprisings were later to be the support of the new military dictatorship, but at this point they were still willing to be the "claws and teeth" of the Fujiwara, who were to remain the leaders of an elegant and cultured society at the capital until well into the twelfth century.

5

THE RISE OF THE WARRIOR CLASS AND THE GEMPEI WAR

End of the Heian Period: 1158–1185

In this period the center of gravity in Japanese political power shifted from the emperor and his court nobles to the heads of warrior families; from the capital, Kyoto, to the country estates; and from those who held ancient, hereditary titles and ruled under the form of a civil administration of the Chinese type to those clan leaders, old and new, who could carve out land and power for themselves by a sword and a strong right arm. In the conservative tradition of Japan all the old features remained—emperor, nobles, titles, and the ancient capital—but they gradually became increasingly empty symbols, for the authority lay elsewhere. As the court became less powerful and as the nobles drew less income from their estates, the country squires were the gainers, not only in money but in knowledge of affairs. These country squires, many of whom started out as estate managers for absentee nobles, had been able to acquire control of land and of the all-important labor force to work the land and to provide a stalwart body of armed retainers.

The name of the war between two great houses with which this period ended is compounded from the Chinese form of their names, "Gen," in native Japanese form "Minamoto," and "Hei," in Japanese "Taira." The compound for phonetic reasons emerges as "Gempei." Other families of military prowess were involved, but these two, the Minamoto and the Taira, were the chief. The period is still known as the Heian, but leadership was clearly passing from the Fujiwara to the warrior families. The Taira were the most powerful at the end of the Heian period. The next era, the Kamakura period, began when the Minamoto became the dominant power in the state.

The origins of both the Taira and the Minamoto go far back in Japanese history. The Taiho Code, doubtless foreseeing large families in the imperial household where wives and concubines were the rule, decreed that descendants of the emperors in the sixth generation were to be deprived of the rank of prince, were to take a family name and start on their own. This rule was observed and began to come into effect in the late ninth century. A younger son of the Emperor Kammu (died 806) had been appointed governor of Hitachi in eastern Japan. His descendants increased their lands and possessions and in due course became an independent family with the name Taira. Taira strength in the eastern part of the country continued to be considerable, for Taira Masakado controlled eight provinces before he was defeated in 940. In a subsequent rebellion led by a Taira, that of Tadatsune in 1028, it is significant that the leader of the government forces sent to suppress the rising was of the rival house, Minamoto Yorinobu.

Taira fortunes rose steeply a hundred years later, for then Taira Tadamori gained the ear of the retired Emperor Shirakawa and strongly supported court policy, especially where the Minamoto could be made to appear in the wrong. Tadamori rendered special aid to the government by controlling piracy in the Inland Sea in 1129. He controlled piracy rather than suppressing it, for he was not above making some deals to his own advantage with local magnates who held coastal property and combined piracy with more legitimate activities. It was largely owing to the success of Tadamori that the center of Taira power moved from its place of origin in the east to central and western Japan. Tadamori, though head of a warrior house, was far from being a mere rough soldier. He was a clever and experienced politician, something of a poet, and not a little sought after as a witty and accomplished companion by the ladies of the court. His younger kinsman, Taira Kiyomori, became a still more powerful figure and dominated the government for twenty years during the second half of the twelfth century.

The Minamoto family also arose on account of the Taiho Code rule, the various branches being distinguished by the inclusion of the name of the particular emperor from whom they reckoned descent, e.g., Saga-Benji, Udá-Genji, and so on. The branch that ultimately succeeded in assuming general leadership of the clan was that of the Seiwa-Genji (Seiwa reigned 858–876), though each branch retained a high degree of independence. The Seiwa-Genji reckoned their origin as a separate branch of the family from the year 961. The Minamoto gave aid and service to the Fujiwara from the beginning, and the great Fujiwara Michinaga (died 1017) depended heavily on Minamoto Yorimitsu and Minamoto Yorinobu, so much so that their enemies referred to them as "running dogs" of the Fujiwara. This derogatory term, however, does not do justice to their qualities as both soldiers and courtiers. The military reputation of the Minamoto was greatly enhanced by Yorinobu's son, Yoriyoshi, and by his grandson, Yoshiiye. Both were involved in bitterly fought wars in the north, known as the Early Nine Years' War and the Later Three Years' War. The Early Nine Years' War was brought on through the ambitions of the Abe family.

This family had for some time held the post of northern commander-in-chief and commissioner for the Ainu, and in 1050 one Abe Yoritoki began exacting taxes and attaching property to which he was not entitled. The governor complained to Kyoto, and Minamoto Yoriyoshi was appointed to bring the Abe clan to heel. When Abe Yoritoki was killed in the course of the protracted campaigns, his son, Sadato, a man of immense strength and courage, took his place. After an unsuccessful Minamoto attack on a stockade fortress, Sadato's men broke out in a surprise attack and pursued the Minamoto forces in a thick snowstorm. Among the few who escaped slaughter on this occasion were Yoriyoshi and his fifteen-year-old son, Yoshiiye, who had followed his father to the wars. Yoriyoshi, undismayed, collected another force and attacked Sadato again. He diverted the water supply of the fortress and managed to set fire to the stockade. After incredible privations, Sadato finally surrendered.

The story of the Later Three Years' War is somewhat similar. In this case the Kiyowara family, who had aided Yoriyoshi and the government side in the last war, themselves began to exceed their authority and mishandle affairs in the north. This time Minamoto Yoshiiye undertook the commission to discipline the Kiyowara in 1083. Difficult terrain, biting cold, and considerable slaughter on both sides made the campaign a desperate one. A certain youth of sixteen received an arrow in the eye. Pausing only to break off the shaft, he fired an arrow of his own back at his opponent and hit him. Then he collapsed on the ground; but when a friend came to pull the arrow out, and put his foot on the youth's face to get a better purchase, the wounded youth threatened to kill him. To trample on a warrior's face was an insult that could only be avenged by death. Finally Yoshiiye's brother brought reinforcements from Kyoto, and with this aid he defeated the Kiyowara. Yoshiiye became a national hero, so much so that the government had to try to put a stop to numbers of farmer-soldiers "commending" their lands to him, not because he was powerful at court but because they wanted to be feudal retainers of so admired a warrior.

These wars in the far north were not in themselves of first importance, though obviously the government was unwilling to allow widespread disobedience even at a distance. But they were significant in the national development because they were hard training schools in the military virtues and in the forging of those intimate bonds of loyalty between leaders and men that would mark the national ethos from that point right up to the present. Yoshiiye, we are told, would assign seats each evening in the barracks to his soldiers in the Three Years' War, the higher places for the brave and loyal, the lower for those who had flinched from the battle. Courage and loyalty, both for good and ill, were soon to outshine all other virtues. Not for nothing had Yoshiiye, when fighting as a youth with his father, been nicknamed by the soldiers "Hachiman Taro," or "Firstborn of the God of War." (See frontispiece.)

A further disturbance, the Hogen Insurrection, took place between 1156 and 1158, led this time by one of the Fujiwara old nobility, Fujiwara Yorinaga. At the deaths of the Emperor Konoye in 1155 and the retired Emperor Toba the next year, an acrimonious dispute broke out over the succession. A woman's name was put forward but did not gain support at court. The regent Tadamichi, who was Yorinaga's elder brother, and the powerful Taira Kiyomori took the side of the man who eventually succeeded as the Emperor Go-Shirakawa, while Yorinaga turned to support another retired emperor, Sutoku. The matter came to an open breach. Yorinaga raised troops and, with Sutoku, fortified a palace in the city of Kyoto, but their forces were heavily outnumbered. Sutoku's palace was burned, and Yorinaga himself killed. The insurrection was not on a large scale and never had much chance of success. Its importance was that it was an omen of things to come, the overwhelming power of the military clans.

Although both the Taira and the Minamoto had their share of power and authority in the provinces, the Taira became the dominant force in the state through the influence of Taira Kiyomori, who became chief of his clan in 1153 and was virtually without a rival until his death in 1181. The groundwork had been laid by the capable and diplomatic Taira Tadamori. Kiyomori was a younger kinsman but not a son of Tadamori. In fact there was a whisper of an imperial sire. In any case Kiyomori gained the ear of the ex-emperor Go-Shirakawa and used to the full his position at court, his increasing wealth, and his clan influence in the region of the Inland Sea. Some of his work there in the construction of harbors, dredging of channels, and development of trade with China was of permanent value to the country.

During the wars in the far north and the power plays in court, life went on fairly peaceably for farmers and the little people in much of the country. There was one rather ominous feature of this period that gravely disturbed the life of all in and around the capital but did not greatly affect the provinces, and that was the endemic warfare conducted by the soldier-monks attached to some of the great monasteries. The situation was particularly bad during the period of the cloister government, in the century 1080 to 1180. In many cases the outbreaks were occasioned by disputes over the appointment of abbots or the right to ordain monks. They seem not to have been the deliberate policy or choice of the leading church dignitaries themselves but to have stemmed rather from the sectarianism and crowd psychology of the somewhat ignorant lay brothers who made up the regiments of temple guards. They were a nuisance rather than a serious threat, but occasionally, as in the Teiji Rising in 1160, their participation did affect the outcome of a revolution or palace plot. A determined military leader from time to time was able without any difficulty to scatter their ill-organized forces; yet many leaders were most unwilling on grounds of conscience or superstition to proceed to extreme measures against those who claimed the protection of Buddha. The soldier-monks were not slow to take advantage of this fact and would sometimes exercise a form of spiritual blackmail by bringing a sacred image with them. If their demands were not met, they would leave the image in its palanquin where it stood on the street and return to their temple. This was thought to expose their enemies to the wrath of the god, particularly if anything were to happen to the image. They would have their demands granted and be begged to come and remove the image to its resting place in the temple.

Farm at Ohara, near Kyoto.
This farm and farmer's family look much the same now as in medieval Japan; but technology has brought improvements in production and convenience.

Japan National Tourist Organization

The last quarter of the twelfth century shows increasing signs of a declining regime, less and less able to keep order. There are notices of famine, great fires in the capital, some of them due to deliberate arson, and piteous tales of infants and their dead mothers and corpses lying unburied in the streets. There was an understandable air of general pessimism, and this in turn was linked to a doctrine of Buddhism prevalent at the time. Popular preachers spoke of a prophecy that the original Buddha Sakya had uttered, predicting that there would come a degenerate age in which men would forsake the Law. It was widely felt that the time of the Latter Day of the Holy Law (*Mappo*) had now arrived, and men were exhorted, by believing in the simple creed of the compassionate Amida Buddha, to save themselves from this untoward generation. The strong presence of Taira Kiyomori doubtless served to prevent even worse disasters; but events seem to have passed the point where one man could patch them up. Taira Kiyomori was not a popular figure, and the Minamoto rivals were always seeking an opportunity to supplant him. Three such attempts were made, the first and the last being the most serious.

In the first, the Heiji Rising of 1160, a Minamoto and a Fujiwara took advantage of Kiyomori's absence from Kyoto to seize the the emperor and the ex-emperor. Their coup seemed to have succeeded, but they were slow to follow up their advantage. Kiyomori returned and acted with his usual decisiveness. He gathered Taira reinforcements and engineered the escape of the ex-emperor. The emperor was disguised as a lady-in-waiting and reached the Rokuhara headquarters of the Taira in Kyoto in safety. The Minamoto leader defended the Great Palace with great bravery but was finally driven out. The final blow to the Minamoto forces was delivered by an army of soldier-monks from Mount Hiei. Go-Shirakawa and Kiyomori were back in the saddle.

The second attempt, the Shishigatani Affair, in 1177, was a plot hatched by leaders who hated Kiyomori and was named for the remote country mansion in which the conspirators met to make their plans. But a junior member of the Minamoto house revealed the plot, and the conspirators were ruthlessly dealt with. The subjection of a Buddhist monk to torture to extract information created a particularly bad impression. It is thought that a serious illness was beginning to embitter Kiyomori and affect his judgment.

The third attempt came in 1179, two years before Kiyomori's death. A call to arms was raised by Minamoto Yorimasa, himself an old man. He was, in a sense, a transitional personality illustrative of the changing times. A poet and a courtier, he had abandoned an earlier military career and had commended himself to Kiyomori as a safe and reliable supporter by taking no part in the Heiji Rising. But apparently clan loyalty was still the dominant factor in Yorimasa's character; and it is certain that Kiyomori was becoming more morose and tyrannical. In any event, in May 1180 Yorimasa sent messages to Minamoto leaders and to the monasteries which Kiyomori had specially alienated. He was joined by a son of Go-Shirakawa, Prince Mochihito, whom Yorimasa planned to make emperor. Kiyomori received word of the plot, brought reinforcements to the capital, and put a close guard on the person of Go-Shirakawa. Prince Mochihito retreated to the monastery of Miidera to escape arrest but had to move on in the direction of Nara. Minamoto Yorimasa, who was now with him, had the bridge at Uji partially destroyed to foil the Taira pursuers. Some of them managed to ford the river, and a battle ensued outside the Byodo-in temple. Yorimasa received an arrow wound and urged the prince to escape, while he himself, to avoid capture, committed *harakiri* in due form right in front of the beautiful Phoenix Hall of the monastery. The prince was later captured and killed, and Kiyomori had the remnant of the insurgents ruthlessly suppressed. Yorimasa's call to arms against the Taira therefore seemed abortive and premature; but it was the last straw. The Minamoto were now burning to avenge the numerous defeats and insults Kiyomori had inflicted upon them.

In the same month of June 1180 in which he had defeated Yorimasa, Kiyomori attempted to secure the persons of the emperor and the ex-emperor more closely under his control—always the key to the legitimacy of a regime—by removing the whole court to his own seat at Fukuwara. This move was not a success. The place did not seem to suit the health of the young emperor, who had never been strong, and Kiyomori was unable to keep an eye on events at the capital, where he knew there was mounting opposition to him. So Kiyomori returned to Kyoto, taking the whole court back with him, at the end of the year 1180.

The shadows were gathering rapidly. Kiyomori fell sick with a serious disease; and in spite of the counsel of his sons and advisers, he seems in a kind of madness to have decided on burning the monasteries of Todaiji and Kofukuji, two of the most ancient and honorable, though by no means peaceful, shrines of Buddhism. By the spring of 1181 he was running a high fever, and on March 21 he died.

The issue was now out in the open and the battle joined in earnest and on a large scale between the Taira and the Minamoto; the Gempei War had begun. Kiyomori had lived to hear of two engagements and had made his sons swear everlasting enmity to Minamoto Yoritomo, the new head of the Minamoto clan. In the first of these battles, a minor one, Yoritomo with only a small force had been halted and turned back in September 1180 at Ishibashiyama as he moved from his eastern base toward the capital. Completely undeterred, he went on gathering forces, claiming that he was the legitimate protector of the Throne and that the dead Prince Mochihito had called upon him to subdue the enemies of the state. In the second battle of 1180, that of the River Fujikawa in Suruga Province, he was more successful, defeating a Taira force in a night attack.

The battles of the Gempei War, which lasted from 1180 to 1185, were fought on several fronts. The Minamoto moved in on the capital from their bases in the east and from the north in the early stages of the war, while the Taira, who had local strength in west Japan and on Shikoku Island, moved in these directions when they were forced to abandon the capital. The Taira were also stronger on the sea than the Minamoto. The Minamoto had the intangible but important advantage of being a rising star, whereas the long dominance of Kiyomori had made the Taira unpopular. Since there was some dissension among the various Minamoto leaders, it is well to note their names and relationships. Minamoto Yoritomo was the commanding general, though perhaps a better statesman than a strategist. His brother, the dashing Yoshitsune, was the best military tactician on either side. Noriyori, the brother who came between the first two in age, also played a significant part in the war. Two other Minamoto generals of great importance were Yoritomo's uncle, Yukiiye, and his first cousin, Yoshinaka, a competent leader but one who tried to play his own hand and failed.[1] It was a war of young generals, for Yoshitsune and Yoshinaka both died at the age of thirty. Yoritomo's famous father, Yoshitomo, had been killed at the age of thirty-seven in the course of the Heiji Rising. Yoritomo himself, after winning the war and designing the peace, died at the comparatively early age of fifty-two.

[1] It may simplify the mastery of Japanese names to note that most consist of four syllables and that the component parts divide into two-syllable pairs, which correspond to two Japanese characters. Many of these two-syllable pairs repeat within a family in various combinations. Surnames are placed first and given names second.

Following the opening battles in 1180, there was a lull in the fighting during the winter of 1181, but the Taira were able to defeat Minamoto Yuki-iye on the Sunomata River in the province of Owari, not very far distant from Kyoto, during the month of May. The Taira were not really able to exploit this victory, and the Minamoto went on recruiting support. The struggle then moved to the north where, in the autumn of the same year, the Minamoto this time were victorious in Echizen under the able Yoshinaka, Yoritomo's cousin.

Very little fighting took place during the whole of 1182, when famine and disease affected large parts of the country. When warfare resumed in early summer of 1183, Taira Koremori was at first successful in reducing certain enemy strongpoints, but his fortune changed when he moved farther north to Etchu Province. Koremori, with superior numbers, was encamped on the slopes of Mount Tonami. Minamoto Yoshinaka, in a carefully coordinated move, surrounded Koremori's army by night, confused it by a series of prodding surprise tactics, and at length put the whole host to flight. This defeat was disastrous for the Taira, since Yoshinaka was now able to move unimpeded toward the capital from a northerly direction, while Yukiiye with another force advanced upon it from the east.

At this point the Minamoto gained a considerable psychological advantage, for Go-Shirakawa, the ex-emperor, threw in his lot with them. He went ostensibly on a religious pilgrimage to Mount Hiei, close by the capital but far enough away to put him out of reach of the Taira and within the protection of the soldier-monks. From this vantage point he was soon brought back in triumph to the capital by Minamoto Yoshinaka's army. Go-Shirakawa was no doubt tired of the heavy-handed "protection" of the Taira, particularly under the domineering Kiyomori, now deceased; but he also had an eye to the main chance, reckoning the imperial house would be better off under Yoritomo, with whom he had secretly been in contact. Portraits of the long-lived Go-Shirakawa show a heavy head, with a large nose, small beady eyes, and a full, down-drawn mouth—the impression is of a crafty man rather than a great one. But there was dire need for shrewdness in the imperial player in this poker game, where others held the main cards of brute force and money and he only those of prestige and his natural wits.

Taira Munemori, chieftain of the clan since his father Kiyomori's death, had now no choice but to retire to the west, and this he did, taking with him the child-emperor Antoku and the imperial regalia. The establishment of the Minamoto in place of the Taira as the dominant power in the capital ushers in the second and final phase of the Gempei War, in the early autumn of 1183.

At first things went well for the Taira. Their retreating army was a formidable force and succeeded in defeating a pursuing detachment of inadequate strength at Mizushima. More important still, Yoritomo had to settle a matter of serious dissension within his own Minamoto ranks. Yoshinaka, now in charge in Kyoto, was plotting to carry off Go-Shirakawa and set up his own regime in the north. Go-Shirakawa himself revealed the plot to Yoritomo, who promptly dispatched his two brothers, Noriyori and Yoshitsune, against Yoshinaka. In an episode famous in Japanese romances, Yoshinaka was brought to book near the renowned Bridge of Uji, where Yorimasa had made his last stand in 1180, and was killed after desperate resistance.

The Taira had established a base in friendly territory at Yashima on the island of Shikoku and were hopeful of being able to restore their fortunes. As the first stage of a possible move back to Kyoto, they took advantage of their naval superiority to cross over the Inland Sea to a point on the north shore at Ichi-no-tani, where they erected excellent defenses along the road running between mountains and sea. But Yoshitsune with great skill devised a plan to turn the terrain to the advantage of the attacking Minamoto forces. Leaving the bulk of his army under the command of Noriyori, he led a small party of disciplined cavalry around through the hills and took up position by dawn above the Taira left flank at Ichi-no-tani. Quieting their restless horses, Yoshitsune and his men lay behind cover of some thickets until they saw Noriyori's attack on the Taira right flank beginning to succeed near the shrine of the Ikuta Woods. Then they broke cover and rode hard down the steep slope, achieving complete surprise. They overran the Taira defenses and set fire to their camp, killing the Taira commander in the melee. Noriyori maintained the pressure on the enemy's right, and the Taira with the sea behind them were unable to maneuver. Numbers were killed and captured, and the remainder fled by sea, leaving the Minamoto in possession of the field.

After this battle of Ichi-no-tani in March 1184, there ensued a lull of six months, in which the Taira were again able to recruit their forces. Subsequent Japanese accounts of the war (often highly colored, for it is the great source of drama and romance) tend to minimize the strength of the ultimate losers, the Taira; yet it is evident that even after Ichi-no-tani they presented a serious threat to the Minamoto. This is clearly seen in the difficulties that attended Noriyori when Yoritomo ordered him to proceed to the far west against the Taira in the autumn of 1184. The mission was dangerous but justified in the result. Noriyori had in front of him Taira Tomomori on an island at the west end of Honshu and Munemori with the boy-emperor on his flank at Yashima, the Taira base on Shikoku, whither Munemori had fled after Ichi-no-tani. The lords of central and western Japan were for the most part adherents of the Taira and in a position to deny to Noriyori both transportation and supplies. Noriyori nevertheless succeeded in reaching the west end of Honshu. He sent desperate appeals to Yoritomo, who was directing affairs from his headquarters at Kamakura far east of Kyoto and at the same time keeping an eye on affairs in the eastern part of the country. Yoritomo, however, could not send reinforcements rapidly or easily because of the Taira control of the Inland Sea route and of the central route to the west. It took six weeks even for a messenger to travel from Kyushu to Kamakura. In the end Noriyori received both food for his men and a fleet of small ships from certain lords in the west and transported his force over to Bungo in Kyushu.

The commanding general Yoritomo's political acumen and caution were very nearly his undoing, for these qualities were strongly mixed with suspicion and mistrust, directed particularly at his brilliant younger brother, Yoshitsune. At this juncture he overcame his jealousy sufficiently to give Yoshitsune an independent commission, and the latter set out about the month of March 1185 with characteristic speed, not to say impetuosity, to deal with the Taira force on Shikoku. A spring storm destroyed a number of the boats he had intended to use for the crossing, but he set out with a small force on the remainder. Taking advantage of the high winds, he made an unexpectedly rapid passage. Yoshitsune mustered his troops and descended on Yashima from the landward side. The Taira defenses were directed seaward, and Munemori gave up and fled to Kyushu—unnecessarily it seems, for he had the larger number of men. Yoshitsune followed at leisure, after securing Yashima as a base for his side and obtaining with considerable difficulty additional ships for transport. His most valuable acquisition, however, was a member of a local clan who joined him and who was familiar with the treacherous currents running between the main island and Kyushu.

Events were now moving rapidly to a climax. Munemori and Tomomori joined forces and offered battle at sea. There has been speculation as to why they did this in view of the dangers to navigation in these narrow waters. Probably they expected to profit from the Minamoto lack of experience in naval warfare; and in any case they had to make some move, for they were caught between Noriyori on Kyushu and Yoshitsune's fresh advance on the mainland from the east.

The Taira took advantage of the flood tide to bear down on the Minamoto ships on the morning of April 25, 1185, near the village of Dan-no-ura on the main island. At first the Taira held their own, but in the afternoon they lost their advantage, for the tide had turned and the Minamoto now had both wind and tide with them. At the height of the battle a commander allied to the Taira deserted to the Minamoto side. Yoshitsune had given orders to all the soldiers on board the Minamoto ships to direct the fire of their arrows at the Taira steersmen in particular. The Taira ships were forced onto the Dan-no-ura shore or caught in the retreating tide, now roaring through the narrows at eight knots. It was a total disaster for the Taira. The boy-emperor Antoku and many of the Taira leaders were drowned. The Dan-no-ura defeat marked the end of effective Taira power.

Much could be written on the military assessment of the Gempei War. The Japanese romances speak of the transitory nature of human glory and of the Taira pride and arrogance which brought nemesis in its train. Personal factors in the characters of the leaders themselves undoubtedly played a large part in the outcome. The Taira showed a lack of skill and determination in exploiting their advantages, for there is no reason to think the quality of their fighting men was in any way inferior to that of the Minamoto. The prudent shift of sides made by Go-Shirakawa in 1183 gave the Minamoto claims a legitimacy that attracted allies to their side. But the greatest single factor was the combination of the political skill and rock-fast determination of Yoritomo with the élan and generalship of his brother, Yoshitsune.

The Minamoto victory marked the political triumph of the warrior class, a decisive event which had important social and cultural consequences. Where Taira Kiyomori, though of a warrior family, had attached himself to the court, Minamoto Yoritomo kept himself and his warriors aloof from court life and maintained his headquarters at Kamakura on his own ground in the east even after victory had made him master of Japan. There were political and personal reasons operating in each case; but the difference between the two men and the milieu in which each chose to exercise power is symptomatic of the cultural changes going on in twelfth-century Japan.

The cultural emphasis moved gradually from admiration of the gentleman, the scholar, and the aesthete to a code of fierce loyalty among fighting men and a worship of honor and the sword. As this martial spirit became more clearly defined, it was known at first as *Kyuba-no-michi*, "the way of the horse and the bow," and later as *bushido*, "the way of the warrior." The actual swords themselves acquired a mystique of their own. In a man's sword resided his honor, and he would sooner die than part with it. When a swordsmith embarked on the forging and tempering of a sword, he would prepare himself by the Shinto religious rites of abstention and purification. Even at the work itself he would wear white clothes similar to those of a Shinto priest. The care put into the craftsmanship in medieval Japan produced swords of a quality and keenness scarcely ever excelled anywhere else at any time, not even by the great artificers of the Muslim world or of Toledo in Spain.

Among the technical reasons for the high quality of the Japanese sword was the care taken to give a different temper to the edge and to the back of the blade. The metal was hammered and wrought to a close texture and density and the edge tempered many times to a great hardness. But each time it was tempered, the broad back of the blade was carefully protected from the heating and cooling process by a layer of clay, making it more resilient and less brittle than the edge. The finished blade thus had both strength and keenness. The swordsmiths also took pride in the workmanship of the sword ornaments, the hilt guards in inlay and gold and silver damascene work, the scabbard ornaments of tiny animals, the handgrips of sharkskin, and so on. These have long been collectors' items both in Japan and the West (see frontispiece).

The other traditional weapon of the Japanese warrior was the bow and arrow. Arrows were discharged by the warrior from on horseback, in the Mongol manner, as well as from the ground. Quivers on the warriors' backs, with the feathered ends of the arrows arranged in a narrow fan shape, figure prominently in contemporary pictures. The armor of a Japanese knight consisted of small, rectangular plates of steel or lacquered wood laced together with red silk or other cords. The armor was lighter in weight than the European suit of armor and gave more mobility to the wearer. The helmet usually consisted of a cap of iron segments skillfully curved to shape, with wide cheek pieces but less frontal protection than in the European helmet, and the whole surmounted by up-curving horns, reminiscent of Viking headgear and presenting a fierce aspect. The aristocratic warrior of Japan rode a horse into battle, was followed by a small company of foot soldiers, and often engaged in single combat with an opponent, as in the medieval West; but he was armed with sword and bow, not sword and lance.

A delight in finery and pride in the accoutrements of war can be seen in the romantic tale *Heike Monogatari*, where the appearance of Taira Shigehira is described:

> He was attired . . . in a hitatare [ceremonial robe] of dark blue cloth on which a pattern of rocks and sea-birds was embroidered in light yellow silk, and armour with purple lacing deepening in its hue towards the skirts. On his head was a helmet with tall, golden horns, and his sword also was mounted in gold. His arrows were feathered with black and white falcon plumes and in his hand he carried a "Shigeto" bow. He was mounted on a renowned war-horse called Doji-kage, whose trappings were resplendent with ornaments of gold.[2]

From this age of the clan wars comes the main source of those romances that have delighted generations of audiences in the popular *kabuki* theater as well as in the classical *No* plays, and have formed an ideal of bravery and loyalty for all Japanese. The effect of this ideal on Japanese thought and on later Japanese history has been very marked, extending right into the twentieth century. The modern situation in Japan is, of course, changing very rapidly under the full impact of technology. But at least until recently the famous names of medieval Japan have probably been more intimately present to the minds of their countrymen than the corresponding figures exactly contemporary with them would be to Western minds. These would include, among many others, twelfth-century figures such as Philip II of France, Frederick Barbarossa, Henry II of England, Eleanor of Aquitaine, Thomas à Becket, Richard I Coeur-de-Lion (King of England from 1189 to 1199, when the Gempei War was just over), Saladin (his opponent in the Third Crusade), and the minnesinger in Germany, Walther von der Vogelweide.

The best known of these stories of romance and adventure is the cycle relating to Minamoto Yoshitsune, the brilliant young leader in the wars against the Taira. When his father was killed, he was only an infant and was placed by his stepfather in a monastery. But as he grew up he felt the urge to avenge the humiliations of his family and made his way, for training and support, to Fujiwara Hidehira, a powerful lord in the north. At the age of seventeen he was in Kyoto. While crossing the Gojo Bridge, he found his passage disputed by a stout and truculent monk, Benkei. The monk thought a few blows of his staff would put the impudent stripling to flight, but he soon

---

[2] Chomei Kamo, *The Ten-Foot Square Hut and Tales of the Heike*, selections from *Heike Monogatari*, tr. A. L. Sadler (Sydney: Angus and Robertson, 1928), p. 154.

found he was up against one of the most accomplished swordsmen in the country. Surrendering at length to his nimble opponent, Benkei swore he would follow Yoshitsune as his master wherever he went. This incident forms the theme of one of the favorite plays, "Benkei on the Bridge." It was Yoshitsune's daring attack that was the decisive factor in the victory of Ichi-no-tani. The highly colored account of the battle in *Heike Monogatari* makes evident even to non-Japanese eyes the popular appeal that these tales of bravery have had from the time they were written.

> Thereafter the battle became general and the various clans of the Gen and Hei surged over each other in mixed and furious combat. The men of the Miura, Kamakura, Chichibu, Ashikaga . . . charged against each other with a roar like thunder while the hills re-echoed to the sound of their war-cries, and the shafts they shot at each other fell like rain. Some were wounded slightly and fought on, some grappled and stabbed each other to death, while others bore down their adversaries and cut off their heads; everywhere the fight rolled forward and backward, so that none could tell who were victors and vanquished.
>
> [At this point the launching of Yoshitsune's attack from the ridge above the Taira left flank at Ichi-no-tani is described.] The descent was of sand and pebbles, and their horses slid straight down and landed on a level place. From thence there were great mossy boulders for fifty yards to the bottom. Soldiers were recoiling in horror thinking that their end had come when Miura-no-Sahara Juro Yoshitsura sprang forward and shouted: "In my part we ride down places like this any day to catch a bird; the Miura would make a race-course of this"; and down he went, followed by all the rest.
>
> So steep was the descent that the stirrups of the hinder man struck against the helmet or armor of the one in front of him, and so dangerous did it look that they averted their eyes as they went down. "Ei! Ei!" they ejaculated under their breath as they steadied their horses, and their daring seemed rather that of demons than of men. So they reached the bottom. . . . They fired the houses and huts of the Heike so that they went up in smoke in a few moments.[3]

Yoshitsune was the main architect of the final Minamoto victory, but the gratitude of his envious and powerful half-brother Yoritomo was not forthcoming. Even when Yoshitsune came to report the victory, Yoritomo would not receive him, and Yoshitsune in the end was forced to flee at times in the guise of an itinerant monk, still accompanied by the faithful Benkei and by Shizuka, his loyal mistress. On the run for over a year, he finally made his way back to Fujiwara Hidehira in the north, where he had stayed as a boy. But the old man was already ninety, and, when his son succeeded him, Yoritomo, ruthless to the last, brought such pressure to bear that Yoshitsune was betrayed and attacked. Rather than surrender, he committed formal suicide. He was only thirty years old.

---

[3] Ibid., pp. 147 ff.

It is this last incident of betrayal which brings the emotion and the cathar-
sis to its height for the Japanese who see the historical drama. For loyalty has
become the supreme virtue and the highest duty of the warrior caste. The
virtue is also a Confucian one and is represented by the character "center"
over "heart," "heart central," or "without deviation"—"his heart is in the
right place." But, though prized in China, this virtue is held in very special
esteem by the Japanese, whose society exhibits to this day a network of obligations and loyalties that serve as an intangible but strong binding force.

Among the fighting men of the feudal period, the Zen form of Buddhism
was the most popular religious belief. Zen (Chan in Chinese) is based on the
early Indian Buddhist practice of seeking release through meditation; but in
China this was amalgamated with a Taoist emphasis on individualism, independence, and a strong identification with nature and the natural order, to
form the Ch'an sect. The doctrine was introduced into Japan by the monk
Eisai, who brought the Rinzai sect of Zen to Kamakura, Yoritomo's headquarters, in 1191, while Yoritomo himself was still alive. Eisai's disciple, Do-
gen, introduced another form of Zen, the Soto sect, a little later in 1227; but
wishing to avoid the distractions of the town and the encumbrances of patronage however advantageous, he went to settle on the remote west coast.
Both sects flourished and continue to be active to the present day.

It is at first surprising that any form of the Buddhist religion, with its
gentleness, reverence for all forms of life, and shunning of desire and hate,
would be practiced at all by warriors. But Buddhism was so well established
and Shinto had so little to offer in the way of a coherent philosophy that those
who were in any way religiously inclined had little alternative to some form
of Buddhism. And such is the power of human rationalization that they probably were scarcely conscious of any contradiction between faith and conduct.

Why Zen in particular? The original Nara sects and the foundations on
Mount Hiei and Mount Koya demanded the study of abstruse doctrines and
scriptures, while the more popular devotional sects, such as the Jodo (Pure
Land) worship of Amida Buddha (see illustration on page 41), tended to
pietism, if not to sentimentality. Zen, on the other hand, was more likely to
appeal to men of action, for its practitioners were offered a direct road to enlightenment and release through discipline and inner control. The aspirants
were given rigorous training in *zazen*, "sitting in meditation." During long
periods of concentration the Zen master would seek to jolt their bodies by a
kick or a cuff on the head, or to jolt their minds by a series of *koan*, "nonsense puzzles," such as, "How do you make a noise by clapping with one
hand?" or "A monk asked Yun-men, 'Who is the Buddha?' 'The dried-up
dirt-cleaner.'" The disciple might then, by these means or independently,
achieve a sudden, intuitional breakthrough and reach enlightenment. A certain austerity, challenge, and mystery about this approach, and especially its
independence of ritual and complicated book learning, intrigued and captivated the warrior mind.

There is another feature of Buddhism in general that may have had a pe-

Garden of the Tenryuji Temple, Kyoto, designed in the fourteenth century by a famous monk, Muso Soseki.

The simplicity of rocks, pond, and raked sand is an aid to meditation in this temple of the Rinzai sect of Zen Buddhism.

Japan Information Center

culiar appeal to men accustomed to taking risks and to staking all on the outcome of a battle or an individual combat, and that is the Buddhist sense of the transitory nature of human life and glory. Many *samurai* (the word means "one who serves" but is used in a proud sense of those in military service as vassals to a lord) were far from being crude, unthinking fighters. Glory and honor were of great importance to them, but they were intelligent and subtle enough to realize that these things were transitory. They welcomed a rationale that would account on a universal scale for the known and experienced fact, *sic transit gloria mundi*—"thus passes the glory of the world." That tinge of Buddhist melancholy which pervades the aesthetic pleasures of the *Tale of Genji* in the early Heian age—"Beauty fades, beauty passes, However rare, rare it be"—is felt again in a different way amid the pawing of horses and the clatter of arms which close the period. For all the *samurai* optimism and confidence, they know that swift defeat and then oblivion can overtake the bravest. Buddhism knows this too, faces it, and seeks to transcend it. The warrior, whose native Shinto is too shadowy and thin to provide an integrated view of the world, is prepared to embrace Buddhism because this faith allows a qualified value to a man's station and duty in life but points him on beyond the vanity of this world to the Buddha whose Law has universal validity. Many warriors who survived the wars took the tonsure and went into a monastery not from convenience, as in the case of some emperors and nobles, but from a conviction that thus they might atone for the sins of their years of battle in the world.

The way of the warrior in Japan is sometimes linked, if only by implication, to the knightly code of honor in the medieval West. There are many genuine similarities, the paramount need for bravery and loyalty being the most important. These similarities arose, it seems, from parallel social circumstances that produced in each case a feudal system in which land was held in return for military service to an overlord who granted protection to all in his domain. The circumstances were genuinely parallel in that a strong lord–vassal relationship was a necessity in both Japan and Europe as the only available barrier to the anarchy and chaos that threatened society after the breakdown of an earlier, stable order. In the West the breakdown was that of the Roman Empire under pressure of the barbarian invasions, while in Japan it was the less spectacular but equally fatal breakdown of the Tang government system borrowed from China.

The physical circumstances of combat also yield minor parallels, such as the terms "chivalry" from the French *cheval* (horse) and the "way of the horse and bow," both expressions with important ethical overtones but both derived originally from the fact that the knights went mounted into battle. But here there is one important difference between Japan and the West.

As G. B. Sansom has pointed out, the quality of chivalry as consideration for women and weaker persons is entirely lacking in the Oriental code. And the very idea of tilting for a woman's favor would be shocking to a Japanese. Courtly love and the worship of womanhood were unknown. The motivation for deeds of incredible bravery and endurance came only from two sources: from personal pride and honor, and from loyalty to one's lord, which took precedence over loyalty to the emperor or to religion. The link with the Homeric hero is closer than with the medieval knight, for as he enters battle the Japanese warrior shouts out his name and ancestry as the gage of honor he will do everything to preserve. His strength is in his pride, and he is fighting loyally for his lord; but he is less apt than the medieval knight to speak of fighting for a cause idealistically conceived. Like the Homeric hero, or Arjuna in the *Bhagavad-Gita,* he is fighting because that is what he has to do. Yet still in the midst of blind destiny there is an inexplicable depth and a certain magnificence in his disregard of death.

> Rising high in his stirrups he cried with a loud voice: "Kiso-no-Kanjai you have often heard of; now you see him before your eyes! Lord of Iyo and Captain of the Guard, Bright Sun General, Minamoto Yoshinaka am I! Come! Kai-no-Ichijo Jiro! Take my head and show it to Hyoye-no-Suke Yoritomo!"[4]

[4] Ibid., pp. 139–140.

6

GOVERNMENT BY THE MILITARY SHOGUN

Kamakura Period: 1185–1336

After the victory of Dan-no-ura in 1185, Minamoto Yoritomo was the virtual master of Japan. He had reached this position by long and thoughtful planning and by being careful always to consolidate his position politically, while delegating the military operations to those, such as Yoshitsune, even better able than himself to carry them out. Yet his position of leadership was still potential rather than actual. He proceeded to make himself unassailable, mainly by administrative measures of a bold and simple design, accompanied by certain judicious assassinations.

Immediately after the Dan-no-ura triumph, whose suddenness apparently took him by surprise, Yoritomo ordered Noriyori to stay in Kyushu and take over the properties of the defeated Taira lords in that area. This was obviously with a view to rewarding his own successful warriors. At the same time he ordered Yoshitsune to bring the imperial regalia and the chief prisoners back to Kyoto. Yoshitsune complied, but had to report that the sacred sword had been lost from the regalia during the sea battle. When Yoshitsune came on from Kyoto to report his victory to Yoritomo himself, Yoritomo, as we have seen, refused to grant him an audience and was soon chasing him for his life. Yoritomo's attitude to Yoshitsune is hard to explain. Personal jealousy played its part. Yoshitsune was popular at court and had received a number of honors and rewards from Go-Shirakawa, whereas it was Yoritomo's policy to forbid all his followers to have anything to do with the court or to receive any rewards or appointments other than from him. In addition a rather disreputable spy appointed by Yoritomo began reporting that Yoshitsune was planning a revolt. It is not likely that this was so, but Yoritomo found it profitable to believe the report. It was an excellent excuse to assert to Go-Shirakawa that the country was in danger from Yoshitsune's activities and that the safety of the realm could be guaranteed only if Yoritomo himself were put in control and allowed to levy a special military tax and to send his own retainers as officials into every part of the country.

Meanwhile, Yoshitsune was unable to raise any sizable force of men to defend himself against his brother and fled in disguise to the north where he met his end. But it did not profit Fujiwara Yasuhira, son of the old man Hidehira, to have carried out Yoritomo's orders and harried Yoshitsune to his death in 1189. Yasuhira was the last great landowner not yet under Yoritomo's control, so in a matter of months Yoritomo attacked him with three large armies, defeated and killed him, acquiring thereby a great addition to the wealth he had available for the granting of rewards. It is evident that Yoritomo was completely merciless, and to this both personal and policy reasons must have contributed. In 1186 his remaining uncle, Yukiiye, was assassinated, and in 1193 Noriyori, his other brother, was arrested on a fabricated charge of conspiracy and executed.

Yoritomo's power was based on the new warrior class. He was careful to establish and maintain it as a privileged order. The status of the *samurai* as a fighting man was defined and regulated, and none could claim this status without permission of Yoritomo. The *samurai* was generally a mounted warrior, with full armor and a flag bearing his insignia. There were, of course, other fighting men of various types who were not of *samurai* status. They fought on foot and had lighter armor.

A smaller and more privileged class was that of the *go-kenin* or "honorable house men," the vassals of Yoritomo. *Samurai* status was necessary to qualify for becoming a member of the *go-kenin*, but actually the two categories were different in origin, *samurai* denoting military rank and *go-kenin* feudal relationship. The "house men," who became a kind of minor nobility, were at first only Yoritomo's own retainers of Minamoto connection, but soon he began to invite allies and finally former enemies into this exclusive group. In the end half of his total number of vassals were of Taira descent.

Much of the time that Yoritomo spent at his Kamakura headquarters before, during, and after the Gempei War was devoted to constructing this system of political and military alliances. He was building for the future by gaining control first in the Kanto. The Kanto Plain is the largest single agricultural area in Japan, situated around the modern Tokyo. It is well to the east of the earlier political and cultural center of Kyoto. The foundation of the Kamakura Shogunate marks a shift eastward in political power which had begun earlier in the economic and military spheres. Yoritomo also increased his control by attaching warriors to himself. Always careful to see to their economic status, he rewarded the loyal with estates and income-bearing offices. Then, at the conclusion of the war, he was able gradually to gain authority over all Japan, including the north, center, and west, by a double process, sending out his own vassals into key positions and securing the loyalty of allies and former foes by making them vassals, always with suitable emoluments. This policy, which seems to have been thought out by Yoritomo in his early years of exile at Izu after his father's downfall, was carried out cautiously and thoroughly.

It made for a stability never achieved by his Taira predecessor in power, Ki-yomori, and resulted in the establishment of the first stage of feudalism in Japan. The necessity of attaching warriors to himself and his house meant that he alone had to be the fount of all honors and appointments, hence the ban on warriors forming links with the court or receiving favors at the hands of the emperor.

Thus Yoritomo's vassals were soon in positions of authority all over the country, and the system he set up to regulate and reward his own retainers and those under them became the effective government of Japan. This system was superimposed upon and not substituted for the earlier imperial structure set up by the Taika Reform, and the latter continued to function, but in an increasingly feeble and nominal manner.

The essence of Yoritomo's system was that one of his own retainers was named as manager of each estate. This manager (*jito*, "steward") was supported by a share of the yield of the estate assigned to him, and in addition he was supervisor of the proper distribution of the other shares of the crop, including those belonging to the owner. He was responsible for keeping the peace and thus came to act as a local magistrate. He was also in charge of collecting and forwarding to Kamakura the "commissariat rice" or special military tax. This was the tax which Yoritomo had represented to Go-Shi-rakawa as being necessary in order to finance the suppression of Yoshitsune's "rebellion." It was not burdensome, being only about 2 percent of the crop; but no exceptions were permitted, and it was levied on public and private land, regardless of whether the land had received exemption from the earlier imperial taxes. Officers known as constables (*tsuibushi*) or protectors (*shugo*) were appointed to provinces. Their duties were to oversee the stewards, assign the vassals in general to guard service, and keep law and order in their domains. They were often given the title of governor in the parallel imperial structure, but this was more a matter of honor than of substantive power. Both these offices, of steward and constable, became hereditary, and both tended to become lucrative posts, combining both civil and military authority.

The central organs of the Kamakura government were of the same simple and practical kind as the local arrangements just mentioned. The first to be set up, as early as 1180, the beginning of the Gempei War, was the *Samu-rai-dokoro* ("service room" or "orderly room"), sometimes translated as the Board of Retainers. This office dealt with the assignment of military duties and the rewards and punishments meted out to the warriors. But its commands extended over wider areas than would be considered proper in the West and covered many concerns in the private lives of the soldiers, their marriages and families, friends and recreation, anything, in fact, which might have a bearing on their ultimate loyalty to their superior. In wartime the *Samu-rai-dokoro* assumed the functions of a headquarters staff.

The second organ of Yoritomo's government was the Mandokoro, or Council, analogous to the secretariat set up earlier to manage the affairs of a great family such as the Fujiwara. The name emphasized the personal character of Yoritomo's rule, but the function of the Mandokoro was that of a policy-making body at the highest level. The Mandokoro was headed by a *shikken*, or "director," and after 1203, when Hojo Tokimasa was appointed to this post, it became hereditary in his family.

The third body was known as the Monchujo or Board of Inquiry. This judicial body was the final court of appeal, administering the Minamoto house law which had gradually accumulated. Strictly speaking this law applied only to the Minamoto and their retainers at first; but since this was the only effective law whose writ ran throughout the land, litigants from all over Japan, even nobles from the capital, began to come to Kamakura for justice. The Board of Inquiry took careful note of documentary evidence and won the reputation of dispensing evenhanded judgments. The fairness of this court in a time of postwar confusion without doubt enhanced the reputation of the Kamakura regime. The customary law administered on the basis of Minamoto house law was later collected and reduced to order as the Joei Code in 1232. These Kamakura boards do not appear to have been dominated by single men for whom they acted as mere mouthpieces. They functioned as committees, giving unanimous public decisions and bearing the responsibility collectively. It has been noted that the Japanese as a people prefer anonymity of this kind and are skilled at reaching collective decisions.

The setting up of the Monchujo provided a link between Kamakura and the court in Kyoto, for certain experienced nobles and legal experts were invited from Kyoto by Yoritomo to assist in drawing up the regulations under which the Monchujo would function. In ways such as this the intentional barrier that Yoritomo erected between the luxurious and corrupt court and his own stern and frugal warriors began to break down. It is evident at the beginning that there was a considerable social gap between the two, for the nobles scorned the military for its uncouth ways, while the warriors despised the nobles for their sheltered lives and their effete manners, and were inclined to say, like Hotspur of the courtier,

> . . . he made me mad
> To see him shine so brisk, and smell so sweet,
> And talk so like a waiting gentlewoman
> Of guns and drums and wounds—God save the mark!
> —(*Henry IV*, Pt. I, I, ii)

But it must be placed to the credit of the soldiers that they were always aware of the values of records, books, and the art of literature.

The arranging of these and other administrative matters kept Yoritomo at Kamakura for a full year after his conquest of the domains of Fujiwara Yasuhira in the north. Only when he felt secure through the distribution of rewards, the disciplining of offenders, and the consolidation of his rule did he proceed to the capital in 1190. In that year he was granted the highest honorific title of *Nairan*. The position he really coveted was that of *shogun*, or "Supreme Military Commander," commanding all military forces on behalf of the emperor. This could be given only by the emperor, and the most powerful figure in the imperial house, Go-Shirakawa, was not willing to grant it to Yoritomo. Finally in 1192 Go-Shirakawa died; and Fujiwara Kanezane, a powerful minister faithful to the imperial interests but ready to cooperate with the new military regime, persuaded the newly retired emperor, Go-Toba, to grant Yoritomo the title. Such was the prestige of the imperial house that Yoritomo, the most powerful figure in the country, felt he had to wait until the emperor bestowed the title on him.

The title of shogun had a history dating from the early wars of conquest against the Ainu. The emperor had then conferred the office on a particular general for a limited period. Yoritomo, however, regarded the title as a permanent mark of his and his descendants' right to rule Japan in the name of the emperor. His government and that of his successors were known as the *bakufu* ("tent government" or military rule).

After shunning Kyoto for so long, Yoritomo made some extended visits there, taking up residence in the Rokuhara mansion, which had been the Taira headquarters. He contributed munificently to the rebuilding of the Todaiji temple and was present at its rededication, for throughout his life he was a devout Buddhist. He died in 1199, without having long enjoyed the fruits of his achievement, yet with his main work essentially done. The portrait of Yoritomo in the British Museum painted by Fujiwara Takanobu shows him in the pose and dress of an official, seated and in black robes. He has a small head and narrow, precise features. The eyes are penetrating, the mouth full and sensual. The whole expression is poised and aloof but with a hint of inner tension. The portrait does not show Yoritomo's iron will and determination, but only their potential presence behind the calm and rather strained expression of the face. Yet the historical record reveals resolute purpose and organizational power of an uncommon order, making him one of the greatest men in the history of Japan. Enough has been said of his cruelty in the struggle for power, a characteristic he shared with others of his age in the West as well as in the East. He was not an attractive personality, but he was extremely successful, an innovator and a combination of thinker and man of action.

After the death of Yoritomo the shogunal power did not long remain in his family line. During a series of sordid struggles his two sons were killed, one after the other, and authority passed to Hojo Tokimasa, Yoritomo's father-in-law and early guardian, and then successively to Tokimasa's son, Yoshitoki, and to his grandson, Yasutoki. In contrast to Yoritomo's Minamoto relatives, who all died young and usually by violent means, the Hojo family was well suited to consolidate the Kamakura Shogunate, for none of its members down to Yasutoki died before the age of fifty-nine and Tokimasa lived to the age of seventy-seven. This consolidation they faithfully carried out, despite the violence with which they began, and gave Japan in the process nearly a century of comparative tranquility. They did not themselves become the shoguns but exercised the real power as the Hojo regents by retaining in their own hands the post of *shikken*, or "head of the Council", first acquired by Hojo Tokimasa in 1203. Ten more members of the Hojo family held the post in succession after him. After a time the position of shogun, now itself a nominal one, was usually held by a prince of the imperial blood.

An extraordinary anomaly thus emerged in the government of Japan, a complicated system of indirect rule probably without parallel anywhere else. In Kyoto a titular emperor had handed over power to a Fujiwara regent, who in turn had yielded to the authority of a retired or cloistered emperor. But even he did not exercise the realities of power, which belonged first to a powerful military shogun and then were exercised on behalf of the shogun by a regent of the Hojo family in Kamakura. Relations between the *bakufu* and the court were on the whole amicable. They were seriously disturbed only once during the height of Kamakura power, and that near the beginning of the long period of peace referred to as characteristic of the Hojo Regency. The Emperor Go-Toba succeeded Go-Shirakawa in 1192, ruling first as titular and then as cloistered emperor until 1221. A man of ambition and charm, Go-Toba flattered and made friends with members of the Kamakura government stationed in Kyoto in a calculated attempt to undermine the shogunate and restore a measure of imperial independence. He gradually determined, against the strong advice of his advisers, to make a strong bid to overthrow the *bakufu* by force. Go-Toba had allies among some of the clans in the north and west who had never become reconciled to the Minamoto dominance. Moreover he showed great skill in his treatment of the monasteries. Ecclesiastical quarrels had broken out again, and in the course of their intrigues the monks had once more tried to blackmail and force the court into supporting one side or the other. Go-Toba, however, was less affected by superstitious dread than his predecessor, Go-Shirakawa, and dispatched guards to scatter the ill-organized troops of the monasteries. But he followed this firmness with conciliation, pointing out to the abbots that they had much to gain by uniting with one another and with himself. And indeed the monasteries had no love for the Minamoto, who had treated them harshly on numerous occasions. There was also a new factor in the church situation. The rise of Amidist (see illustration on page 41) and Zen sects in the eastern region was offering serious competition to the older sects in and around the capital. For several reasons, therefore, the abbots of the older monasteries were ready to listen to Go-Toba.

With the support of certain clans and the leading monasteries, Go-Toba made his move in 1221 and summoned all the eastern warriors to a great festival in Kyoto, in order to draw them away from their base. He declared Hojo Yoshitoki an outlaw in June and gave notice that all of the eastern region was officially in a state of rebellion. The *bakufu* received a last-minute warning of the state of affairs. They gathered three armies and marched on the capital by different routes. There was considerable sympathy for Go-Toba's cause, and, given better leadership in the field, he might have made a sufficiently good showing to have reached a compromise arrangement with Kamakura. But neither his generals nor his troops were up to the standard of the experienced Kamakura fighting men, and his side was defeated. Go-Toba failed to get help from the Mount Hiei monastery when he needed it, and he resolved to make a last stand on the river between Seta and Uji, the scene of earlier battles. After inflicting heavy losses on the Kamakura forces, who had to contend with the difficulties of the river crossing, Go-Toba's men were surrounded and vanquished. A few of the leaders were executed, but in general the *bakufu* had the good sense not to press the matter of punishment for this revolt too far. Go-Toba and the titular emperor were sent into exile in remote parts of Japan, and their estates and those of many court nobles were confiscated. This incident was known as the Jokyu Disturbance. Thereafter the *bakufu* watched the court much more closely, even determining the succession to the positions of titular and cloistered emperor; but they were always correct and careful in respecting the sacred prerogatives of the Throne. The distribution of the confiscated estates proved very useful in allaying discontent among the vassals of the *bakufu*.

During the remainder of the thirteenth century the Hojo regents maintained domestic peace. They themselves set an example of frugal living and faithfulness to duty. The structure set up by Yoritomo proved a durable one, and the vassals were assured reasonable justice and security in their holdings. But in the last quarter of the century a serious threat developed from abroad. The Koreans had not been strong enough and the Chinese not ambitious enough to attack Japan. But the Mongols were a different matter; their restless zeal for conquest knew no bounds. The Yüan or Mongol dynasty came into full control of China in 1280, after the defeat of the Southern Sung dynasty, and thus the dates of the Yüan dynasty are usually given as 1280–1368. But the Mongols were already in control in North China from about 1230, and Kublai, the Great Khan of the Mongols, established his capital at Beijing in 1264. Korea proved quite incapable of resisting and succumbed to the conqueror. In 1268 Kublai sent an embassy to Japan demanding submission. The court would probably have compromised, but Hojo Tokimune and his Council of State decided to resist and sent the envoys back without an answer or even an acknowledgment. Hojo Masamura, an experienced general of sixty, was put in charge of the defense. The Mongol preparations had been delayed but were sufficiently advanced by 1272 to cause Masamura to order all Kyushu vassals who were residing elsewhere to return to their estates. He commanded that they and the Kyushu constables see to the manning of the western defenses.

Another Mongol envoy was expelled from Japan in 1272, which amounted to a declaration of war. The attack came in 1274 by a force of some 25,000 Mongols and Koreans, who made a landing at Hakata Bay in North Kyushu. The Mongols were a terrifying enemy and had the advantage of skill in the use of massed cavalry and heavy catapults flinging explosive bombs. But they had little room to maneuver, and the Japanese, fired by desperate zeal to defend their homeland, used their swords and bows to such good effect that they were able to hold off the Mongol attack at least partially on the first encounter.

When night fell, the Japanese retreated a few miles inland and lay behind dikes erected as defenses in earlier times. Bad weather was brewing, and the Korean pilots advised urgent reembarkation lest the ships be caught on a lee shore in a storm. For some reason the Mongol commanders feared a night attack by the Japanese in wind and rain, though in fact the exhausted Japanese were in no position to deliver one. Fortunately for the Japanese defenders, the Mongols did decide to retreat after just one day's fighting. A number of ships were lost in the ensuing storm, and many soldiers drowned.

The Japanese had gained a respite. They took full advantage of it by beginning immediate construction of a stone defensive wall all the way round Hakata Bay, by calling up troops for garrison duty on a regular roster, and by making arrangements for the drilling and movement of reinforcements in the event of a second attack, which they felt sure would follow. It was to be five years before Kublai was ready with a much larger force. Japanese vigilance did not slacken, and preparations went on unabated, with a dedication and united sense of patriotism which the country had scarcely known hitherto. One of the items that proved most important among the defense preparations was the building of a large number of small warships. Envoys sent again from Beijing were this time summarily executed in defiance. The court led in offering prayers to the deities, especially the Shinto gods. Special measures were taken to encourage loyalty and efficiency among the vassals.

In 1281 the Mongols made their second and more determined attempt. They had gathered an immense force of 140,000, but it should be noted that some 100,000 of these were Chinese from South China, a region only recently conquered by the Mongols. These men had little stomach for a fight on behalf of their Mongol masters. The invaders made several landings along the Kyushu coast, but Hakata Bay was the most strategic location, and there the Japanese wall was effective in preventing the deployment of cavalry. The Japanese warriors in a heroic defense held the Mongols at bay for two months, from June to August, and denied them any significant expansion of their beachheads. Meanwhile the smaller and more maneuverable Japanese warships inflicted serious damage on the Mongol war junks in the narrow waters of the bay. On August 15 and 16 deliverance came. A tremendous typhoon blew in and wrought havoc on the Mongol fleet. In such tropical storms winds of 120 miles per hour are not uncommon, and the fleet of the Chinese contingent received the worst damage. They were in a bay farther down the coast to the west and caught the full force of the onshore hurricane. Ships were jammed together in the narrows, and the loss of life was appalling. The large number of Mongol and Chinese soldiers left on shore fell prey to the swords of the exultant Japanese. The typhoon was hailed as an answer to prayer, the "wind of the gods," *kamikaze*. The *bakufu* maintained their Kyushu defenses for twenty years more, but the Mongols never returned.

From the Mongol point of view this failure was not important. There was little incentive for the Mongols to press the matter of the conquest of Japan to a conclusion. The Chinese emperors heretofore had never viewed these offshore islands as either a threat or a valuable prize. For the Mongols the reduction of Japan was a matter of prestige, an attempt to round off their conquest of East Asia, not a matter of economics or necessity. They already had all the land they could exploit or administer, right down to South China and into Indochina. But for the Japanese the victory was a miraculous deliverance. This was the first attempted invasion of the sacred soil of Japan in historic times, and the last until the end of World War II. It is little wonder that the experience made a lasting impression and that the memory of *kamikaze* was reinvoked in World War II as the name for suicide pilot attacks. In view of Japan's later achievements, the defeat of the Mongols must be considered one of the decisive battles of world history.

The religious aspect of this deliverance from the Mongols was emphasized in the enthusiasm generated by a priest, Nichiren (1222–1282). He claimed that he had prophetically foretold the foreign attack, as a punishment for the country's leaders, and the eventual triumph of Japan. His doctrine was a combination of Buddhist beliefs and fervent nationalism, and his fiery personality seems to have inspired in his followers a fanaticism in keeping with the crisis of the times. Nichiren exalted the Lotus Sutra as containing all the truth needed for salvation. He summarized this in the phrase *Namu myoho rengekyo*, "Hail to the Wonderful Law of the Lotus Sutra!" which his followers would chant to the beat of a drum, "dondon dondoko dondon." He showed more intolerance of other sects than any Buddhist leader hitherto and criticized the authorities for supporting false teachers. He was sentenced to death for open censure of the Hojo regents but escaped, according to his disciples, by a miracle when a bolt of lightning struck the executioner's sword. "Banished then to a lonely island in the Sea of Japan, Nichiren wrote, 'Birds cry but shed no tears. Nichiren does not cry, but his tears are never dry.' "[1]

With no lack of self-confidence he saw his own mission in terms of two saints mentioned in the Lotus Sutra, the Bodhisattva of Superb Action, a pioneer in propagating the Perfect Truth, and the Bodhisattva Ever-Abused. "How much more, then, should this be the case with Nichiren, a man born in the family of an outcast fisherman, so lowly and degraded and poor!"[2] Completely convinced of his mission, he could say:

> I, Nichiren, am the master and lord of the sovereign, as well as of all the Buddhists of other schools. Notwithstanding this, the rulers and the people treat us thus maliciously. How should the sun and the moon bless them by

[1] Ryusaku Tsunoda, William De Bary, and Donald Keene, *Sources of the Japanese Tradition* (New York: Columbia University Press, 1958), Vol. 1, p. 215.
[2] Ibid., p. 221.

giving them light? Why should the earth not refuse to let them abide upon it? . . . Therefore, also, the Mongols are coming to chastise them. . . . It is decreed that all the inhabitants of Japan shall suffer from the invaders. Whether this comes to pass or not will prove whether or not Nichiren is the real propagator of the Lotus of Truth.[3]

The name that the prophet adopted symbolized his love of Buddhism and of Japan, for *nichi* (sun) stands for both the Light of Truth and the Land of the Rising Sun, while *ren* means "lotus." He sees Japan as the center from which Buddhism will spread to the whole world.

> Then the golden age, such as were the ages under the reign of the sage kings of old, will be realized in these days of degeneration and corruption, in the time of the Latter Law. . . . The Holy See in Japan will then be the seat where all men of the three countries India, China and Japan and the whole Jambudvipa world will be initiated into the mysteries of confession and expiation; and even the great deities, Brahma and Indra, will come down into the sanctuary and participate in the initiation.[4]

Nichiren was by no means the only prominent Buddhist teacher active in this era, for there was a considerable revival of Buddhism during the Kamakura period. The coming of the Zen sects to Kamakura has already been mentioned, but it was in the Pure Land sects that two of the most influential priests, Honen (1133–1212) and Shinran (1173–1262), were to be found. Trust in the mercy of Amida Buddha for entry after death to the Pure Land had been a feature of other sects of Buddhism for some time. But Honen laid exclusive emphasis on this Way and on the repetition of Buddha's name in faith as the supreme means of salvation, thus for the first time marking off the Pure Land as a distinct and separate sect. He was extremely successful in winning converts, especially among the common people. It is said that ex-Emperor Go-Toba was annoyed at the fact that two of his maids of honor were among those who were converted and became nuns and that this was a contributory reason for the exile of Honen in his old age.

An extract from his famous *One Page Testament,* written two days before his death, will give an idea of the essence of his teaching:

> The method of final salvation that I have propounded is neither a sort of meditation, such as has been practiced by many scholars in China and Japan, nor is it a repetition of the Buddha's name by those who have understood the deep meaning of it. It is nothing but the mere repetition of the *"Namu Amida Butsu"* without a doubt of His mercy, whereby one may be born into the Land of Perfect Bliss. The mere repetition with firm faith includes all the practical details. . . . Those who believe this, though they clearly under-

[3] Ibid., pp. 219–220.
[4] Ibid., p. 224.

stand all the teachings Shaka taught throughout his whole life, should behave themselves like simple-minded folk, who know not a single letter, or
like ignorant nuns or monks whose faith is implicitly simple. Thus without
pedantic airs, they should fervently practice the repetition of the name of
Amida, and that alone.[5]

Shinran was banished, at about the same time as Honen, for taking a wife in
violation of the vow of celibacy. This action, his followers claimed, was part
of his identification with the common man and demonstrated the belief Shinran held that monastic discipline was not essential to salvation and that family and home formed the right setting for the religious life.

He [Shinran] was, he admitted, a lost soul, unsure of himself and of all else
in this life except the abiding grace of Amida. His only aim was to bring this
faith in Amida to those like himself who needed it most, to those ignorant
and illiterate souls who could not distinguish good from bad, to "bad
people" rather than "good people." Shinran even went so far as to say that
wicked men might be more acceptable to Amida than good men, since the
former threw themselves entirely on the mercy of the Buddha, while the latter might be tempted to think that their chances of salvation were improved
by their own meritorious conduct. "If even good people can be reborn in
the Pure Land, how much more the wicked man!"[6]

The parallel in this last passage to the parable of the Pharisee and the tax gath-
erer in the New Testament (Luke 18: 9–14) is striking. Successors of Shinran organized the scattered groups of converts into a solid body called the
True Pure Land sect. Under the name Ikko, "the Single-Minded," they later
formed communities and fought frantically in the wars of the sixteenth century. This True Pure Land sect, known in Japanese as Shinshu, is now the
largest Buddhist sect in Japan.

Many features of popular Buddhism in this era exhibited close similarities to religious developments in Reformation Europe, notably married clergy,
the use of scriptures in the vernacular, emphasis on salvation through faith in
divine grace, and even the religious divisions and intolerance. These divisions
in Japan were now more over points of doctrine and less over questions of
prestige and politics than had been the case with the intermonastic quarrels
of the earlier sects.

The Mongol War had proved a severe strain on the finances of the Hojo
Regency, and after about 1284 its power began to decline. Always uncertain
as to whether the Mongols might return to the attack, the Hojo had had to
maintain the Kyushu defenses for twenty years, and this had been a very costly
burden. Moreover they had not acquired in this war any fresh captured territories with which to reward their fighting men, such as those Yoritomo had

---

[5] Ibid., p. 202.
[6] Ibid., pp. 203–204.

been able to dispose of after the defeat of the Taira. Discontent was slowly growing, particularly since the monasteries had had first chance at what rewards were available in return for their prayers for victory, and there was then little left for the soldiers. As time passed, warriors who had felt a close personal tie with Yoritomo came to feel much less intimately attached to a succession of shoguns who were mere figureheads. Justice in the Kamakura courts began to be administered less promptly, fairly, and efficiently than in the early days. Finally quarrels among the Hojo themselves weakened their position. The Hojo regents, in fact, had compiled a remarkable record of good administration and an example of high personal character; but inevitably there were exceptions. It did not enhance the reputation of the *bakufu* when one of the regents, though a monk, kept forty concubines and was passionately addicted to dogfights, making the populace bow down to the champion dog when it was paraded in the streets of Kamakura.

The country as a whole had an expanding economy; but many individual retainers were in financial distress. There was no law of primogeniture, which would have retained estates intact in the hands of the eldest son, and, as the warrior class increased in this time of peace, the holdings of each member tended to decrease by constant division. In 1297 the *bakufu* tried the somewhat desperate expedient of passing a law of "virtuous administration," which was in effect a cancellation of debts owed by the retainers to those outside their class. This proved to be no help, for they still needed money, and new loan contracts began to carry a clause specifically excluding cancellation by future acts of "virtuous administration." The result was that money became tighter and loans harder to obtain. The rich became richer, and the poor poorer. The stewards throughout the country tended to fall lower on the property scale, and the higher officials, such as the constables, to rise. This social change presaged the rise later on of the great territorial lords known as *daimyo*, or "great names."

These general causes of decline in the power of the Hojo regents came to a head in certain specific events which occurred when Emperor Go-Daigo came to the throne in 1318, not as a child but as a grown man of thirty. He planned neither to abdicate nor to remain as a mere titular emperor, but to rule as the reigning emperor. A considerable measure of power might have been his, since the Hojo regents were no longer strong; but he incited their opposition and in a sense compelled them to take a stand because of a succession dispute. In the mid-thirteenth century ex-Emperor Go-Saga had left a will that was bound to cause future trouble for the *bakufu*. Each of his two sons had been titular emperor in turn, and the will carefully divided his property between them but was silent on the question of the succession, in effect leaving the choice to the *bakufu*. In the intervening period up to Go-Daigo's time, the lines descending from these two sons had provided emperors in turn; but Go-Daigo, in his newfound resolution, planned to keep the succession in his line only. He was opposed, somewhat naturally, by the *bakufu*.

This dispute began the Genko War in 1331. Repeating the earlier pattern of Go-Toba, Go-Daigo enlisted the help of some of the monasteries around the capital and of certain clan leaders who had become disillusioned with the Hojo regime. Go-Daigo himself was soon captured and sent into exile; but one of his supporters, a famous and unselfish warrior, Kusunoki Masashige, held out in a mountain fortress near Nara and kept the cause alive.

Then events took an odd turn. Go-Daigo escaped from his place of exile in 1333. The general sent by the *bakufu* to recapture him, Ashikaga Takauji, head of a distinguished branch of the Minamoto, changed sides and seized Kyoto in the name of Go-Daigo. The Hojo regents were becoming increasingly unpopular, and Takauji's success in taking the capital was the signal for others to join him. Most of the Kanto region rose in revolt and found a leader in Nitta Yoshisada, who marched upon Kamakura, suddenly defeated the last of the Hojo regents, and consigned the city to flames.

Go-Daigo was triumphant. He made a thoroughgoing attempt, in what is known as the Kemmu Restoration, to put the old imperial system of government back into operation, reviving all the former ministries and official positions. But the attempt was an anachronism. The power still lay with the wielders of the sword and the holders of land, and the emperor had neither. The resolution of the situation came through a further twist in the warrior struggle for power. Ashikaga Takauji and Nitta Yoshisada each had too much ambition to brook the presence of the other, and they became involved in conflict in the Kanto region in 1335. Go-Daigo sided with Nitta Yoshisada, but he had made the wrong guess. Ashikaga Takauji suppressed his rival during the next year, removed Go-Daigo, and installed an emperor of the rival branch. Go-Daigo, however, once more escaped and proceeded to a place called Yoshino, in the mountains south of Kyoto, where his supporters established him as emperor of a southern line. For the next fifty-six years, from 1336 to 1392, there were thus two imperial lines claiming legitimacy, the southern at Yoshino and the northern at Kyoto. The war of the two dynasties was the outward form of the struggle; the real issue was which warrior group would dominate the court and control the country as had the Hojo regents. Ashikaga Takauji was the victor, and this ushered in the Ashikaga Shogunate, the first part of which, up to 1392, was called after a period in Chinese history, the Nambokucho, the South and North period, when a similar situation had prevailed.

7

THE ASHIKAGA SHOGUNATE

Nambokucho: 1336–1392
Muromachi: 1392–1573

The devious shifts and complicated power struggles through which Ashikaga Takauji rose to the summit of authority in the early fourteenth century continued to characterize the political scene throughout the Ashikaga Shogunate. The Ashikaga, in contrast to Yoritomo, never controlled all of Japan. They maintained a grip on eight eastern provinces but could not hold down the rest of the country by placing their own retainers in key positions, as Yoritomo had done. They had rather to resort to bargaining with powerful landowners and warlords for support. The age was therefore one of constant war, with alliances dissolving and re-forming, and the center of gravity in the nation shifting away from the capital to the great landed estates and feudal domains of a new type. This shift incidentally distributed to other parts of Japan many of the benefits hitherto enjoyed exclusively by the dwellers in the capital region. There was no strong, central, feudal court of justice, such as had given cohesion to Yoritomo's rule, and the diminishing authority of the emperor was further weakened by the split between the factions of the northern and southern courts.

The distribution of the *shiki*, "rights or shares in the produce of estates," was no longer carried out, for the stewards had become outright owners or, in many cases, lost their land to a superior. The feudal pattern had therefore altered to a direct overlord-vassal relationship, operating locally with no strong central authority. The income from estates was not remitted to absentee owners, with the result that the emperors and court nobles were seriously impoverished. In 1500, for example, the funeral of an emperor had to be delayed for six weeks until enough money could be collected to pay the funeral expenses. Emperors were actually reduced to selling their autographs. Anyone could leave a written request and a small amount of money, and the emperor would be willing to copy out in his own hand a verse from one of the poets or a section from one of the warrior romances. There was no re-course for those thus deprived of customary income, for the shogun was not strong enough to compel his followers or allies to give up any of their wealth.

Fortunes rose and declined within short periods of time. The Yamana family, for instance, originally allies of Takauji, became dissatisfied and changed their allegiance to support the southern court. After a while they withdrew from the fighting to consolidate their family position and came to an agreement with the second Ashikaga Shogun, who made the head of the Yamana clan constable of no fewer than six provinces. By 1390 the family controlled eleven provinces, but they broke their oath to the Ashikaga two years later and in overweening confidence attacked the shogun. They were defeated and deprived of all but their own original two provinces.

The Yamana, though outstanding, were but one among many families whose fortunes fluctuated wildly. The romances spoke of loyalty to the death, but opportunism and treachery seem to have been equally common. One leader, however, Kitabatake Chikafusa, proved unswervingly loyal to Go-Daigo and the southern court. Learned and a man of many parts, he felt Go-Daigo to be the legitimate emperor and devoted his life to the cause of his master. Kitabatake's bravery and brilliant planning kept the southern cause going long after Go-Daigo's death in 1339. He gathered intelligence from all over Japan and kept dividing and confusing the forces of Takauji and the northern court by guerrilla tactics. The cause was maintained successfully even after his own death in 1354 by his stratagem of having sons of Go-Daigo stationed in various parts of the country to form rallying points of loyalty to the southern line.

The confusion of the period may be seen from the fact that Kyoto changed hands four times between 1353 and 1355. The Ashikaga would have been able to maintain firmer control had Takauji and his brother not fallen out. When Takauji died in 1358, the dire results of their dispute continued, for their quarrel weakened the cause of the northern court. Lords in various parts of the country continued to keep the struggle between the northern and southern courts alive, supporting one side or the other. They did this not so much out of conviction as from the hope that fighting would bring them improved fortune in the form of booty or land.

In accordance with Kitabatake's policy for the southern court, Prince Ka-nenaga had gone to Kyushu and by 1365 had gained control of the whole of that island. He was opposed by a talented general of the Ashikaga side, Imagawa Sadayo, who was a scholar-poet as well as a soldier, and similar to Kitabatake in that he took an overall view and planned carefully every detail of his campaign. Both in this respect showed an advance in generalship and strategic grasp over the commanders of the Gempei War era, who were coura-geous and dashing, with an eye to tactical advantage, but less able to plan thoughtfully for the effective use of numbers in a whole campaign. Imagawa won back the northern part of Kyushu by 1372, but the southern loyalists held out for nearly twelve years more and surrendered only upon the death of Prince Kanenaga. Finally the third shogun, Yoshimitsu, prevailed on the southern court to give up the struggle and return to Kyoto in 1392. The regalia were to be brought back by the southern court, a division of property was agreed to, and the succession was to alternate between the two lines. The regalia were duly surrendered, but the shogun broke his promise about the succession; the line of Go-Daigo was excluded and supplied no future emperors. The reunion of the courts in 1392 marked the beginning of the political subperiod known as the Muromachi, which was named after a district in Kyoto and which continued until the end of the Ashikaga period in 1573.

After the union of the courts, the first half of the fifteenth century was a period when no major wars were fought between territorial lords. But it could not be described as a time of peace, for it was marked by serious agrarian unrest. The peasants were becoming more conscious of their strength and less satisfied with the conditions of their lives. They found leadership among those warriors who had taken to farming or who had, by some accident of fortune, lost their place in the territorial power structure. Since the weak *bakufu* could give them no redress for their grievances, they formed leagues, *ikki*, for self-protection. The word *ikki* underwent a transformation from meaning "league" to meaning "a revolt promoted by a league." There was a famine in 1420, another famine followed by plague in 1425, and the first armed peasant rising on a large scale near the capital in 1428. Thereafter such risings became extremely frequent. Mobs broke into buildings owned by sake brewers, pawnbrokers, and monasteries, all of whom were engaged in money-lending, in order to destroy evidence of their debts. The *bakufu* tried the expedient of cancellation of debts on more than one occasion but with little effect, and its authority became minimal after 1441. Two years later the capital itself was attacked by rioters.

The ultimate in tragic futility was reached in the Onin War of 1467–1477. Yoshimasa, the eighth Ashikaga Shogun, was overwhelmed by problems of government he could not solve and was in any case more interested in the enjoyment of art than in the exercise of power. He wished to retire at the age of thirty, and the two most powerful families, the Hosokawa and the Yamana, became involved with rival claimants to his vacant seat. In the course of the maneuvering, the Yamana chieftain requested permission to punish Hosokawa Katsumoto for interfering in a matter concerning the shogun's deputy. He was refused, but Katsumoto saw which way the wind was blowing and began to mobilize troops. The rivals were content to glare at each other for a time, since neither wished to be officially branded as a rebel and thus to offer his enemies a chance to annex his property without penalty. In May 1467 fighting broke out in the city of Kyoto itself.

This was no longer single combat between mounted knights but fierce slaughter in streets and alleys, arson and looting by a new type of soldier, the *ashigaru* or "light infantry." These men, often absconding peasants, were armed with one weapon, a spear, halberd, or sword, and were expert in the art of street fighting. The results of months of battle and burning in the civilized and beautiful capital of Kyoto were disastrous. The temple of Shokokuji was burned down during intense fighting in the northeast quarter, whole sections of the city were gutted by fire, and the slaughter at close quarters was fearful. After one engagement eight cartloads of heads were collected, and this represented only some of those killed. The fighting was not continuous. Forces were withdrawn from the capital to fight elsewhere. Lulls occurred in the struggle, during some of which poetry contests were held to relieve the tedium of waiting under arms.

In 1473 the original opponents, chieftains of the Hosokawa and Yamana, both died. The spark went out of the useless struggle, and Ouchi, now leader on the Yamana side, at length withdrew from Kyoto in 1477 and submitted to the shogun. One result of the Onin War was to make men sick of civil strife; but there was still to be a century of disunity before the rise of any power strong enough to provide unquestioned central authority. The Ashikaga ceased altogether to be effective after the end of the Onin War. Such government as there was came from their deputies in the Hosokawa family, who were left as dubious victors when the Yamana retreated.

The period of decentralized feudalism under the Ashikaga, which forms the second stage of feudalism in Japan, coincided with and in part caused a considerable economic expansion. The earlier feudalism of the Kamakura period under Yoritomo and then the Hojo regents in their days of strength had already seen a movement of goods and people much greater than in the early times of Nara in the eighth century and the beginning of Heian in the ninth. Technological skills such as those required for making pottery and paper and casting iron had spread during the Kamakura period. Taira Tadamori and Kiyomori slightly before that time were interested in trade with China and did a good deal to promote it by improving harbor facilities in the Inland Sea. But an increase in wealth and a rise in the standard of living become much more marked during the Ashikaga period. This is sufficiently proved by one fact alone: Agricultural production per acre increased two- or even threefold in many parts of the country due to better farming methods and to larger economic units in the new type of feudal estate.

In spite of disturbed conditions, there was economic advance during this period, both domestically and in foreign trade with China. The wars of the fourteenth and fifteenth centuries created demand in remote parts of the country and also rendered better transportation a necessity, both by land and by sea. Handicraft industry expanded to meet the requirements of war, in arms and armor, and of peace, in agricultural implements and in the creation of those luxuries—textiles, lacquer, and numerous other goods—which the territorial lords could now better afford. At the same time the disturbed conditions of the country made it advisable for merchants and craftsmen to band together for mutual protection. There was a system at hand for this purpose in the *za*, or "guilds," which had existed since the twelfth century but were now strongly developed. The word *za* means a "seat or pitch at a marketplace," usually associated with a temple fair and under the protection of a powerful religious institution. This symbiotic arrangement between monks and merchants was mutually profitable, for it was well worthwhile for the merchants to pay fees to the temple for their stalls in the nearby market area in return for the support of the temple in cases where the merchants had to complain to court or *bakufu* concerning some invasion of their rights. It is even said that temple support was of aid in the collection of debts.

Businesses and trades associated with a particular region would turn to a prominent shrine in that region for protection. Thus in the course of time the guild dealing in cotton clothes became associated with the Gion shrine, the brewers of yeast with the Kitano shrine, and so on. The warehouse keepers were also the pawnbrokers, and they, too, were connected with a religious institution: the Enryakuji on Mount Hiei, one of the most powerful monasteries in Japan. Great families played a similar role as patrons: the Bojo associated with the papermakers, the Konoe with the craftsmen in gold leaf, and the Kuga with the guild of courtesans.

The proliferation of independent estates resulted, exactly as in Europe, in the multiplication of tolls and customs dues collected at barrier points between different regions of jurisdiction. One main reason for the rise of the *za* was to facilitate the movement of goods by paying a fee to secure exemption from tolls. Armed with this exemption from their powerful patron, individual merchants in a guild could move their products more freely from the place of manufacture to distant places of sale. The securing of a local monopoly in the sale of certain articles is a well-known feature of medieval European guilds, and this factor also operated in Japan.

The shrine patrons mentioned above were in the Kyoto area, but guilds were to be found in other parts of the country. There is evidence of interconnection between the guilds of one craft in different places, though such alliances were not nearly so tightly knit or so powerful as the great combination of the Hanseatic League in northern Europe. The presence of guilds outside the capital, however, indicates the rise of provincial and castle towns, a feature of this period in Japan. Only one of these new towns, Sakai (the modern Osaka) at the head of the Inland Sea, developed such privileges and immunities as to make it a "free city," able to bargain as a corporate body with the *bakufu*. Sakai had its origins in a salt-producing manor and went on to become a port for the capital area. During the wars of the Kamakura and Ashikaga periods it gained in importance by providing military supplies and also became a port for the China trade rivaling the nearby Hyogo (the modern Kobe), whose early leadership in commerce with China can be traced to Taira influence. The *bakufu* borrowed money from the Sakai merchants in 1543 and secured their loan by pledging the tax returns from the Ashikaga domains. Sakai must have proved attractive to merchants seeking security for their operations, for it obtained certain freedoms in administering its own laws, and it drew to itself a number of *ronin*, or "masterless *samurai*," a class of fighting men who could defend the city and who were to become an important factor in later Japanese history.

One of the main imports from China was copper cash in response to new demands for money in place of barter as a medium for internal exchange. Japan had minted coins earlier but had ceased to do so in the tenth century and did not resume until the sixteenth. During this time of expanding trade Japan therefore depended on Sung and Ming coins from China. Other imports were iron, textiles, drugs, and items to satisfy a growing luxury trade: books, pictures, and embroideries. Japan, in turn, exported to China copper and sulfur as raw materials and luxury goods in whose manufacture it excelled, such as fans, lacquerware, and weapons, particularly swords and halberds. In 1483 the astonishing total of 37,000 swords were exported to China. The export trade was very profitable, Japanese goods selling in China for four, five, and even ten times their value in the home market.

The trade with China was opened up by merchants who doubled as pirates: the line between the two professions was never very clearly drawn in any part of the ancient world. China always attempted to keep government control over foreign trade, and it was suffering from the activities of the Japanese "pirates," sometimes violent, sometimes no doubt merely extralegal, along most of China's coastline in the fourteenth century. Yung-lo, the emperor of the Ming dynasty under whom China's own overseas trade was vastly expanded, then came to an agreement with Ashikaga Yoshimitsu, the third shogun, concerning Japanese privileges for a limited, regulated trade in return for suppression of piracy by the shogun and the acknowledgment by the "king of Japan" of the usual "tributary" status under which China recognized her neighbor countries. This agreement in 1404 provided for two Japanese ships to trade with China every ten years, but in fact, with Chinese connivance, the number of ships was larger. They carried "tallies" to establish their identity and authenticate the exchange of goods. After 1469 a virtual monopoly of the China trade was obtained by a family, the Ouchi, prominent in the western part of the main island, and it continued in their hands until they were overthrown by one of their own vassals in 1557.

Although the shogun made the trade agreement noted above, the *bakufu* was not involved in the actual commercial transactions. Much of this was carried on under the aegis of certain Buddhist temples—one more instance of the important role of the Buddhist church in Japanese society. A famous statesman-monk, Muso Soseki, of the Zen sect, organized the sending of a ship to China as far back as 1342, with the backing of the first shogun, Ashikaga Takauji, and from the profits of this voyage he was able to build the Tenryuji temple (see illustration on page 66). "Tenryuji ships," as temple ships were thereafter called, continued to make successful voyages, and other monasteries followed this example. Among the reasons for the involvement of the monasteries in the trade were their knowledge of China and the Chinese language through Japanese monks trained in China, the amount of surplus capital from endowments and other sources which they had to invest, their political power derived from religious immunities and from their access as trusted advisers to those in power in both court and *bakufu*, and finally, no doubt, their education and experience in planning and decision making. In the changing fortunes of the period, the monasteries benefited from the stability and comparative freedom from interference accorded them through their sacred character. Thus monasteries not only financed trading ventures but also developed port facilities. The Sumiyoshi shrine, for instance, had a controlling interest in the port of Sakai, and the ancient Kofukuji monastery of Nara in the port of Hyogo.

The collapse of central authority, which began before the Onin War but was more marked after it, did not mean the advent of total chaos. Local law and order were maintained by the house laws of the territorial lords, often rigorously administered. Economic gains and a new self-realization among the warrior-farmer class brought about changes in the structure of society and a certain degree of social mobility. One example of such a change took place in 1485 in the restless province of Yamashiro where peasant rebellions had already occurred. The farmers were incensed at the damage caused by war and arson on the part of two groups fighting in their province. They themselves raised an armed force under reliable leaders and denied all supplies to both sides in the fighting. On receiving an ultimatum backed by force, the intruders withdrew and a provisional government of the province was chosen, with a clause requiring a monthly rotation of executive officials. This interesting semidemocratic experiment lasted for eight years.

The foregoing pattern of warfare and shifting alliances marked the whole of the sixteenth century. In the absence of acknowledged authority, the character of war itself changed and gave rise to an increased emphasis on fortified castles and methods of siege warfare to capture them. The period from 1534 to 1615 is known as the Sengoku-Jidai, or Period of the Country at War. Meanwhile in the midst of the inconclusive fighting and widespread unrest of the Ashikaga period, a limited circle of scholars and aesthetes around the shogun's court was producing new art forms and evolving canons of taste that were to be definitive for the future.

8

THE GOLDEN AGE OF JAPANESE ART

1378–1490

The Ashikaga Shogunate wore a very different complexion from the shogunate of Yoritomo and the Hojo regents, and this was partly due to the location of each. Yoritomo had selected Kamakura in the eastern region as his base because it was a center of his own feudal power and far from the distractions and intrigues of the court at Kyoto. Military power and feudal justice were his interests and in the main those of his successors, the Hojo regents. But when Ashikaga Takauji rose to prominence, the center of gravity in national affairs was once more of necessity in the Kyoto region. The long dynastic struggle between the northern and southern courts, and the Ashikaga attempts to build up their power and oppose the southern court in all parts of the country, meant that Kyoto as a center became the key to control.

The literary and artistic life which had always centered around the court would have held little attraction for the first shogun, Takauji, even if he had had time and leisure for such pursuits. But the third in the Ashikaga line, Yoshimitsu, who became shogun in 1368, and the eighth shogun, Yoshimasa, who succeeded in 1443 and died in 1490, were both devoted to the arts and generous in their patronage. Yoshimitsu was lavish in his expenditures on building to the point of exhausting the treasury, but Yoshimasa was much more able and creative as a critic and discerning patron of architecture, painting, and drama. Yoshimasa carried on these activities and gathered round him a remarkable group of scholars and artists at the very time when the horrors of the Onin War were at their height. He did this no doubt partly as an escape from a military and political situation which had gone far beyond his control, but Japan since his time has reason to be grateful, for he was instrumental in forming what is acknowledged to be the greatest age in Japanese art.

After Takauji, his generals, and his immediate successor, Yoshiakira, had painfully disposed, for the time being, of all effective opposition, the century

Flower arrangement.

It is an art of theoretical complexity in Japan, but one which is appreciated worldwide simply for its aesthetic value.

Japan National Tourist Organization

of Ashikaga rule was ushered in by the accession of Yoshimitsu. The headquarters of the Ashikaga were located in the Muromachi district of Kyoto, and there, in 1378, ten years after he became shogun, Yoshimitsu built the Hana-no-Gosho, Palace of Flowers, with its magnificent gardens. This marks the beginning of the art period known as the Muromachi.[1] He went on to build a sumptuous villa for religious retreat at Kitayama, erecting on its grounds the famous Kinkaku or Golden Pavilion, which was destroyed by fire in 1952 but restored in exact replica of the original.

The Silver Pavilion, Ginkaku, on the other side of Kyoto, was commissioned by the later shogun, Yoshimasa, as part of his retreat, the Higashiyama.

---

[1] The points of division between Japanese periods, and indeed the whole subject of Japanese chronology, are confused and controversial. The political beginning of Muromachi was marked by the reunion of the northern and southern courts (see. pp. 82–83), but the building of the Hana-no-Gosho was a decisive point in art history and as such is selected as the beginning of the art period known as Muromachi. (The name Muromachi is sometimes used as an equivalent to Ashikaga for the whole period 1336–1573.)

Ginkakuji (Silver Pavilion Temple) in Kyoto.
This was the retreat of the eighth Ashikaga Shogun, Yoshimasa, the great art patron in the fifteenth century.

Japan Information Center

These grounds and gardens were the scene of the contemplation and creative activity of men celebrated in several fields of art and drama—Noami, Geiami, Soami, Kanze, and the great painter Sesshu—in the last decades of the fifteenth century, and as such they merit a brief description.

The Silver Pavilion itself, delicate and simple, is two stories high and contains a shrine and rooms for rest and recreation with views over the garden. The word "silver" refers to some of the planned decoration which was never carried out. This quiet and restrained pavilion was built on the edge of a miniature lake, whose steppingstones, islets, and bridges consist of stones contributed by lords from all over Japan. There is a temple on the grounds and near it a mound of white sand piled up in a regular, conical form to make a "moon-viewing platform." And just beyond the temple is the small building of four and a half mats[2] which claims the distinction of being the first tea-

---

[2] Rooms in Japan have their floor area measured in terms of the standard six by three foot (Japanese measure) *tatami*, or "woven grass padded mats."

ceremony room in Japan. Its outlook well illustrates the quiet, understated, almost severe canon of taste which ruled at this time and which came to form the highest standard in all subsequent Japanese aesthetics. The view from the teahouse reveals no flowers, no bright colors, not even a glimpse of water, but only pine trees and underneath them undulating stretches of moss on the ground. Observing more closely one notices that these moss beds differ subtly in hue—some green, some brown, other parts russet or almost red—and this is all that meets the eye. This quiet taste the Japanese call *shibui*. The word means "astringent," puckering the mouth, as persimmons do when they are barely ripe. It is the direct opposite of the taste of the succeeding era, the Momoyama. Momoyama was all strawberries and cream, preceding slightly in time the baroque era in Europe, a style which it distantly resembles.

The quiet, modest nature of the prospect from the teahouse was exactly suited to the attitude of mind cultivated in the tea ceremony itself. The pomp and circumstance of the world must be left behind when one enters the teahouse, for its low door will permit entry only on hands and knees in an attitude of humility, and without the projecting sword and dirk which the samurai were accustomed to wear. Having entered, the participants behave in a formal and reserved but inwardly relaxed manner as they inspect and comment upon the ancient kettles, pots, and bowls used in the ceremony or admire the simple flower arrangement or single hanging scroll. It is less customary to comment upon the kimono and the skill of the hostess, *simplex munditiis*, "simple in her neatness." But participants note the play of her hands and all her gestures as she carries out the anciently prescribed movements of preparing and offering the green tea, whisked to a froth, to each guest in turn. These movements are like a progression and sway of an antique ritual dance. The whole experience, though strange and rather flat to a Westerner, is charged with significance to a Japanese. The combination of withdrawal from the cares of the world, artistic appreciation, intellectual conver-

Tea ceremony (*chanoyu*).
Note the iron kettle, water jar, cup, bamboo whisk, and ladle.
Japan National Tourist Organization

Tea jar (*chatsubo*) by Nomura Ninsei, active mid-seventeenth century; light grey stoneware with decoration in overglaze polychrome enamels.

Ht., 12 in. Seven quarrelsome crows (a bird of good luck in East Asia) are disposed around the jar in such a way as to leave plenty of restful space among them.

The Asia Society, New York: Mr. and Mrs.
John D. Rockefeller 3rd Collection.
Photography by Otto E. Nelson

sation, and observance of a restful and loved pattern or ritual—and all of this in the atmosphere of Buddhist contemplation—gives to the Japanese soul a sense of refreshment and well-being. Perhaps it is that very formalism antipathetic to a Westerner which enhances the ceremony in Japanese eyes, for the Japanese, more than most, find security in prescribed patterns of behavior. Seen in this setting, a moss garden is precisely what is required in front of the teahouse. Overstatement in color or line makes its appeal to the eye. But Buddhists are trying to get beyond the senses altogether, and understatement speaks more directly to the mind.

The Muromachi period is remarkable because so many arts flowered at once. Some of them were very minor, such as incense-judging competitions. Even the burglar alarms of medieval Japan were given a poetic art form. The corridors leading to the monks' dormitory in some temples were called nightingale walks, the heavy floor beams being set on supports in such a manner as to give out thin musical notes or chirrups when trodden upon, thus compelling night intruders to give audible warning of their approach.

At the center of all this intense artistic activity was a succession of three remarkable men: Noami (1397–1476), a monk and companion of the Shogun Yoshimasa; his son, Geiami; and his grandson, Soami. All were versed in Chinese learning, were practicing artists themselves, and acted as arbiters of taste at the court of the shogun.

Two earlier men—Kanami (1333–1384), a Shinto priest, and his son Zeami (1363–1444), of common origin but dramatic genius—were favored by the third shogun, Yoshimitsu, and encouraged to develop the *No* drama as a classical form, using earlier materials of dance, music, and poetry and combining them in a new and distinctive manner. The character *no* is the same as the Chinese *neng*, meaning "to be able," "ability," hence "the skill of a virtuoso." *No* plays are virtuoso performances combining poetic chant, mime, and slow posture-dance with accompanying music and elaborate costumes and masks. The subjects treated come from the realms of legend, history, and magic; and all the atmosphere and action are impregnated with Buddhist thought. The origins of *No* go back much earlier than the times of Kanami and Zeami to sacred dances or mimes performed on an open-air stage raised up so that the performers were visible both to the notables and the populace. Parts of the performance were known as *sarugaku*, "monkey plays," indicating an element of ribald buffoonery probably associated with fertility rites. At a later point in the development, the comic element is preserved separately in the *kyogen* plays put on in the intervals between the serious *No* performances. This feature is a parallel to the evolution of tragedy and comedy in Greece, which in origin were twin developments of the religious Dionysiac festival. In the case of both Japan and Greece, comedy came to serve an artistic purpose of providing light relief, after the religious function of comedy as promoting fertility and warding off evil influences had been largely forgotten.

   No plays are traditionally performed in sets of five categories: a god play, a warrior play, a woman play, a miscellaneous or contemporary play, and a

No play on stage.
There is no scenery except for the customary pine tree painted as a background.

Japan National Tourist Organization

demon play. The stage is a rather small, square platform, raised some four feet off the ground and connected by a sloping bridge at the left of the audience to the green room from which the actors emerge through a curtained doorway. The principal actor (*shite*) makes a slow and impressive entrance down the bridge and performs for the most part near the pillar at the left front, one of four pillars supporting a roof over the stage. The right front pillar is associated with the *waki*, or "second actor." Supporting characters as chorus may be seated in a line on the right, while the musicians occupy the rear.

There is no scenery save a pine tree painted on the rear wall, and there are almost no props. The gorgeous antique costumes, wigs, and masks provide the required interest and color. The effect of the intoned chanting and the slow, controlled, occasionally violent gestures is immensely heightened by the orchestra, consisting of flutes and drums. The percussion effects and gradually accelerating rhythms can create an almost unbearable tension at moments of crisis in the action.

The use of masks—masterpieces of artistry in lacquer; quiet, oval features for a young girl or contorted, wrinkled features for an old man or a demon—raises interesting dramatic and psychological considerations which might apply to both Japanese and Greek tragedy. In both instances the audience is perfectly familiar with the plot and already knows the denouement. There is no need to have surprise reflected on the faces of the actors. The element of

Gigaku Mask. Nara period, c. A.D. 754. Wood with traces of polychromy.

Such masks were used in the ancient *gigaku* ritual dance-drama, a forerunner of the *Nō* plays.
Arthur M. Sackler Art Museums, Harvard University; Bequest of Grenville L. Winthrop

the dance, originally of paramount religious importance, acts as the channel for the highly charged emotions of actors and audience. It is better *not* to see the faces of the actors. Costume and mask lift the actor onto another plane, heroic and larger than life. The force of word and gesture is heightened by the mask, remote and unmoved in its antique beauty, while the person who wears it goes through exalting or crushing experiences of hope and love, of despair and death. He is anonymous, and he goes through these experiences for all of us.

In both Greece and Japan, classical tragedy shows man struggling with his destiny and involved in the great realm of the gods, shot through with sunlight and shadow from beyond this world. The role of the chorus, however, is very different. The Greek actor declaims his part in the story, but the chorus dances it out, its members expressing their own feelings and those of the audience. In the intimate theatre of *No* the Japanese chorus has a smaller part, while dance and chant are both assigned to the main actors.

Zeami in *The Secret Traditions of No* refers to "the flower," a quality in the acting which produces in the spectator a sure but indefinable aesthetic pleasure. It is like watching a flower unfolding its petals; that precise moment of blooming is something unusual, unexpected. To produce these moments an actor must train long and hard. He must master the reproduction of reality; but that is not enough. There is something beyond, *yugen*, which results in the quality of "the flower." *Yugen*, originally "dark" or "obscure," by Zeami's time is equivalent to "elegant." Zeami gives the word a deeper meaning, "mysterious or subtle charm." This quality, he insists, is to be found not only in a scene we should expect to be charming but also in a scene, which he describes, of an old man acting the part of a youth, perhaps the youth he used to be. He wants to look young; but his limbs are heavy and he is a little hard of hearing. So the actor in the dance should beat his foot on the ground and move his arm in a gesture just a fraction of time after the beat of the music, just minimally off rhythm.

Even in Japan, however, *No* is an entertainment for the sophisticated. The average person prefers the more direct "blood and thunder" statement of *Kabuki* theater.

In Japan and especially in the Muromachi period the ambience of all these quiet but rich developments in art was the Buddhist worldview, for Buddhism influenced Japanese art profoundly. This was evident from the very beginning in the sophisticated combination of artistic force and spiritual tenderness seen in the sculpture of the Tempyo era, when Buddhism was first introduced. Now in the Muromachi period the Buddhist philosophical concepts of nature and man were more thoroughly mastered, and they affected directly the most highly regarded art form, that of landscape painting.

One of the best-known artists of Japan, Sesshu, has already been mentioned as belonging to this period. Leaning heavily on Zen training and inspiration, his work has an impressionistic character. With hard, decisive, an-

The Four Seasons, manner of Kano Motonobu (1476–1559). Pair of six-panel screens *(byobu)*. Ht., 5 ft 1 in.; ink and light color on paper.

First screen (pp. 96–97), spring (left) and summer. Second screen (pp. 98–99), winter (left) and autumn.

The Asia Society, New York: Mr. and Mrs. John D. Rockefeller 3rd Collection.
Photography by Otto E. Nelson

gular brush strokes and superb balance, Sesshu captured not only the form but also the essence of a landscape and a mood, and so his work becomes a channel for the great insight of Buddhism. This insight is notoriously hard to trap in words. It has to do with the fact that this world has value, but only relative value, while the abiding essence that gives meaning to all things is to be found only in the Buddha and his all-pervading Law.

Buddhist influence went behind Japanese art to its origins in China. The famed landscape painting of the Song dynasty (907–1260) had an exciting effect on the Japanese artists of the important Kano School. Examination of a Song or other classical landscape painting usually reveals a small focus or two of human interest, a man with a donkey crossing a bridge, or a scholar reading in a mountain pavilion. But the persons are dwarfed by the grandeur of the scenery of mountain or river. Humanity is subordinated to nature. Man is present, but only as part of a greater whole.

This attitude to man and his place in the scheme of things shows a marked difference from the Hebrew view, where man is represented as having a dominion over all other creatures given him specifically by God. Adam and Eve in Genesis *name* all the creatures, and to know the name of something is to have power over it. Man is supreme in creation. A contrasting Buddhist story, in quite a different vein, appears in the *Hsi Yu Chi* ("Record of the Western Pilgrimage"), a favorite tale known to all Chinese (translated by Arthur Waley as "Monkey"). The hero, a monkey who is always up to mischief but is potentially worthy of being changed at last into a man, has been bragging to Buddha in his usual fashion. He says that by his magic jumping somersault he can reach the end of the world; in fact, he says he has been there. Buddha smilingly shakes his head in disbelief and reproof, so Monkey says he will do it again. He makes his fantastic leap and, when he comes down, signs his

name on the great Pillar at the End of the World. He comes back, stands on
Buddha's hand, and says that if Buddha does not believe him, he can look at
his signature. Buddha in reply merely holds up his middle finger and shows
Monkey the signature written there. For all his vaunted leap he had never
been out of the hand of God, for the whole world is God's hand. Man has a
place in the universe, but to the Buddhist any exaggerated idea of his role is
absurd.

The second influence of Buddhist thought on Chinese and hence on
Japanese painting was the creative use of space. In the subtle changes which
overtook Chinese Buddhism in its passage from the earlier Indian form,
Daoist nature-mysticism played a part. The Daoist classic, the *Tao Te Ching*,
speaks of space as a positive, a creative factor in Chapter 10:

We put thirty spokes together and call it a wheel;
But it is on the space where there is nothing that the usefulness of the
    wheel depends.

We turn clay to make a vessel:
But it is on the space where there is nothing that the usefulness of the
  vessel depends.
We pierce doors and windows to make a house;
And it is on these spaces where there is nothing that the usefulness of the
  house depends.
Therefore just as we take advantage of what is, we should recognize the
  usefulness of what is not.[3]

Painters steeped in Daoist and Buddhist thought "recognized the usefulness
of what is not." With an elevated perspective, as though looking at a view
from the slopes of an opposing mountain, they eliminated teasing and unnecessary detail and presented the essentials in a serene and pleasing sim-

[3] *The Way and Its Power: A Study of the Tao Te Ching and Its Place in Chinese Thought*, by Arthur
Waley (London: George Allen and Unwin, 1949), p. 155.

plicity. In a landscape by Dong Yüan (active c. A.D. 1000) a boat is floating alone on a vast expanse of river. Water merges with sky, and a hill in the background is faintly sketched in. The skiff and the lonely figures just discernible in it carry a nostalgic significance, a Buddhist tinge of melancholy, they could never have in a crowded picture. The same effect is found on a smaller scale in a picture of two birds on a bough by Mu Ch'i (1181–1239), also of the Song dynasty. A plum branch thrusts up in uneven naturalness and upon it is a pair of small birds huddled very close together. They are viewed as they are in nature, without the obtrusion of man's feelings. Yet they seem to nestle more closely together, to need each other more, to be more true to their bird nature, because they are surrounded by ample space. The temperate use of line and emphasis, the large amount of space "left over," deliberately unfilled, even in a narrow hanging scroll, represent a profound and philosophical reflection by the artist, a reverence for life as it is in itself, not life as dominated by egotistical man. It was qualities such as these in the great Chinese tradition of painting that appealed to the Japanese. The tea ceremony and still more Zen Buddhist meditation were further examples of space created in the crowded press of life. And these qualities, interpreted by Buddhist masters such as Noami and his successors, captivated by their restrained and astringent discipline the minds of the Muromachi period and set a standard of artistic taste which Japan has never lost.

9

THE UNIFICATION OF JAPAN

Sengoku-Jidai, the Period of the Country at War:
1534–1615

Some unity of emotion and loyalty had always existed in Japan, fostered by the national legends and later promoted by Confucian ideals. Developments of literature and thought during the Heian period must have given birth to a sense of cultural unity. A degree of political unity had been forged by the powerful Minamoto Yoritomo after the clan wars of the twelfth century. But a period of constant war and frustrating rivalry between innumerable grasping warlords had intervened and had lasted for about 250 years. At length, at the end of the sixteenth century Japan became unified and pacified in a much more definite and complete sense. This period in Japan[1] happened to coincide roughly in chronology with the solidifying of the nation-states in Europe, and particularly with the centralizing power and skill of the Tudor monarchs in England. However in Japan it was not the monarchs but the generals who were the architects of unity. This unification ushered in the most peaceful and homogeneous period in Japanese history, the Tokugawa Shogunate, lasting also for 250 years. It must be recognized, nevertheless, that this internal peace was characterized by some of the rigidity of a police state and was purchased at the cost of free development and unhampered intercourse with other nations. Japan went into an isolation that was almost but not quite total.

Although the civil wars of the Ashikaga period and the Onin War (1467–1477) in particular were bloody and wasteful, there were also factors leading to positive growth and development which were, as so often in history, operative at the same time. A notable increase in domestic and foreign

---

[1] The dates for this period of unification begin before the end of the Ashikaga line of shoguns, who became steadily weaker and ceased altogether in 1573. The Sengoku-Jidai dates run from the birth of Oda Nobunaga to the final establishment of the Tokugawa Shogunate. The year of the decisive battle of Sekigahara, 1600, is sometimes substituted for 1615.

trade, the rise of commercial towns, and improvements in agriculture began to cause far-reaching changes in the framework of society. Class lines between aristocratic warriors on the one hand and the common people, merchants, and peasants on the other were becoming much less distinct. All this led to the decline of feudalism, with its self-sufficient and mutually hostile enclaves, and rendered both possible and desirable a move toward unification of the country. It is significant that after the end of the Onin War there were only about twenty major *daimyo* (territorial lords) left. Many of these were new-comers who had supplanted the older noble and feudal families.

In three distinct ways the commoners were beginning to acquire a power and influence they had never known before. First, battles were being decided by large bodies of foot soldiers and no longer by mounted knights of the warrior aristocracy. Second, some *daimyo* found it to their profit to encourage rather than suppress the activities of merchants in the new commercial towns. And third, fanatical Buddhist sects, such as those founded by Nichiren and the Ikko or "single-minded" sects of the Shinshu persuasion, whose strength was drawn from the common people, asserted themselves successfully against some of the *daimyo* and even acquired territory of their own. An Ikko group conquered the province of Kaga in 1488 and held it for a century. These factors in social change corresponded closely to similar factors in Europe at about the same time. In one important respect, however, Japanese history took a different course; unification was accomplished not by abolishing feudalism but by "freezing" it, using certain elements in it, and at the same time isolating the country from outside influences making for further change.[2]

Those who practice the art of history are only beginning to discover how sweeping are the changes brought about by advances in technology. The startling and swift changes that took place in the Japan of the late sixteenth century would not have been possible had it not been for the advent of the smoothbore musket. In one of the ironies of history its arrival in Japan co-incided with the coming of Christianity. A Portuguese sailing ship bound for the China coast was wrecked on the shores of Kyushu in 1542, and the muskets on board were soon expertly copied by the Japanese. Just seven years later, in 1549, Francis Xavier, the pioneer Jesuit missionary, also landed in Kyushu and began his work, which soon met with great success. Not for the first or the last time did the West bring to a non-Western land the powerful and explosive forces of its inventions and its ideas, so often in contradiction to one another. Yet the contradictions were usually not felt either in the West or in the East of the sixteenth century to the extent that we feel them in the twenty-first.

The Roman Catholic Jesuit order was of such immense importance in the early history of the contacts between Europe and East Asia that it is necessary to glance briefly at its origins and ideas. The Jesuits were not the first

---

[2] For an interesting discussion of the similarities and differences between Japanese and European feudalism, see Reischauer and Fairbank, *East Asia, The Great Tradition*, pp. 579–581.

Christian missionaries to reach East Asia. The Nestorian form of Christianity had been successfully propagated in Tang China but then had died out completely, though it was later reintroduced among the Mongols. Franciscan friars arrived in China just prior to the time when Marco Polo spent his seventeen years of service at the court of the Mongol emperor, Kublai Khan. But in length of stay and depth of influence in both China[3] and Japan the Jesuits were by far the most effective of the early representatives of Christianity.

One possible reason for this effectiveness was that they were a modern order, only just founded, with strong emphasis on academic, scientific, and practical knowledge, and a high degree of discipline. The founder, Ignatius Loyola, was a Spanish nobleman who had an experience of identification with the sufferings of Christ as he lay in his castle recovering from a wound. The spiritual exercises he practiced at that time and later wrote out for his followers have been a formative influence in the order up to the present. Aware of his need for intellectual training, Loyola became a student at the University of Paris and there gathered round him a group of men of outstanding ability. After the pope had accepted their offer of special service for the Church anywhere in the world, they were constituted the Society of Jesus. One of the original Paris band, Francis Xavier, became a missionary to the Far East. When he discovered that the Japanese derived much of their culture from China, he set out with incredible daring and that sense of strategy which has always distinguished the order to make an entry into China, but died on an island off the coast.

The advance of Christianity in Japan, which Francis Xavier initiated, was favored by one or two special features in the Japanese situation at the time. Good feeling existed between Japan and Portugal, particularly in the early days. The Portuguese liked the Japanese better than any other Asian nation, perhaps because they sympathized with the Japanese code of honor. The Japanese, on their side, admired the Jesuits because they exhibited a discipline reminiscent of the best Zen monks. Many converted *daimyo* were sincere and loyal Christians; others had more mixed motives, concerned with trade and technological advantages. They found the Jesuits had considerable influence with the Portuguese merchants and were also possessed of scientific and technical knowledge which could give them an edge over their rivals in the interclan struggles that were still going on. Once a *daimyo* embraced the faith, all his retainers tended to follow suit. Thus where Christianity gained an entrance at all, its advance was rapid; and this seems particularly to have been the case in Kyoto.

Francis Xavier had gone to Kyoto in 1550 but found in the midst of war and destruction no effective authority to whom he could make an appeal. He was invited by a *daimyo* of Bungo in Kyushu, Otomo by name, to visit him,

---

[3] The most noted Jesuit pioneer in China was Matteo Ricci. After infinite pains he reached the court at Beijing in 1600 and became so expert in Chinese that he was accepted as a scholar colleague by many of the literati. He was succeeded by Father Adam Schall, the astronomer, and other Jesuits, who continued to be an influence at the Chinese court for nearly 200 years.

and there the work prospered. A Father Vilela went later to Kyoto and in 1560 secured a guarantee of good treatment and tax exemption from the shogun. He was reinforced by the arrival of Father Frois, who made friends with several leading figures in the capital. Both priests operated not only in Kyoto but also in Sakai, Nara, and other places in the environs.

So successful was the work of the Jesuits that the Buddhist authorities became alarmed and brought sufficient pressure to bear on the government to have the priests ousted from the capital. They withdrew to Sakai, the independent city, and, although safe there, found little response among the merchant class. Father Frois succeeded in returning to the capital in 1569 after four years' absence. He had interviews with Oda Nobunaga and secured a license to preach. There is no doubt that his message had the more appeal in that Buddhism at this time had sunk to a very low point in public esteem.

The Jesuit Visitor-General Valignano reported to the Society in Rome in 1582 that there were 150,000 Christians and 200 churches in Japan. The vast majority of these were to be found in the western part of the country. It is no wonder that Valignano was encouraged by the situation, for Nobunaga had been gracious and invited him to spend several weeks at the new and splendid castle of Azuchi on Lake Biwa. It appears that Nobunaga was much intrigued by Valignano's black servant.

A good many *samurai* and some *daimyo* were among the Christian converts. They adopted Christian names, such as Simeon and Francisco, the latter being the name chosen at baptism by Xavier's host, Otomo. They wore the cross on their helmets and even used to go into battle with war cries such as "Jesu" and "Santa Maria." Four Japanese youths of noble lineage were sent as a delegation to visit the pope and the king of Spain. The common people also had an opportunity to hear the doctrine in church and Christian schools. As has been found to be the case in other parts of the world, they derived both comfort and a new sense of dignity and personal worth from their Christian belief. Many remained faithful to their vows through the severe persecution that was to follow.

There were thus a number of factors both internal and external, concerned with trade, firearms, and foreign ideas, which combined with profound weariness of civil war, to make Japan ready for certain fundamental changes. The country was in a sense ripe for unification, but the task was not easily accomplished. Three strong men—Oda Nobunaga (1534–1582), Toyotomi Hideyoshi (1536–1598), and Tokugawa Ieyasu (1534–1616)—accomplished it, the last two building upon foundations laid by their respective predecessors. Their common task and personality differences are symbolized in two anecdotes. In the first, Nobunaga is said to have quarried the stones for the imaginary castle of a unified Japan, Hideyoshi to have shaped them, and Ieyasu to have laid them in place. In the second, the three discuss what to do about a songbird in a cage who will not sing. Nobunaga says, "I'll make it sing"; Hideyoshi, "I'll kill it if it doesn't"; but Ieyasu, "I'll wait until it does sing." The three worked together in spite of serious differences and rivalries; but fundamentally they had the same aim, the pacification and unification of the country. It was well for Japan that they did, for one man alone in the span of a lifetime could scarcely have accomplished the task. And without a long period of security and quiet after so much turmoil, it is doubtful whether Japan would have been ready for its sudden and dramatic entry into the competitive world of the late nineteenth and twentieth centuries.

Oda Nobunaga's family was minor in rank and importance but began a rise to power by becoming deputy constables for the lords of Shiba in the province of Owari. Nobunaga's father increased the family estates, and on his death the youthful Nobunaga gathered a force of fighting men to secure a strong position in the province. At this point a powerful neighbor, Imagawa, began a drive on Kyoto with some 25,000 men and had to pass through Nobunaga's province. One of Imagawa's lieutenants, later to take the name of Tokugawa Ieyasu, captured the fortress of Marune, and Nobunaga's advisers became despondent. But Nobunaga himself resolved on a bold attack, even though he could command a force of only about 3,000 men. The Imagawa forces were relaxing and drinking in an ill-chosen campsite situated in a narrow defile. After a heavy rainstorm Nobunaga executed a brilliant surprise attack, routed the enemy, and killed Imagawa himself. This battle of Okehazama in 1560 proved decisive. Nobunaga felt the time was ripe for him to begin a gradual and calculated move on the capital.

He secured his rear somewhat by a pact with Tokugawa Ieyasu, his former opponent, and disarmed the opposition of neighboring *daimyo* by alliances and suitable marriages. Strong resistance was offered by Saito Dosan and his son in Mino province, which lay on the route to Kyoto. This was a parvenu but powerful clan who had made money in vegetable oil. Their castle at Inabayama was at length reduced in 1567 in maneuvers directed by Toyotomi Hideyoshi, who had risen rapidly from a common foot soldier in Nobunaga's service.

There was still some resistance to Nobunaga's ambitions in Ise and Omi, but the fall of the castle of Mizukuri meant that by 1568 the way was open to the capital; and in that year Nobunaga was welcomed there and lauded by the emperor. The advance of Nobunaga demonstrated that the reduction of fortresses was now the key to successful warfare.

Nobunaga had Yoshiaki appointed the fifteenth Ashikaga Shogun, but when he proved intractable, drove him out in 1573 and did not trouble to choose a successor, thus bringing to an end the Ashikaga line. Neither Nobunaga nor Hideyoshi after him attempted to acquire the title of shogun for themselves but preferred to support and protect the imperial line and use such court titles as seemed suitable for themselves, knowing that their real power lay in military control. They did, however, restore moderate incomes to the court and relieve emperor and nobles from the abject poverty they had suffered under the Ashikaga.

Oda Nobunaga was now established in Kyoto and had clearly won the first round in the struggle. He was a warrior first and foremost and determined to rule by military force. But there was still a large part of the country not by any means under his control. With some difficulty he subdued two *daimyo* threatening him in provinces north of the city. He then ensured for himself greater security at the center by a ruthless destruction and burning of the large Enryakuji complex of monasteries on the hills outside Kyoto, which had for so long been a thorn in the side of the government. Next he turned his attention to another branch of Buddhism, the fanatic Ikko sect, whose strongholds at the mouth of the Kiso River, east of Lake Biwa, had given him constant trouble. He besieged the last two of their fortresses there, refused an offer of surrender, and put the crowded forts to the flames with enormous loss of life. He was moving to the north against other Ikko adherents when he had to turn back to help Tokugawa Ieyasu hold off the powerful Takeda chieftain in the east. Together they defeated Takeda in the battle of Nagashino in 1575. This battle marked an important new departure in the fact that it was the intelligent use of firearms which decided the issue. The mounted enemy force was brought up short by a high stockade and then shot down by musketeers sheltered behind it. Since loading and firing were such clumsy processes, the troops were divided into three sections, who fired volleys in succession while the others reloaded. But even so the results among the enemy were devastating, while Nobunaga's losses were minimal.

Nobunaga had little time between campaigns to devote to civil affairs, but he put in force some economic measures, notably provisions for free markets and free trade, currency regulations, and arrangements for the erection of bridges and repair of roads. He devoted special attention to attracting merchants to the new town built around his strong headquarters castle of Azuchi, completed in 1579.

The west was not yet brought under control. Hideyoshi was entrusted with this task, and he undertook it on behalf of Nobunaga with characteristic skill and thoroughness. Again fortresses were the key, and one of them Hideyoshi reduced by diverting the course of a river and flooding the place. But Nobunaga's time was running out. He had taken the sword, and he was to perish by it. In 1582 one of his generals, Akechi Mitsuhide, turned on him and took him completely by surprise in a temple in Kyoto when Nobunaga was passing through on his way to take a short holiday. Nobunaga committed suicide to avoid capture, and his body was destroyed in the flames of the burning temple. On hearing the news, Hideyoshi brought compromise negotiations with the powerful Mori in the west to a quick conclusion, rode for the capital at breakneck speed, and utterly defeated the rebellious Akechi.

The vengeance exacted by Hideyoshi for the treachery of Akechi might appear to be one more personal conflict in the dreary record of ambition, rivalry, and blood. It is true that all three of the great leaders of this period, Nobunaga, Hideyoshi, and Ieyasu, were determined to rise to the top. Yet they differed from the adventurers of the Ashikaga period in a number of important ways. They showed some continuity of plan, much good sense, political as well as military ability, evidence of economic planning, and, above all, intelligent application of principles of law and order.

Hideyoshi acted with his customary decisiveness immediately upon the death of Oda Nobunaga. The provinces which Nobunaga had held were divided up among a few loyal generals, Hideyoshi retaining a goodly share for himself. He called a council of the four leading commanders, but it soon became clear that he would be the dominant member. The sons of Nobunaga and one of the four commanders, Shibata, each made bids for independent power but were defeated within a year of Nobunaga's death. Hideyoshi reached the site of the culminating battle at Shizugatake in one of his swift night rides, covering about fifty miles in six hours. He rallied his hesitant officers and made a prompt end to Shibata's threat.

Hideyoshi now had control, directly or indirectly, of thirty provinces out of a total of some sixty in the country, including the twenty it had taken Nobunaga so long to dominate. A further important factor in his strength was that the provinces not under his control were at a distance from the center of the country and did not pose any immediate threat. Tokugawa Ieyasu, his powerful ally in the east, however, was something of a problem. Ieyasu had not been present at the first council of four commanders, and was now sufficiently jealous and alarmed at the extent of Hideyoshi's power to take up arms against him. Ieyasu in fact gained a small advantage in two battles; but both were men of sense and decided they could profit more by cooperation than by rivalry, a pregnant decision by which neither lost and the country gained immeasurably.

When matters were settled between them, Hideyoshi proceeded to consolidate his position and evolve a peacetime policy. He felt that Osaka on the Inland Sea near the capital would be the best center for control and built a strong castle there, a move which was feasible now that the Ikko monastery fortress of Honganji at Osaka had been destroyed. He had already ordered a land survey, a step that may be compared in significance to the Domesday Book of William the Conqueror. The survey began in 1583 and continued until Hideyoshi's death in 1598, by which time all the provinces in Japan had been covered. The size and yield of every rice field in the country was set down (though in practice some areas were inevitably left out), and the permanent tenancy of a plot guaranteed to the actual cultivator, who was then entirely responsible for the tax. This move of simplification did away with the jungle of *shiki*, "rights, dues, and proportions of the crop owing to various officials and owners." The rate of tax was high, as much as 50 percent of the crop, but there were no further dues or obligations. The land was divided into two types, wet and dry fields, and each of these into three categories by yield. The calculated yield of the lowest category was 28 percent less than that of the highest.

The fiefs which Hideyoshi thus had at his disposal were granted, along with their accompanying taxes, to his vassals and varied in value of yield (irrespective of acreage) from 10,000 koku to over 1,000,000 koku. (The koku measure is equivalent to five bushels and was supposed to feed one man for one year.) In return the vassal pledged fealty to Hideyoshi and promised to supply military aid on demand, usually up to two-thirds of his income. The land survey was conducted by Hideyoshi's own officials and was ruthlessly enforced. In an attempt to correct decades of self-protective evasions of tax, he even threatened to crucify the inhabitants, including women and children, of villages which falsified their returns.

Although Hideyoshi's central position was secure, he could neither rest nor feel safe until the outlying parts of the country were also under his control. In 1587 he himself commanded an expedition against Shimazu, the *daimyo* of Satsuma at the extreme south of Kyushu. After a leisurely advance in enormous force, Hideyoshi won a decisive battle near the Sendai River. One of his contingents was at the same time coming in by sea, and Shimazu was completely at his mercy. With a wise combination of firmness and clemency he did not press matters to a conclusion, but allowed Shimazu to keep his own territory and a part of what he had won in previous fighting. The rest of Kyushu was secured by being granted to loyal commanders and allies. After returning to his base, he enacted a pacification measure known by Hideyoshi's title as the "Taiko's Sword Hunt," the object of which was twofold. The confiscation of swords from all except *samurai* deprived peasants, gentlemen-farmers, and soldier-monks of the means of raising armed rebellion, and it also served to make a clear distinction between the *samurai* and the farmer classes.

There remained the Kanto Plain and the far north to be brought into subjection. The refusal of a proud Hojo chieftain to come to Kyoto and offer submission gave Hideyoshi the needed excuse to mount an expedition to the Kanto region. Since he now had ample resources, he was able almost to guarantee the outcome by assembling a force estimated at 200,000 men and planned to reduce the central Hojo citadel of Odawara by a siege conducted for as long as was necessary. To keep up the morale of his troops, he allowed them to bring their wives on the expedition, and he himself provided musicians, dancers, and other forms of entertainment. Odawara was surrounded by May 16, 1590, and what followed was almost an anticlimax. There was treachery within the gates, and the fortress surrendered by August 4 of the same year. The major *daimyo* in the north were summoned and made their submission. By the end of 1590 Hideyoshi was supreme in all Japan. The eight rich Kanto and surrounding provinces were offered to and accepted by Tokugawa Ieyasu in exchange for his own family territory and subsequent acquisitions. This was an advantage for Hideyoshi in that it moved the powerful Tokugawa farther away from the capital and detached them from the old family ground where they could count on traditional loyalties if they should attempt revolt. On the other hand the Kanto was of great value to Ieyasu because it had been well developed both agriculturally and industrially.

There is a story concerning the grant of the Kanto land which deserves to be true—*si non e vero, e ben trovato.* Hideyoshi one day dismissed his followers and rode out alone with Ieyasu. Without a word, in the taciturn spirit of *bushido*, Hideyoshi drew out from his sash his sword and scabbard and handed them over to Ieyasu, indicating that he trusted him completely. The two men discussed the future of Japan, and then Hideyoshi, waving his arm toward the head of Edo Bay, said, "Make your capital there." The significance of this advice lay in the fact that the center of gravity of the country had been moving eastward over the past centuries, and Edo (the modern Tokyo), surrounded by the largest single stretch of agricultural land in the country and geographically near the center, could in the future become the best point of control. Whether Hideyoshi entirely trusted Ieyasu or not, he probably reflected that the Kanto was better placed in his hands than in those of any other. In any event Ieyasu moved into the castle of Edo well content.

As the edict concerning the sword hunt followed the Kyushu campaign, so in 1590 following the Kanto campaign an expulsion edict was promulgated. The land survey had uncovered the existence of a number of *ronin* or vagrant warriors. A list of houses and occupants was to be prepared under this new edict, and all who entered a village from another village or an outside province were to be expelled.

Hideyoshi's organization of government consisted in general of the feudal system of vassals under strict discipline with Hideyoshi at their head as suzerain. The ultimate authority, as always, was that of the emperor in the background; but he had almost no freedom of action or independent initiative. When affairs had been sufficiently settled by military action, Hideyoshi appointed a Commission of Five to govern the capital and home provinces, but he himself issued orders and edicts in both civil and military matters for the country as a whole. A body with more of a policy-making character was that known as the Five Elders (Go-Tairo), but it was only appointed toward the end of Hideyoshi's life and for the purpose of guarding the status quo and preventing changes that would threaten Hideyoshi's family after his death. The Elders were assisted by the Junior Advisers, but the task of these latter, to settle differences arising among their seniors, was an impossible one. Lower but important officials were the *daikan*. These were deputies for Hideyoshi in the extensive territories directly owned by him. They were as often as not rich merchants who acted as managers but were also appointed to watch the activities of nearby *daimyo*.

Christianity, meanwhile, continued to prosper under Hideyoshi's rule as it had under that of Nobunaga. Takayama Ukon, one of Hideyoshi's leading generals, was a Christian and helped Father Organtino secure a site for a church and a house near the great Osaka Castle. Nagasaki city was practically run by the Jesuits, and Portuguese trade was increasing. In 1587 the viceprovincial, Coelho, came from Nagasaki to pay a state call on Hideyoshi, and the talk was amiable. There was further friendly contact the next year after Hideyoshi's successful Kyushu campaign, and the Japanese leader paid a visit on board a Portuguese ship. But the very next morning the missionaries learned to their dismay that an edict banning Christianity had been published and that they were ordered to leave the country within twenty days. Two of the reasons given in the edict were that Buddhist shrines had been damaged and that Japanese were being sold abroad as slaves. Some enthusiastic converts had smashed images, and certain Portuguese traders were known to have purchased and exported slaves. But the real reasons behind Hideyoshi's decision are not known. He may have regarded the slave trade, though small, and the independence of Nagasaki as defiance of his authority, and he may have considered the success of Christianity a possible source of disunity in the country, particularly in view of the attack on Korea which he was contemplating.

This was a severe setback, but the missionaries kept their heads. They gave every appearance of complying with the order and gathered their whole body at the port of Hirado. Some sailed away, but possibly as many as 100 stayed behind, went underground, and carried on their work in secret, aided by loyal converts. They found in the course of time that the ban was only sporadically enforced. The number of converts continued to increase, until by 1596 the total was reckoned to be 300,000. These included some in high places, such as Gracia Hosokawa, daughter of that Akechi who had killed Nobunaga, and Maria, sister of Hideyoshi's favorite consort, Yodogimi. There cannot have been any extensive alarm at associating with Portuguese, for the gilded youth of the capital began to copy Portuguese fashions and even to carry rosaries and crucifixes. A number of Portuguese words were adopted into the Japanese language, such as *pan* for bread, *karuto* from *carto* for playing cards, and, more farfetched than these, *tempura*, for shrimp fried in batter, derived from the fact that on the Ember Days, *quattuor tempora*, the Jesuit fathers ate seafood. But another reversal of policy occurred in 1597, the year before Hideyoshi's death. In a fit of rage he ordered the torture and death of twenty-six Christians, six Spanish Franciscans, three Portuguese Jesuits, and seventeen Japanese believers. They were mutilated and paraded through a number of cities and then crucified in an upside down position at a site near Nagasaki.

The last great event in the long, arduous, and successful career of Hideyoshi was the invasion of Korea. Counting the reserves at the campaign headquarters at Nagoya, over a quarter of a million men were involved. The logistics of supplying such an army would have been unthinkable in earlier days, but the army staff had gained experience in decades of warfare and more recently in the ambitious campaigns in Kyushu and Kanto. The invasion was launched in April 1592, and a landing successfully made. The Japanese naval convoy was unaccountably late in arriving, but the Korean Navy did nothing to stop the invasion because its admiral had received no orders. Pusan was captured, and the Japanese columns moved swiftly north. They encountered little resistance and captured Seoul, the capital, without much difficulty. Having advanced to the Manchurian border, they spread over most of Korea. They tried to conciliate the populace and persuade them to throw in their lot with Japan. They even began a land survey.

But the Koreans, recovering from the first surprise, began to offer some serious resistance. They organized guerrilla bands and would have been even more successful if their government had not been so weak and confused. Sickness and the severe winter took their toll on the Japanese forces, until by 1593, the second year of the campaign, perhaps one-third of the Japanese in Korea had succumbed.

China claimed suzerainty over Korea, and at this point an army dispatched by the Ming emperor entered the struggle. The Japanese were compelled to fall back. A war party and a peace party developed within the ranks of the Japanese commanders. Ming envoys came to Kyoto in 1596 to arrange terms of peace and to invest Hideyoshi with the title "king of Japan" from the emperor of China. But Hideyoshi, incensed by the condescending tone of the emperor's letter, lost his temper with the envoys and made preparations to launch a new campaign in 1597. The Chinese sent in a fresh army, and the Japanese, though reinforced, were compelled to retreat all the way to the south coast. The majority were evacuated, but a rear guard of picked troops, mostly from Satsuma, held positions around Pusan and inflicted severe casualties on the Chinese and Koreans. The long war was reaching a stalemate, and the death of Hideyoshi in 1598 gave the Japanese a reason to make a final evacuation and end the war.

Measured by standards of achievement, power, and wisdom, Toyotomi Hideyoshi was probably the greatest individual in the history of Japan. He was capable of swift decision and action, as at the time of the unexpected death of Oda Nobunaga. But he was not rash or impetuous. He would not waste lives making frontal attacks on fortresses when he could reduce them by siege or stratagem. His origins among the common people gave him an understanding of character and a certain sympathy which tempered his ruthlessness. He knew better than his predecessor, Nobunaga, when to follow firmness with mercy, as when he spared the Satsuma house at the conclusion of the war in Kyushu. His combination of thoughtful planning and abounding self-confidence carried him to the summit of affairs. At the end, when he attacked Korea and suffered from the delusion that he could take on China as well, this confidence turned into megalomania. He loved pomp and display, was overly fond of women, and was subject to fits of rage; but by any count he was a great man.

There is a portrait in the Itsuo Art Museum in Osaka, painted within a year of Hideyoshi's death by an unknown artist. It shows a face almost emaciated, with hollows beneath the high cheekbones, as of one who has been ill. Since it is not a complimentary likeness, it may well be true to life. The head is bent slightly forward, and this, with the keen and glittering eyes, gives an impression of great concentration and nervous energy. The chin is pointed, and the wide mouth set in a determined line. The man radiates an air of decision and capacity, above all capacity. Voluminous black court robes give, as they are intended to, an air of great calm; but in Hideyoshi's case this attitude is entirely belied by the head and eyes, trying to stare into the future.

He died at sixty-two after an illness of two or three years. In his last weeks he had spent much time in lucid intervals having Ieyasu and all the great vassals sign oaths vowing to support the Toyotomi family and his son Hideyori when he came of age. As events turned out, what Hideyoshi had built on Nobunaga's foundations did remain; but it was under the firm hand of Tokugawa Ieyasu and not that of Hideyori, as Hideyoshi probably guessed that it would be.

Tokugawa Ieyasu had been born in 1543 into a small *daimyo* family, Matsudaira, situated between the more powerful families of Imagawa and Oda. He had spent no less than thirteen years of his youth as a hostage with one or the other of these houses, and it may not be fanciful to suppose this was a source of his caution and close attention in later life to political methods of control of his *daimyo* rivals. He had benefited from his association with both Oda Nobunaga and Toyotomi Hideyoshi and gained an immense amount of battle experience. On several occasions he lay low instead of rising to challenge Hideyoshi; but all the while he was consolidating and adding to his own domains in the east. At the death of Hideyoshi he was by far the most powerful of the Council of Regency, holding estates worth 2,500,000 koku in revenue, or more than double the wealth of any of the other four members. Incidentally, the five members of the Council together held fiefs of one-third of the value of all fiefs in the country.

Ieyasu had as his main object to preserve the unity of Japan. From this unity he naturally stood to benefit; but also his outstanding position made him the object of envy and intrigue. His most dangerous enemy was Ishida Mitsunari, who did everything possible to cause bad blood between Ieyasu and his colleagues, and even made two attempts on Ieyasu's life. In 1600 another opponent, Uesugi, raised a rebellion in the north, and Ieyasu marched against him. But Uesugi was held in check by two *daimyo* loyal to Ieyasu, and Ieyasu's own advance was in the nature of a feint. He was watching Mitsunari, who now gathered allies and made an advance from the west. Battle was joined on October 21, 1600, at the pass of Sekigahara, a strategic defile between the plain east of Lake Biwa and the plain surrounding Nagoya. Each side had mustered approximately 80,000 men, but Mitsunari did not succeed in bringing all his forces into action, and the loyalty of some was doubtful. At the beginning of the fight at dawn the advantage went to Mitsunari. At a crucial moment one of his commanders, Kobayakawa, was supposed to charge down a hill onto Ieyasu's rear; but he remained inactive and then changed sides and attacked other regiments of Mitsunari's. Although the commanders of these regiments were veterans of the Korean War and had large numbers of men at their disposal, the element of surprise and shock must have been great, and they were pushed back. There was considerable slaughter, and Ieyasu emerged with an overwhelming victory. This was the final battle in the long and exhausting series of civil wars, and the last major engagement fought on Japanese soil to the present day.

Ieyasu at once set about the matter of punishments and rewards. By con-

fiscating ninety fiefs and reducing the size of many others of his recent enemies, he had land worth 6,500,000 koku to dispose of. A good part of this
he kept in the Tokugawa family, but rewarded his retainers and allies generously. He was careful to assign estates near the main routes in the center of
the country to those whom he considered absolutely reliable. He was cautious in actions affecting certain powerful feudatories, most of them distant
from the center, in order not to drive into the arms of his enemies those faithful to Hideyoshi's memory and to his young son, Hideyori. He then spent
the next years strengthening his castle at Edo, whose inner ramparts now enclose the emperor's palace in Tokyo, in protecting Edo by erecting a series
of fortresses around it, in building the Nijo Castle as headquarters for his
deputy at the capital in Kyoto, and in providing for the growth of industry
and foreign trade.

By 1611 the old supporters of the youthful Hideyori had been removed
by death, and by 1614 Ieyasu had decided, in spite of his repeated oaths to
Hideyoshi, not to permit the continued existence of the house of Toyotomi
in case it might still become a rallying point for the disaffected. No *daimyo*
were prepared to come out in the open to Hideyori's aid, but *ronin*—masterless *samurai*—rallied to him. This increased the garrison available to
Hideyori in the castle of Osaka to 90,000. Hidetada, appointed by his father,
Ieyasu, to conduct the attack, could not breach the defenses of this famous
stronghold, so, after a period of siege in the winter of 1614, he induced
Hideyori's advisers to sign a compromise peace, whereby Hideyori would
keep his domains and castle, while Hidetada would demolish the outer works
of the castle. Hidetada did not keep to his part of the bargain, had his men
fill in the inner moat as well, and attacked again without any justification in
the summer. The defenders sallied out and were overwhelmed. Hideyori
committed suicide, and Yodogimi, his mother, was killed by a retainer to fore-
stall capture. The whole episode was the more disreputable as Hideyori's wife
was Hidetada's own daughter and had sent a last appeal for the lives of her
husband and Yodogimi. The message was totally ignored.

Ieyasu was now the unchallenged leader of the country. He had already
revived the institution of the *bakufu* and been made shogun by the emperor
in 1603. He retained the office for only two years and then handed it over
to Hidetada, his son. He thus signalized the fact that the office was to continue in the Tokugawa family and at the same time set himself free to devote
time to a system that would preserve his house from overthrow. The details
are considered in the next chapter, but in essence the plan consisted in treat-
ing the powerful *daimyo* with firmness and respect, and placing his own family members and close allies in estates in key positions to keep an eye on them.
His greatest weapon was his wealth, which was constantly increasing through
the operation of gold and silver mines, through foreign trade, and through
taking the main cities of Japan under his direct jurisdiction.

The system mentioned above was a system of control, but not an administrative pattern of government. Of that there was very little. Ieyasu gov-

erned by giving direct orders, as one would govern a fief. His subordinates then carried out the orders as circumstances seemed to dictate. In the early period Ieyasu had no involved scheme of boards or government offices. At a later stage in the Tokugawa rule a more detailed and quite unbending organization was worked out. Ieyasu laid down general principles, especially for the control of the "outside lords," the great feudatories, in the *buke sho-hatto* of 1615, the "ordinances for military houses." This document forbade these lords to marry without approval of the shogun, did not allow them to repair or enlarge their castles without a permit, and ordered them to denounce subversive activity. The details of administration were in any case handled locally by the *daimyo* in each fief, so there was little need for an elaborate central structure of government.

Ieyasu was a shrewd judge of men but had a curiously casual way of employing some persons. He used talent wherever he saw it. Thus he employed a falconer on diplomatic missions and an actor as director of his mining operations because they had a flair for these things. It was by a strange accident that he found one of his most valuable experts, a shipbuilder, Will Adams, pilot-major of a small Dutch flotilla, who was one of a few survivors of a typhoon which severely damaged the flagship, the *Liefde*. The little group of foreign sailors landed in Kyushu, and in due course Ieyasu came to hear of Will Adams. He was a native of Kent in England and had served a thorough apprenticeship as a shipwright. He built several small ships for Ieyasu and explained Western methods of navigation. He arranged for the salvaged guns and ammunition of the *Liefde* to be used in the siege of Osaka Castle. Ieyasu admired Adams' determination and native shrewdness and held frequent conversations with him. In the course of their discussions Adams persuaded Ieyasu to grant the English trade privileges, a move which commended itself to Ieyasu, who was anxious for competition to offset the Portuguese monopoly. Adams warned him against the potential dangers of relations with Spain and Portugal and pointed out that there were other European nations, England among them, who did not insist on propagating their faith but were content with trading privileges alone. The Dutch received permission to trade in 1609. The British East India Company was at this point offered a gilt-edged opportunity to acquire a favored trading position. But the company official in charge, possibly jealous of Will Adams, selected an unsuitable site for his trading station against Adams' advice. The British "factory" never really prospered and was closed down after some years, leaving the Dutch the only gainers from the whole affair. Will Adams acquired a considerable estate and married a Japanese woman. He ultimately died in Japan, somewhat homesick for England but full of honors, and is commemorated by a monument that looks out over the sea, which was his livelihood and his sorrow.

From his own observations as well as Adams' advice, Ieyasu was well aware of the rivalries among European nations in securing trade openings. He thought he could profit from these rivalries and treated all nations impartially. He hoped to gain technical aid and was in correspondence with the

Spanish governor of the Philippines, to whom he suggested trade arrangements and from whom he requested the help of mining and shipbuilding experts. The governor was slow to respond, and, when he sent a ship, the personnel proved to be more missionaries than either traders or experts. This annoyed Ieyasu. He welcomed Dutch and English trade and felt less dependent on the ships of Portugal and Spain. He had long been tolerant of Christianity, but toward the end of his life he became more suspicious. He seems to have felt that Christian allegiance might make some *daimyo* less loyal to his regime, in view of the fact that foreign policy was becoming a more complicated matter with more European nations involved. In 1614 he had an edict issued suppressing Christianity. Churches were destroyed in the capital at Kyoto, prominent Japanese Christians exiled, and foreign missionaries placed under arrest. No missionaries were killed at this time.

In the winter of 1614–1615 he took the most difficult step to secure the future, namely, the attack on Osaka Castle and the elimination of Hideyori and the house of Hideyoshi. He must have long considered this move and been reluctant to make it, at least until he was quite sure he could do it with impunity and without risking revolt. He was just in time. The year following, 1616, he died, aged seventy-five. His life was the most fitting to close the work of the three men who had succeeded in unifying Japan, for he was as strong in politics as he was in military affairs. He had the patience and determination for the one as well as the physical stamina and strategic brilliance for the other. He fought over forty-five battles in his time. In his case the portrait appearance is deceptive. He was small in stature and rather stout. His face looks like that of a *petit fonctionnaire*, round and rather ordinary, except for the eyes. But in fact he liked riding and swimming and was accustomed to fatigue and hard exercise, enjoying excellent health right up to the time of his last illness.

The artistic climate during the sixteenth century, the Period of the Country at War, shows a contrast almost as great as can be imagined to the earlier Muromachi period under the Ashikaga Shoguns. The pendulum of taste has swung from restraint to exuberance, from chaste and cultivated simplicity to the florid use of gold and color. Inside the buildings the screens have larger, bolder designs and much gilt background, while outside the roof lines have been altered to the rounder, swelling, and somewhat ostentatious forms connected with the art period of Momoyama (1573–1615). The very name Momoyama, "Peach Mountain," taken from the site of Hideyoshi's villa, suggests a lush opulence quite different from the understatement of the earlier period.

This marked artistic shift had at least something to do with the tastes of the political leaders themselves. Hideyoshi once gave a tea ceremony party to which everyone, from the greatest to the humblest, was invited. The affair went on for ten days, with art exhibits, concerts, plays, and dance performances. Every device of ostentation was employed to enhance the public image of the leading military figure who was aiming to unite Japan under his personal banner. Hideyoshi enjoyed entertaining and took pride in showing visitors around his Osaka Castle, where the bowls, tea kettles, and other vessels, and even the hardware on the doors, were all of pure gold. No greater contrast could be found than that between this magnificent rococo display and the deliberately quiet and spare character of the tea ceremony in the original small room in the grounds of the Silver Pavilion.

The Western world also exhibited a change in the favored style of art from the classic and restrained to the extravagant and theatrical at about the same time, the latter half of the sixteenth century and the beginning of the seventeenth, when the painting and architecture of the Renaissance gave way to those of the Baroque era. Yoshimitsu, the third Ashikaga Shogun, who governed latterly from his retreat at the Golden Pavilion and died in 1408, falls in time just before the active period of the Early Renaissance painters, Fra Angelico, Masaccio, and Fra Filippo Lippi. Yoshimasa, builder of the Silver Pavilion and patron of the great monk-artist and connoisseur, Noami, corresponds roughly with the age of Giovanni Bellini, Sandro Botticelli, and Leonardo da Vinci. But by the time the swashbuckling Hideyoshi gave his gigantic tea party, Rubens as a young man was forming his style of glorious exuberance; and the elaborate allegorical ceiling paintings of overblown Baroque in the Italian mansions and churches, such as Pietro da Cortona's "Triumph of Divine Providence" (between 1633 and 1639) in the Palazzo Barberini, coincided with the final consolidation of the Tokugawa regime.

The progress of elaboration in Europe was more gradual and steady, and transition from the simple to the magnificent in Japan more sudden and more marked. The severity of Giotto in the fourteenth century and the simple dignity of Masaccio in the fifteenth yielded by gradations to the magnificence of Leonardo, Raphael, and Michelangelo in the High Renaissance of the sixteenth century, before the mannered painting of the Baroque came to fill the center of the stage. The period of restraint, even of severity, in Japan owed its origin to the artists of the Song dynasty in China (960–1280), but its most famous Japanese practitioners came much later. They were Josetsu (c. 1410), Shubun (active from 1414 to 1465), and Sesshu (1420–1506), most renowned of them all. All three were deeply influenced by the philosophy of Zen. (The name of the first, Josetsu, means "as if unskillful," reflecting a Zen notion of direct spontaneity.) Sesshu, with his strong, severe style, was still active at the beginning of the sixteenth century; but by the second half of the century the painter Kano Eitoku (1543–1590) was at work on such commissions as screens for Nobunaga's new castle at Azuchi. One of these, with the title Karashishi, "Chinese Lions," offered both in theme and execution a marked contrast to the earlier simplicity. Painted on a background of gold, it is full of flamboyant curves and mock fierceness. In an exaggerated Chinese convention the animals' tails are so bushy they could be mistaken for flames of fire or waves of the sea.

Although the shifts in style took place in the East and West at about the same time, the two movements seem to be quite independent of each other.

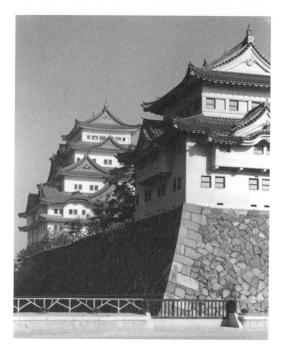

Nagoya Castle.

The castle has formed the center of this castle-town since Tokugawa Ieyasu constructed it in 1612 (restored 1959). Nagoya is now the third-largest city in Japan. Castles such as this provided the clan leaders (*daimyo*) with strong fortifications and a degree of interior luxury. Sloping roofs prevented the lodgment of fire arrows.

Japan Information Center

The parallel changes in artistic taste do not show any evidence of a causal connection. The Portuguese visitors, as curiosities, were made the subjects of a few Japanese paintings. There was for a time a superficial fashion, already noted, for things Portuguese. But the influence of the Jesuit missionaries and a handful of merchants, Portuguese and Dutch, was too marginal to have had any real effect on the course of Japanese art.

In one field, however, that of architecture, the influence of European technology is clearly to be seen, though the outcome is distinctively Japanese in style. The advent of firearms made necessary an entirely new form of fortification, and Oda Nobunaga made a characteristically thoroughgoing response to the problem. In 1576 he erected the castle at Azuchi on Lake Biwa which dominated central Japan. Hideyoshi followed with the great stronghold of the castle of Osaka in 1583–1585, and Tokugawa Ieyasu with the rebuilding and enlargement of the castle of Edo. In these and subsequent castle buildings an immense square with sloping sides formed of large stone blocks gave an unbroken foundation extending up to fifty or sixty feet in height. Upon this was erected the castle proper, constructed of wood and plaster with wall faces and gables between layers of small projecting roofs. The towering structure of five or six stories gradually diminishes in size as it rises. The gables and projecting roofs are designed to give advantageous lines of fire to the defenders but to provide no horizontal valleys in the roofs in which incendiary materials could easily lodge. The castle at Azuchi is aptly named "The White Heron," for the massive stone base surmounted by white walls and gray roof tiles, visible from far away, gives an impression of surprising lightness and airiness considering the functional strength and power of the structure. The interiors of the castles were sumptuously furnished with screens and decoration in the ornate Momoyama style. (The full name often given to this period in art is Azuchi-Momoyama, to include Nobunaga's castle at Azuchi as well as Hideyoshi's villa at Momoyama.) The considerable sums spent on these fortified dwellings were a calculated expense incurred to help the leaders establish their dominant position among the *daimyo*. The exterior would overawe the visiting lords with its impregnability, and the interior impress them with the owner's vast reserve of wealth.

10

JAPAN IN ISOLATION

The Tokugawa Shogunate: Part I, 1615–1715

Japan in the seventeenth century was at length peaceful and prosperous. The *Tokaido*, "the eastern road by the sea," between the old capital at Kyoto and the new one at Edo, was thronged with people, some traveling on business, some on pilgrimages combined with pleasure and sightseeing. If they noted the procession of a great lord moving up to Edo, they would scatter and kneel prostrate on either side of the road till the lord had passed. First came the *samurai* warriors, wearing the traditional long sword and short dirk, the first group of them a bodyguard surrounding one of the important officials of the lord's estate, mounted on horseback. Then followed servants carrying boxes and baskets of treasure and supplies, more *samurai* with banners, then the *daimyo* himself, borne in a palanquin, with whole regiments of *samurai* and servants forming the rear of the procession. The entire equipage might amount to hundreds or even thousands of men. It went ill with any bystander of the common people who did not show proper respect, for the *samurai* had the legal right of *kirisute*, "to cut down and leave," the right to kill with impunity, without questions asked or explanations offered.

Constant processions of this kind to and from Edo were the most characteristic part of the contemporary scene. They were occasioned by the practice of *sankin-kotai*, "alternate attendance," first a custom then a requirement of the shogunate, whereby the *daimyo* spent four months of each year, or sometimes of every second year, in attendance at the shogun's court and the remainder of the year on their estates. But when they returned to their estates, they had to leave their wives and families in Edo as hostages for their good behavior. The word "alternate" referred to the fact that each category of *daimyo* was divided into two groups, one of which was in attendance while the other was in the country. In this way the shogun was able to prevent the lords from plotting those uprisings which had disturbed the peace for so long in the past. He was also able to divert the spending of the lords' finances from military purposes into peaceful, if wasteful, channels by forcing each lord to keep up two establishments in a style befitting his rank.

The *daimyo* were divided into three categories: the *shimpan*, "related fiefs," belonging to collateral branches of the Tokugawa family itself, the chief of these being the *go-sanke*, "three houses," the estates of three of Ieyasu's sons in Owari, Kii, and Mito provinces respectively; the *fudai*, or "hereditary vassals," who had been allied with the Tokugawa house before the battle of Sekigahara; and the *tozama*, "outside lords," who had sworn fealty to Ieyasu only after Sekigahara and the fall of Osaka.

The Tokugawa family took full advantage of the prestige and position given by the title of shogun, which was secured by Ieyasu as a member of a branch of the famous Minamoto, to which Minamoto Yoritomo, the first shogun of the new, permanent style, had belonged. The title had never been claimed by Nobunaga or Hideyoshi. The importance of the *go-sanke* lay in the fact that they were eligible to supply a member for the office of shogun if a son failed to the direct line. The *fudai daimyo* were located for the most part in central Japan and held fiefs averaging about 50,000 koku, though a few were much larger. Although holding the privileged place of loyal vassals, they had often to undergo the hardship of being moved from one estate to another, for the shogunate used them to keep watch over outside lords of doubtful fidelity. The outside lords themselves were originally the equals of the Tokugawa, and some of them held very large fiefs. The Maeda held estates worth over 1,000,000 koku, and Mori of Choshu at one time controlled thirteen of the sixty-six provinces in the country. They could do little outside their fiefs but were largely autonomous within them. They had to be handled tactfully by Ieyasu at the beginning, but subsequent shoguns found the methods of control evolved by the *bakufu* to be increasingly effective.

These methods of control included not only the alternate attendance, hostage system, and encouragement of heavy financial expenditure on the part of the lords but also a ban on any repairs, strengthening, or enlargement of fortresses by any *daimyo* without express permission and the device of compelling the outside lords in particular to undertake public works, including the rebuilding of Tokugawa fortresses. Two further measures were in the nature of police control, namely, the upper and lower ranks of *metsuke*, or "censors," who supplied secret intelligence to the *bakufu* concerning *daimyo* and lesser ranks of landholders, and the institution of *gonin-gumi*, "five-man groups" among the farmers. The five-man groups were mutually responsible for keeping the peace and seeing that taxes were paid and obligations discharged within their own group. Another precaution, drawn from the lessons of the civil wars, was to forbid any *daimyo* to enter into direct communication with the emperor; everything had to be done through the shogun's deputy in Kyoto.

The lesser vassals who held land under 10,000 koku in value were called *hatamoto*, "bannermen" (originally the bodyguard of a general). Many held land worth only 500 koku or less. It became customary to withdraw such men from the land altogether and pay them a fixed stipend instead. The *bakufu* was anxious to dissociate the warrior class as much as possible from the peasants, so as to avoid the agrarian revolts under *samurai* gentleman-farmer leadership which had presented such a problem in the recent past. But the presence of idle warriors in the castle towns, living on an income that fluctuated with the price of rice, began before long to cause embarrassment of another kind to the regime.

The organization of the Tokugawa government, minimal under Ieyasu, became gradually more elaborate and formalized under his successors, until it attained the following form under Iemitsu, the third shogun (1623–1651):

The Tairo, "Great Elders," advised the shogun on important matters of policy and ruled as regents during the minority of a child. At first there were three Tairo, but later only one.

The Roju, "Council of Elders," originally two and finally four in number, served on a rotation system for one month each. In addition to some advisory duties they were responsible for the direction of the bureaucratic machine. Their administrative supervision covered a wide range, the affairs of the *daimyo* and of the monasteries, relations with the emperor's court, the affairs of the shogun's own vast domains, public works, and coinage.

The Hyojosho, "Judicial Council," was formed by the addition of certain commissioners to the Roju councillors. These commissioners were in charge of various government departments and had both executive and judicial functions in areas such as city government, reporting on *daimyo* activity (the commissioners known as *metsuke*, mentioned above), control of the bannermen and of religious organizations, and responsibility for the finances of the Tokugawa domains.

It was not necessary for the central government of the shogun to provide labor or funds for local government, since this was decentralized in the hands of the various *daimyo*. But commissioners for the large cities were always appointed by the shogunate from among the *fudai daimyo*, their own vassals. The resultant whole was quite evidently a police state with tight supervision, organized to preserve as closely as possible the status quo.

This strong impulse to preserve the country exactly as it was explains in part the mounting persecution of the Christian church in Japan, viewed with ever-increasing suspicion as the agent of foreign powers. During the rule of Hidetada (1616–1623), Ieyasu's son and successor, some 700 Christians were executed. An English merchant reported seeing children burned alive in their mothers' arms, while the women prayed to Jesus to receive the children's souls. Many more than the number killed must have had to leave their homes and been reduced to abject poverty. Those enforcing the edicts against Christianity tried to induce their victims to place their feet on a sacred picture or image—*fumi-e*, "treading picture"—and so to renounce their faith. A remarkable number refused.

The climax of persecution came in the years 1637–1638, during the reign of Iemitsu, third shogun, when 37,000 peasants, the majority of them Christians, were joined in armed rebellion by *ronin* and others driven to desperation by bad local government and poor economic conditions. All made a stand in an old fort on the Shimabara Peninsula, an area near Nagasaki which had for long been a Christian center. The *bakufu* could not fail to take strong action in the face of this threat to the peace of the realm; but it took the authorities three months, 100,000 troops, and the help of Dutch naval bombardment from the sea to reduce the rebels. The slaughter was hideous, and only a handful escaped with their lives.

The failure of the Shimabara Rebellion was decisive. Christianity in Japan was compelled to go underground and in many areas was rooted out altogether. The Roman Catholic Church officially lists 3,125 individual instances of martyrdom (the unrecorded deaths at Shimabara being omitted) between 1597 and 1660. And yet, when the country was opened to foreigners after 1868, Christian families were discovered who had handed down the faith in secret from father to son. The savage suppression of Christianity was not unrelated to the internal political situation in Japan. Foreign and Christian influence had always been strong in Kyushu and the western end of Honshu, and it was precisely here that some of the greatest *tozama* ("outside lords") had their seats. There can be no doubt that the *bakufu* feared that these lords might at any time offer trade privileges to Portugal or Spain in return for foreign weapons and even military reinforcements of troops and naval vessels to overthrow the regime. Following the Shimabara Rebellion, therefore, the *bakufu* took the final steps of expelling all Portuguese merchants and missionaries, imposing the death penalty on all Japanese attempting either to go abroad or to return, and placing a limit of 2,500 bushels capacity on the construction of new ships, a size suitable only for coastal and not overseas trade. The Chinese merchants were kept under strict supervision, and the only Europeans admitted were the Dutch. The Dutch traders were granted limited privileges only, being confined from 1641 onward to a small, artificial island called Deshima in Nagasaki Bay. There they lived in cramped conditions and without their families for the long months between the annual trading exchanges. Their massive and well-armed vessels were slow but for their day reliable and able to carry a large amount of cargo. The round trip could be made only once a year, and the risks from pirates and from tropical storms were great. But if the voyage was successful, the profits were very high. In the corresponding trade of the British East India Company with Canton, a captain could sometimes retire comfortably on the gains secured from three or four voyages, if his luck held. The parallel is not an exact one, and the height of the British trade occurred at a later date, in the second half of the eighteenth century. But the low-bulk, high-value cargoes from Asia were generally a profitable venture. The profits of the Dutch seem to have made their endurance of the hardships of Deshima worthwhile. In any event it was soon evident that the *bakufu* meant business by their new regulations, for all the members of a Portuguese diplomatic group which came in 1640 to negotiate the resumption of trade were summarily executed.

Ship engaged in trade with Luzon, Annam, and Siam in A.D. 1633, just before the exclusion order closing down foreign trade.

Tablet dedicated by merchants to the Kiyomizudera Temple, Kyoto, in prayer for a safe voyage. Note natives from Southeast Asia working on the sails aloft.

Japanese National Treasure. From the author's collection

Thus Japan decided neither to admit foreigners to free and open trading nor to continue the overseas trade ventures to Southeast Asia which Japan itself had undertaken with considerable success in the sixteenth century. By this decision for retreat and isolation Japan gained stability and internal solidarity at a time when these factors were urgently needed in its society. But there was a certain irony in the fact that this closing down and sealing off took place just when the rest of the world was being opened up to an interchange of goods and ideas incomparably more thorough and extensive than had ever been known before. The rate of social and technological change in the West became rapid in the two centuries following 1640, whereas in Japan the rate of change was deliberately slowed down by Tokugawa policy. Thus when Japan reopened its doors, it had much lost ground to make up; but it was in a stronger position to do so when the time came.

The main roots of the strength which Japan exhibited in the crucial period of modernization in the latter half of the nineteenth century lay in the *samurai*. This class provided a labor source with a strong sense of duty, courage both physical and moral, and a thorough, if narrow, experience in handling public business in the various fiefs. These valuable qualities were developed by generations of training in the hard school of war; but they derived also from the Confucian ethic which had been introduced when Chinese culture was first acclimated to Japanese soil in the sixth century.

Ieyasu had issued in 1615 his *buke sho-hatto*, "ordinances for military houses," in which the *samurai* were bidden to give themselves equally to the practice of arms and the pursuit of polite learning. Polite learning in actual fact meant Confucianism. Buddhism, earlier a main factor in cultural advance, was now declining. Shinto played its part as an ally of Confucianism against the power of Buddhism. But Confucianism, with its conservative qualities and its stress on loyalty, was ideally suited to the static pattern of Tokugawa rule. The pattern was further reinforced by the form which Confucianism had already assumed in China, namely, the Neo-Confucianism of Chu Hsi (1130–1200), a state orthodoxy that became increasingly rigid with the passage of time. Neo-Confucianism had been the subject of discussion in Japan at the court of the Emperor Go-Daigo as early as 1333; but it came into its own in Tokugawa times.

One of the great proponents of the Neo-Confucian philosophy was Hayashi Razan (1583–1657), a scholar who acted as secretary to Ieyasu and helped with the drafting of laws at the beginning of the Tokugawa Shogunate. It was due to him in the first instance that Neo-Confucianism became almost equivalent to a state orthodoxy in Japan. He encouraged the shogunate to become independent of the West and to lay stress, in the traditional Confucian manner, upon farming, not trade, as the foundation of the state. There was, however, a change of emphasis. In the Confucian ethics of the *samurai*, loyalty to one's lord took precedence over all other considerations, even over the family loyalty and filial piety which were such a feature of the Confucianism of China. Hayashi Razan was immensely learned and a prolific writer in the fields of history, literature, and Shinto studies, as well as Confucian philosophy. A drawing of his face shows deep lines of concentration on the brow and around the eyes, while a small, pursed mouth suggests a legal mind of rigid precision. His house in Edo became a center of Confucian studies, and the tradition was carried on by his son and grandson. The latter, with the enthusiastic support of the fifth shogun, Tsunayoshi, became the president of the Shohei Academy, a Confucian university providing for instruction in philosophy and the performance of a ritual cult centered on Confucius.

The Tokugawa government preserved a firm social stability in Japan, but it was always plagued by an inner contradiction, namely, the need to maintain peace and at the same time preserve in the *samurai* a stance of military preparedness and an attitude of pride, not to say of bellicosity. The *samurai* could find no avenue for military action outside Japan, for the country was insulated from almost all contact, positive or negative, with other powers. The warning of Hideyoshi's misadventure in Korea had been heeded. Those *samurai* not employed in administration could find little outlet for their energies inside Japan, for a social freeze between peasant and warrior and between warrior and merchant had occurred. Class distinctions were intentionally fostered by the government and had been ever since Hideyoshi's sword hunt. Upward social mobility was very difficult, in part owing to lack of money among the lower grades of *samurai*. Indeed fluctuations of the rice market, in which their stipends, paid in rice, were converted to cash, made any social movement for the *samurai* likely to be a downward one. The classic means for a warrior to enrich himself by fighting to gain possession of the lands of others was totally denied to him by the overwhelming power of the Tokugawa police state. It is no wonder there was a deep sense of frustration in the *samurai* ranks.

Some enterprising *samurai* founded military academies where the practice of arms and the theory of strategy were taught. These schools naturally became social centers where many of the warrior class congregated and discussed all manner of topics, not excluding politics. It was at one of these academies in Edo that a *ronin* conspiracy was planned. The objective was to set off an explosion in a government powder magazine on a night when a strong wind would start a large fire. In the ensuing confusion the conspirators proposed to break into the shogun's castle and kill the highest officials. Simultaneous arson and violence was to take place in Osaka and Kyoto. The plot took a long time in preparation during the last years of Iemitsu and was not ready for execution until 1651, the first year of the rule of Ietsuna, the fourth shogun. Even then there was a further postponement due to the illness of one of the leaders. He was heard to mutter details of the plot during a bout of fever, and the authorities were forewarned. The rising proved abortive. The leaders committed suicide or were punished by crucifixion and their relatives by decapitation.

Some change in the attitude of the government had, however, already taken place. The young Ietsuna (in office 1651–1680) was fortunate in having good advisers. The regime felt secure, and a change from the military government of the first three shoguns was now initiated. Policy began to be directed from this time on into civilian channels. Enlightened attempts were made to find openings for *ronin* in constructive work. Many of them were not eager to assume clerical tasks, and others had not sufficient education to enable them to do such work. But better education and the gradual growth of a central government bureaucracy enabled most *ronin*, with the exception of the most restless and the least reputable, to be taken up into useful employment by the early 1700s.

The fifth shogun, Tsunayoshi (1680–1709), who succeeded his brother, Ietsuna, was a curious character. He supported Confucianism, as his patronage of the Shohei Academy showed, and was himself a scholar of some ability. But he was all his life under the influence of his mother, a strong and ambitious woman, who was a fanatical believer in Buddhism. She persuaded him to issue in 1687 an edict protecting all living things, especially dogs, since he had been born in the Year of the Dog in the traditional calendar. Those mistreating dogs were punished, and the city officials ended by building shelters outside Edo which housed 50,000 of these animals. The ultimate absurdity was reached when citizens were required to address dogs as O Inu Sama, "Honorable Dog."

The years of Tsunayoshi's rule coincided with the important cultural period known as the Genroku Era (1688–1704). This period was associated with a new urban culture and the flowering of a new type of art and literature whose patrons were no longer the court nobles, great monasteries, or powerful *daimyo*, but the merchants, the *samurai*, and the townspeople.

The peaceful years and expanding economy of the Tokugawa period had led to a remarkable urban growth. Although the financial distress of the *samurai* was real, the economy as a whole was prosperous and more diversified. Cash crops such as sesame oil, mulberry, indigo, sugar cane, and tobacco supplemented the staple, rice. Cotton accounted for 25 percent of the produce of four provinces by the first quarter of the eighteenth century. Large ancestral farms were breaking up into smaller units which could be run by single families, whose members, in the current shortage of labor, were able to increase their earnings by work in village and town industries. Some small businesses burgeoned into large merchant enterprises. The house of Mitsui, for example, started by brewing *sake* in Ise. The family opened a pawnshop and then began dealing in rice. A member of the family founded a retail textile store in Edo in 1673, which proved so successful that branches were opened in Kyoto and Osaka. The Mitsui house then conducted the banking business required both by the shogun and the emperor. The Mitsui firm adapted itself more successfully than some other merchant houses to the changes that came later with the Meiji era and went on to become one of the great industrial companies of modern Japan.

In the course of this urban growth the three great cities were Kyoto, the old capital, Edo, the new capital, and the combination of four towns which formed the city of Osaka—"the kitchen of the world," as it was called. There the Dojima Rice Exchange was set up in 1697, though trade in rice had been a feature of the city previously. By 1710 the exchange was operating with warehouse notes in place of actual grain and was dealing in futures. Numerous towns, some of considerable size, grew up in the centers of the various fiefs, towns such as Nagoya, Sendai, Kumamoto, Kagoshima, Kanazawa, Hiroshima, Hakone, and Kofu, as well as over 100 other towns of smaller size. Road transportation improved under the Tokugawa, but the mountains and headlands of Japan make road construction peculiarly difficult. The cheapest and most efficient form of transport was by sea. An eastern circuit and a western circuit were developed for coastal trade by sea on a regular basis. Without seaborne traffic it would scarcely have been possible to deliver to Osaka the 4 million bales of rice which were reaching that port annually by the time of the Genroku Era.

The merchants, until now despised as a class, began to assume an altogether new importance. The surplus wealth in the hands of these new merchants and their servants was sufficient to support a type of urban living almost unknown hitherto except possibly around the fringes of the court in

Contemporary seafront architecture in the port of Osaka.

Japan Information Center

Kyoto. A life of leisure, particularly evening leisure, now became available at a price to the city dweller. There were teahouses and taverns, many of which also served as places of assignation for lovers. The pleasure quarters of Edo and Osaka became famous and provided for the enjoyments of unrestrained good company as well as for those of sex. The theaters and public baths were more frequented; and tourism, travel for pleasure and sightseeing, became more common.

The popular *Kabuki* theater in its early phases had a bad moral reputation with the result that the *bakufu* forbade women to be associated with the theater as actresses (see illustration on page 128). The challenge of having men present female parts helped to form a highly stylized dramatic art. This fully developed *Kabuki* theater satisfied the common people's love of gaudy and bright costumes, violent action, and strong emotional tension. The parallel art of *Bunraku*, the popular puppet plays, also affected *Kabuki* in the exaggerated and sometimes jerky gestures adopted by the actors (see illustration on page 129).

Chikamatsu Monzaemon (1653–1724), one of the most notable figures of the Genroku Era, wrote both for the *Bunraku* puppet stage and for the *Kabuki* popular theater. His plays were of two types, those depending on historical events for their themes and those dealing with contemporary and domestic affairs. In both cases the dramatic tension emerges from the conflict of duty and affection, of the social code and the impulses of the heart. There are records of discussions which Chikamatsu had with his friends concerning the difficulty of writing for the puppet stage. He said in effect that the dialogues

The *Kabuki* play *Musume Dojoji*, centering around a temple bell.

Chorus of monks in the foreground and orchestra behind them. *Kabuki*, which became popular in the Tokugawa period (1615–1867), has more characters and more action than *No* drama.

Japan National Tourist Organization

and descriptions had to be more than usually vivid and alive to compensate for the fact that the actors were inanimate creatures. The best-known of his *Kabuki* plays is *Chushingura*, the tale of the forty-seven *ronin*. Their lord had been unbearably provoked by the deliberate taunts of another *daimyo* and had drawn his sword to kill the man while both were within the confines of the shogun's court. For this crime against the shogun's majesty he was condemned to death. His forty-seven loyal followers vowed they would avenge him. To divert suspicion they scattered and took up employment in different places, biding their time. At an agreed moment they gathered, marched through a snowy night, caught their enemy off-guard, and killed him. They then gave themselves up to the authorities. They should have been executed, but in view of the faithfulness to *giri*, "duty and obligation," they were allowed to commit suicide, the lesser punishment of a more honorable death.

The most famous novelist of the Genroku Era was Ihara Saikaku, who died in 1693. The theme of his tales, one of which was entitled *Five Women Who Loved Love*, was bourgeois life, with all its materialism and love of pleasure realistically and amusingly portrayed. His stories are filled with idle young men about town, miserly merchants, ladies of easy virtue, simple folk, and priests with dubious past histories. The style is light but the characterizations masterly. There are touches of poetry sufficient to give charm and a feeling of continuity with the past to what was at the time a very modern genre in literature. A complete contrast is to be found in the work of a later Tokugawa novelist, Takizawa Bakin (1767–1848), whose father was a *ronin* and whose many popular books reflect the traditional virtues of the *samurai* class.

Undoubtedly the most beloved and most quoted literary figure of the pe-

Bunraku (puppet) play.

The puppet-master (left) manipulates the half life-size puppets, while the storyteller chants an account of the action.

Japan Information Center

riod was the poet Matsuo Basho (1644–1694). He was chiefly renowned for the short poetic form known as *haiku*, in which he had many successors but few equals. The traditional *tanka* lyrics, found as early as the seventh century in the Manyoshu collection, were short enough, thirty-one syllables only, arranged in lines of 5-7-5-7-7. But the *haiku* made its point in only seventeen syllables, 5-7-5. This extreme brevity demanded a bright wit and was the invention of the "cockney" city society of the sixteenth and seventeenth centuries. The form began as the opening section of a chain type of poem known as *haikai* but soon became established in its own right. It has remained popular down to the present day and now enjoys a considerable vogue in the West as well as in Japan. It depends for its impact on a vignette, the fragment of a scene, usually from nature, and then a sudden subjective turn indicating the effect upon the poet. The literary force which the form generated at the time of its invention was considerable, for its gaiety and impudence offered an implied challenge to staid aristocratic art and feudal society. The *haiku* is deliberately open-ended; it begins in the middle of a scene and ends, perforce, immediately when the contrast has been pointed up or the turn of thought indicated. The artist depends upon the imagination of the reader to apply the image the poem brings and complete its effect in his or her own mind. This unfinished nature of the *haiku* may be said to correspond to the creative use of space in the best landscape painting, for it too is a positive use of what is *not* there.

One or two actual examples may make these points clear.

> On the moor: from things
> detached completely—
> how the skylark sings!
> —Matsuo Basho,
> tr. Harold G. Henderson

> My hut, in spring:
> true, there is nothing in it—
> there is Everything!
> —Yamaguchi Sodo
> (1642–1716),
> tr. Harold G. Henderson

The poem is miniature; so, often, is the subject.

> In its eye
> the far-off hills are mirrored—
> dragon-fly!
> —Kobayashi Issa (1763–1828),
> tr. Harold G. Henderson

> A one-foot waterfall
> it too makes noises, and at night
> the coolness of it all!
> —Kobayashi Issa,
> tr. Harold G. Henderson

The small serves to illustrate beauty as well as, perhaps better than, the great; and the poet takes a cultivated delight in simplicity.

In suggesting moods, *haiku* offer an Oriental alternative to the pathetic fallacy so common in Western literature. Instead of the Western habit of transferring the poet's feelings to Nature—"the angry waves," "the sullen clouds"—man's mood and nature's face are kept separate but linked. Basho, in his prose poem "The Unreal Dwelling," says:

> Mountain wisteria hung on the pines. Cuckoos frequently flew past, and there were visits from the swallows. Not a peck from a woodpecker disturbed me, and in my joy I called to the wood dove, "Come, bird of solitude, and make me melancholy!" I could not but be happy—the view would not have blushed before the loveliest scenes of China.
>
> —tr. Donald Keene

The state of solitude is natural for the bird; the feelings of happiness and melancholy may be induced by surrounding nature, but they take place in the spirit of the man. In one of Basho's most famous *haiku*, no feeling whatever is attributed to the grasses; but they are a symbol powerful in their simplicity.

> The summer grasses—
> of brave warriors' dreams
> all that remains.
> —tr. author

Or again:

> The place where I was born:
> all I come to—all I touch—
> blossoms of the thorn!
> —Kobayashi Issa,
> tr. Harold G. Henderson

The increased wealth of the merchant class and their pleasures, in which many of the *samurai* also took part, are all reflected with great clarity in the popular art of the time, the wood-block prints. These prints, brought to the Western world by ship captains and traders, became collectors' items in Europe and America. They had a marked effect on the work of Toulouse-Lautrec and other artists of his time in France. Although popular in Japan, they were despised as inferior and vulgar in their subject matter by Japanese connoisseurs of traditional painting in the Chinese style. Collectively these prints are known as *ukiyo-e*, "pictures of the floating world," a Buddhist term denoting the impermanence and fleeting nature of human pleasures. Hishikawa Moronobu (1638–1714) is accounted one of the founders of the *ukiyo-e* style, but the form continued to develop and flourish throughout the eighteenth century, and some of its greatest artists were still alive in the middle of the nineteenth.

The possibility of reproducing many copies from one set of blocks enabled the prints to be sold at a very reasonable price, and they found a ready market. The prints have a peculiar charm and show great technical skill, not only on the part of the original artist but also in the work of the wood-block carver and the printer, who applied the colors to the blocks by hand. The blocks required—one for each color used in addition to the master block with the black outlines of the drawing—range in number from three or four to as many as fifteen. In all cases the registration of one block printing over another is perfect. The favorite subjects are pictures of the pinup type, well-known actors in their celebrated roles, famous courtesans and their attendant maids, geisha entertainers, and celebrated landscape scenes, such as "Thirty-Six Views of Mt. Fuji" by Hokusai or "The Fifty-Three Halting-Places on the Tokaido" by Hiroshige. Prints depicting the various activities of women give an insight into the processes of home industries such as silk culture and dyeing. In addition to such social scenes many artists also drew for their publishers erotic scenes which were circulated as "spring books."

The variety of colors, the flow of line, a high standard of taste, and the natural human appeal of the subject matter all combine in the great age of the Japanese color print in the second half of the eighteenth century and first half of the nineteenth to form a body of popular art almost unrivaled in the world. The individual artists and their schools are too numerous to mention; but some of the greatest names are Hokusai and Hiroshige for landscape, Sharaku and Toyokuni I for pictures of actors, and Utamaro, Harunobu, and Shigenobu for the charm of their delineation of women.

The art of printing from wooden blocks was, of course, not new in Tokugawa times. The Chinese had used it for centuries for reproducing written characters and pictures of human and landscape subjects. The rapid mass production of Buddhist charms was made possible in ancient Japan by the woodblock process. Characters and a frontispiece of gods and saints were combined in some of the earliest printings of Buddhist sutras. A complete sutra was printed from blocks, one block for each page, in A.D. 868. Even after the introduction of movable type in China about the year 1030 (four centuries before Gutenberg), the method of using a wood block for an entire page was continued, especially in the printing of sacred books.

Many examples exist of Chinese landscape prints with very fine lines in black and white. What was distinctive of the great age of Japanese woodblocks was the masterly use of color, subtle effects being obtained by the mixing of colors and by gradation and the wiping away of color already applied. Groups of subscribers would combine to commission sets of New Year greeting cards, and these would often incorporate elaborate effects obtained by sprinklings of gold, silver, and mica dust. Certain artists became famous for the skill with which they could represent images extremely difficult to portray through the medium of woodcutting. Hiroshige (1797–1858), for instance, was celebrated for his showers of rain, and Utamaro (1754–1806) for his figures seen behind a bamboo screen or through a diaphanous gauze, as in a print where women are depicted drying dyestuffs.

No artist excelled Hokusai as a colorful personality, and anecdotes from his life are numerous. He is said to have provided himself on one occasion with a barrel of ink and a broom and to have rushed around to complete an enormous painting in a few moments. The spectators could make nothing of it until some went up to the roof of a temple and saw that the design was the face of the Buddhist saint Daruma. The mouth was as large as a gate, and each eye had room in the center for a man to sit down. To show his command of the other extreme, Hokusai painted a picture of two sparrows on a grain of rice. Summoned to an artists' competition before the Shogun Ienari, Hokusai asked for a paper screen door, laid it down, and painted a broad, waving stripe of blue upon it. He then produced a cock, dipped its feet in scarlet color, and made it walk down the blue band. That was his picture—

the title, "Maple Leaves Floating Down the Tatsuta River." Hokusai had risen by constant struggle from a life of poverty, but by the end he was in great demand. He was chosen to illustrate the *Life of the Hundred Heroes*, one of the works of the famous author Bakin. The two fell out; but when the matter came to the ears of the publisher, he dispensed with Bakin and found another author to finish the text rather than lose Hokusai.

11

THE WINDS OF CHANGE

The Tokugawa Shogunate:
Part II, 1716–1867

The eighth shogun Yoshimune sat up late one night in 1719 talking animatedly to a man called Nishikawa Joken, an interpreter for the Dutch traders near Nagasaki. He was asking for an explanation of a terrestrial globe Nishikawa had constructed and pressing for more details of the celestial wonders revealed by a Dutch telescope his guest had used. And, like all responsible rulers in China and Japan, he was anxious for religious reasons to have the calendar made as accurate as possible. Only thus could the proper time for sowing and reaping be observed and the true harmony between heaven and earth maintained. That was why the shogun sent to Nagasaki for a copy of an astronomical work which Father Adam Schall had compiled for the court of Beijing a century before. As a result of these scientific interests and his sense of the value of Western knowledge, Yoshimune lifted the ban on the importation of foreign books, provided they did not teach Christianity. Thus a movement for acquiring Western or "Dutch" learning, *rangaku*,[1] which already existed in a clandestine manner, came out into the open and made considerable progress.

The Japanese had derived from the Portuguese some acquaintance with Western practice in firearms and cannon, maps, navigation, and naval affairs generally, and, perhaps most important of all, the existence and nature of the European world. But the West had made vast strides between the first arrival of the Portuguese at the end of the sixteenth century and the shogunate of Yoshimune (1716–1745) at the beginning of the eighteenth. In between lay the achievements of Galileo, the polite but ultimately earth-shaking conversations in the Royal Society (founded 1662) and the Académie des Sciences

---

[1] *Ran* is the middle syllable of *Ho-ran-da* for Holland, and *gaku* means "study" or a "branch of learning."

(founded 1666), the chemical experiments of Robert Boyle, and the solid theoretical work of Sir Isaac Newton. His *Philosophiae Naturalis Principia Mathematica* was published in 1687 and did more than any other single treatise to form the scientific worldview of the West. Once this worldview was established in the physical sciences, it was not long before it was applied to the social sciences. After the Enlightenment the world would never look, nor be, the same again.

The earlier Japanese scholars who had suffered imprisonment and death to gain a knowledge of Western technology and those who were at this time taking advantage of the new freedom permitted by Yoshimune were pragmatic in their approach. They were not at first primarily interested in theory. They studied, through the medium of the Dutch language, such practical subjects as botany, medicine, gunnery, Western drill, and tactics, but included also some theoretical subjects such as mathematics and astronomy. The last, as we have seen, had a useful application to the calendar. The Japanese had little means of knowing the theories that lay behind the improved technology of the West; but they sensed that the new discoveries were significant for Japan and that it would be perilous to neglect them. They were intensely curious and faced with determination obstacles which might have been thought insurmountable. Pioneer physicians with great difficulty obtained Dutch works on medicine and in 1771 dissected the body of a criminal by reference to the illustrations in one of these books. They then slowly and painfully translated the text of the work at the rate of ten lines a day.[2]

One such scholar, Aoki Konyo, helped Yoshimune, who was concerned with improving the food supply, by introducing the sweet potato to Japan. He thus earned the nickname Doctor Potato. Yoshimune commissioned him to work on a Dutch-Japanese dictionary which was published in 1758. The majority of these scholars worked in one or two specific areas; but one of the most famous, Hiraga Gennai (1728–1779), made contributions in such varied fields as botany, iron ore, electricity, and European-style oil painting. He was interested in improving the economy overall, both in agriculture and in industry, and coined a Japanese word, *bussangaku*, the "science of production," to express his aim. By the close of the eighteenth century books on astronomy, medicine, botany, and mathematics, which were considered standard works in Europe, had been translated and published in Japan. In 1811 an official translation office was instituted by the government and came to be known later by the title Institute for the Investigation of Barbarian Books. Some twelve years before the arrival of Commodore Perry and his American squadron a demonstration was given in Edo of Western gunnery and drill using Dutch words of command. Japan thus reacted much more promptly and thoroughly to incoming Western knowledge than did China, although China had the incomparable advantage of the presence of the Jesuits, most of them highly trained scientists or technical experts. Japan had thrown out the Je-

[2] G.B. Sansom, *The Western World and Japan* (London: Cresset Press, 1950), p. 217.

suits for political reasons but made use of every other available source of information, however meager. It was to the credit of Yoshimune and his advisers that they saw, however dimly, the shape of things to come and made it possible for the trickle of scientific and other Western books to become a flow and thus to lay the foundation of Japan's present greatness.

Yoshimune was the most noteworthy and successful of the shoguns after Ieyasu. By a combined policy of retrenchment in expenditure and the opening up of new land, he strengthened the shaky economy. Better irrigation, more efficient farming, and the introduction of mechanical devices to aid in threshing and in raising water from a lower level to flood the fields—all helped to increase the agricultural yield. But an attack of insect pests ruined much of the rice crop in 1732, and this was followed by alarming fluctuations in rice prices, which in turn led to riots.

Following Yoshimune the effectiveness of the *bakufu* declined. Neither the ninth nor the tenth shogun was strong enough to cope adequately with affairs. A liberal statesman, Tanuma Okitsugu, held office under the tenth. He did much to encourage foreign trade and, in contrast to the conservative Yoshimune, stressed the industrial and mercantile sector of the economy. He promoted mining and state monopolies to strengthen the government's fiscal position and had the vision to attempt the development of Hokkaido, the northern island. But he was a controversial figure and was attacked by the conservatives on the grounds of dishonest administration. Another conservative reaction set in under the eleventh shogun, Ienari (1787–1837). Matsudaira Sadanobu was the Elder responsible for this reactionary policy, known as the Kansei Reforms. Sabanobu cut back on foreign trade and had strict sumptuary laws enacted severely limiting expenditure on luxuries, even to the extent of forbidding the use of barbers and hairdressers. He arranged for the cancellation of the debts of the poor among the warrior class and restored emphasis on farming as the mainstay of the state. His measures were effective at first and brought back some confidence in the government. In the long run, however, they were economically stultifying, being based on traditional Confucian theory and not on empirical economic results.

The Kansei Reforms were followed by ten years of acute famines. Peasant uprisings became frequent, and the violence spread to the towns. The *bakufu* reacted with a certain desperation in a third series of reforms, those of Mizuno Tadakuni in 1841 and 1843. To the standard procedures of government economy and cancellation of debts were added measures such as price regulation and orders to absconding peasants to return to their farms. These orders proved ineffective.

The rural economy of Japan from the seventeenth to the middle of the nineteenth century showed both positive and negative features. On the one hand, the total crop yield increased in the seventeenth century alone from 18 million koku to 25 million. Better irrigation, more intensive farming, and an increase in cash crops other than rice made possible a rising standard of living. But the government's financial difficulties led to increased taxation.

Where peasants were harshly treated, many absconded to the towns, while those who were left had to bear the same total tax as before but divided among fewer workers. Three major famines, or famine series, in 1732, 1783, and 1832, respectively, caused intense and prolonged suffering. In the famine which began in 1783 and continued for five years there were reports of cannibalism and thousands of deaths by starvation in the north. In good years many landowners and even small farmers did well. But the farm laborers suffered a great deal of hardship. The *bakufu* professed to regard the farming class as the foundation of the state; but they treated its members with little mercy nonetheless. The theory was to allow the farmer just enough to live on and to set aside as seed for the next spring, and to take the rest of his produce from him in tax. In a sententious edict of 1649 the peasant was bidden to save leaves for fuel or to serve as food in time of famine; he was forbidden to drink tea or sake, and if his wife went sightseeing or even walking on the hillsides and neglected her household tasks, she was to be divorced. In 1652 the headman of a village appealed strongly for a reduction of tax on the village. The reduction was granted, but the headman was executed for his temerity in asking. It is small wonder that there were frequent peasant rebellions—as many as twenty in different parts of the country in one year—and "smashing raids" in the cities. Improvements in the lot of the small farmer and the yield of his land led, in a manner not unfamiliar elsewhere, to a glimpse of better conditions and rising demands for greater freedom and further improvements.

There were thus a number of converging factors which tended to undermine from within the carefully constructed solidarity of the Tokugawa regime—the presence of numbers of *ronin*, unemployed and congregating in the large cities; the rise of the merchant class, for which the Japanese feudal system provided no recognized place; the introduction of Western knowledge and techniques, which were of their nature disruptive to the traditional Japanese way of life; and the peasant unrest breaking out into open rebellion. The *bakufu*, already faced with these internal problems, had now to face another, this time a threat from outside, with the arrival of Commodore Matthew C. Perry of the United States Navy in 1853.

Commodore Perry's mission has sometimes been treated as though it were the sole reason for the change in Japan's attitude from one of seclusion to one of participation in the modern world. That this is an oversimplified interpretation may be seen from the foregoing account of internal changes within the country. Nor was Perry the first to knock on the door of a closed Japan, though he was the first to gain an entrance.

Russian geographers learned about Japan only in the late seventeenth century, and in 1702 Peter the Great interviewed a shipwrecked Japanese sailor. In spite of the Japanese ban some secret trading took place in the eighteenth century between Japanese and Russians, whom the Japanese called the "Red Northern Islanders" (from the Kurile Islands). A Russian officer, Lieutenant Adam Laxman, was sent to Hokkaido by Catherine the Great to try to open trade negotiations in 1793, but he was told he must go to Nagasaki to gain a hearing. When a later ambassador went to Nagasaki in 1804, however, he met with no more success. The British sailed a frigate, H.M.S. *Phaeton*, into Nagasaki harbor in 1808 in chase of a Dutch vessel during the Napoleonic Wars, demanded and received supplies, and sailed away. A British survey vessel in 1845 reported courteous treatment by the Japanese; but in neither case did the British attempt to make any trade arrangements. The *Morrison*, a ship chartered by American missionaries, had been fired upon when attempting to return Japanese castaways in 1837. The only approach made by the U. S. government prior to Perry's mission had been an abortive one under Commodore James Biddle in 1845.

Commodore Perry's success in using negotiation backed by force to compel Japan to open her doors has received more than usual attention in Western history because it was one of the rare occasions at that early date in which America rather than one of the European powers took aggressive action. The action itself took its rise from causes which might seem at first relatively minor. The United States was very dissatisfied with the treatment being meted out by the Japanese authorities to shipwrecked sailors and to ships in need of shelter and supplies. Whaling ships and vessels involved in the fur trade of the American west coast required victuals and fresh water when they faced the vast and typhoon-ridden stretches of the Pacific Ocean. With the coming of steam, coaling stations in Japan were going to be of increasing importance. But from the beginning, other and larger factors were also operative. Expansion of overseas trade was made possible and necessary by surplus goods turned out by the new manufacturing methods of the Industrial Revolution. New markets were vital. America had extended her frontier to the West Coast; the next logical extension was over the Pacific Ocean. The example of Britain's easy success a decade earlier in forcing China to open her gates to trade was not lost on the other great powers. Moreover, the United States was well aware that Russia had designs on the Japanese market. Commodore Perry's instructions from President Fillmore therefore covered the immediate matter of the treatment of distressed mariners and also the question of a trade treaty.

Perry himself had not wanted the command of this squadron. As a senior officer he had hoped for a pleasanter assignment in European waters; but he was admirably cut out for his delicate task in Japan. He combined tact with dignity and firmness and had sufficient patience to counter the delaying tactics of the Japanese. He had as his interpreter S. Wells Williams, a pioneer American missionary in China, who had been on the *Morrison* and had acquired some knowledge of Japanese. As it turned out, most of the negotiations were carried on in Dutch. When Perry's squadron, consisting of two steam frigates and two sloops, sailed up to Uraga near the mouth of Edo Bay, there was consternation and curiosity among the Japanese. In a short time the common people began swarming out in small boats to view the strange warships, but Perry gave orders that no one was to be allowed aboard. Commodore Biddle in an earlier attempt to establish relations had made the mistake of allowing the people to take liberties and thus had lost the respect of the officials. Those in authority were deeply concerned. They were impressed by steam propulsion, and they knew enough about artillery to realize the greatly superior fire power of the American vessels. They also knew, better than the Americans, how dependent the large capital of Edo was upon seaborne supplies.

Commodore Perry wished to deliver President Fillmore's letter to "the emperor," by which he meant the effective ruler, who was really the shogun. The Japanese appeared to agree but kept sending junior officials with whom Perry wisely would not deal. At length an official of adequate rank received the letter with its demands, and Perry, with a shrewd concession to Oriental face, said he would give the authorities time for consideration and return in a year for their answer. He made it clear, however, that when he returned it would be with a more powerful force.

The shogunate was now in a dilemma. Patriotism, national pride, and the policy of isolation all pointed to a strong negative to the American demands. But the shogun's advisers were well aware that America possessed superior weapons; the question was whether it would use them or not, and all indications were that it intended to back up its demands by force, as the British had done in China. In this situation the shogun took the unprecedented step of consulting the emperor's court and all the *daimyo* throughout the country. He must have known that this would further weaken his position of control, which was already much less strong than in the early days of the Tokugawa Shogunate. But Abe Masahiro, his principal adviser, felt that it was absolutely necessary in the national interest to have as much agreement as possible on the correct policy toward the aggressive foreigners. The majority of those who replied to the shogun's question were in favor of resistance, though some *daimyo* who had already had Western contacts showed an awareness of the need to temporize. The emperor's court was strongly in opposition to any concessions. However, Abe felt that his assessment of American power and determination made it necessary to compromise. Thus, when Perry returned in 1854, as he had promised, the shogun's officials employed the usual delaying tactics but ultimately conceded the main items of the American demands. By this Treaty of Kanagawa two rather inadequate ports were opened to limited trade—Shimoda, small and isolated, and Hakodate, far away on Hokkaido; American shipwrecked sailors were to receive good treatment; and an American consul was to be permitted residence at Shimoda.

The signing of the treaty and the attendant celebrations proved to be a colorful affair. Honor guards from both sides were drawn up on the beach at Kanagawa. There was an elaborate exchange of presents and entertainment. Sumo wrestling and a minstrel show were the forms of amusement each nation thought suitable to offer the other. The *pièce de résistance* was an American scale model of a steam locomotive and train large enough to ride upon. The track was laid out on the seashore, and officials in Japanese dress were

Commodore Matthew C. Perry at Uraga, July 14, 1853. The first landing of the American expedition.

The commodore is immediately behind the two sailor boys. Note two of the ships have both steam power and sails, the remainder sails only.

Courtesy U.S. Naval Academy Museum

to be seen flying around curves on the cars in evident pleasure, the more so as they had been enjoying the champagne and whiskey which also figured prominently among the American gifts. Another present was a Morse electric telegraph system, which was set up and demonstrated. It may be imagined that the lesson of these modern marvels of steam and electricity was not lost upon the observant Japanese.

The Perry squadron departed, but the implementation of the new treaty proved to be a long and laborious business. In the man chosen to represent the United States in the new relations with Japan, America was again fortunate. Unlike Commodore Perry, the first American minister, Townsend Harris, had actively sought the post. He was fascinated by Japan and possessed the necessary tact and patient determination to carry his work to successful completion amid the most harassing and frustrating conditions. The book *Shimoda Story* by Oliver Statler represents Harris as arrogant, small-minded, and given to deceit. There is doubtless an element of truth in this view, but a large amount of proper pride was an asset, not a liability, in dealing with the Japanese at this juncture. As part of the Perry treaty a plot of land and a house for a resident minister had been stipulated. But when Harris arrived, the Japanese claimed nothing had been said about servants. The possession of a sufficient retinue was necessary not only for the household tasks but for the maintenance of such style as would entitle the minister to respect for his position. So Harris doggedly set about winning permission to employ servants. He then had to secure an audience with the shogun to present his credentials. In the end the persistence of Harris and the good sense of the more moderate Japanese officials prevailed; at the close of 1857 Townsend Harris proceeded in style from his residence at Shimoda to the shogun's court at Edo and was duly received.

Negotiations for a full treaty of commerce had already begun. During these, Harris made full use of the argument that it would pay the Japanese to conclude an agreement with a nation as reasonable as America rather than submit to the imperialist ambitions of Britain and other European nations, as seen in China. Nothing was said of the fact that all Western nations, including the United States, had benefited from the concessions extracted from China by the British. In July 1858 a commercial treaty was signed between Japan and the United States which included among its terms the opening of additional ports, the rights of extraterritoriality and foreign residence in Edo and Osaka, and agreement on custom dues and provision for the United States to supply Japan with ships, armaments, and technicians. Subsequent treaties were concluded with four other Western powers: Russia, Britain, France, and Holland. The terms of these were similar, and in some cases they tended to favor the foreign merchants—20 percent import duty, lowered to 5 percent on all goods in 1866, was a cheap price to pay for the opportunity of a new market. From the beginning the Japanese sought a graduated scale of import duties and the abolition of the galling provisions of extraterritoriality, the foreign right to have all cases involving their nationals tried in consular courts outside the jurisdiction of Japanese laws. These objectives were at length gained with the abolition of extraterritoriality by treaties in 1894, becoming effective in 1899, and with complete tariff autonomy in 1911. Tariff autonomy became effective in China in 1933, but extraterritoriality was not abolished there until the end of World War II in 1945.

The Harris commercial treaty engendered considerable controversy in both shogun and imperial court circles. Political attitudes were now crystallizing—the hereditary lords (*fudai*) along with the shogunate favoring foreign trade, and the collateral (*shimpan*) and outer (*tozama*) lords rallying round the emperor and fostering resistance to foreign demands. This latter policy was summarized in the slogan, *Sonno-Joi*, "honor the emperor, expel the barbarians." In 1858 Ii Naosuke, one of the most powerful of the hereditary *daimyo*, put into effect strong measures to reassert the power of the shogunate. His work was effective enough to provoke violent opposition, and his enemies took advantage of a snowstorm to set upon him and kill him while he was on his way to attend the shogun. The *ronin* were becoming more and more truculent. Heusken, Harris's Dutch interpreter, was killed at night in an Edo street, and in 1863 a band of *ronin* set fire to the British legation.

Meanwhile the authority of the shogun was being attacked on theoretical as well as on practical grounds. The Mito fief had for some time been known as the home of a group of nationalist historians who asserted the native traditions and values over against the Confucian learning from China.

Their work had been reinforced by the research of Motoori Norinaga (1730–1801), who published an extensive commentary on the text and meaning of the Shinto classic, the *Kojiki*. Although early Japanese history had not been forgotten during the long years of the Tokugawa, new research made it ever more evident that the original authority of the state had been vested in the person of the emperor and not in the shogun, and that in fact the total control exercised at this time by the shogun was illegal. The historical and legal foundation for a restoration of the power of the emperor was thus clearly laid down. To the *samurai*, with their strong sense of precedent and tradition, the idea had a growing appeal.

The difficulties of the shogunate were increased by the heavy indemnities demanded by the foreign powers for breaches of the peace which the declining authority of the shogun's government was powerless to prevent. Attacks upon foreigners and proforeign Japanese were being made not only by isolated *samurai* but even by *daimyo* beyond government control and acting with the support of their domain leadership. It was this independent action of prominent *daimyo*, particularly the clans of Choshu and Satsuma, which finally precipitated the fall of the Tokugawa regime.

The clans of Choshu and Satsuma were hereditary enemies of the Tokugawa, and their geographical position in the extreme west made them hard to control. They could each dispose of considerable military forces; Satsuma had 27,000 warriors, and Choshu 11,000. Moreover their *samurai* had not been softened by the easy living of Edo and had retained their martial spirit. Traditional in outlook, they yet commanded the use of Western-type weapons, since their domains included the ports of entry of Chinese and Dutch trade. Satsuma also controlled the Ryukyu Islands, which acted as a transfer port for the entry of foreign goods. Both clans suffered, along with many others, from financial stress, but both were able by wise management to overcome the problem. Choshu developed an office for aid to needy *samurai* which added to its other functions the profitable investment of clan funds. Satsuma under able financial leadership in the 1830s and 1840s had been able to improve the quality of its crops, reduce waste, and exercise a closer control of the valuable sugar crop from the Ryukyu Islands. The clan thus succeeded in reducing its debt and also paying for military modernization.

A fresh stimulus to the independent fighting spirit of Satsuma and Choshu came from a remarkable personality, Yoshida Shoin (1830–1859). Son of a Choshu *samurai* of modest rank, small and not very healthy as a boy, he became during and after his short lifetime a strong patriotic influence in his own clan and far beyond. He studied assiduously and traveled widely in Japan, forming in his own mind an explosive combination of Dutch learning and the fervid nationalism of the Mito school. At one point he tried to smuggle himself out of the country on board one of Perry's ships, armed with a plentiful supply of paper and brushes to make notes on the ways of the foreigners. When discovered, he was returned to his own clan and placed under house arrest. He then proceeded to open a small school. He was an excellent teacher, and his enthusiastic discussions of the meaning of loyalty to the emperor in the new context of a Japan being opened to foreign influence deeply affected some young *samurai* students. Among these were Inoue Kaoru, Ito Hirobumi, and Yamagata Aritomo, who were very shortly to become three of the most prominent leaders of the new Japan. Yoshida had more fire than sense and became involved in a plot to assassinate a Tokugawa official in Kyoto. The plot was discovered, and Yoshida was taken to Edo and executed in his thirtieth year. Robert Louis Stevenson heard about Yoshida from a Japanese friend and in 1880 wrote of him and a fellow prisoner, Kusakabe, in *Familiar Studies of Men and Books.*

> He [Kusakabe] was led toward the place of death below Yoshida's window. To turn the head would have been to implicate his fellow-prisoner; but he threw him a look from his eye, and bade him farewell in a loud voice, with these two Chinese verses:
>
> > "It is better to be a crystal and be broken,
> > Than to remain perfect like a tile upon the housetop."
>
> So Kusakabe, from the highlands of Satzuma, passed out of the theatre of this world. His death was like an antique worthy's.

Yoshida was then tried and executed, and Stevenson sums up his character thus:

> It is hard to say which is most remarkable—his capacity for command, which subdued his very jailers; his hot, unflagging zeal; or his stubborn superiority to defeat. He failed in each particular enterprise that he attempted; and yet we have only to look at his country to see how complete has been his general success. His friends and pupils made the majority of leaders in that final Revolution, now some twelve years old; and many of them are, or were until the other day, high placed among the rulers of Japan.[3]

The stage was thus set for the last series of events that were to lead to the downfall of the shogunate, the restoration of the emperor's power, and the modernization of Japan, already begun but soon to gain momentum as a matter of deliberate policy. In this last struggle there were five groups in constant and confusing interaction: the shogunate, the imperial court, the Choshu clan, the Satsuma clan, and the foreign powers acting in concert. A key to the understanding of these crucial years 1858–1868 is an awareness of the rivalry of Satsuma and Choshu, both demanding change and both in a better position than any other clan to bring it about, but neither wishing to yield primacy of leadership to the other. When these two clans agreed to combine their efforts, events proceeded to a climax. The victim was the

---

[3] Nottingham Society, N.Y., edition of *Collected Works*, Vol. X, p. 127.

shogunate; the means to victory was to possess military power and to become, in the ancient pattern, the spokesman for the emperor; and the shifts of policy were determined by the iron necessities of confrontation with the foreigners.

Satsuma at first favored the union of court and shogunate; but Choshu, not to be outdone, took the line of out-and-out support for the emperor against the shogun. Choshu won over some of the court nobles and received important, though temporary, support from extremist *samurai* in the domain of Tosa in Shikoku. Thus fortified, Choshu succeeded in getting the emperor to compel the shogun to fix the date of June 25, 1863, as the day on which all "barbarians" would be expelled from Japan. As the fateful day approached, it became evident to most *daimyo* that this patriotic resolution could not be carried out. The Choshu clansmen, however, fired their cannon against American, French, and Dutch ships in the Shimonoseki Strait. The Americans retaliated by shelling the Choshu forts and sinking two new ships. A few days later French forces made a landing and demolished the forts and their stores.

At this point a *coup d'état* led by Satsuma restored more moderate forces to power at court. But Choshu on its own ground continued intransigent and began forming "mixed units" of *samurai* and commoners, armed with modern rifles, under one Takasugi Shinsaku (1839–1867). The morale and effectiveness of these units was very high, and their success was decisive in convincing conservatives throughout Japan of the necessity of modernization. Choshu's constant antiforeign provocations led to a second international action. In 1864 seventeen English, French, Dutch, and American warships again destroyed the rebuilt Choshu forts and forced the reopening of the Shimonoseki Strait to international traffic. The Choshu *samurai* Inoue Kaoru (1835–1915) and Ito Hirobumi (1841–1909), earlier students of Yoshida Shoin, had illegally left the country and spent some time studying in London. They had but lately returned and were able to exercise some influence as interpreters in relations with Western powers. Their persuasion and the cold logic of events now convinced the Choshu authorities that the expulsion of foreigners was an impossible dream.

Satsuma, meanwhile, though less openly antiforeign, had become involved in trouble with the British. A cultural misunderstanding, typical of the times both in China and Japan, had developed in 1862, when an Englishman, Charles Richardson, out riding with some companions, had failed to dismount and show proper respect by making an obeisance to the lord of Satsuma as his procession passed by. Angry Satsuma *samurai* guards had set upon and killed him. The British government demanded a large indemnity from the shogun and a further sum from the Satsuma *daimyo*, along with the punishment of the guilty parties. A British naval force of seven ships stood off Kagoshima, the Satsuma capital, to enforce payment and were fired upon. They replied with a severe bombardment of Kagoshima and the sinking of a large number of ships in the harbor. The reaction of the Japanese was not one of grievance but of unbounded admiration for the efficiency of British naval power. British warships were subsequently purchased by Satsuma, and a number of volunteers were trained by the Royal Navy. When the new Japanese Navy was formed, the majority of its officers were British-trained Satsuma *samurai*, while a large number of army officers came from Choshu and were trained by the French.

The Choshu clan had clearly shown its opposition to the shogunate. Punitive action had to be taken, and in 1864, on the authority of an imperial order, the *daimyo* of Nagoya was chosen to lead a large combined force from several domains against Choshu. The moderate group in Choshu was ready to come to terms, and an agreement was made through the offices of a Satsuma warrior, Saigo Takamori (1827–1877), risen from humble origins but now prominent in the shogun's service. The terms arranged were not harsh, probably because Saigo, as a Satsuma man, had no desire to see the shogunate too powerful or Choshu too weak. But the terms did include the disbanding of the "mixed units," and these units were in no mood to obey. Instead, after several successful engagements against the moderates of their own clan, they took possession of the Choshu capital of Shimonoseki and formed a new domain government in which the extremists were the dominant force. Their independence of authority led to a second punitive expedition against them in the summer of 1865. But this time Choshu was in an even stronger position. A member of the domain government, Kido Koin (1833–1877) had proved an effective leader, tightened discipline over the independent "mixed units," and modernized the whole of the domain forces. The Satsuma and other *daimyo* withheld or withdrew their support from the shogun, whose government was at the same time embarrassed by the economic burden of the expedition against Choshu and by rice riots in several cities. Choshu emerged victorious, and the shogun's forces withdrew.

Two *ronin* from Tosa now began to work for a coalition between Satsuma and Choshu. A secret agreement was entered into in 1866, and this marked the beginning of the end for the Tokugawa Shogunate. The thirteenth shogun Iemochi died that year and was succeeded by Keiki, a wise and vigorous leader. Léon Roches, the French minister, supported Keiki in the reorganization of his administration and military forces and in the building of a modern dockyard at Yokosuka. Sir Harry Parkes, the British minister, in a rival move, supplied Satsuma and Choshu with arms. It was now too late for the shogunate to stage a recovery. On January 3, 1868, Satsuma and Choshu, aided by the collateral domains of Echizen and Nagoya and the outer domains of Tosa and Hiroshima, took possession of the palace and proclaimed an "imperial restoration." Keiki himself was inclined to capitulate, but some of his supporters insisted on making a fight of it. Shogun forces marched up from Osaka toward Kyoto. They were superior in numbers but inferior in modern equipment and were defeated at the hamlets of Fushimi and Toba south of Kyoto on January 27.

The imperialist forces pressed straight on to Edo. Most of the *daimyo* submitted to them. Keiki forbade resistance, but there was some fighting in

Edo near the present site of Ueno Park. Keiki was treated generously. He retired and was confined to his estate in Mito. His successor in the family title
was allowed to keep one-tenth of the Tokugawa lands, but even this
amounted to 700,000 koku, about the same revenue as that of Satsuma and
almost twice that of Choshu. The Aizu domain leaders continued to hold out
in northern Honshu until November, and the last embers of resistance were
stamped out in Hokkaido in May of 1869. This marked the end of the Tokugawa rule which had begun with Ieyasu's victory in the battle of Sekigahara
in the year 1600.

12

THE MEIJI RESTORATION AND THE MODERNIZATION OF JAPAN

1868–1914

A boy of sixteen was given a document of five medium-length sentences to sign in April 1868. The sentences consisted of pious hopes and unexceptionable statements—"all classes . . . shall unite," "no discontent," "the just laws of Nature." It is true there was one mention of "public discussion," but subsequently this feature was not encouraged. Nevertheless the Charter Oath was a revolutionary document and the consequences of it enormous, for the signatory was the Emperor Meiji ("Enlightened Rule").[1]

The young and vigorous *samurai* leaders of the new state had immense problems to face, but they lost no time in addressing themselves to the task. Edo was not subdued until July 1868, but already in April the first principles of the new regime had been enunciated in the emperor's name in the Charter Oath, also known as the Five Articles Oath. In general moral tone, in intentional lack of specifics, and in deliberate borrowing from another culture, it was faintly reminiscent of the "constitution" of Prince Shotoku in the seventh century.

ARTICLE 1. Deliberative assemblies shall be widely established and all matters decided by public discussion.

This would appear to indicate a first step toward full democracy, but such was not its intention. It was rather a bid to rally support for the new government. Since the main policymakers came from not more than seven domains, this clause allowed the leaders from other parts of the country to feel they could have a part in forming national policy. Later, when the govern-

---

[1] There was opposition to Japanese government plans to hold celebrations of the two-hundredth anniversary of the Meiji Restoration in view of its bourgeois nature.

147

ment felt more secure, the practice of holding these assemblies was discontinued.

> ARTICLE 2. All classes, high and low, shall unite in vigorously carrying out the administration of affairs of state.

This appeal for unity had more significance then than now in view of the strict class structure of Tokugawa Japan.

> ARTICLE 3. The common people, no less than the civil and military officials, shall each be allowed to pursue his own calling so that there may be no discontent.

More definite than Article 2, this was a promise that the frustrating class barriers of feudalism would no longer be in force and that all careers would be open to those with talent. The whole country, in fact, would become a labor pool for the immense effort of modernization.

> ARTICLE 4. Evil customs of the past shall be broken off and everything based upon the just laws of nature.

Among the "evil customs of the past" the authors intended to include the Tokugawa Shogunate and all its works. The "just laws of Nature" is a universal phrase with a mystical appeal. The concept was familiar in the West but was also known to the East in fundamental Confucian and Daoist thought.

> ARTICLE 5. Knowledge shall be sought throughout the world so as to strengthen the foundations of imperial rule.

Here was the most deliberate break with the past. Modernization was to be a main, calculated, and official aim. The old and the new were combined in one phrase: "imperial rule" was the heritage of the past, but for the future it would be promoted by "knowledge . . . sought throughout the world." In another famous slogan it was to be "Eastern ethics and Western science"; ancient patriotism and modern, scientific application were to be the secret of Japan's rapid rise to power.

CONSTITUTIONAL PATTERN

The first efforts of the reformers to construct a new machinery of government show the marks of improvisation, for changes were made four times between January 1868 and September 1871. Finally a Council of State (*dajo-kan,* an ancient name) and six ministries were set up. The Council of State under the chairmanship of a reformist court noble, Sanjo Sanetomi

(1837–1891), had three divisions: the Left Chamber was concerned with legislation, the Right Chamber supervised the ministries, and the Central Chamber held control over the work of the other two chambers as well as over the recently created Office of Shinto Worship. The last provided a means for stressing publicly the divine descent of the emperor. This system of government lasted until a cabinet was introduced in 1885. But whatever the system, the stability of the government came from the fact that it was run at the beginning by a group of men similar in age (the youngest was thirty-one, the oldest forty-one), in social rank (generally the lower *samurai*, with one or two court nobles), and in political training (all with experience in their own domains in a period of upheaval and change). They were an unusually brilliant company. At first they ruled as assistants to figurehead chiefs, then gradually took the higher offices themselves, and ended for the most part as respected "Elder Statesmen," *genro*, a position of unofficial power which had no real parallel outside Japan.

CENTRALIZATION

Edo was chosen as the new capital, and the emperor was installed in the shogun's castle, which underwent suitable alterations. To mark the break with the past, the city was renamed Tokyo, "Eastern Capital." The main obstacle to centralized government was a psychological rather than an administrative one, namely, the proud separate existence of the numerous domains. The first steps to centralization were taken in the ex-Tokugawa domains, which were very extensive and entirely at the disposal of the government. These were divided into prefectures. The administration of the other domains was then gradually brought into line with the system used in the new prefectures. Tolls and economic barriers between domains were abolished.

The leaders of the central government had already been policymakers in their home domains and were therefore able to exercise considerable influence. Kido Koin of Choshu and Okubo Toshimichi (1830–1878) of Satsuma persuaded their respective *daimyo*, as well as those of Tosa and Hizen, to give back their lands to the emperor in March 1869. In one sense this was a token change, for the *daimyo* were reappointed as governors of the territories. Many other *daimyo* followed this lead, because they did not want to incur the displeasure of the government or lose any future privileges or benefits under the new regime, which had obviously come to stay. The central government, moving with caution but increasing confidence, sent special envoys to the leading domains of Satsuma, Choshu, and Tosa to assess the degree of support for their policies. One of the envoys was the court noble Iwakura Tomomi (1825–1883), who had close associations with Okubo. Both were to hold very important posts in the Meiji government in the next few years. Then in August 1871 the emperor announced on behalf of the government the abolition of all the domains. The ruling came as a shock, but there was no major resistance. The country was divided into seventy-five prefectures (three of them urban), but this number was later reduced to forty-five. These form the present-day units of local government.

COMPENSATION AND FINANCE

That there was so little resistance to changing the age-old feudal pattern is surprising, but the domains were not organized to combine against a central government riding the crest of a popular, patriotic movement. The absence of resistance must also be taken as an index of the penetration of Western knowledge and its international implications among the educated local leaders throughout the whole of Japan. Moreover the compensation to the former *daimyo* was generous. The majority of them, as governors of prefectures, received 10 percent of the area taxes as personal income. Most were actually better off financially, since they were relieved of the *samurai* payroll responsibilities, administration costs, and especially the domain debts.

The *samurai* were not treated so well; their stipends were cut by 50 percent. They had been paid less than the full book value of their salaries by the former *daimyo*, but the new salaries still represented a considerable drop from what they had actually been receiving before the change in 1871. This caused considerable discontent and some real hardship, particularly among the lower *samurai*.

Paying salaries, taking over the obligations of the domains, and at the same time building up modern defense forces placed upon the central government a heavy financial burden for which tax income was inadequate. Japan did not want to become dependent on foreign capital, but a small loan of £2,400,000 ($6,000,000) was contracted with Britain in 1872, in addition to another British loan of less than half that amount already entered into for the building of a railway between Tokyo and Yokohama. These loans and considerable sums raised from Japanese merchant houses enabled the government to carry on during the first few crucial years. Internal trade, now free of restrictions, showed marked improvement and was further stimulated by the new export-import commerce. Within ten years the government had begun to reach a sound financial position.

Feudal taxes and restrictions on land use and sale were removed, and the taxpayer on any given piece of property was constituted the owner. A new land-tax system, based on money not crop yield, came into operation in 1873. The tax was fixed at 3 percent on current assessed land values, but this was later reduced to 2½ percent. Four years were taken up in assessing the arable land of Japan and four years more in applying the system to mountain and forest land. There was some peasant unrest at first, since it proved harder to evade the new regulations than the old.

In 1876 all *samurai* stipends were transferred into the form of government bonds; but the interest on the bonds amounted to only about half the value of the already reduced stipends. The *daimyo*, again, were treated more generously in the bond amounts they received. In 1871 *samurai* were permitted and in 1876 compelled to cease wearing the pair of short and long swords which had been the jealously guarded social privilege of their class.

THE ARMY AND NAVY

The overthrow of the shogunate had been accomplished with the aid of forces from the domains and only a small nucleus of imperial troops. But once the Restoration had been effected, the new leaders at once began to build up the imperial forces. The pioneer in this was Omura Masujiro, who set up arsenals and military academies. He was assassinated by conservative *samurai* in 1869, and his work was taken up by Yamagata Aritomo (1838–1922). After studying under Yoshida Shoin and commanding the Choshu mixed units, he spent some time in study in Europe. He became commander of the Imperial Guards, nucleus of the new army, a force of over 9,000 recruited from Satsuma, Choshu, and Tosa domains and organized on the French model. In 1873 he was made army minister and was prominent in the government for many years. When the domains were abolished, the country was divided into four garrison regions and standard regulations were enforced in order to unify the diverse domain forces now incorporated into the army.

Shogunate warships and flotillas from various coastal domains formed the first units of the new navy, which took the British Royal Navy as its model. The former Satsuma fleet for many years supplied the majority of senior officers for the Japanese Navy. A fishing and seagoing tradition in Japan was of help in the rapid development of an efficient modern navy, as a similar island-nation tradition had earlier helped Great Britain.

Yamagata in 1873 introduced a revolutionary law of universal conscription. This spelled the ultimate end of *samurai* military privilege, but it was a necessary part of the modern state which Japan aspired to become. The measure was incidentally useful in extending government control into the most remote hamlets of the countryside. It also provoked considerable peasant discontent but no serious incidents. All, regardless of social origin, were liable to call-up for three years of active duty and four years in the reserves.

The Japanese leaders intended not to Westernize, but to modernize; that is to say, they decided to choose the best model in each field of technology and administration which would make Japan powerful and a match for other nations. They did not intend to sacrifice or to alter fundamentally "the spirit of Old Japan," *yamato-damashii*, the soul of the nation, or the basic structure of their society under the emperor through which this spirit was expressed. Deputations of leading statesmen and students were sent abroad to bring back information and ideas upon which the reforms could be based. The shogunate and certain domains had already sent individuals such as Ito and Inoue abroad prior to the Restoration, and this process was stepped up after 1868. The largest and most important group to go abroad was the Iwakura Mission, which left in 1871 and spent two years in the United States and Europe. The delegation was composed of forty-eight members and fifty-four students and included, in addition to the leader, Iwakura, such prominent government figures as Okubo and Kido, as well as future leaders such as Ito. They gathered extremely useful information but failed completely in their second objective, to persuade the Western powers to alter the unequal treaties entered into by the Tokugawa.

In this process of conscious cultural borrowing in the nineteenth century—undertaken not for the first time in Japanese history (see Chapter 2)—two points are noticeable: first, the impartial selectivity of the Japanese, and second, their willingness to change their plans if they found a better model in another country. For the formation of their navy, they looked to Britain, as has been noted. For the army, France was the model; but Yamagata made important changes in 1878 when he adopted the German general staff organization. A French legal expert, Gustave-Émile Boissonade, assisted the patient committee that worked out a new civil code of law, beginning in 1875 and issuing a final draft in 1888. Further alterations stemming from German law were made, and the resulting code was put into effect in 1896. Beginning in 1871, German doctors were brought to Japan to give instruction in medical schools. As a result, German language and practice became predominant in Japan during the Meiji.

Several government departments made use of experts invited from abroad. The Bureau of Mines, for instance, employed 34 foreigners, and the Ministry of Industry spent a large proportion of its budget in 1879 to hire 130 Western advisers. Efforts were made to replace the foreign experts as quickly as possible with trained Japanese, since the foreign salaries were so high.

EDUCATION

In order to bring about a basic and permanent change in the attitude of the Japanese toward modernization, reforms in the field of education were of the first importance. A Ministry of Education was set up on the Western pattern in 1871. The French system was adopted at first, with eight school districts and compulsory elementary education for boys and girls for three years of schooling, later increased to six. Here again a change in Japanese policy occurred, and more liberal ideas of education from America supplanted the rigid French pattern. Dr. David Murray of Rutgers University, New Jersey, exerted a profound influence on the educational system during the six years he spent in Japan. The missionary societies from America were also influential, especially in pioneering higher education for women.

The Confucian University in Edo was amalgamated with the shogunate medical school and the language study at the Institute for the Investigation of Barbarian Books to form in 1869 a new government university, later named Tokyo University. Other government universities were added, from Kyoto University in 1897 to Hokkaido University in Sapporo in 1918. All main-

Sapporo, capital of Hokkaido.
The modern development of the city has filled all the plain between the mountains.
Japan Information Center

tained a very high standard. In the 1880s a further change in educational style took place: a convergence of nationalistic, Confucian, and German influences emphasized the supremacy of the state. The highest value was put upon the good of the nation as a whole, while the free development of individual personality through education was accorded a lower place. An Imperial Rescript on Education was issued in 1890 in which harmony and loyalty were stressed above all else. The schools thus became a means of official indoctrination available to future governments.

The man who did most to popularize Western knowledge in Japan was Fukuzawa Yukichi (1835–1901). His books, *Conditions in the West* and *Encouragement of Learning*, were bestsellers, for he described the ordinary social customs of the West, concerning which the average Japanese felt a consuming curiosity. His engaging autobiography, recently reissued, is an epitome of his age. His father was a *samurai* with scholarly tastes, belonging to the Okudaira clan in Kyushu. He sent his children to a teacher for calligraphy and general education.

> The teacher lived in the compound of the lord's storage office, but, having some merchants' children among his pupils, he naturally began to train them in numerals. "Two times two is four, two times three is six etc." This today seems a very ordinary thing to teach, but when my father heard this, he took his children away in a fury. "It is abominable," he exclaimed, "that innocent

children should be taught to use numbers—the tool of merchants. There is no telling what the teacher may do next."[2]

Yukichi was sent to Nagasaki in 1854 to study Dutch and gunnery. After further study in Osaka, he was called to Edo to act as Dutch interpreter in the business of his clan. He was shocked to find in Yokohama that all the foreigners spoke English, not Dutch. With some fortitude he immediately embarked on the study of English. Since foreign books were in very limited supply, students had to copy laboriously by hand the section of the common textbook which they wished to study, writing out as best they could "the strange letters written sideways."

Considering Yukichi's determination and competence, it is not surprising that he was sent by the shogun on two missions abroad, to the United States in 1860 and to Europe in 1862. He says he was not taken aback in these experiences in the way his guides expected. He was already familiar with the principles of the electric telegraph and understood the method of refining and bleaching sugar. What astonished him was the waste of iron, which he saw lying about in garbage piles and on the seashore, and the lack of reverence for the descendants of George Washington, even the lack of knowledge of their whereabouts. On his return he found the antiforeign feeling running so high that the captain of his ship was advised not to show a foreign umbrella in the streets for fear he would be cut down by *ronin*. Yukichi went further than most in his hatred of the Chinese Confucian heritage and the dead hand of the past. He met a farmer one day riding along the seashore. On seeing a *samurai*, the farmer dismounted at once in order to show respect; but Yukichi explained that under the new laws this was not necessary. Much against the man's will, he forced him to mount again and drove him off, Yukichi reflecting sadly "what fearful weight the old customs had with the people." He devoted the rest of his life to writing and translating and to the affairs of the school he founded, which became Keio University, the first private university in Japan. He summed up his aim in life as follows:

> After all, the purpose of my entire work has not only been to gather young men together and give them the benefit of foreign books but to open this "closed" country of ours and bring it wholly into the light of Western civilization. For only thus may Japan become strong in the arts of both war and peace and take a place in the forefront of the progress of the world.[3]

Gradually the people of Japan as well as the leaders became aware of changes in the air. New fashions in dress and style, in habits and customs, began to enjoy a great vogue, the high point being reached in the 1880s. The

[2] *The Autobiography of Yukichi Fukuzawa*, tr. Eiichi Kiyooka (New York: Columbia University Press, 1966), p. 3. In the book title the surname Fukuzawa has been placed second to accord with Western practice.
[3] Ibid., p. 246.

samurai haircut, with the top of the head shaved and the rest of the hair brought up into a topknot, proved quite impractical with the introduction of the modern army uniform cap, so Western-style haircuts were adopted. The term *haikara*, "high collar," was used to mean "fashionable"; "business suit" appeared in Japanese as *sebiro*, a corruption of the words "Savile Row," the tailors' street in London, leading city for men's clothes. The emperor was even induced to eat beef in order to overcome in the average Japanese a prejudice derived from Buddhism against this diet. Prints are to be found from this period showing modern young men about town eating beef, sporting umbrellas and big "turnip" watches. Women learned to use the new sewing machines to turn out Western-style dresses with large bustles. There was even a short period when leaders of Tokyo society felt it incumbent upon them to attend Assemblies every Sunday night in the Rokumeikan, a building put up by the government, to dance waltzes and quadrilles. They were prepared to dress up in uncomfortable evening dress; but fancy dress was something else. When an elaborate fancy-dress ball was held in 1887, attended by members of the government, Japanese opinion was so shocked by the undignified absurdity of the proceedings that the whole practice of ballroom dancing was dropped.

In literature there was a growing demand for translations of Western works. Among the earliest translations were *Robinson Crusoe* (1859), Samuel Smiles's *Self-Help* (1870), and John Stuart Mill's *On Liberty* (1871). Jules Verne's writings were among the most popular. Novels were written by Japanese depicting new and daring behavior, and one of them dealt with revolutionary movements in different parts of the world. Few were of any literary merit.

It is possible, amid the amusing vagaries of fad and fashion, to miss the serious purpose behind the efforts at social modernization, for the motive was an important one. It was to become accepted by the leading nations of the world so that the unequal treaties would be revised, tariff rates improved, extraterritoriality abolished, and Japan accorded its full place in the comity of nations.

The course of reform and modernization was by no means all clear sailing. Peasant unrest has already been mentioned; it was considered an acceptable risk by the government. But the distress of the former *samurai* gave grave concern to the leaders, themselves for the most part from the same class. The launching of an overseas venture was discussed as a possible means of employing the *samurai* and restoring their morale. Diplomatic missions had already been sent to Korea after the Meiji Restoration to renegotiate trade and foreign relations and bring them more into accord with the new situation in Japan. When these approaches were rejected by the conservatives in Korea, Saigo Takamori actually suggested that he be sent over alone so that his expected murder might give a valid excuse for Japan to attack. This offer was not accepted, but a chance to act seemed to come when the Iwakura Mission drew off to the United States and Europe the more moderate members

Traditional *kimono* and *obi* (sashes) worn by young women on special occasions.

Japan National Tourist Organization

of the ruling group. The remainder, including Saigo, decided in the summer of 1873 that a military force should be sent to Korea. Members of the Iwakura Mission returned just in time to have this provocative decision reversed. It was clear to them, after comparing Japan with Western countries, that the plan was premature and most unwise. Saigo resigned and returned home to Kyushu.

As a milder show of force, an expedition was sent against Taiwan to exact punishment for the murder of some shipwrecked seamen from the Ryukyu Islands. China gave in and agreed to pay an indemnity. Later a naval force was sent to Korea; and, by the Treaty of Kanghwa of 1876, two ports in addition to the existing one at Pusan were opened to Japanese trade and Korea was declared independent, although without any attempt to secure the agreement of China, the nominal suzerain.

To the discontented *samurai*, however, conquest by treaty was no substitute for the glories of war. Following Saigo's resignation from the government, there were several revolts in Satsuma, Tosa, and Hizen over Korean policy, the commutation of *samurai* stipends into government bonds, and the ban on wearing swords. In these revolts Saigo himself took no active part, for he was unwilling to come out against the government and his former colleagues. He built up a chain of schools in the south devoted to military training and the fostering of conservative *samurai* ideals. In the end these became so successful and so powerful that he could no longer control the more eager of his followers. When the government took the precaution of removing military stores from Kagoshima, the provincial capital, supporters of Saigo seized the government depots there, put their hero at their head, and began a march on Edo with 40,000 troops. They did not get very far. They were held up by local government forces at Kumamoto, and the central authorities had time to muster an army. Conscript regiments with naval support fought a hard campaign of six months and forced the rebels back on Kagoshima, where Saigo and his chief supporters were killed after desperate resistance. Saigo Takamori became a legend, but there were no more feudal rebellions. The Meiji government was undisputed master of Japan.

Rebels such as Saigo had neither the foresight nor the political realism of the government leaders whose cardinal policy was summed up in the contemporary slogan *fukoku-kyohei*, "rich country—strong army." These leaders early grasped the fact that modernization was a total and indivisible process and that certain constitutional, legal, and economic ideas and methods from the West would have to be incorporated into their new system, even though they intended to retain "the Japanese spirit." Above all they realized, in contrast to the limited modernizers in China, that a modern war machine required not only arsenals and shipyards but the whole apparatus of modern industry to undergird it. Their slogan led directly to what is now known as a military-industrial complex, though they would not have necessarily approved the uses to which their more chauvinistic successors put the military-industrial tool which they so skillfully forged.

INDUSTRY

The Meiji government provided secure political conditions and a reliable financial framework in the country. It also sponsored and supported early developments in some industries, especially the heavy industries needed to fill modern army and navy requirements. The private sector was nevertheless responsible for the major development of industry in Japan.

A modern furnace for iron smelting was constructed by the Hizen domain as early as 1850 from instructions contained in a book from Holland. Soon afterward the iron from this furnace was used to cast cannon which were more efficient than the older bronze models. Tokugawa Nariaki, lord of Mito, was running a small iron and shipbuilding concern in his own fief by 1858. The new government built on these foundations by developing large arsenals in Tokyo and Osaka, and by adding to the two earlier shipyards at Nagasaki and Yokosuka a new one at Hyogo (Kobe). Even before the new government began operations, there were already, by 1868, 138 modern ships in use, some bought from abroad and some made in Japan.

The early railroads showed only a slow growth in mileage of track laid down owing to the mountainous terrain and the high cost of tunnels and bridges; but such track as there was immediately began to bear heavy traffic. The short Tokyo-Yokohama railway built in 1872 was carrying 2 million passengers by 1880, in addition to large quantities of freight. Kobe was linked to Osaka in 1874 and to Kyoto three years later. Small sections of the Tokyo-Kobe projected line were completed by 1877. After this date private companies began to enter the railroad field, which had hitherto been government-financed, and private construction soon outstripped that of the government, as the following chart indicates:

Year	Private Company Track	Government Track	Total
1881	none	76 miles	76
1885	130 miles	220 miles	350
1895	1,500 miles	580 miles	2,080

After 1906 the railroad system was nationalized for strategic reasons in times of national emergency.

A coal mine was started by the Hizen domain in 1869 and operated at first with British assistance; but the government took it over in 1874 and was soon operating eight other mines. This and some significant development in textiles occurred under the direction and with the encouragement of Ito, who was minister of the newly created Ministry of Industry from 1870 to 1878. The textile industry provides the clearest pattern of cooperation between the government and the private sector. Woolen manufacture, required for uniforms for the military and for government employees, was entirely a government responsibility. Silk, on the other hand, required much traditional handwork, the only major innovation being machine reeling. Enough private capital was available to finance the expansion caused by heavy foreign demand, and the government took very little part in this industry. In 1880 silk formed 43 percent of Japan's export trade. In the cotton industry, one of the greatest growth industries of the period, both government and private finance were involved. Private capital was attracted since the factories could be large or small and the technology was comparatively simple. The Satsuma domain opened a factory in 1868, and there were three government mills by 1880 as well as numerous private concerns. Cotton machinery was purchased from abroad in 1878 with a large government loan of 10 million yen and then sold on easy terms to private companies. The growth of the cotton industry as a whole is indicated by the number of spindles being operated, as follows:

1877	8,000
1887	77,000 (equivalent to the number of spindles in one Lancashire mill)
1893	382,000

Cheap labor was forthcoming for both cotton and silk manufacture from the daughters of poor farmers, who were indentured to the factory owners, housed in dormitories, and made to work long hours with very little freedom. Conditions in the factories themselves, however, were probably no worse than at the corresponding stage in Europe during the Industrial Revolution. The girls in the cotton and silk mills of Japan undoubtedly suffered from virtual imprisonment and from tuberculosis, as is vividly portrayed in Kagawa Toyohiko's novel *A Grain of Wheat*; but their fate in the factories was better than the earlier destiny of girls from impoverished families who were sold to brothel keepers.

The industrial development sponsored and financed by the government proved a costly item. It was made possible only by a deliberate decision to favor industry at the expense of agriculture. In 1880 about 75 percent of the population was engaged in farming, and 80 percent of the tax revenue came from the agricultural yield. This tax revenue enabled the government, among other things, to pay for imported industrial machinery and the services of foreign experts. Foreign loans could be negotiated, but these were expensive and involved an unacceptable measure of dependence on foreign governments; no one had invented foreign aid, and Japan had to pay as she went. The 1870s had been a decade of unprecedented expenditure. In addition to the payments to *samurai* and *daimyo* and the industrial financing, it had been necessary to make new outlays for the development of Hokkaido, the northern island. These had included subsidies to immigrant farmers, whose influx in considerable numbers successfully held off Russian encroachment which was threatening from the north. Then at the end of the decade came a period of serious inflation, which added to the difficulties of the government. In 1877 the price of rice was 5.7 yen per koku, but in 1880 it had risen to 12.2 yen. The members of the government considered requesting a foreign loan, which they could have secured from London, but on the advice of the able finance minister, Matsukata Masayoshi (1835–1924), they decided on a policy of retrenchment and economy instead. This policy was firmly carried out and gradually improved the government's financial position, until by 1886 the state of affairs could be considered normal.

Among the economy measures introduced by Matsukata was the sale to private buyers of factories and enterprises which had originally been financed by the government. For some of these enterprises it was not easy to find purchasers, and the prices were not advantageous to the government as sales were made at figures varying from 11 to 90 percent of the original investment. Ready cash, however, was made available to the government, and the losses were more than balanced by the advantage of new industries to the nation as a whole. Manufacture involving national defense remained in government control. There was inevitably a certain amount of political graft bound up with these sales arrangements, factories being sold at low prices to friends of those in the relevant government ministry. In some cases these were the very men best able to carry on the industry in question; in other cases they had to wait for years for the ultimate profits. In one instance at least, involving government property in Hokkaido, the price was so absurdly low that a scandal erupted and the sale was blocked.

Some of the firms which benefited most from the purchase of government-financed concerns were the great business houses which emerged as the so-called *zaibatsu* ("financial clique") firms. The first in order of size was Mitsui, which started in Tokugawa as a *sake* brewery and branched out into the sale of dry goods and into banking. In the mid-nineteenth century a brilliant manager, Minomura Rizaemon, had the firm adopt modern banking methods and diversify its operations. His friendship with Inoue gave him valuable government connections. The firm bought the Tomioka silk-reeling mill from the government, began to engage in heavy industry, and set up the great Mitsukoshi department store business as a separate entity. The second *zaibatsu* firm of Mitsubishi owed its origin to a Tosa *samurai*, Iwasaki Yataro (1834–1885), who, with the help of the resources of the Tosa domain and government subsidies, set up his own shipping line. From this in turn developed the famous N.Y.K., Nippon Yusen Kaisha, or Japanese Mail Line. The third largest firm was founded by a well-to-do peasant of consuming ambition, Shibusawa Eiichi (1840–1931), who rose to prominence under the patronage of Keiki, the last shogun. Shibusawa engaged in banking and trading, served in the government, and became president of the First National Bank. He founded the Osaka Spinning Mill, which became in the 1880s remarkably successful by reason of its large size, up-to-date technology, and efficient management. In addition to these activities Shibusawa played a part in the affairs of some hundred other companies. Two other main *zaibatsu* firms were Yasuda in banking and railroads, and Asano, the firm which purchased a government-built cement factory and turned its losses into profits.

POLITICAL EVENTS: TOWARD A CONSTITUTION

In the realm of politics the movement toward representative government was slow and tentative; indeed at one point President Ulysses S. Grant of the United States advised the emperor to make it slow. The government of Japan from the Meiji Restoration in 1868 to the promulgation of the Meiji Constitution in 1890 was in the hands of a few men, an enlightened and progressive group but a distinct oligarchy nonetheless. It is doubtful whether any other political arrangement would have worked. A demand for representative institutions, however, was steadily growing, stimulated by the study of Western models.

When Saigo Takamori left the government in the 1873 crisis over Korean policy, Itagaki Taisuke (1837–1919) went with him; but thereafter the two men moved in very different directions, Saigo toward an unwilling military resistance and Itagaki toward progressive political action. With support from his own clan of Tosa, Itagaki formed a political club called the Society of Patriots. From local beginnings it reached national proportions and formed a valuable training ground for the future political party movement. Any training in legitimate activity of this kind was of benefit, for the notion of "a party" was still an unfamiliar one. The authorities tended, in the traditional manner, to regard associations of persons advocating change as automatically subversive, while those zealous for change wanted to proceed immediately to extremes and had no concept of a "loyal opposition." The limits of valid political activism had still to be discovered and laid down, as may be deduced from the tenor of a newspaper headline of the time: "Tyrannical officials must be assassinated."

While Itagaki and others were carrying on the movement for "people's rights," the government was making experiments of its own. In 1879 prefectural and later town assemblies were elected. There was a small property qualification to determine electors, and only matters concerning taxes and budget were permitted on the agenda; but it was a beginning in representative government. Yet again the leaders were revealed as a true oligarchy, for they were determined to keep control in their own hands and decide the pace of advance. Newspapers had been increasing in numbers and influence during the seventies, and from the start they exhibited the tendency they still display, of being antigovernment and antibureaucratic. Reacting to this, the government passed a Press Law in 1875 which gave wide powers of censorship. The law of libel was made strict, and police permission was required for public gatherings. All this apparatus was used against the budding parliamentary movement on numerous occasions. On the other side, the movement for the "people's rights" was strengthened by the translation of Jean-Jacques Rousseau's *Contrat Social* which appeared in 1877. Intellectuals inspired by it formed a radical wing depending on French rather than on British parliamentary ideas.

The conflict between the conservative government leaders and their opponents came to a head in the crisis of 1881. Okuma Shigenobu (1838–1922), who was heading the parliamentary movement from within the government itself, proposed that elections be held in 1882, that a parliament meet the next year, and that a cabinet be responsible to parliament in the British manner. This was most alarming to the oligarchs, and after some discussion Okuma was dismissed from office. As a concession to the parliamentary party it was arranged that the emperor should announce that a constitution providing for a parliament would be set up in the year 1890. Regular political parties were now formed: the Jiyuto, or Liberal Party, under the leadership of Itagaki and Goto Shojiro and with some of the characteristics of French radicalism, and the Rikken Kaishinto, or Constitutional Progressive Party led by Okuma and more akin to English ideas. A warning had already been issued in the emperor's name against "those who advocate sudden and violent changes." In 1887 a Peace Preservation Law authorized the police to remove from the area of the capital any person "judged to be scheming something detrimental to public tranquillity." This wide provision was obviously subject to abuse, but in extenuation of the government's action it must be said that assassination was a constant threat; Okubo Toshimichi, a highly respected member of the government, had been murdered in 1878. Furthermore, though the government had its own cautious timetable, its members did agree in principle to the establishment of a representative national body; the disagreement was over the date and the nature of the body and its powers. Democracy in some form was felt by all to be a reason for the success of the Western nations. Representative government was something you had to have, like *moningu*, "morning coat," the formal Western dress officially adopted during this era.

Ito now began serious work on the drafting of the promised constitution. He led a mission to Europe in 1882 to make a comparative study of government systems. He already knew in broad outline what he was looking for and spent most of the time in Prussia, where he met Bismarck and studied under Albert Mosse, and in Austria, where he received the advice of Lorenz von Stein. He spent only six weeks of the eighteen months abroad in London, for the Germanic system, with tighter centralization and greater powers for the monarch and the bureaucracy, seemed to him better suited to the needs of Japan than the British parliamentary system, which involved political parties of some experience and self-restraint.

When Ito finally returned to Japan, he superintended several steps leading toward the controlled democracy he was so carefully planning. In 1884 a new peerage, required to form the Upper House in the proposed constitution, was created. It had five ranks—prince, marquis, count, viscount, and baron. Five hundred persons were included in the first grant of titles of nobility, of whom no fewer than 470 already belonged to the old court nobility. The remaining thirty belonged mainly to the government group, and leaders of the new political parties were intentionally left out. Then the civil service was reformed, with the institution of examinations and the passing of regulations designed to prevent nepotism. The Law School of Tokyo University became the chief avenue of entrance into the higher echelons of the civil service, and the bureaucracy gained steadily in political significance. Next a cabinet replaced the *dajo-kan* as the supreme organ of government under the emperor. This gave the premier, Ito, more power; and since the cabinet was set up prior to the constitution, the precedent was the more easily established that the ministers should be responsible to the emperor and not to the elected representatives of the people. Finally, in 1888, a Privy Council was created to advise the emperor. Since its first task was the final drafting of the constitution, it seemed to Ito to take precedence over everything else and he resigned the premiership to take over its chairmanship. Most of the members were in agreement with Ito's views, and they had an unrestricted field of action, since the Privy Council was specifically enjoined from receiving petitions from the public.

The Meiji Constitution was promulgated in February 1889, the first system of representative government to be adopted in Asia. In spite of numerous safeguards it was regarded by many as too liberal; but Ito ingeniously warded off criticism by the conservatives through his arrangement that the constitution was made as a gift from the emperor to the people of Japan. Sovereignty was fixed in the person of the emperor, declared to be "sacred and inviolable." He was to convene and dissolve the Diet of parliament and could pass emergency laws when the Diet was not in session. These, however, had later to be submitted to the Diet. He was supreme commander of the army and navy, and the government ministers were individually responsible directly to him and not through the cabinet as a whole. The constitution set up a Diet with a House of Peers, appointive, and a House of Representatives, elective. Each was of equal status, which meant that the upper house had the power of veto in addition to the veto power vested in the emperor. The House of Peers consisted of the upper nobility, representatives of the lower nobility (counts, viscounts, and barons), distinguished public figures, often scholars, and representatives of the highest taxpayers. The House of Representatives consisted of 300 members, later raised to 466, elected by all adult males in Japan over the age of twenty-five and paying at least 15 yen per annum in taxes. In practice this turned out to be at first only 1 percent of the population. The premier was to be appointed by the emperor on advice from the elder statesmen. An important provision was inserted in order to ensure to the government some freedom from Diet control, namely, the power reserved to the government to carry on with the budget of the previous year if the Diet failed to pass the new budget proposed.

Since the time of their formation the political parties had declined rather than gained in influence. They suffered from internal factions, felt the adverse effects of public opinion after the riots of 1884, and were harassed by the operation of the Peace Preservation Law. Nevertheless, when the first Diet was elected in 1890, the members proved much less amenable to government persuasion than Ito had expected. The Diet used its budgetary powers to show its resistance to the government; but the government found that the weapon it had counted on, namely, the right to operate in case of need with the budget of the previous year, proved almost useless for the simple reason that, in an expanding economy, the previous year's budget figure was never enough. A succession of premiers fell back upon their second weapon, the proroguing or dissolution of the Diet. The government leaders, in their frustration, did not hesitate to use more extreme methods. The second election, which took place in 1892, was accompanied by bribery and the use of police force, in which 25 persons were killed and almost 400 wounded. Two factors, however, made for a series of uneasy compromises: the government leaders were unwilling to see the new constitution fail, and the parliamentary party leaders did not want to incur the constant expense of new elections. (There were four premiers and two elections in the year 1898, but this was exceptional.) The machinery of representative government, although creaking, did function, and gradually the political parties began to operate more normally by opposing each other rather than by combining to hamstring the executive branch. The pattern of control already established in the hands of the members of the Choshu and Satsuma clans continued, for the premiership alternated between Choshu and Satsuma men from 1885 to 1898, the former being represented by Ito and Yamagata and the latter by Kuroda Kiyotaka and Matsukata Masayoshi.

EXPANSION OVERSEAS

Japan's turbulent and phenomenal advance in both the economic and political realms inevitably created new pressures and new demands. This growth, combined with national pride and ambition, produced a drive to control or acquire new territory overseas, which is the salient factor in Japanese history from the 1890s until the end of World War II. Korea, traditional target of Japanese conquest, was the starting point. In 1894 the king of Korea, involved in factional strife at the court, appealed to his suzerain, China, and a small contingent was sent in answer to his plea. The Japanese then sent a larger army and demanded reforms in Korea on behalf of the progressive party which they were supporting. China refused agreement, and war was declared in August. The Japanese were successful on land, and their troops penetrated into Manchuria. The decisive action took place at sea, off the mouth of the Yalu River. Japan was again victorious and went on to destroy the rest of the Chinese fleet at Weihaiwei in Shantung province and to capture Port Arthur on the Liaodong Peninsula. China had been easily defeated. The spoils of war obtained by Japan at the Treaty of Shimonoseki in April 1895 were considerable—the islands of Formosa and the Pescadores, the recognition of Korea's independence, an indemnity of 30 million pounds, and a commercial treaty. During the negotiations the Japanese had also secured the cession of the Liaodong Peninsula in South Manchuria; but before the treaty was ratified, Russia, France, and Germany combined to compel Japan to relinquish that claim. The Japanese bowed to the inevitable, but the insult rankled, the more so as Russia proceeded to develop her own interests in Manchuria. Japan annexed Korea outright in 1910 and meanwhile found the indemnity very useful in expanding her foreign trade.

The last years of the nineteenth century were comparatively quiet. Ito at length secured the consent of his *genro* colleagues to form a new party favorable to the government, naming it Rikken Seiyukai, Friends of Constitutional Government, thus recognizing what had long been the case, that the original dream of having a cabinet above and independent of the political parties was an impossible idea. In the same year, 1900, Yamagata, while premier, had a ruling adopted that those appointed as army and navy ministers in the cabinet must be officers on active duty. This was to have ominous consequences, for its effect was to increase the leverage of the military upon the political process. At the same time the sense of grievance at the terms of the Treaty of Shimonoseki had made it easier for Yamagata and his military colleagues to raise the figure for the defense budget.

The significance of Japan's easy victory over China in 1895 was not lost upon Western observers; but the point at which the nations of the world recognized that Japan had joined "the club" of powers possessing modern weapons was the occasion of the Relief of the Legations which marked the end of the Boxer Rebellion in Beijing in 1900. The full story of that tragic but understandable anachronism belongs to the history of China. The shrewd and formidable Empress Dowager had skillfully turned the hatred of the Boxer rebels away from the Manchu regime and toward the foreigners. When to the persecution and killing of Christians was added the murder of the German ambassador and the subsequent siege of the legation quarter in Beijing, world opinion was fully aroused and summary action taken. A Japanese contingent formed half the international force which set out from Tianjin and succeeded in relieving the beleaguered legations on August 14, 1900. A speech of Kaiser Wilhelm II on July 27 to the troops of the German contingent sheds an interesting sidelight on his mentality and his outlook upon Asia:

> Let all who fall into your hands be at your mercy. Just as the Huns a thousand years ago, under the leadership of Attila, gained a reputation by virtue of which they still live in historical tradition, so may the name of Germany become known in such a manner in China, that no Chinese will ever again dare to look askance at a German.[4]

By taking its place at this juncture alongside the Western powers, Japan felt it had successfully claimed recognition as a modern, industrialized nation. It is ironic that the possession of armed might was the chief passport to recognition. To be fully in fashion, trade and territorial ambitions were expected to go along with military potential. Japan was well established in Korea. Russia's expansion eastward and its attempted domination of Manchuria were considered a threat not only by Japan but also by the major powers. By a secret treaty of 1896 and a handsome bribe to Li Hong-zhang, Russia had secured from China the right to build the Chinese Eastern Railway across Manchurian land, thus saving the expense of the longer and more difficult route north of the Amur River, and connecting the Trans-Siberian Railway with the port of Vladivostok on the Pacific. At about the same time Russia obtained a lease of the Liaodong Peninsula, with the port of Dairen and the Port Arthur naval base, as well as the right to connect these ports with the railway in the north by means of the South Manchurian line. This was a vital concession, for the port of the Vladivostok is ice-free for only about four months of the year, while Dairen is open to navigation all the year round.

Manchuria has figured prominently in the international rivalries between Japan, Russia, and China from the end of the nineteenth century until the present. It is significant that both Manchuria and its chief city, Mukden, are designated in the West not by Chinese but by Russian words, based on the original Manchu language. (The Chinese refer to Manchuria as the "three eastern province," Dong San Sheng, or more often simply as "the Northeast" Dongbei) Geographically the region consists of a great and fertile plain, in which large-scale land development was begun only in modern times at the hands of Chinese farmer immigrants, mainly from Shandong Province. This plain produces the staple grain of the north, millet, and soybeans,

---

[4] W.L. Langer, *The Diplomacy of Imperialism*, Vol. II (New York: Alfred A. Knopf, 1935), p. 699.

legumes of high nutrient and vitamin value used also in the manufacture of paint and many other industrial products. The plain is surrounded on the east by virgin forests near the Korean border, by the Mongolian steppes to the west, and by the Great Wall and the Gulf of Zhili to the south. It has valuable deposits of gold, iron, soft coal, and other minerals, the largest open-surface coal mine in the world being situated at Fushun near Mukden. Both the situation and the undeveloped resources of Manchuria, therefore, made it a most desirable area for exploitation by the Japanese.

There were two views in Japan as to how it might best proceed in the complicated diplomatic maneuvering going on at this time for "spheres of influence" on the Asian continent. Ito favored an alliance with Russia on the basis of a simple division: Korea for Japanese development, Manchuria for Russia's share. Yamagata and Katsura Taro, on the other hand, felt that a military showdown was the only way to halt Russia's expansion. They concentrated on still further strengthening the army and navy, which were already by 1894 receiving one-third of the national budget. Yamagata's hard-line policy won out, and the Anglo-Japanese Alliance was signed in 1902. By this agreement the Japanese gained prestige and security, while the British were glad of an ally as further insurance in their rivalry with Germany and Russia. The new alliance did not require Britain to intervene in a purely Russo-Japanese conflict but guaranteed British aid if any other power joined Russia.

Japan and Russia then entered into direct negotiations in 1903, in which Russia recognized Japan's right to freedom of action in Korea; but Japan, with Britain at its back, sought to restrict Russia's sphere of action in Manchuria to the railway zone only, while the rest of Manchuria was to remain under Chinese control. While the bargaining dragged on, Tsar Nicholas II began pouring a steady stream of troops into the East via the Trans-Siberian Railway. Japan was unwilling to lose the military advantage and broke off the negotiations in February 1904. It immediately struck at the Russian fleet in Port Arthur by a night attack and succeeded in blockading the enemy ships in the harbor. Japanese land forces crossed the Korean-Manchurian border at the Yalu River, while other Japanese troops occupied the port of Dairen and besieged Port Arthur from the landward side. The Japanese forced the Russians to withdraw northward along the railway line by repeated flank attacks. Port Arthur fell in January 1905. Casualties on both sides had been heavy, and casualties among Chinese civilians would have been still heavier than they were had it not been for the efforts of a Scottish missionary doctor, riding ceaselessly on a Mongolian pony between the lines to arrange for civilian evacuations. The land war culminated in the Battle of Mukden, which lasted for over two weeks in March 1905 and produced a stalemate.

Meanwhile the Russians had dispatched their Baltic fleet to reinforce the squadron at Vladivostok. Britain refused to allow the fleet to use the Suez Canal or any British ports en route. The Russian admiral had to round the Cape of Good Hope and refuel at French ports in Madagascar and Indochina. Admiral Togo Heihachiro guessed, correctly as it turned out, that the Russians would take the shorter route inside the Japanese islands, and he lay in wait with a powerful battle fleet in the Tsushima Straits between Korea and Japan. He achieved surprise and executed the tactic known as "crossing the T," namely, moving his ships in column across the enemy line of advance, which enabled him to fire successive broadsides while the rear ships of the enemy, blocked by their own vessels in front, could not bring their guns to bear. Torpedo boats then went in to administer the *coup de grâce*. The result was an overwhelming disaster for the Russian fleet, in which thirty-two out of thirty-five ships were put out of action. This naval battle, in May 1905, ended the war.

Western public opinion had been pleased to see the plucky Japanese stand up to the great Russian bear. At the conclusion the British Navy was proud of its brilliant students, but the powers generally were shocked to see a European nation so thoroughly and rapidly defeated by an Asiatic race. Some swift reappraisal had to be undertaken in the chancelleries of Europe and the United States. President Theodore Roosevelt arranged a peace conference in Portsmouth, New Hampshire, which agreed to recognize Japan's "paramount interests" in Korea and handed over to Japan the southern half of Sakhalin, the Russian lease on the Liaodong Peninsula, and the South Manchurian Railway as far north as Changchun. But the Treaty of Portsmouth gave Japan no indemnity, a fact which aroused intense feeling in the country. The Russian people had never been in sympathy with the war; defeat precipitated the Revolution of 1905.

When it was announced that Japan was not to receive an indemnity from Russia, there was rioting in the streets of Tokyo, which produced 1,000 casualties, and the premier, Katsura, was compelled to resign. An associate of Ito in the Seiyukai party was appointed to the post. The new incumbent, Saionji Kimmochi (1849–1940), a member of the former court nobility, had had a varied career. After ten years' study in France, he returned to publish his liberal ideas through the medium of journalism. This was considered undignified for a man of noble family, and he was persuaded to join the government. He served as education minister and later as president of the Privy Council. Similar opposition was voiced to his activity in political party affairs, but he maintained a close connection with the Seiyukai, and it was in this capacity that he succeeded to the premiership, although the oligarchs brought forward other reasons. Katsura had been premier from 1901, and Saionji held the office from 1906 for two years. Thereafter the two, by an amicable arrangement, occupied the post alternately until 1913.

Ito Hirobumi, by now Prince Ito, had just laid aside his last office of resident-general in Korea when he was cut down at the age of sixty-eight by a Korean assassin's bullet in Manchuria in 1909. The lifetime of this man of peasant birth, who had reached a place second only to the emperor himself, had seen his country pass from being an almost unknown land to the position of a world power. The Emperor Meiji, also a man of vigor and talent, died in 1912, thus bringing this remarkable era to a close.

13

EXPANSION, LIBERALISM, AND MILITARISM

1914–1931

The planned revolution carried through by the Meiji leaders and the obedient, even enthusiastic, response of the people had by 1912 proved an outstanding success. The political outlook was uncertain as the original Elder Statesmen were removed by death; but Japan had gained impressive military strength, and its economy had reached what is now known as the takeoff point. Hard work and thrift enabled Japan's industry to reinvest as much as 15 percent in plant and machinery in good years, after 1900, and still have enough left over to raise the standard of living of the country as a whole. Japan thus proved able to support its growing power upon an adequate industrial and commercial foundation.

The quarter of a century prior to World War I was the period of a worldwide scramble for colonies, concessions, and spheres of influence in Asia and Africa. As the accompanying table shows, Japan joined the other great powers in making very considerable expenditures on "defense" from 1890 to 1914. The Japanese total was increased fourfold, and the amount per capita rose from 60 cents to $1.75. While the latter amount was less than the American figure of $3.20 and far below those of the major competitors for world power, Great Britain and Germany, it represented an impressive effort considering the fact that Japan had only begun to attempt modernization as a definite policy after 1868.

When World War I broke out in August 1914, the Okuma government immediately entered on the side of the Allies, declared war on Germany, and sent a force to attack the German holdings in Shantung without any regard for China's neutrality at that time. The British cooperated in the capture of the port of Tsingtao, and within three months Japan had obtained possession of the German assets in Shantung and had placed police along the railway lines to secure them. In this campaign, incidentally, military aircraft were first used in warfare. Japan at this time also occupied the Pacific Islands formerly held by Germany, namely, the Mariana, Caroline, and Marshall islands.

The moment seemed propitious for Japan to follow up these gains by consolidating her power on the continent. The government in 1915 secretly presented Yüan Shih-k'ai with Twenty-One Demands in five groups. Groups 1 through 4 concerned rights of limitations in Shantung, Manchuria, the central Yangtze valley, and on the China coast. Group 5 involved the appointment of Japanese as advisers in Chinese government affairs, joint Sino-Japanese control of police, and certain conditions affecting arsenals and the purchase of arms. This last group was such a clear infringement of China's sovereignty that the Western powers, preoccupied though they were with the war, could not possibly ignore the matter. When Yüan Shih-k'ai intentionally informed the world press of the contents of the Twenty-One Demands, Japan was forced to withdraw the more controversial of its "requests," but it obtained valuable concessions in Shantung, South Manchuria, and the eastern part of Inner Mongolia. Japan's aim in all this was mainly economic, but there were serious political repercussions in China, where Japan was suddenly marked out as the main imperialist enemy. Japan had secured agreements one by one from the main powers to have a special position accorded her in China in exchange for help in World War I. The climax came in 1917 in the exchange of the Lansing-Ishii Notes with the United States. By this agreement the parties were to respect the territorial integrity of China but recognized that the "territorial propinquity" of Japan gave it "special interests" on the Asian continent which it was entitled to protect.

In the Peace Treaty of Versailles Japan succeeded in obtaining the League of Nations mandate over the former German Pacific islands and the recognition of special rights in Shantung. Japan failed to have a clause guaranteeing racial equality included in the League of Nations Covenant, owing to opposition to nonwhite immigration into Australia and California. This caused no little resentment in Japan. Japan, however, was recognized at the end of the war as one of the "Big Five" powers, with a seat on the Council of the League of Nations, and emerged, after very little expenditure of men or money, more powerful than before.

The chief gains of the Japanese were not political but economic. They were aware that they had done very well from World War I. They had made immense strides in the building and operating of a great merchant fleet, having, in fact, become one of the world's great carriers through the heavy shipping losses experienced by Britain, Germany, and the United States in submarine warfare. The Japanese had been able in their new construction to take advantage of the latest technical advances. They never, for instance, had to invest much capital in ships with reciprocating engines but moved directly to steam turbines and then to diesel engines. During World War I Japanese merchant marine income had multiplied ten times. Japan had captured a large share of the world textile trade and had ended the war as a creditor nation with gold reserves which had increased sixfold in six years.

Military Expenditures of the Great Powers*

	Standing Army (000)	Army Appropriation ($000,000)	Naval Tonnage (000)	Naval Appropriation ($000,000)	Total Defense Expenditure ($000,000)	Growth Factor	Cost per Capita Home Population ($)
Japan							
1890	70	18	41	6	24		.60
1914	250	48	700	48	96	X4	1.75
Germany							
1890	487	121	190	23	144		2.95
1914	812	442	1305	112	554	X3.1	8.52
British Empire							
1890	355	88	679	69	157		4.03
1914	381	147	2714	237	384	X2.4	8.53
France							
1890	502	142	319	44	186		4.87
1914	846	197	900	90	287	X1.5	7.33
Russia							
1890	647	123	180	22	145		1.32
1914	1300	324	679	118	442	X3	2.58
United States							
1890	27	45	40	22	67		1.06
1914	98	174	895	140	314	X4.7	3.20

*Adapted from Black and Helmreich: *Twentieth Century Europe*, Alfred A. Knopf, New York, 1966, pp. 25–26.

Such were the events and the changed directions brought about by the participation of the new Japan in the international arena. A change had also come over the domestic political scene. The small, gifted, and comparatively stable group of the Meiji oligarchs had guided affairs all the way from the Restoration until the outbreak of World War I; but by the end of the war authority was more widely distributed over a much larger number of persons grouped in sets of the elite, such as the bureaucrats, the businessmen, the military leaders, the Privy Council and peers, and the intellectuals. No one of these sets had the degree of authority which the oligarchs had been able to command, and therefore all had to rely on the various combinations of power that could be set up and traded through the machinery of political parties. The Diet was the mart in which this bargaining took place; or rather, the Diet was the place in which speeches were made for public consumption, while the bargaining went on in the back rooms. Although not always harmonious, the process led to the participation of many more Japanese in the operation of government. The decade of the 1920s, and especially the earlier half of it, was the era of liberal politics in Japan, and this tendency to rely to a greater extent on political parties was reinforced by the fact that the democratic countries had been seen to be the victors in the recent war.

The new tendency found expression in the premiership of Hara Kei (born 1856), president of the Seiyukai party and the first commoner to become premier. He held the post for three years until murdered by a rightist.

In the circumstances of party politics business interests tended to dominate, sometimes by means which were more than dubious, for frequent cases of corruption were uncovered in both main parties, the Seiyukai and the Kenseikai, the latter named Minseito after 1927. The businessmen were opposed to expansionist military schemes because they cost money in taxes and because they led to boycotting of Japanese goods by Chinese nationalists. Thus part of the Seiyukai program in 1922 was to withdraw the Japanese forces that had gone to Siberia with an Allied anti-Bolshevik expedition in 1918 and had remained on with a vague hope of territorial gains after the other Allies had recalled their troops.

The cabinets of the 1920s represented on the whole the complexion of the political parties, and both of these were pacific rather than warlike and cautious rather than adventurous. There was little ideological difference between them. Although the parties received financial support from the big business sector, their membership was drawn from the smaller businessmen and the rural landowners, who had no other means of political expression. The poorer urban workers were even worse off politically; being below the property level that would have entitled them to vote, they had neither the experience nor the expectation of governing themselves. However, they had an advantage for their future: their numbers were growing. Agricultural production, after an extraordinary rise of 59 percent in yield per acre from 1880 to 1914, was now leveling off. In 1883 only 16 percent of the population lived in towns of over 10,000. By 1913 this had risen to 28 percent, and by

1920 only about half the people remained in the countryside. The figures for the production of goods manufactured in the towns tripled between 1914 and 1929.

The workers' cause was championed by new political parties. Oi Kentaro, an early radical pioneer and supporter of Sun Yat-sen, had founded the Oriental Liberal party in 1892, but it was short-lived. The Social Democratic party, founded in 1901 under mainly Christian auspices, had a program which today seems eminently reasonable, namely, free education, an eight-hour day, and the abolition of child labor; but it was suppressed by the police on the day following its founding. The Communist party, established in 1921 (the same year as the Chinese Communist party), suffered from faction as well as the attentions of the police and went into voluntary liquidation in 1924. (It was revived the next year, but as an illegal, underground organization.)

It was the labor unions rather than any political party which gave the workers their means of self-expression. The booming war years supplied an impetus to the formation of these unions in industry, and membership reached 300,000 by 1929. Strikes, beginning in 1919, recurred throughout the 1920s. Moreover the poorer classes began to find aid in several quarters, in a combination which was typical of the early twenties and was never to occur again in the same form. The varied elements in this combination included the intellectuals and liberal party men, the spokesmen of the labor unions, the Christians with an active social concern, and the political leftists. One of their goals, universal adult (over twenty-five) male suffrage, was attained in 1925, which at one stroke increased the voter rolls from 3 to 14 million.

One of the most outstanding of the liberal party politicians was Ozaki Yukio (1859–1954). It was he who, as mayor of Tokyo, presented Washington, D.C., with the famous cherry trees. His career as a national politician began in association with Okuma. In 1898 he was forced to resign from the cabinet on account of a speech in which he mentioned republicanism in Japan. He touched again on the delicate subject of the emperor's position when he led the Seiyukai party opposition to Premier Katsura in the Diet in 1912–1913. He was working on behalf of a strongly supported movement for a democratic Japan, timed to coincide with the accession of the Emperor Showa. Katsura, to gain time for party maneuvering, had used the weapon of an imperial rescript to prorogue the Diet for fifteen days, and Ozaki challenged him in a famous speech which contained the words: ". . . they hide themselves behind the Throne, and shoot at their political enemies from their secure ambush." Ozaki was protected by his own sincerity, for no one ever doubted his personal loyalty to the emperor, and he lived to a ripe old age. But in these actions he laid his finger upon the central question of Japanese history, from the times of the Fujiwara through the shogunate to the Meiji oligarchs and the party politicians, namely, "Who really speaks for the emperor?" The main point of Ozaki's life was made when some power to affect national decisions was given to all the men of Japan in 1925.

Among the radical Christian leaders were Suzuki Bunji, Kagawa To-

Calligraphy.

1940 poem by Kagawa Toyohiko, representing the idealistic hopes of many Japanese for the peaceful development of
Manchukuo. (Translation: "As I visit, after a long interval, the northern land of
Manchuria, in the smiling faces of my
friends the sun too smiles for me.")

*From the author's collection. Photography by
Keith Scott Morton*

yohiko, and Abe Isoo. Suzuki, an attorney, founded a labor organization on
a national scale, and Abe was on the faculty of Waseda University. The most
colorful and many-sided personality of the three was Kagawa. Illegitimate son
of a cabinet minister and a geisha girl, he became a Christian pastor and
worked in the slums of Kobe, living for a time in a room six feet square. Socialist thought was introduced into Japan mainly by Christian leaders, and
Kagawa aided Suzuki in his labor union work. Kagawa began writing, and his
novels became bestsellers. He was offered a high government post, but felt
he could serve his country better in the freedom of the pastorate. He was active in rural cooperatives and founded a chain of sanatoria for the large number of workers who contracted tuberculosis in the unsanitary conditions of
the factories. (The law fixing eleven hours as the maximum working day for
girls in the cotton mills was not put into force until 1916.) In spite of poor
health he undertook arduous preaching and lecture tours, and found time to
establish and edit the *Kingdom of God Newspaper*. His writings included
philosophical works as well as popular novels with a social theme. He was imprisoned in 1921 for his part in a strike of Kobe workers and was again placed
under house arrest by the military near the end of his life, this time for attempts to promote reconciliation with the Chinese during World War II. But
when the High Command became alarmed at the excesses committed by
Japanese rank and file in the rape of Nanking in 1937, it was Kagawa they
called upon to visit the troops and speak to the men about self-discipline. Although Kagawa was clearly exceptional, his life indicates the reasons why the
ideas of Christianity have been influential in modern Japan to an extent far
greater than would be expected from the membership of the Christian
churches, today less than 1 percent of the population.

The more pacific and liberal feeling among Japanese statesmen during this era was an aid to the settlement of East Asian affairs which emerged from the Washington Conference of 1921–1922. In succession to the Anglo-Japanese Alliance, which had been renewed in 1911 but was now terminated, Great Britain, France, Japan, and the United States entered into a Four Power Pact to respect one anothers' rights in the Pacific area and to consult in the event of a crisis. Further, a critical clause was acceptance of a limitation on capital ships in the ratio of 5 : 5 : 3 for Great Britain, the United States, and Japan, and 1.67 each for France and Italy. Accompanying this were limitations on the tonnage of warships and the caliber of guns, and a guarantee that no new naval bases would be constructed nearer to Japan than Singapore or Hawaii. Japan had wanted the ratio of ships to be 10 : 10 : 7, but even with the slightly lower ratio, the inclusion of the naval bases clause and the fact that Japan needed to deploy her naval strength only in the Pacific Ocean gave her predominance in a large area and control of the China coast. Japan then agreed to withdraw both from Shantung in China, returning the port of Tsingtao, and from Siberia, as already mentioned. A Nine Power Treaty was also signed in 1922 in favor of the Open Door policy and the territorial integrity and administrative independence of China. In all these arrangements, however, no provision was made for adequate enforcement of the agreements.

A major disaster overtook Japan in 1923 when an earthquake of extreme severity and subsequent fires destroyed half of Tokyo and almost all of Yokohama. The catastrophe continued for three days. Gaping cracks opened in the ground and swallowed up people. Fires raged out of control through acres of wooden houses. A hundred thousand lives were lost, and the damage was incalculable. The ground was cleared for a new city, and when Tokyo was rebuilt, its center was transformed by the erection of modern steel and concrete office buildings, theaters, and stores, a pattern soon followed by other cities.

The era of the twenties also saw changes in the social fashions and modes of living. Women attained a new independence as secretaries and office workers. Family living began to change as fathers became less autocratic and husbands more understanding. Some were even prepared to treat their wives as their equals. There was golf and skiing for the rich and baseball for everyone. The books of all countries were available in translation in greater profusion than ever, and the Japanese became the greatest newspaper-reading public in the world. Symphony orchestras and Western classical music enjoyed a great vogue, while films, jazz, and cafés (really taverns) catered to the tastes of the *moga* ("modern girl") and *mobo* ("modern boy").

These gilded youths were too much for the conservative farmers and the earnestly patriotic young army officers. To many Japanese the behavior of the young people was a sign of the decadence which crept in when the old authoritarian ways were given up in favor of liberalism and internationalism. They felt that the party politicians with their newfangled ideas were not fit to advise the emperor. Who could do this better than the army? It was the repository of the ancient *samurai* virtues, and it alone maintained in purity the pristine loyalty to the person of the emperor and to *yamato-damashii*, "the spirit of Old Japan."

Such a vast and sudden change as that dividing the militaristic 1930s from the liberal 1920s has to be accounted for. It is appropriate to begin with such vague and emotional reasons as those just mentioned, for the rise of militarism in Japan was accompanied, as it has been elsewhere, with unreasoning elements of feeling and prejudice, leading ultimately to mass hysteria. The background of family and circumstance among the younger officers and the common soldiers was a further factor in the strong drive behind the increasing power of the military. The young officers tended to be the sons of officers, of small landowners, or of peasant farmers. They began a rigorous military training with little intellectual content at the age of fourteen and had no understanding of the principles of democracy or representative government, which was something entirely new to Japan. The rank and file from peasant homes, unlike the city youth, were perfectly willing to be conscripted. The army gave them not only a better life physically than they had ever known but also an emotional security under authority more comforting than Dostoevski's Grand Inquisitor could offer. As peasants they were nobodies; as soldiers of the divine emperor, directly descended from the Sun Goddess, they felt a mysterious personal dignity. To lay down their lives for their country was not hardship but glory. Not since ancient Rome had so many at one time felt such powerful truth in the sentence *Dulce et decorum est pro patria mori* ("It is sweet and fitting to die for your country"). Everything in their elementary schooling and their military training served to reinforce this motivation. The higher officers were of the same mind but for different reasons. They read the writing on the wall of liberal policy, if it were allowed to continue. In 1925 the army strength had been reduced by a total of four out of twenty-one divisions.

The army seemed to be gaining influence with the appointment of General Baron Tanaka Giichi as premier in 1927. However, he chose an unwise China policy of trying to stop the northern advance of Jiang Jieshi (Chiang Kai-shek) and the Nationalist government and was compelled to abandon the attempt. Then some extremist Japanese officers in Manchuria caused him acute embarrassment. They murdered the warlord Zhang Zuolin (Chang Tso-lin) by blowing up his train, with the idea that his son, the Young Marshal, Zhang Xueliang (Chang Hsüeh-liang), would be more amenable to Japanese aims in Manchuria. Tanaka demanded that they be disciplined, but the High Command ignored his demand, and this loss of face compelled him to resign.

Secret societies of an ultranationalist type were becoming increasingly active. The best known was the Black Dragon Society, called after the Chinese name for the Amur River. The name indicated an emphasis on Manchuria, and one of the society's avowed objects was to incite trouble among the Chinese so that the Japanese Army would have an excuse to come in and restore law and order. Such societies were successful in fostering among the more hotheaded officers the idea of Japan's manifest destiny to rule in Asia and the notion that the army, as the direct servant of the emperor, entrusted with carrying out his will, had a right to act independently of the civilian government.

Baron Tanaka was succeeded as premier in 1929 by Hamaguchi Osachi of the Minseito party. The London Naval Treaty, a sequel to the Washington Conference and concerned with limiting cruiser strength, was signed in 1930. Hamaguchi's willingness to make concessions in regard to the Japanese Navy was considered reprehensible by the hawks. Worse still, the world depression hit Japan during his period of office. He had already been pursuing a deflationary money policy and had returned Japan to the gold standard. This magnified the devastating effect of deflation caused by the depression. Hamaguchi was shot in a Tokyo railway station and died soon afterward. His successor, Inukai Tsuyoshi, was assassinated in 1932 in a coup organized by a young officer group. The days of the liberals were at an end, and "government by assassination" had taken their place.

Japan in the years 1929 to 1932 was beset by problems, and the military extremists felt that desperate remedies were called for. The depression was a worldwide phenomenon, but it had certain repercussions in Japan which were peculiar to that country. Exports declined by 50 percent in the two years following 1929. The greatest suffering fell on the farmers and peasants, with silk cocoon prices dropping 65 percent in one year, 1929–1930. The real incomes of industrial workers fell from an index of 100 in 1926 to 69 in 1931; but the corresponding figures for rural incomes went from 100 to 33. Peasants had to eat the bark of trees and sell their daughters to city brothels. The rage of the people was directed against the *zaibatsu*, the "large business interests," identified with the landlords in the popular mind. The suffering of the farm families was felt keenly by the army officers, many of whom came from a rural background. The army men were totally opposed to that cooperation with the international economic order which seemed inevitable to the party politicians and the businessmen, but which to the young officer group appeared as the malign source of the depression and all its evils that had swept over its country.

They had the idea that the army, known for its loyalty and honor, could devote itself selflessly to carving out on the Asian continent an empire that would be independent of the rest of the world and that would ensure a stable livelihood to the farmers and industrial workers of Japan. Thus the turbulent events of recent years seemed to these patriotic idealists to have given unmistakable signs that they were meant to be the saviors of their country. All the necessary elements were present. The mystique was supplied by their sense of being empowered to carry out the emperor's will; the external enemies were the decadent democracies (the Japanese, always sensitive to world trends, had noted that Mussolini had made good his criticism of democracy by the march on Rome in 1922 and his seizure of total power in 1924); the internal enemies frustrating Japan's search for its destiny were the business

interests and the venal politicians; and the means at hand were ﹍
of violence already so successful against Zhang Zuolin (Chang Tsu﹍
their own high government officials. There were few theoretical restraints
upon direct strong-arm methods for men who had never been trained to consider the military power as subordinate to the civilian government.

Premier Inukai made prompt moves to overcome the effects of the depression. He took Japan off the gold standard again. Exports rose sharply,
and Japan began to recover more quickly than any other industrial country;
but an irreversible trend toward militarism had already set in. The Fates had
begun to spin their threads.

14

MANCHUKUO, THE CHINA WAR, AND WORLD WAR II

1931–1945

The crack corps of the Japanese Army, the Kwantung Army in Manchuria, was growing impatient. The Nationalist Government of China was becoming stronger, and the day of the warlords who could be bought or intimidated was rapidly passing. Two Kwantung Army officers of colonel rank, Itagaki and Ishiwara, decided it was time to strike. They had the support of the commanding general in Manchuria, but his chief of staff wanted to know the attitude of the Tokyo General Staff. A Major General Tatekawa was sent with a letter forbidding any provocative action; but then some curious things happened. He cabled to say he was coming, and the colonels at the other end advanced their timetable. Tatekawa did not fly but took the train through Korea, and on arriving in Mukden (Shenyang) on the evening of September 18, 1931, he went straight to a geisha house and made no effort to deliver the letter. That night a bomb exploded on the railway line just north of Mukden.

Colonel Itagaki ordered his troops to attack the Chinese forces in the city. The arsenal, airfield, and radio station were captured before dawn. By September 21 the army had taken Kirin in the northeast and was fanning out all over Manchuria, far beyond the railway zone where alone they had jurisdiction. The embarrassed government in Tokyo was explaining, first, that the troops had acted in self-defense and, second, that they were returning to the railway zone. But there was never any question of their retreating; they had the war minister's support. It was later established that the whole incident, including the bomb, had been deliberately staged.

The ostensible reason for these moves was the suppression of "banditry." A certain amount of actual banditry, it is true, was endemic in the Manchurian countryside, as Owen Lattimore's studies have shown—poor farmers turning to violent means of livelihood in seasons of crop failure. The millet stalks growing five to eight feet tall provide excellent cover and make surprise attacks by bands of desperate men relatively easy. But this type of unrest posed little threat to the industrial and transport operations of the South Manchurian Railway. The Japanese were patently seeking to extend their control over the whole country, and by early 1932 this objective was attained. They then felt themselves in a position to set up the puppet state of Manchukuo, securing the services of the last Ching emperor of China, Henry Pu Yi, as ruler, and seeking to maintain the fiction that this was the will of the "Manchu" people. (The Manchus had, in fact, merged with the Chinese and had almost ceased to exist as a separate race.) In September 1932 Manchukuo was recognized by the government of Japan. The pattern of government throughout the new state was simple and uniform. The number one positions, from prime minister to local mayor, were held by Chinese, but they acted merely as rubber stamps. The real power was held by their assistants in the number two position, who were invariably Japanese. The true character of the regime was indicated by the fact that His Imperial Majesty's ambassador to the new court at Xinjing "New Capital," formerly Changchun, was coincidentally the general commanding the Kwantung Army.

The Nationalist Government of China appealed this illegal seizure, and the League of Nations sent out the Lytton Commission under Lord Lytton of the United Kingdom to investigate. On the evidence of the facts and on information secured from patriotic Chinese intellectuals and others in Manchuria, it was made clear that the state of Manchukuo had not been set up by the will of its inhabitants. Upon the presentation of the commission's report in September 1932, Japan was condemned by the League of Nations for its actions in Manchuria. Japan replied by walking out of the meetings and leaving the League; but no sanctions were applied by the other member nations. The scene of the affair seemed remote from the centers of Western power, but the weakness of the League of Nations and its great-power member states was to have disastrous consequences. There is little doubt that Mussolini in his adventures in Ethiopia (1935) and Hitler in his occupation of the Ruhr and subsequent mounting acts of aggression looked upon Manchuria as a test case which failed to produce anything beyond harmless verbal condemnation. But it was not only the League which was powerless; the Japanese Foreign Ministry and civilian members of the government were able to do little to stem the advance of the fire-eaters among the military. They did not even know of the plans leading up to the Manchurian Incident until it was a *fait accompli*.

Manchukuo did not become a colony of Japan in the sense of attracting farmers to settle on the land. Neither the climate nor the crops were of a type with which the Japanese were familiar. But the new territory was an ideal proving ground for the new imperialism of the army. Here there was space for maneuvers and training far away from the eyes of the Japanese people and the remaining liberals in the government. There were ample natural resources which could be used as incentives and rewards for exploitation by new industrial firms. (The old established *zaibatsu* concerns were neither inclined nor encouraged to take part.) Above all a strong base on the mainland could be built up from which the Kwantung Army could move against North China when the moment was ripe.

The military leaders, however, were not by any means prepared to confine their activities to military matters. Phobias concerning "dangerous thoughts" multiplied, and intellectual leaders among the Chinese came under increasing attack. Prominent persons in the Christian churches who had contacts with foreigners, professional men such as doctors and others whose connections with the Chinese nationalists were close, all found themselves under increasing suspicion. Certain intellectuals who had given evidence before the Lytton Commission were arrested in the small hours of the morning, imprisoned by the *kempeitai*, the dreaded "military police," and subjected to refined torture, including a new electric shock treatment, as well as the old water torture, which involves almost drowning the victim and then bringing him around for further questioning. Many Chinese suffered severely, and all Chinese felt humiliated by the contempt in which they were held by the Japanese military and police. Revelation of these facts later caused consternation among liberal and pacific Japanese at home, who could scarcely bring themselves to believe that their countrymen had acted in this brutal fashion.

It was comparatively easy for the military to carry through at home a process of "spiritual mobilization," for in Japan the people were disciplined and dedicated to the service of emperor and country. But similar attempts in Manchukuo met with little success. The Chinese made an outward surrender to *force majeure*, but inwardly they were not convinced that it was Japan's destiny to unite all countries in a "Greater East Asia Co-Prosperity Sphere." The Japanese military authorities, attempting to promote this line of thought, compelled all school authorities, both in public and in private or mission schools, to conduct the children to worship, first, at the Confucian temples in an artificial bid for a new "Manchu" nationalism and, in a later phase, to the Shinto shrines as a sign of loyalty to the emperor of Japan, to whom, understandably, the Chinese felt no loyalty whatsoever.

More sinister was the widespread use of narcotics, not merely the traditional smoking of opium but the increasing addiction to the more deadly heroin and morphine. Keepers of opium dens were afraid of the consequences of having dead men found on their premises, and so used to get rid of the moribund addicts by giving other addicts a free shot of heroin as a reward for carrying out the dying and leaving them on the garbage heaps of the city of Mukden. After the 20 degrees below zero cold of the winter night such men were, of course, corpses by the next morning. Little attempt was made by the Japanese authorities to halt this traffic, and this contrasted with the considerable efforts of the Chinese Nationalists toward stringent control of the drug market, which had flourished in the warlord era. Some Chinese in Manchuria charged the Japanese military with the deliberate distribution and sale of narcotics in Manchukuo in the 1930s in order to corrupt and weaken the morale of the people. It would be hard to substantiate this charge; but it is certain that drugs were relatively inexpensive and very easy to obtain, even in remote villages in the countryside. Over-the-counter sales were made to anyone without question.

Meanwhile, Manchuria was being developed industrially, and many technical improvements were being introduced. At Fushun the large, open-surface coal mine was expanded and a power station established at the pithead for the cheap distribution of electric power over a wide area of South Manchuria. At Anshan on the Mukden-Dairen section of the South Manchuria Railway the iron and steel works set up by the Russians made considerable increases in production. The South Manchuria Railway was the hub and center of technical improvements in many fields; indeed it constituted a small empire in itself. The president of this remarkable institution was Matsuoka Yosuke, who later became Japanese foreign minister. The railway in the mid-1930s ran a stainless steel diesel-powered train daily as a superexpress from the capital at Xinjing to the port of Dairen. It was scheduled with arrival and departure times printed in half-minutes on official timetables, but this utopian practice had later to be abandoned. The hospital maintained by the South Manchuria Railway in Mukden was conducted on modern lines and produced competent doctors from its affiliated medical school.

A steady transformation had been taking place in the public health situation in Manchuria ever since the disastrous bubonic plague of the early years of the twentieth century. The pioneer agent in this transformation was the Christie Memorial Hospital and Medical College operated jointly by missionaries from Scotland, Ireland, and Denmark. Men and women graduates from this college in the fields of medicine, nursing, and pharmacy staffed hospitals and set up practices all over Manchuria and gradually raised standards of hygiene, diagnosis, and treatment both in towns and in remote rural districts. After the foundation of the state of Manchukuo the college was severely restricted and downgraded because of its international contacts. Japanese medical efforts, however, hastened the adoption of modern methods of public health control throughout the country.

Japan in its policy, though not always in the sentiments of its people, continued to move toward the right. Marxism, which since World War I had made an increasing appeal to intellectuals, was ruthlessly suppressed. Some 3,000 Socialists, Communists, and labor organizers were arrested in 1932 and 1933. Many of them were imprisoned and a few tortured to death. Direct action and violence were increasingly used, accepted, and even condoned as expressions of political opinion. A financier, Inoue, and Baron Dan, chief executive of the Mitsui firm, were assassinated early in 1932, as was Premier Inukai himself some months later. The subsequent trials of the army and civilian extremists responsible for these outrages were used as platforms for the statement of their views, and the sentences passed were often absurdly light. It was felt that their patriotism, "sincerity," and "pure motives" justified their acts of terrorism. The army itself suffered from faction, one of the main divisions being between those who had attended the War College and those who had been thwarted in this prestige-carrying ambition. General Nagata Tetsuzan was responsible in 1934 for the dismissal of an extremist general. An officer of lieutenant-colonel rank simply walked into Nagata's office and killed him with his sword. At the trial he said he was only sorry he had not been able to accomplish the slaughter with one stroke. The witch hunt extended into academic circles, the most celebrated case being that of Professor Minobe Tatsukichi of Tokyo University. This distinguished professor was ousted from his job and all of his works banned, though they had been standard texts for years, because, in his books, he had referred to the emperor as an "organ of the government" instead of in more laudatory and exclusive terms.

The army did not have matters all its own way. Elections, particularly that of 1937, returned in large numbers liberal members and those opposed to the actions of the army. The navy was less extreme, and army activists were forced to accept two moderate premiers who were admirals, Saito Makoto and Okada Keisuke, for the years between 1932 and 1936. The method the army used to control the government went back to the Meiji Constitution and its Prussian model, with the emperor's position as head of the armed services clearly marked out. The result was that the General Staff was placed directly under the emperor, and the army minister became directly responsible to the emperor as well as having a place in the cabinet which was chaired by the premier. The service ministers' direct responsibility to the emperor and their right of access to him gave them a measure of control over the cabinet and the civilian ministers which was impossible, for instance, in Great Britain, where the cabinet functioned as a body under the prime minister and was responsible as a whole to Parliament. In 1936 the rule that the service ministers had to be serving officers on the active list was revived. This in turn placed these ministers under the control of army and navy opinion, and made it impossible in effect for anyone to hold those officers who did not enjoy the confidence of the main body of the officers. Since the extremist faction was always invoking the name of the emperor, they made it difficult for anyone to oppose their choices for the highest posts. If a civilian premier was unacceptable to the dominant forces in the army, the nomination of an officer to the post of army minister was delayed and thus the formation of the cabinet could be hung up indefinitely. At the same time and as a result of these processes, the Diet was becoming less and less effective. Thus, no matter what the outcome of the elections, the drift to the right continued.

The climax of direct action came with the Tokyo Revolt of February 1936. Not content with the great measure of control the army had already attained and desiring the elimination of all opposition to military policy, some junior officers of the First Division with 1,400 troops staged a coup in the capital itself. They assassinated certain cabinet ministers and members of the Imperial Household Ministry, and occupied some government buildings in the center of the city, including the Diet and the Army Ministry. The navy and other important groups were completely opposed to the coup. The only surviving Elder Statesman, Saionji, supported the emperor in a firm stand, and the men who had led the coup were adjudged rebels. Troops were called in from other commands, and the revolt was crushed. This time there was no propaganda performance but a prompt trial and execution of thirteen of the leaders.

Japan signed the Anti-Comintern Pact with Germany in December 1936, and this was a signal that the army considered Russia a definite threat to Japanese security. Nevertheless in 1937 the army, with Manchuria now secured, embarked on a venture into China proper. This was the next step in the outline of conquest contained in the Tanaka Memorial—Manchuria, China, Southeast Asia, Australia, India. This document reflected the thinking of army imperialists, even though it is now thought not to have been a genuine state document of the government of Baron Tanaka, premier in 1927. The aim in 1937 was to lop off China's five northern provinces, in the sense of rendering them neutral and outside the control of the Chinese Nationalist Government, and thus more open to Japanese commercial penetration. Preparations with this end in view had been going on for some time. Japanese railway police were exercising controls over the movements of persons and freight beyond the Manchurian border into North China as far as Tianjin and Beijing in the supposed interests of security. Trade was extended, and capital invested in North China by Japanese industrial firms with the encouragement of the army. The Nationalist Government of China, involved in the enormous problems of modernization and warlord control and committed to a long-continued course of resistance against the Chinese Communists, felt powerless to prevent these stage-by-stage encroachments by Japan. Finally in July 1937 the Japanese forces mounted maneuvers in the Beijing area, and a clash with the Chinese garrison troops took place at the Marco Polo Bridge.

This clash has been compared to the Manchurian Incident, but it was probably not planned, at least not at high level, for the authorities hoped to secure North China without armed conflict. Their calculations proved wrong, and in the end fatal. Once committed, the Japanese brought in heavy reinforcements; but the Chinese commander in Beijing resisted strongly, even though his military resources were quite inadequate. The Japanese had moved also in Shanghai, but there too encountered spirited resistance. The limited war, if war it had to be, in which the Japanese High Command had hoped for a quick victory, also proved illusory; and both sides settled down to a long struggle. Thus the real beginning of World War II was not in 1941 when the attack on Pearl Harbor brought America decisively into the war, nor in 1939 when Britain and France resisted Hitler, but in 1937 when China decided she would not submit tamely to Japanese aggression.

It was ironic that Jiang Jieshi's (Chiang Kai-shek's) foreign military advisers were Prussian officers from the country allied with the enemy, Japan. These men served China well, advocating the strategy that Jiang followed, that of trading the vast space of China for time, in which it was hoped allies would come to China's aid. Pitched battles with Japan's superior forces were avoided, and a strategic withdrawal gradually executed behind the mountain barriers of Sichuan. During this retreat extraordinary efforts were made to salvage both material and labor. Textile factories and arsenals in Shanghai and other coast cities were dismantled and the machinery transported inland in carts, on riverboats, and on the backs of coolies in an unending chain. Students and professors picked up books and laboratory equipment and set up their universities again in temporary quarters a thousand miles away.

The Japanese were never able to take possession of the country as a whole. They could bomb but could not penetrate with ground forces the mountain provinces of the southwest in sufficient strength to force a decision; but they overran the main part of the country, holding all the principal cities and lines of communication. For Japan as well as China it was a costly war. Chinese guerrilla forces, organized mainly by the Communists operating out of Yenan in the northwest, constantly attacked and overcame small, isolated garrisons of Japanese, disrupted transport, and succeeded in supplying themselves with trucks, arms, ammunition, and even uniforms from the small enemy units they had defeated. In particular, the Communists succeeded in organizing resistance and intelligence systems among the peasants of China, thus gaining experience in community organization and control at the grass-roots level which was to prove invaluable to the Communist cause at the end of the war.

With American and British aid reaching free China in small but significant quantities, first by the Burma Road and, when it was closed, by airlift from India "over the hump" of impassable mountains, China was able to hold out and a stalemate was produced.

Once the China campaign was launched in 1937, the Japanese Army obtained full national support and was able to obtain almost any arrangements it wished. The National Mobilization Law of November 1938 gave the government wide authority in price and wage control, a plan for national registration and compulsory savings, direction of materials and labor, and the government operation of some industries. A Manchurian Industrial Development Corporation with government capital was set up in 1938, and additional supplies of coal, iron, and chemicals were obtained through the North China Development Corporation established two years later. The political parties were swallowed up in 1940 in a type of wartime coalition known as the Imperial Rule Assistance Association. In the same year even the cabinet became almost a nonentity, for key decisions were now to be made by a Liaison Conference attended by the premier, war and navy ministers, foreign minister, and service chiefs of staff. Other ministers could attend only by invitation.

In its efforts to find some way out of the stalemate position in the China War, the Japanese government at length prevailed on a Chinese politician of sufficient stature to head a puppet government in Nanking. Wang Ching-wei agreed to fill this role in 1940, but this move did not have the effect Japan desired. There was no diminution of China's will to resist, and the specter of Russia still loomed at Japan's back. There was a group of leaders in Tokyo who felt that accommodation with Britain and America offered the best counterweight to the Russian threat. Matsuoka Yosuke, however, now foreign minister in the cabinet of Premier Konoe Fumimaro, was completely convinced that Germany would be the ultimate victor in Europe. He had evidence in plenty to support his case in the year 1940. May 10 to June 4 had seen the phenomenal success of the German blitzkrieg in the Netherlands, Belgium, and France, culminating in the Allied evacuation from Dunkirk. The air Battle of Britain was then joined and lasted from August to November 1940. The peak came in September, when Goering and the Luftwaffe failed by a very narrow margin to break the power of the Royal Air Force, and thus could not clear the way for an invasion of the British Isles, which would probably have finished the war. The impetuous Matsuoka did not wait quite long enough; he had Japan sign the Tripartite Pact with Italy and Germany in the same month of September 1940. In November, when the Battle of Britain was decided in Britain's favor, his colleagues would probably not have allowed him to sign.

In April 1941 a neutrality agreement between Japan and Russia was signed—a triumph for Matsuoka—and Japan felt it could breathe again. It was not to be for long. In June of the same year Hitler suddenly turned to attack Russia without giving warning to Japan. The Japanese were now faced with the choice of honoring the Tripartite Pact with Germany or the more recent neutrality agreement with Russia. Memories of a 1939 summer war with Russia in the Nomonhan area of Outer Mongolia were still fresh in their minds. The superiority of the Russian tanks had become clearly evident before the affair was settled by an armistice. They decided to stick with the Russian agreement. In a rearrangement of the cabinet, the pro-German Matsuoka was dropped as foreign minister.

The economic situation was now causing the Japanese leaders some anxiety. They had been stockpiling throughout the China War, but supplies of oil in particular were urgently needed. The United States in 1940 banned exports to Japan of certain strategic materials, first scrap iron, then steel, and finally oil. Indeed it was surprising that the United States allowed exports of these items to go on as long as it did. A sour joke among the New York GIs in bombing raids later on was, "Well, here comes the Third Avenue El [elevated railroad that was demolished] back at us." In order to secure supplies of oil, the Japanese sent two missions to the Dutch in Indonesia; but the Dutch temporized and agreed only to the delivery of small amounts. In spite of the urgency of the situation the Japanese Navy counseled caution. It was not prepared to risk hostilities with the Netherlands, Great Britain, and the United States to take the oil by force. Admiral Nomura Kichisaburo was therefore sent to the United States to negotiate. But the army was impatient and confident. A decision was taken to invade Southeast Asia in July 1941, and Vichy France was forced to agree. As soon as troops were sent in, the United States froze all Japanese assets and trade between the two countries came to a standstill.

Tension now increased in Japan between the war party and those favoring negotiation, while Premier Konoe tried to hold the balance between the two. It was decided to begin preparations in September for eventual war against the United States, but meanwhile the Nomura talks in Washington were to go on. America was well aware that an explosion might occur at any time. Both American and British nationals in Japan had received warnings from their respective governments to evacuate, the first at the end of 1940, another in the spring of 1941, and a final peremptory warning in September of that year. Konoe was forced to resign, and General Tojo ("Razor") Hideki became premier on October 17. Tojo, a military man first and last, at once began general mobilization and the planning of war strategy. American terms now proposed in the Nomura talks were too stringent for Japan—nothing less than withdrawal of all Japanese troops from Indochina, China, and Manchuria. On December 1 an Imperial Council again voted to go to war with the United States if it should prove necessary. President Roosevelt made a last appeal to the emperor, but it never reached him. The attack on Pearl Harbor by Japanese Navy planes took place early on Sunday morning, December 7. In view of all the diplomatic activity which had preceded it, the achievement of complete and deadly surprise by the Japanese is the more amazing. But Nomura himself was informed of what his government had done only when he returned to the Japanese Embassy in Washington after a session with Secretary of State Cordell Hull, who was outraged by what he thought was colossal duplicity.

The Japanese Navy had conducted intensive practice for the Pearl Harbor raid in Kagoshima Bay, and the operation from their point of view was a brilliant success, the more so as the United States Navy paid no heed to the radar warnings of approaching planes. Seven battleships, numerous other vessels, and about half the United States aircraft on Hawaii were destroyed or so seriously damaged as to be useless. Simultaneous attacks were delivered on the Philippines, Hong Kong, and Malaya. In the Philippines American aircraft were caught on the ground, all neatly lined up, and off Singapore the British battleship *Prince of Wales* and battle cruiser *Repulse* were steaming out of range of air cover and were ignominiously sunk.

Free for the time being of the threat of American naval power, the Japanese moved with speed over the whole Pacific area. Hong Kong fell on Christmas Day and Manila on January 2, 1942, Bataan holding out till April and Corregidor till May. The defense of Singapore was all oriented toward the sea, as the jungle to the rear was supposed to be safe and impenetrable. But the Japanese had been training troops in the jungles of Thailand, and Singapore was captured from the landward side on February 15. The Dutch East Indies fell in early March and Burma by the end of April. Within six months of the initial attack Japan was making serious preparations to advance against Australia. Her lines of communication were now, however, very far extended, and the American buildup for a counteroffensive was under way.

The naval Battle of the Coral Sea was approximately a draw, but its effect was to call a halt to any attack on Australia. The Battle of Midway a month later in June 1942 gave an advantage to the United States Navy, for it had had warning of the attack and was able to destroy four Japanese aircraft carriers, which seriously affected the key factor of air power. It is said that the Japanese Navy was so humiliated by the defeat at Midway, which actually proved a turning point, that they did not inform Premier Tojo of the outcome until a month after the event. On land New Guinea was gradually recaptured by Allied forces; and Guadalcanal, after bitter and prolonged fighting, was regained in February 1943.

The economy in Japan had been performing prodigies of production. The engineering firms were able to meet their own needs in the domestic manufacture of machine tools before the war started in 1941. By decentralizing production in small workshops, in a typical Japanese pattern, and by working a fifteen-hour day, the new aircraft industry was able in the course of the war to manufacture 62,400 aircraft. But raw materials were growing scarce. The Greater East Asia Co-Prosperity Sphere—Asia for the Asians under Japanese leadership—was strong in propaganda appeal but often short in performance, as the Southeast Asian inhabitants and others found that the profits accrued to Japan and that the Japanese in running affairs were tactless and overbearing. Supplies of oil, rubber, tin, and other vital war materials did not flow back to Japan in the quantities required. Moreover, American submarine strength was growing, in spite of the urgent demands of the European theater of war, and Japanese merchant marine losses were mounting. (By the end of the war Japan had suffered the loss of over 75 percent of her shipping; some estimates go as high as 90 percent.) In fact the early estimates of the Japanese naval strategists were proving approximately correct. They had informed the government at the beginning that the war could be won by a quick campaign, but they could not guarantee to maintain the effort after eighteen months.

One permanent result of the rapid and decisive Japanese victories in the early stages of the war was that the myth of white supremacy was forever exploded. The Japanese treated the defeated Dutch, British, and American prisoners with intentional contempt and callous cruelty in front of the native inhabitants of the whole Pacific area, in Indonesia, in Thailand, in Malaya, on the so-called Railway of Death ("Bridge over the River Kwai"), in Hong Kong, in the Philippines, and elsewhere. After this and after three years of intensive anticolonial propaganda, it was well-nigh impossible for the colonial powers to reassert their authority in these regions, or anywhere in the world, at the conclusion of the hostilities.

By 1943 the pressure on Japan was becoming gradually more intense. Overall strategy was not as effectively coordinated between Japan and Germany as it was between Britain, the Dominions and other Allies, and the United States. The Chinese maintained pressure on the mainland. The unorthodox British General Orde Wingate and his successors penetrated Japanese lines in Burma with small but effective forces of Chindits, as the specially trained jungle troops were called. Above all, American forces pressed a

relentless campaign of island hopping, capturing certain predetermined islands and ignoring others, which then become isolated and unimportant. After months of fighting, Saipan in the Marianas was reached in July 1944, and
from there the islands of Japan were within bombing range. Industrial plants,
especially in Tokyo and Nagoya, were severely bombed, for Japanese air defense was quite inadequate to protect them. The Tokaido main railway line
was constantly disrupted and constantly repaired; but the lack of alternative
rail routes was a serious handicap to war production. When Okinawa was captured in June 1945 after appalling losses on both sides, the bombing became
much more intense, and almost all the main cities of Japan were heavily damaged by fire bombs. As the enemy closed in on Japan, resistance was fanati-
cally brave. Few Japanese prisoners were taken throughout the entire war. Pilots flew planes to destruction, aiming their bomb or torpedo loads directly
at the target and perishing in the explosion. They were named *kamikaze*
("wind of the gods") pilots, after the typhoon that had destroyed the Mongol invaders in the thirteenth century.

The Casablanca Conference of the Allies had laid down unconditional
surrender as the aim in the defeat of both Germany and Japan. At the Yalta
Conference of February 1945 Stalin agreed to enter the war against Japan
three months after Germany had been defeated. In return Russia was to be
granted the southern half of Sakhalin and the lease of the Port Arthur naval
base in Manchuria, approximately what Russia had had to give up at the
Treaty of Portsmouth in 1905. The Allies at this point were reckoning on
having to fight yard by yard through the Japanese islands and thought they
would require Russia's help.

Japan attempted to secure better terms than unconditional surrender
through the good offices of Russia. Tojo had resigned as premier in July 1944;
and his successor, General Koiso Kuniaki, in the next April to be succeeded
in turn by Suzuki Kantaro, was less intransigent and more ready to make
peace on any terms. But the Allies had no reason to modify their demands
and expressed themselves unequivocally at the Potsdam Conference of July
1945 as determined to do away with the "irresponsible militarism" by which
the people of Japan had been misled. With knowledge of the new and deadly
weapon in their hands, the Allies conveyed their answer to the Japanese over-
tures through Russia: unconditional surrender or "prompt and utter destruction." They gave the Japanese ten days and then dropped the first atom
bomb on Hiroshima, the southern Army Headquarters, on August 6. Russia entered the war on August 8, and the second bomb was dropped on Nagasaki, a major port, on August 9. Although the targets had some military
importance, the two bombs were dropped with the idea of breaking the civilian will to fight and thus, it was hoped, saving the casualties of a long battle
in Japan itself.

The Kwantung Army in Manchuria had been depleted to reinforce other
areas and could not resist the Russian advance. Units of the Russian Navy attacked Sakhalin and the Kuriles.

On August 10 Emperor Hirohito was asked by the cabinet, which was deadlocked on the question of surrender, to give his counsel. He opted for surrender, and this was offered to the Allies "provided the Emperor's status is preserved." The Allies would entertain no conditions whatsoever, so, on a second intervention of the emperor, a complete capitulation was made. On August 15 the emperor made a broadcast speech announcing the surrender to the whole of his people, saying they must "endure the unendurable" and bidding them work together for reconstruction. The people and the area commanders accepted the situation, for further resistance was evidently hopeless. There was a small mutiny among some military leaders who broke into the palace and attempted, unsuccessfully, to steal the recording of the emperor's speech to prevent its being broadcast. The war minister committed suicide. Prince Higashikuni was appointed premier in order, by the imperial prestige, to secure order and obedience, and on September 2 the instrument of surrender was signed in due form on the deck of the flagship, the U.S.S. *Missouri*, in Tokyo Bay.

15

POSTWAR JAPAN

The wisdom of the decision to use the atomic bomb has been long debated. Dropping the bomb probably did shorten the war; nevertheless Asians cannot forget that this new and frightful weapon of destruction was loosed upon them by the Christian West. Conventional weapons since the beginning of time, from the stone ax through the spear and sword to the rifle, had killed men of one generation only. Mysterious horrors were now added by the fact that the atomic bomb had the power not only to destroy large numbers instantly but also to affect future generations through the damage caused to the human reproductive system by fallout. After the war the mayor of Nagasaki made clear the fact, attested elsewhere also, that the Japanese population were shocked and dazed by the bomb, but less resentful against America than might have been expected. They were deeply disillusioned by the morass into which their own military men had led them, and they experienced a complete revulsion against war and the use of force.

The defeat of Japan in World War II involved the first invasion and occupation in their entire history of the soil this proud people had been taught to consider sacred. The effect of defeat was therefore traumatic, the more so as the courage and loyalty of the officers and men of the Imperial Army had been phenomenal. Very few prisoners indeed from the officer class had been captured, death in the *samurai* tradition being preferred to capture. Since this preference of death to surrender had been strongly reinforced by orders of the High Command throughout the war, it was felt necessary to make perfectly clear the official nature of the call to surrender by sending imperial princes and members of the emperor's family to the various theaters of war with the capitulation orders.

The Japanese people were extremely apprehensive as to what occupation by foreign troops would mean. The wildest rumors circulated about expected rape and looting, and many women left town and retreated to the country. The population was therefore pleasantly surprised when the GIs, and the smaller number of British, Australian, and New Zealand troops involved, proved to be not only correct but friendly in their behavior. As fraternization gradually increased, the authorities on both sides became somewhat alarmed by the dangers attendant on the rapid growth of bars and brothels catering to the occupation troops. But on the whole it may be said that this occupation was one of the best prepared and best conducted in the history of warfare. At the conclusion of the seven years, from 1945 to 1952, during which it lasted, few of the reforms introduced at the beginning were rescinded, and the general lines of the course charted for Japan were accepted by parties of both the right and the left. The mood and reaction of the Japanese people toward the occupation went through the phases of fear, relief, gratitude, boredom, and finally a predictable but tolerably mild resentment.

The machinery of the postwar control of Japan was supplied by a thirteen-nation Far Eastern Commission in Washington and a four-power Allied Council in Tokyo, with representatives from the United States, the Soviet Union, the British Commonwealth, and China. The Allied Council meetings frequently degenerated into futile argument, and in practice the direction of affairs was in the hands of SCAP, Supreme Commander Allied Powers, on the basis of a short document called "Initial Post-Surrender Policies for Japan." A decision was taken to work through a Japanese government and not to replace it, partly owing to the simple logistic fact that not enough Japanese-speaking personnel could be found to staff a nationwide operation. Contact with the Japanese government was maintained through a Central Liaison Office until 1948, and thereafter directly with the various Japanese government departments.

The position of Supreme Commander Allied Powers was given to General Douglas MacArthur, who had fought in the Pacific theater all through the war. He was well suited by nature and by professional training to fill his role of supreme arbiter and effective ruler. Somewhat in the style of a shogun he was punctilious in the performance of his duties, but in his bearing rather dignified and aloof. He turned up at his office in the modern Dainichi Insurance Building near the emperor's palace promptly each morning in a black limousine and returned to his quarters after a hard day's work, without any attempt at fraternizing or even going about the country on inspection tours. This was precisely the conduct expected and appreciated by the Japanese. MacArthur's sense of history and of destiny seemed at times pompous and egotistical to the egalitarian sentiments of Americans; but these very qualities, combined with his essential fairness, impressed the Japanese and gave them a needed feeling of confidence.

The period immediately after the end of the war was a time of great hardship and difficulty for the nation. There was widespread devastation and shortage of food. City dwellers packed the trains and fanned out daily into the countryside to try to barter a few possessions for food. The number of unemployed rose to 13 million. Repatriated Japanese swelled the population requiring to be fed, and large numbers of demobilized soldiers, so far from being heroes, found themselves unwanted and despised in the aftermath of defeat. Many of them, wounded and clad in tattered uniforms, begged alms on the streets and watched the conquerors go by with Japanese girls on their arms. Even those who obtained food were liable to be arrested for dealing on the black market. Gradually American aid and Japanese hard work improved the situation, though it was to be some time before industry could begin to show significant production.

The directives from Washington required demilitarization and democratization. The first was carried out with smoothness and dispatch. Troops were demobilized, and military installations dismantled. War trials and purges were conducted between 1946 and 1948 at various levels. Twenty-five were accused of major war crimes, and of these seven, including General Tojo, were hanged and the remainder imprisoned for life. Prince Konoe, former premier, committed suicide rather than submit to the disgrace of entering Sugamo Prison. Five thousand war criminals were tried in countries of Asia outside Japan, and 900 were executed; 200,000 were purged from their jobs as bureaucrats on the basis of the type of work they had done rather than for any reasons of personal responsibility.

In the process of seeking to make Japan into a democracy in the fullest sense, the first question to be decided was the position of the emperor. Here MacArthur carried out a wise decision reached earlier at a high level and did not indict him as a war criminal in spite of the clamor for this action by hotheads in America and among the Allies. He was retained in his position as a symbol of the nation's unity and as the keystone of the social arch which would preserve the country from chaos and disintegration. Emperor Hirohito was personally quite willing in the year 1946 to make a public renunciation of claims to divinity. Thereafter he made tours of the country and began to show himself to the people in a new light as a constitutional monarch and a sympathetic and modest individual of scholarly tastes, whose hobby was marine biology.

The new constitution, passed in 1946 and taking effect in May 1947, made clear in the Preamble and Article 1 the sovereignty of the people and the position of the emperor as a constitutional monarch.

> We, the Japanese people, acting through our duly elected representatives in the National Diet, . . . do proclaim the sovereignty of the people's will and do ordain and establish this Constitution, founded upon the universal principle that government is a sacred trust, the authority for which is derived from the people, the powers of which are exercised by the representatives of the people, and the benefits of which are enjoyed by the people; and we reject and revoke all constitutions, laws, ordinances and rescripts in conflict herewith.

ARTICLE 1. The emperor shall be the symbol of the state and of the unity of the people, deriving his position from the will of the people with whom resides Sovereign power.[1]

In a prominent position in Chapter 11 of the Constitution came Article 9 on the renunciation of war:

ARTICLE 9. Aspiring sincerely to an international peace based on justice and order, the Japanese people, forever, renounce war as a sovereign right of the nation, or the threat or use of force, as a means of settling disputes with other nations.

For the above purpose, land, sea, and air forces, as well as other war potential, will never be maintained. The right of belligerency of the State will not be recognized.

In other articles the peerage was abolished, the Diet made the only source of legislation, and provision made for the cabinet to be selected from the majority party or coalition in the Diet, on the British model. Important provisions concerning the cabinet were contained in Article 66:

The Prime Minister and other Ministers of State shall be civilians. The Cabinet, in the exercise of executive power, shall be collectively responsible to the Diet.

Both Houses of the Diet were to be fully elective, and the franchise was extended to all men and women of twenty years of age and over. A Supreme Court was set up on the United States model, but with a provision for popular review of its membership:

ARTICLE 79. . . . The appointment of the judges of the Supreme Court shall be reviewed by the people at the first general election of the House of Representatives following their appointment and shall be reviewed again at the first general election of the House of Representatives after a lapse of ten (10) years, and in the same manner thereafter.

ARTICLE 81. The Supreme Court is the court of last resort with power to determine the constitutionality of any law, order, regulation or official act.

The powers of local self-government were considerably increased by such provisions as:

ARTICLE 93. . . . The chief executive officers of all local public entities, the members of their legislative assemblies, and such other local officials as may

---

[1] These and subsequent quotations from the constitution are taken from *Political Handbook of Japan*, 1949. Tokyo: The Tokyo News Service.

be determined by law shall be elected by direct popular vote within their several communities. . . .

ARTICLE 95. A special law, applicable to only one local public entity, cannot be enacted by the Diet without the consent of the majority of the voters of the local public entity concerned, obtained in accordance with law.

Guarantees were given in the constitution not only for the customary freedoms of person, domicile, and religion but also for academic freedom (Article 23) and the right of collective bargaining (Article 28).

As part of the process of democracy it was the policy of the occupation authorities to encourage the trade union movement. Labor legislation between 1945 and 1947 granted rights to organize in unions, to bargain collectively, and to strike. Union membership rose within a year from approximately 1 million to 4.5 million. Not all of this could be considered a genuine increase, since unions within some firms had the employer as president of the union. Former Marxist and Communist labor leaders, released from the imprisonment to which they had been condemned by the former military regime, began to assume positions of leadership in the unions, to such an extent that the authorities became concerned and introduced changes into the labor field after 1948. In the countryside a successful democratic base was formed by a program of land reform. In order to eliminate absentee landlords, the government would purchase all land and sell it to the tenants on easy terms. *Resident* landlords were allowed to retain an average of seven and a half acres, of which they could rent out only two and a half. Tenants were to pay rent in cash, not in kind. This law of 1946 resulted in a more contented farming population and in the reduction of tenancy from nearly half to one-tenth of the farmers. The big landlords, no longer so dominant in the economic and social spheres, lost some of their political power to manipulate the village vote. In this respect the success of the Japanese land reform may be considered a model for underdeveloped countries, though it must be admitted that such results would not have been possible in Japan without the considerable advances in democracy made prior to World War II.

SCAP also arranged for antimonopoly legislation directed against the commercial empires of the *zaibatsu*. Eighty-three holding companies were broken up, and family fortunes confiscated by a capital levy. In education, compulsory schooling was increased from six to nine years, and new textbooks written embodying democratic rather than authoritarian trends. Emphasis was directed away from official dogma and toward the training of children to reach their own conclusions and form their own convictions. Courses in morality and ethics were dropped, and courses in social science substituted for them. American policy in this last respect may have gone beyond the point of wisdom and contributed to the malaise and uncertainty of postwar Japan. Japan was used to a state orthodoxy, while America rejects any such thing. Yet social science provides no way of life to live by.

The imprint of American ideas is clearly to be seen in the educational reforms and in such important documents as the constitution. Yet these ideas found a strong echo in the minds of the Japanese themselves, for they were seeking something very different from the ideology behind the former *kokutai* or "national polity" of the days before the war. An impressive, though unofficial, delegation of seventy leaders of politics, industry, and labor left Japan to visit Europe and the United States in 1947. The delegation was received on the floor of Congress in Washington, and in Berlin and London they presented to the mayors of these cities small crosses made of olive wood from the heart of a blasted tree near the epicenter of the Hiroshima bomb explosion, in token of the need for reconciliation. When they set out, the Prime Minister reminded them that former delegations had gone abroad in Meiji times to return with Western technical know-how, but he asked them to try to find out how democracy worked in practice, and what was its spiritual basis. He was aware that a democratic constitution on paper was of little use unless men had the spirit which would make it function.

Although the period of occupation was not yet halfway over, a marked change came upon the international scene in the years 1948–1950, which in turn had its effect on Japanese-American relations. In 1948 Manchuria fell to the Chinese Communists, and in the next year Jiang Jieshi (Chiang Kai-shek) was forced to flee the mainland and set up his government in Taiwan. Positions were being defined in the cold war, and Japan was moving from the role of a former enemy to that of a needed ally for America. By 1950 the United Nations, with America in the forefront, were at war with North Korea and Communist China. General MacArthur oversaw the civilian government of Japan, but he was also commander-in-chief of the American forces in the whole Pacific area, and his responsibility all along had been primarily to the Defense Department and only in the second place to the Department of State in Washington. In light of the realities of world power-politics some far-reaching alterations were made in American policies. Successive Japanese governments accepted these alterations as necessary, but many Japanese regarded them as cynically opportunist. Thus was built up a resentment against America, which was exploited by the Japanese political left and which has persisted in varying degrees right up to the present.

In the first place, American authorities encouraged the growth of the Self-Defense Forces of Japan, in police reserves and in land, sea, and air arms, in spite of Article 9 of the constitution renouncing war. Action against the *zaibatsu* was abandoned, and the dismantling of plants ceased. Retrenchment and government economy were instituted on American advice. One hundred thousand government workers were laid off. A no-strike law was passed for civil service and industrial workers, and although a Public Arbitration Board was set up, SCAP would not back up the decision of this board in the case of the railroad workers' strike in 1948. The result was that the workers received a raise of only 3 percent and not the 25 percent which the board had recommended. Some government saving was undoubtedly necessary in an overextended economy, but the angle of view had shifted. Defense and rapid recovery had taken the place of demilitarization and democratization as the primary goals. Labor agitation was now dangerous, and left-wing radicals had to be controlled. In one respect, however, America provided a valuable object lesson in the working of democracy and the superiority of the civil over the military power, even in wartime. President Truman, to the astonishment of the Japanese, dismissed General MacArthur in 1951 because of the general's expressed wish to carry the war into Manchurian territory in spite of the president's instructions to the contrary. His replacement as Supreme Commander was General Matthew Ridgway.

The march of events indicated above made it desirable to conclude a peace treaty with Japan, but when this was attempted through the channels of the Far Eastern Commission, Stalin and Jiang Jieshi (Chiang Kai-shek) objected. President Truman then appointed the international attorney John Foster Dulles to make individual approaches to the various nations concerned. Dulles worked hard during 1950 and 1951. By September of the latter year the representatives of fifty-two countries gathered in San Francisco to sign a peace whose terms had been in the main settled already. Russia tried to confuse and divide the delegations, but all signed save Russia, India, and mainland China. Japan renounced her claims to Korea, Formosa, the Pescadores, the Kuriles, South Sakhalin, and the former Pacific mandated islands. Reparations were to be negotiated with the separate countries that wished to receive them. Both the Peace Treaty and the whole occupation policy were nonpunitive and nonvindictive. Prime Minister Yoshida Shigeru was satisfied that the treaty was "fair and generous" and made it clear that Japan aligned itself with the non-Communist world. At the same time as the signing of the Peace Treaty, America and Japan concluded a Security Treaty, which provided for the stationing of United States forces in and around Japan for purposes of the internal and external security of the country. A separate agreement to resume diplomatic relations with Russia was signed in 1956, and at that point Japan was admitted to the United Nations.

A review of the economy of Japan shows phenomenal growth in the postwar years, once the initial difficulties were overcome. As in the Meiji era, economic growth was fostered by a combination of government and private enterprise. United States assistance, both governmental and private, was of decisive importance. The Japanese banks made commercial loans easy to acquire, and the government offered tax incentives and high depreciation allowances. The overall rate of economic growth averaged 10 percent annually from 1950 up to 1965, with a high of 12.1 percent in 1963 and a low of 7.5 percent in 1965. Comparative figures for other countries' growth are West Germany, 6.1 percent; France, 5.3 percent; England, 2.4 percent; and the United States, 2.3 percent. The gross national product, only $1.3 billion in 1946, rose to $15.1 billion in 1951, then in an upward surge more than tripled to $51.9 billion in 1962, and shot up to $167 billion in 1968.

The story of the average Japanese wage earners is told by the figures for per capita real income. If 100 is taken as an index for the year 1934, they lost half their income in the year after the war (1946, 51.9) and did not clamber back to the original figure until 1954 (99.5); but by 1962 their earning power had more than doubled (215.2).

Japan's constantly rising prosperity has undoubtedly favored a conservative trend in politics. Up to 1993, all the premiers since the war have been conservative, except Katayama Tetsu, Socialist in politics and Christian in religion, who held office in 1947–1948. Yoshida was longest in office (1946–1947 and 1948–1954) and bridged the period between the Occupation and independence. He was prepared to cooperate with the Occupation authorities out of a genuine conviction that Japan's destiny lay with America and its allies. He retained the support of his people and disarmed some of the opposition by what was known as the "reverse course." This phase, a turning point in Japanese-American relations, was a criticism and modification of some of the occupation policies, which could be seen in Yoshida's plans to control subversive activities, his support of a restructuring of the *zaibatsu*, and his restoration of the police force to a measure of central control. This move toward greater central control and less local autonomy was continued, particularly in the field of education, by Yoshida's rival and successor as premier, Hatoyama Ichiro (1954–1956). During his period of office, relations with Russia were resumed, trade with Communist China grew in volume, and the divided conservative wing in politics was reunited into the Liberal Democratic party. The next premier to hold office for any length of time was Kishi Nobusuke (1957–1960). He was caught in a wave of feeling against American policy, which had already gone through various stages. Beginning in 1952 with the Security Pact and American pressure for Japanese rearmament, it had been notably increased by the incident of the *Lucky Dragon* fishing vessel in 1954. The unfortunate crew of this ship was affected by radiation sickness due to radioactive fallout in the atomic test at the Bikini Atoll. The subsequent explanations were badly handled by the American authorities, and Communist propaganda made the very most of the ensuing resentment. Then during Kishi's premiership the Security Treaty came up for review, and he was accused of forcing a renewal of the treaty through the Diet for his own political advantage. So great and so violent were the demonstrations by students in the Zengakuren, a student federation to the left even of the Communist party, that the projected visit of President Eisenhower to Tokyo had to be canceled and the Kishi government had to resign. Resentment was directed not so much against America as against the Japanese establishment and its ties with America.

Premier Ikeda Hayato (1960–1964) then adopted what he called a "low posture" of caution in foreign affairs and concentrated on furthering still greater growth in the Japanese economy. He did not, however, make any fundamental change in policy and in fact tightened the regulations on internal law and order. When he had to resign the premiership because of illness, Sato Eisaku took over. Sato crowned a number of successes with a visit to President Nixon in November 1969, during which he secured American agreement to the return of Okinawa to Japanese rule, to become effective in 1972. He was rewarded by seeing his party, the Liberal Democrats, make notable gains in the elections of January 1970 at the expense of the Socialists.

Thus, in spite of fluctuations in the degree of cooperation between Japan and the United States, and in spite of severe internal problems in the rebuilding of Japan (physically and socially) after World War II, the country by 1970 had attained a position strong and stable enough to enable it to expand in influence and to take its place as a world power.

16

JAPAN TODAY—ECONOMY

On a hill high above the harbor of Nagasaki there is a charming small house and garden built in the late nineteenth century for a British engineering adviser to the Japanese, Thomas B. Glover, whose Japanese love became the heroine of Puccini's tragic opera *Madame Butterfly*. From this vantage point, symbolically connecting East and West, one looks down on one side to the former island of Deshima, now landlocked, where Dutch traders were immured from 1641. On the other side the view is quintessential twentieth century, one of vast shipyards with the latest technology. There giant supertankers were constructed on such a scale that bow and stern had to be launched separately and welded together in the water.

THE ECONOMIC MIRACLE

Japan had consistently impressed European observers. The earliest Jesuits appreciated their cleanliness, aesthetics, and cultural refinement, comparing Japan favorably with their homelands. Western observers during the Meiji period welcomed Japan into the community of modern nations following its early imperial wars against China and Russia in 1895 and 1905, respectively, and its impressive role in the International Force sent against China's Boxers in 1900. Japan's unprecedented achievement of rapid transformation from a traditional, rural, feudal economy into a modern industrial state bore the familiar bitter fruit of massive war and defeat along with the fragrant flowers of success. Its cities and industrial plants broken, and millions of citizens lost to the carnage of war, Japan nonetheless amazed the world repeating the Meiji miracle with a second "economic miracle," transforming itself into the world's second largest economy and an engine that helped to drive the transformation of Asia throughout the second half of the twentieth century.

199

Shipbuilding.
The supertanker "Tokyo Maru," 150,000 tons, was built in Yokohama.

Japan Information Center

　　This so-called "economic miracle," which includes Japan's industrial and technological advances from the end of World War II to the present, has been a source of pride and, in recent years, frustration as well. Its accomplishments, crafted from hard work, distinctive institutions, beliefs, and historical factors produced an economic expansion that profoundly influences its politics and society.

　　Within the broader scope of economic development, prior to the bursting of the bubble and the "lost years of the 1990s," Japan had experienced linear growth characteristic of postindustrial societies. The process of post-war linear growth benefited from the collective national will to rebuild and rebound and the "conscious planning" of elites determined to redeem themselves from the disasters of war and defeat. Japan's workers, while continuing production as farmers in the primary sector of the economy, propelled the nation, creating perhaps the most sophisticated advanced industrial and technological engine of the twentieth century. By the 1970s Japan's dual agricultural-industrial economy had advanced into a new or postindustrial phase in which more than 50 percent of the labor force was engaged in the tertiary or service sector. By 1990 the tertiary labor force had expanded to more than 60 percent and Japan, long the second-largest market economy, had become one of the wealthiest and most advanced societies in the history of the world.

Japan's achievements in material and economic development which so astonished contemporaries in the second half of the twentieth century reflect the Japanese genius for optimizing use of the collective achievements of the international enterprise and distinctive strengths of its indigenous culture and values. Students of Japan's economic success story have identified several corporate and personal qualities that help to explain the distinct strengths of a Japanese as opposed to Western economic organization.

LIFETIME EMPLOYMENT OR LAND OF MERCENARIES[1]

Japanese-style management has been defined by a distinctive symbiotic relationship between labor and management. From the factory floor through the upper tiers of management, among white- and blue-collar workers, postwar corporate life embraced an ideal of "companyism," a style that included elements of Japan's Confucian paternalism and practical considerations. This corporatist culture with features such as lifetime employment, advancement according to seniority, and cooperation between management and the single-company union is a defining part of the Japanese model of management.

> Lifetime employment together with seniority-based wage scale and promotion provided the capstone to the human resources management in the postwar Japanese economic model replacing a fluid prewar model. Along with lifetime employment the Japanese coined a neologism, sarariman or salaryman to designate this new kind of employee. Generally on the management side of a corporation, salarymen in fact, extend down to the factory floor. Within this system, the destiny of employer and employee was bound together in a symbiotic knot. A loyal workforce was paired with a generally paternalistic management, both enjoying limited but secure incomes and other benefits of company largess. In the immediate postwar years when survival was problematic, security and income in exchange for loyalty and devotion was a good bargain for all. As the economy flourished, so too did the number of "sarariman" from 30 percent of the total work force in 1950 to 70 percent in 1995.[2]

Lifetime employment engendered an intense company loyalty resonating with traditional and even feudal values found in the *bushido* and Confucian traditions. There was a culture of mutualism that infused the eternal struggle for survival with a pattern of self-respect and dignity. Mutualism bound the entire corporation into a shared destiny. There was shared responsibility

---

[1] Kusaka Kimindo, "Demise of the Salaryman," translated in Masazoe Yoichi, *Year of Trial: Japan in the 1990s*, Tokyo: Japan Echo Inc., 2000, pp. 200–209 (p. 208).
[2] Ibid., p. 202.

which meant that management became extremely reluctant to lay off workers even during the most severe downturns, preferring hiring freezes, transfers, and reduced schedules. As company fortunes improved, beginning during the 1950s, management made sure to share the new wealth with employees while keeping its own salaries within reasonable limits. In addition to yearly salary increases, employees enjoyed other benefits like free housing, vacations, company recreational facilities, team sports, and traditional arts, such as flower arranging and tea ceremonies for young women and housewives. Such benefits were not limited to the large corporation; second tier and smaller companies, on a smaller scale, provided benefits as well. For the Japanese, beyond the necessary material benefits, the company played a critical social role in their lives—bosses and managers served as spokespersons at weddings and funerals where they contributed important prestige as well as financial support to their underlings.

In its ideal form, lifetime employment was a pragmatic device in a labor-scarce market as the nation put its collective shoulder to the tasks of rebuilding and catching up with and surpassing competitors in the international industrial world. One should appreciate, however, that Japanese companyism, mutualism, and paternalism were always more than a pragmatic solution to scarce labor; these qualities arise from deep historical values and traditional culture. They had been shaped into a modern ideology during the late Meiji and Showa periods. While Americans discarded "the company towns" and most paternalistic management in favor of a "frontier capitalism," the Japanese continued to embrace their paternalistic model during the postwar years. Though the shocks of the decade of decline during the 1990s forced a shift toward an Anglo-American corporate model, perhaps effectively transforming the Japanese model, there has been an inertia and reluctance to discard corporate welfarism. Aspects of feudalism, Confucian paternalism, *bushido* loyalty, devotion, and industriousness continue to inspire behavior into the twenty-first century. And while a new work ethic and individualism blossoms in the soil of global, postindustrial Japan, the Japanese retain a strong need for group identity within corporate social culture. Company songs, badges, logos, uniforms, social gatherings, and recognition remain. Colleagues still gather after work and on weekends for recreation and bonding. Similar corporate culture remains in academia as well, where academic *batsu* or "cliques" define university identity as well as economic and social networks. In spite of this strong corporate culture the Japanese model described has been seriously affected by the challenges of global competition. Firings, suicides of salary-men, the increasing use of part-timers in both rural and urban economies are all symptoms of the tectonic plate of postwar values grinding against the imperatives of the global economy.

On the management side, Japanese corporations had developed specific policies to forge a distinct culture. A central policy was the consistent annual recruitment of employees from a select group of distinguished universities.

In Japan, school ties have remained critical in personal networking and identity; corporate recruitment strategies facilitated a seamless march from university to corporation. Obviously the new recruits shared professors and a uniform training. This continued as each year's recruits advanced together through the same corporate training programs, promotions, and ultimately retirement. Most of their leisure hours, after work or on weekends, were spent associating with colleagues. In time a few exceptional individuals were selected for power positions, while most of their group continued, following familiar and timeworn paths. While it is true that similar systems do exist in other corporate cultures, it is generally accepted that the Japanese case has been extreme. In the past ten years, with the unraveling of the Japanese corporatist model, elite recruitment is still a strong feature, though seniority is no longer a guarantee of security or advancement. Ability, innovation, and performance have become important. While the demographics of aging force the retention of some employees beyond the traditional mandatory retirement age of 55–60, hundreds of thousands of middle management salarymen have been fired, replaced by part-timers, the "mercenaries" of contemporary corporate life in the twenty-first century.

Mandatory retirement was a logical finale to yearly recruitment and lifetime job security. As long as there was a sufficient supply of replacements, all companies with 100 persons or more used mandatory retirement between the ages of fifty-five and sixty. Very few have had a cutoff point extending beyond sixty. Recent demographics characterized by a steadily declining birthrate have, however, begun to force some corporations to retain older workers. Conversely, corporate restructuring, noted above, has resulted in the massive layoff of less essential managers and workers as they approach retirement. Forced early retirement has resulted in disastrous personal and social consequences. Until recently retirement was not usually the end of one's working life. Many retirees stepped almost immediately into another job as consultants or part-timers, often in smaller companies or new positions. This transitional work life eased the financial and psychological burden of retirement. This same transitional phase applied in both bureaucratic government and academic professions as well. Government bureaucrats have been especially favored by this system. Having served in a bureaucratic position, they regularly "descended from heaven"(*amakudari*) to arrive at a management position in one of the companies they had recently been "regulating." More than likely they would find a familiar social group there with classmates and colleagues to greet them. Acceptable to the Japanese, this cozy situation could produce irregularities. Among academics, mandatory retirement usually launches one into a new university career, on a part-time basis, where perks and prestige might serve mutual interests, and a scholar's mature talents could continue to benefit society. Overall, then, the early retirement within the Japanese corporate personnel model was never a ticket to leisure but rather a chance for a gradual transition to one's "golden years."

SUBCONTRACTING

A second distinguishing feature of Japanese industry is the extensive use of subcontracting to small firms, each of which manufactures one part only of the finished product. This business structure, known as *keiretsu*, has grown out of premodern home and village industry, which was greatly expanded under the pressure of military procurement in World War II. It is a practice well known in the West also, particularly in the automobile industry, but it has been developed to a higher degree in Japan. The small firm is relieved of certain overhead expenses and often benefits from the research conducted by the larger business. But it is also involved in risk, for the ancillary company becomes entirely dependent on the success and goodwill of the larger firm. The *keiretsu* system—with its pyramidal structure resting on hundreds of thousands of small firms—has been under serious stress since the onset of the prolonged recession of the nineties. While the small and middle-sized companies took the direct pounding in the economic wars, the large, globalized industrial corporations have been able to restructure and expand. Well over 1,500 small and medium-sized companies declared bankruptcy in 2000 compared to only 500 or so in 1990. Japan's contracting economy of the nineties and early twenty-first century would exact a heavy toll in collective and personal suffering.

LABOR UNIONS

Japan's labor unions also played an important role in the years of the miracle economy. While there were national union confederations linking units in transportation, mining, and industry, the foundation of the postwar labor movement was built on company unions, in-house organizations designed to harmonize labor-management relations and channel labor feedback into the management process. This had not always been the case. In the months just after occupation began, carried by the euphoria of liberation from wartime controls and imprisonments, Marxists and Socialists in particular led a wave of strikes and demonstrations that triggered arrests and suppression by the SCAP (Supreme Commander for the Allied Powers) authorities. While Marxists and Socialists continued to have influence in a number of public unions, this diminished in time. Major union activity settled into the company union format. The result was a docile, cooperative and loyal workforce. Union efforts were reciprocated by paternalistic management as well as by regular salary increases, bonuses, and longer vacations along with other company benefits noted above.

In considering the symbiotic labor-management relationship, it is important to include the postwar idea of "honorable poverty," that is, the general embrace of a simple, frugal, hard-working lifestyle by Japan's managers. Honorable poverty had a corollary in a general disdain for *narikin*, "any taint of nouveaux riches and extravagance." Labor, sharing the hard and simple life with its postwar managers, found it easier to shoulder the burdens of the age. Thus collective bargaining could be done in house. Industrial strikes were extremely rare. Writing in 2000, Ushio Jiro noted that there had not been a significant strike in forty years. In a general climate of shared hardships and shared rewards, one can imagine the stability and harmony that helped propel growth and progress.

There was, however, a flurry of national strikes in the 1970s in the aftermath of the increased wages and their accompanying hyperinflation of 30 percent plus. These strikes for higher wages mostly hit the national transportation unions, which were dominated by the Socialists. Other strikes hit railroads, the postal service, telephones, airlines, and buses. The Ministry of Labor responded by negotiating salary increases to match inflation. Subsequent demands then dropped between 1974–1977 to a still substantial 9 percent. The so-called "spring labor offensive" became a yearly ritual that allowed public workers to keep pace with their counterparts in the industrial sector, keep up with inflation, and see a consistent, if modest, improvement in their quality of life. This process also increased the purchasing power of the working class along with the expansion of the economy, generating a base of consumers, which then added to demand stimulating economic growth.

This comfortable relationship and its mutual benefits continued throughout the 1980s bubble economy. The 1990s cycle of recession, restructuring, deflation, and periods of negative economic growth diminished the relevance of the unions. Workers received only modest salary increases of 1.5–2.5 percent. The important bonuses were reduced and savings diminished by the stock market collapse. Even worse, the unions were unable to save their members from the massive effects of a decade of economic collapse; between 1997 and 2000 close to 2 million jobs were lost, and unemployment reached an unprecedented 4.9 percent. Like the other two "sacred treasures" of Japan's human resources management model, lifetime employment and seniority-based promotions, the union-management symbiosis has been seriously threatened.

SAVINGS

Another characteristic of Japan's economic formula during the boom years of the 1960s through the 1980s was the high rate of personal and familial savings. Emerging from an economy of scarcity and a long Confucian tradition of frugality, the Japanese were able to forgo personal gratification for the collective needs of their families. They put aside income for housing, transportation, and education as a cushion against the unknown. These same habits of frugality helped the economy to accumulate a substantial, indigenous pool of capital to finance industrial development and expansion. The fact that savings provided capital was important to the Japanese as a kind of insulation against fluctuations in the global economy and a means to assuage somewhat their longing for an autocracy.

The household savings rate in Japan from 1961 to 1979 ran between 18.2 and 22.1 percent, versus 5.4 to 8.8 percent in the United States. As a percentage of GNP the Japanese saved 12 percent in 1960 and 17 percent in 1973 compared to 6 percent in the United States. By 1988 the figures for savings went down all around: in Japan to 14.8; in France, a country generally known for popular thrift, to 12.1 percent; and to 6.6 percent for the United States. These declines followed the heated consumerism that took place during the peak of the bubble years. In 1991, caught by the bursting of the bubble, Japanese savings plunged to a record low of 6.5 percent. By 1999 Japanese household savings had rebounded once again to 18.5 percent. This recent savings boom is driven by several postbubble imperatives, including the desire of families to rebuild savings following bank losses and the stock market collapse, a declining confidence in the ability of the government to provide needed services, the concerns of an aging population, and the need for some kind of financial cushion against job insecurity.[3]

In addition to benefiting from substantial household savings as a source of capital to fuel the miracle economy, Japanese corporations borrowed heavily, limited payments to shareholders and salaries to employees, and kept inventories lean by using the *keiretsu* system of relying on countless small and medium suppliers. These suppliers to larger corporation operated within the "just in time" model, providing materials and parts as needed. Engaging these various gears generated power for the Japanese production miracle.

Banks played an unusually critical role, recycling household savings into the capitalization of business expansion. Whereas stocks and bonds provided the bulk of investment capital in Western economies, in Japan banks were more important. Beginning with Japan's first phase of industrialization during the Meiji period, the government used banks as tools to finance industry. They regarded them somewhat like a public utility with an unspoken assumption that they could not fail and that the government would intervene in the event of a serious threat to any major bank. Clearly the Japanese preferred a close, symbiotic relationship between the government and banks. In the aftermath of World War II this system was reborn, to some extent encouraged by SCAP policies, which dismantled the old *zaibatsu* conglomerates. Capitalization of the industrial miracle was mostly paid for by taxes and savings channeled through the banking system under the guidance of the state financial bureaucracy. Taking unimaginable risks, banks provided companies with loans sometimes reaching 80 percent of assets. This tightrope walking was possible only because the banks' solvency was guaranteed by the government. Even if a company folded, the bank could count on a bail-out by the Bank of Japan. In this cozy triangular relationship between banks, business, and government bureaucrats, guarantors of last resort had the final say and ultimate control. The result was that prior to 1993 there were no major

[3] Jean-Marie Bouissou, *Japan: The Burden of Success* (Boulder, CO: Lynne Rienner Publishers, 2002), p. 258.

bankruptcies in Japan. Things changed, however, during the bubble economy years of the 1980s. Awash with seemingly unlimited wealth generated during the booming previous decades, bureaucracy, banks, and business colluded in "creating wealth out of air," pumping up the bubble of real estate and stock speculation to absurd heights. With the bursting of the bubble, major banks, burdened by the immense debt of nonperforming loans and overinflated stocks, collapsed and tore through the bureaucratic safety net, pulling down the entire Japanese economy by the early 1990s. November of 1997 was especially disastrous with three of Japan's major brokerage houses collapsing, including the oldest in Japan, Yamaishi Securities (the other two were Sanyo and Hokkaido Hakushoku). In spite of bureaucracy-managed consolidations and buyouts, in 2003 Japanese banks still had approximately $3 trillion in outstanding nonredeemable loans.

It is important to appreciate how pervasively and, one might say, insidiously, the state bureaucracy came to control industrial development through the 1980s. Rebuilding during the immediate postwar years was financed through the Reconstruction Bank, which mutated into eight specialized banks. Capital for the eight came from household deposits in post office savings accounts. Individuals who deposited in the post office were permitted to hold multiple accounts, which were tax exempt to a certain limit. This incentive helps explain how the post office came to hold 40 percent of total national savings. The MITI (Ministry of International Trade and Industry) and the Finance Ministry distributed postal savings funds to target corporations that fit into current plans. Needless to say the close relationships among corporations, bureaucrats, and banks offered irresistible opportunities for questionable activities beyond public scrutiny.

Since capital was available in banks at good rates, corporations did not have to be overly concerned about market capitalization or payment of dividends to shareholders. In fact the general rule was to retain profits for reinvestment, thereby holding dividends down. The system thus relied on a "production"-based economic model that consistently prioritized development while squeezing wages as well as dividends. The same squeeze was applied to the thousands of small firms. These formed the foundation of the *keiretsu* and supplied the large corporations with "just in time" components, further reducing costs by keeping down the need for large inventories or in-house production. During recession, it was small firms and their employees that absorbed the most immediate blows. Of late the number of small business bankruptcies has increased significantly.

NATIONAL COOPERATION

The last element of the miracle economy, which runs throughout as a sort of leitmotif, is national cooperation. Each of the preceding sections discusses the tight links between discrete sectors of Japanese society and the economy. Government, management, and labor held together through the most difficult times—first to rebuild, then to expand, and finally to surpass the competitor economies of the world. At the core of this cooperative structure has been the so-called "iron triangle" of big corporations, politicians, and bureaucracy. The strong and tight links among these potentially contentious sectors had a long history. Forged in the Meiji and World War II eras, they took for granted a managed economy in which government, more specifically, the bureaucracy, was expected to play a decisive role formulating and directing a national economic policy. These Japanese expectations, which cede considerable power to the state, stand in contrast to the market-driven preferences of the West, especially the United States. In Japan's case, on the level of values and culture, one could find among the taproots of a greater tradition an intense awareness of shared destiny. From mythico-Shinto emperor genetics through Confucian familial-patriarchal cosmology, the Japanese had fused the Meiji-militarist ideology of war. The effect of these values and ideology were individuals and institutions that unified in the face of any real or perceived external threat. Japan could constitute a military or economic monolith under certain circumstances. Elite groups martialed this effect with particular intensity.

Japanese national cooperation in the economic sphere and the modern ideology of nationalism complement each other. There has always been a widespread awareness of the necessity for unity in order for the national economy to compete with rival economies. Loyalty to the state meant working in cooperation toward a shared national destiny. During the Meiji era *samurai* gave up feudal class identity to work for the state in government and industry; so from the first days of industrialization, Japan had already begun to form a consensus regarding the essential unity of the iron triangle and the identity of the self with the modern nation state.

Understandably, as Japan's economy rose to challenge the West during the second half of the twentieth century, the monolithic front formed by the iron triangle caused widespread resentment and accusations of unfairness as competitive balances shifted. When Japanese dominance in heavy industries evolved into fierce competition in high value-added, high-tech products like consumer electronics, autos, memory chips, etc., it triggered trade wars with Europe and the United States. Western competitors coined the pejorative "Japan Inc." As Japan's dominance in consumer electronics began to threaten domestic industries in Europe, the response exploded in angry rhetoric. In 1987 France's prime minister, Edith Cresson, described Japanese workers as "ants" and their tiny company-provided housing as "rabbit hutches." But, while the Japanese were surely hard workers who sacrificed creature comforts, in fact, state-of-the-art technology had already given Japan a competitive edge.

At the heart of Japan's development strategy was careful government planning, along with the aggressive pursuit of outer-focused (OF) expansion and the protection of the inner dependent (ID) or domestic economy. Thus, Japan took full advantage of the world's free markets while putting its competitors at a disadvantage by seriously restricting access to Japan's markets. This strategy included the management of tactical policy and was controlled by the MITI. MITI bureaucrats in cooperation with the Ministry of Finance and important industrial and financial leaders from the private sector shared responsibility for economic development. They focused resources on promising products and development, conducted crucial market and product research, and identified and facilitated the triage of weakening or dated sectors like the indigenous coal industry. In general MITI provided the institutional structure that held together the miracle economy.

The MITI presided over a tight-knit and exclusive club of bureaucrats, politicians, bankers, and businesspeople, most from a handful of elite public and private universities. As mentioned previously, horizontal transfers between these political and economic units were frequent and considered usual. Familial alliances and personal networks further bound the destinies of the inner core. Devoted, diligent, and extremely capable individuals were able to steer Japan through the postwar years. It was difficult, however, to avoid the temptations of corruption inherent in such a system. As the bubble economy burst in the late 1980s, it pulled down the walls concealing problems, which had contributed to the artificial expansion and collapse. Throughout the 1990s the pervasiveness of cronyism and corruption continued to break through the surface, seriously compromising the iron triangle and forcing restructuring and reform.

Today the cooperative links within the old iron triangle still hold. The MITI, renamed METI (Ministry of Economy and Industry) in a 2000 reorganization of the government, presides over Japan's globalization initiatives, IT (Information Technology), and other high-tech development. Its role is changing however as Japan opens to the outside. Foreign investment, management, and outright ownership of key Japanese corporations, banks, and investment firms are changing economic structure. With the Trojan horse of non-Japanese inside the walls of the triangle, the postwar model will continue to be transformed.

ADVANTAGES AND DISADVANTAGES OF THE JAPANESE MODEL

While the decade of the nineties and the first years of the twenty-first century have cast a shadow over Japan's postwar achievements, Japan remains the second largest economy in the world with its GDP per capita in 1998 at $32,350, far beyond that of the EU $22,119 or the US $29,240. Back in 1988 seven of the ten richest banks in the world were Japanese (now, 2004, reduced to one) and six of the ten richest men, according to *Forbes* magazine, were also Japanese. The Japanese model of those halcyon days was much emulated throughout Asia and in the West as well.

In 1991 Ardath Burks hit upon a succinct formula to summarize Japan's success: "Japan's high growth rate was the product of the rate of investment, the high quality of the labor force, the acumen in business organization, and the diffusion of technology."[4] One might add to Burks's formulation that in Japan there was a "national solidarity in the single minded pursuit of economic development." The times were also favorable as there was a world order (that part dominated by the market economies of the West) that welcomed Japan's growth and competition. Unquestionably, corporate Japan's ability to harness technology to produce outstanding, durable consumer products at a reasonable cost has been critical. Early in 1992 as Japan's banks and corporations were drawn deeply into the collapsed bubble economy, Akio Morita, cofounder, with Ibuka Masaru, of the Sony Corporation in 1946 (then known as the Tokyo Telecommunications Engineering Corp.) singled out technology as the primary ingredient in the miracle economy. A decade later, Yamada Shinjiro, a president of INCS, one of the world's premier IT (information technology) corporations, reaffirmed Morita's opinion asserting that Japan had been able to surpass America industrially because her machine tooling and precision molding industries had become the best in the world.

In light of the above, then, what were some of the advantages and disadvantages of the Japanese model we have discussed? The advantages are compelling. First of all, managers, although tough in their demands, are careful to keep in touch with the workers in the plant. Their company uniform is the same, and their offices are used by a number of people, being open and near to the factory floor, not placed in remote luxury in a top floor suite. Managers are often to be found talking to workers at the machines and showing a readiness to adopt suggestions for improvements from workers' group discussions, both on grievances and on possible new technical methods of production. While labor-management relations remain important, restructuring and globalization have changed the conditions that made this distinctive brand of harmony possible. In particular, massive offshoring of production, the need to use immigrant workers as the current work population ages, the replacement of labor by IT and robotic systems, and the adoption of Western-style management erode the old system. The last, in particular, commodifies the working class as "a head count" rather than a precious ingredient in a larger corporate culture. Resulting layoffs have shaken the ideal of harmony and cooperation.

Perhaps most important, the gap in pay between workers and managers is not as wide as it is in many Western firms. In March 1986, in a time of crisis caused by a steep rise in the value of the yen, some firms felt compelled to move part of their production to Singapore, Hong Kong, and Taiwan, to the disadvantage of their workers; but at the same time they cut the pay of their executives. By offering security of employment, incentives, and a pervading sense of teamwork, managers seem able to promote in the workplace a feeling of harmony and consensus. An adversarial relationship is to be

---

[4] Ardath W. Burks, *Japan—A Postindustrial Power* (Boulder, CO: Westview Press, 3rd, updated ed., 1991), p. 159.

avoided wherever possible, for it would run totally counter to the expected Japanese social norm. Where layoffs are necessary, as in the 1986 dislocations just mentioned, every attempt is made to find work in other factories of the same firm or elsewhere. This egalitarianism is still idealized in the examples of labor leaders like Miyata Shoji, who led Sohyo (General Council of Trade Unions of Japan), and Usami Tadanobu of the Domei (Japanese Confederation of Labor), and business leaders like Sakurada Takeshi, who led the Nikkeiren (Japan Federation of Employers' Associations), and Doko Toshiwo in charge of the second Ad Hoc Commission on Administrative Reform. These men set the standard for labor-management cooperation in the seventies and eighties, helping to pull Japan out of the oil shock-induced recession and into the new era of corporate and government restructuring. Doko and Sakurada in particular lived the simple life according to the ideal of "honorable poverty,"as an example for society as a whole. Indeed, the model of the mid-eighties has given way to a record high unemployment rate of 5.6 percent in 2003, suggesting a shift to commodification of labor.

Yet there are notable disadvantages in the Japanese business system. One of these is the reverse side of the much prized consensus in decision making, namely, the long time it takes to arrive at it. Memorandums concerning future plans are circulated widely in a department of business or government. Employees at all levels are given the chance to see and understand these documents. They sign off on them, not necessarily as supporting but as understanding and not objecting. (When proposals are made in a Japanese consultation with foreigners and a Japanese person says "Yes," he or she may only mean "Yes, I understand," but the foreigner may assume he or she means "Yes, I fully agree.") Juniors are welcome to discuss the matter in question with superiors and may offer their own input. But they must do this quietly, with respect, and not in a self-assertive or arrogant manner. Each is part of a team and must not stand out above other workers. Modifications may be made by those in charge, and upon consensus, the final decision is made and promulgated. It may be unwelcome, but it is not a total surprise. Naturally the cogs move slowly. In the speed of international business some Japanese are seeking to accelerate the process. But teamwork, harmony, and the inclusion of everyone are still highly valued in the corporate enterprise.

Consensus decision making along with the rest of the Japanese model of corporate management is being transformed in the context of globalization and the restructuring of Japanese corporate life. The need to use local management in Japan's global production system utilizes local non-Japanese who are unable to operate in the consensus mode. The purchase of Japanese corporations and banks with the opening of domestic markets beginning in the late 1980s has transformed management to the Western style. For example, Carlos Ghosn was assigned by Renault of France to turn around Nissan (Japan's second largest auto manufacturer, purchased by Renault of France in 1999). Ghosn put company profits first, closed five factories in Japan, and reduced the labor force by 21,000 in his first years. His consensus-defying approach has, however, turned Nissan from the brink of bankruptcy to profitability.

New voices are demanding attention within the Japanese business world. Women, now more than 48 percent of the labor force, make up an increasingly important segment of Japan's workers. The aging population with fewer young replacement workers, reductions in force, which hit middle-aged men the hardest, as well as the skills and high educational level of many women, have transformed them from part-timers and tea pourers into an indispensable component of workers outside the household. There remains a strong male bias excluding women from better jobs and management positions. The response of talented women has been to seek jobs and education overseas or to work for international corporations where their talents are highly valued. Some have also broken from the established corporate world and founded their own companies, though this option seems very difficult given male dominance in general.

As for lifetime employment, obviously, from what has been said above, this pillar of the Japanese model of corporate culture is clearly crumbling. While skilled workers and managers in big corporations will retain tenured job security, restructuring with downsizing, mergers, and the triage of Japan's non-competitive small and medium-sized companies being kept alive with infusions of government support, referred to as "zombie industries," along with new managerial goals as discussed above, have destroyed this benefit (though some would argue that the end of lifetime employment liberates both the worker and the corporation from the straightjacket of the unimaginative and humdrum life of routine and prescribed expectations). In fact, it is important to note that most Japanese workers never did enjoy this benefit. Part-time workers (many of them women), workers in ancillary *keiretsu* companies, foreign workers in Japan, particularly Koreans and Chinese, and workers in small businesses were always vulnerable. In the recent rounds of layoffs, the middle-management ranks and older workers are most often the victims. In their forties and fifties, they lose expected income and pensions and are unable to find new jobs because of their age. Sadly the suicide rate among these dismissed salarymen is exploding.

Along with restlessness among women and the growing numbers of the unemployed, the young generation of Japanese is also increasingly alienated from the existing system. While the vast majority still seeks conventional employment from school to work, job markets are changing along with attitudes. Many simply refuse to enter a seniority-based system in which they might slowly advance in rank based on years of service; some reject the life style of the salaryman and its total demands on an individual. The low pay in early years is not attractive either. When it comes to attitude, many young Japanese reject the old hierarchical systems, sublimations, and loyalty with its implied destruction of the individual. A new itinerant crop of young people prefer living from hand to mouth and from temporary job to temporary job while living at home with their parents and leading a simple, hedonistic life. Called "freeters," they resemble the detached characters in the works of contemporary writers like Murakami Haruki. They look with horror on the not unusual example of the older generation of salarymen working themselves to death (*karoshi*), a phenomenon which has become so widespread that the government passed a law making it a crime for a corporation to work its employees to death. The alienation of youth from conventional corporate culture has caught the attention of management, especially as competition for talent now involves foreign companies operating in Japan. Talent-based promotion, better pay during the earlier years of work, and a loosening of after-work and weekend demands on young employees are among new policies.

Shortly before his death, Akio Morita of Sony, whose company embraced the Japanese model and successfully used it to become one of the premier corporations in the modern technological economy, understood that the model was flawed and that there was a critical need for change. He admitted that there was an exploitative dimension to the system, hidden perhaps in the general improvement of life for the Japanese in the postwar period. The long hours, strict rules, and snail-paced advancement had been a painful sacrifice for many. The low salaries and margins had perhaps squeezed the working class in the interest of growth too much. The rabbit hutches and lifetimes of toil six or seven days a week were realities. Morita understood that the world economy was changing and that it was time for Japan to change as well for practical as well as moral reasons. In fact he knew that the post-post-industrial economy of the nineties and the twenty-first century was ending the Japanese model as it had existed. From his point of view this was not to be lamented; systems naturally changed and evolved, as the Meiji created the prosperity of the prewar years. The Showa era had contributed to that of the postwar period. Morita hoped, however, that the new economic order would be a more humane one while retaining the good aspects of the old.

THE ROLE OF HIGH TECHNOLOGY

High technology is not a luxury but a necessity for Japan. For an island country with limited natural resources to survive in the contemporary world, it is necessary for its manufacture to have a very high value-added factor; that is, more and more skill, knowledge, and sophistication must be added to less and less raw material in the course of making a product if that product is to be sold at a high profit. That profit is required in order to pay for the importation of scarce raw materials and to maintain the standard of living to which the new society has become accustomed. This was the case of Great Britain in the nineteenth and twentieth centuries and is the case in Japan now to an even greater degree. A remarkable disparity between the sectors in the Japanese economy is shown in the percentage figures for the year 1988: primary (agriculture), 2.3 percent of the total economy; secondary (manufacture), 34.9 percent; tertiary (services), with the highest value-added factor, 62.8 percent. This last stage has given rise to the name "the postindustrial society."

It is in this field of high technology, including automobiles and electronic products (digital equipment, videocassette recorders, robots, and computers), that Japan has excelled. And since Japan's main trading partner has been the United States, there has been much rivalry and some cooperation in this area. The same tendencies have been increasingly seen of late in Japan's relations with the European Union and Asian competitors. All this simply underlines the emergence of an interrelated world trading community. The interrelation is nowhere more clearly seen than in a common dependence on the supply of crude oil.

It is useful at this point to contrast the dominance of the high-tech industry with the dramatic decline in the relative importance of Japan's agricultural sector. By 1993 agriculture made up only 1.5 percent of the GDP. Of Japan's 3,440,000 farming families, only 430,000, or 12.5 percent, in 1995, relied solely on farming income. In the remainder, at least one family member had a part-time job in another industry. In fact, at present, Japan is the world's largest net importer of agricultural products.

The technology issue is vital to Japan's past success and critical to its future survival. Beginning in the late 1950s decisions were made to achieve international dominance in advanced technology. Sheltering under the American military umbrella, the Japanese in the civilian sphere were able to concentrate on technology. To develop advanced technology, the Japanese have heavily funded research and development from private industrial sources. The proportion of GNP spent in this way has increased from .84 percent in 1955 to 2.9 percent in 1993. The earlier figure is less than 1 percent of the amount spent by the Federal Republic of Germany, while the latter figure surpasses that spent by the United Kingdom, France, Germany, or the United States. The amounts have continued to rise even in the face of the prolonged depression in the economy, reaching 4.7 percent of GDP by 1997. The latest research and development investment is targeted in the super-high-tech

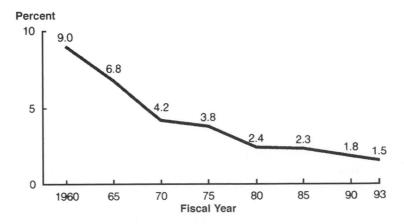

Share of Agricultural Production in GDP.

SOURCE: Ministry of Agriculture, Forestry, and Fisheries.

areas of IT, the space industry, new materials, software, biotech, artificial intelligence, and robotics. The labor force devoted to this effort includes 641,000 researchers in Japan (1999), second only to the United States with 949,000 (1989). These are mainly engineering graduates working on high-tech basic research. They have produced more journal articles than all other countries with the exception of the United States, and likewise in the number of registered patents for new products as of 1997.

THE OIL SHOCK

Japan has long understood that national survival in the industrial era depends on the availability of oil. By 1905 following its earth-shaking naval victory over Russia in the Tsushima Straits, the Imperial Navy converted its propulsion systems from coal to oil. By the 1930s the United States had become the chief supplier of oil to the Japanese Navy. Policies in the years leading up to World War II were driven by the strategic assumption that Japan would confront the United States and that there was a need to secure a reliable alternative supply of oil for industrial and military purposes. Engagement of the United States in 1941 was driven in part by the Imperial Navy's voracious appetite for oil. Postwar reconstruction and reindustrialization were even more dependent on oil to fuel the machines of production and product, such as plastics, chemicals, synthetics, fibers, fertilizers, and pesticides, not to mention the national and international transportation networks. By the early 1970s Japan's fleet of supertankers made a circle from the Persian Gulf to the home islands.

Japan was receiving 83 percent of its oil supply from the Arab countries and Iran. In November 1973 the Arab nations brought pressure on Japan to cut off diplomatic and trade relations with Israel and agree to supply the Arab nations with arms. In return for this Japan would be declared a "friendly nation" and receive uninterrupted supplies of oil. Japan refused. The government had already put into operation an anti-inflation plan, tightened credit, instituted emergency petroleum regulations, and frozen the price of rice. The budget for 1974 was called an "austerity budget," although it was still higher than that of the previous year. Inflation, however, running at 19 percent, was a serious problem for Japan. And in 1974 the country had a record deficit balance of payments, due mainly to the high price of oil.

The situation improved markedly from 1976 to 1978, and inflation rates dropped to 3.5 percent. An increase in Japan's favorable trade balance even led to problems with the United States; Japan was doing too well. Premier Fukuda promised President Carter in mid-1978 to reduce the trade surplus and hold down exports. Participants of the Bonn economic summit the same year brought pressure on Japan for this very policy; but performance was limited, and these promises had to be renewed on subsequent occasions. The lack of oil was a constant problem, causing a deficit balance of payments again in 1979. There were plans to expand the use of nuclear energy beyond the twenty-one nuclear power plants operating in 1980. Eleven additional units were then under construction, and three more were planned, which in all would increase output by two-thirds. In June 1990 there were thirty-nine nuclear power generators operating, with sixteen more planned. Electrical output from nuclear plants in 1990 was approximately twice that of the United Kingdom and one-third that of the United States. By 2003 Japan was operating fifty-eight nuclear reactors, including the revolutionary fast-breeder reactor, Monju, in Fukui prefecture.

The oil shocks and expansion of nuclear power did not, of course, end Japan's thirst for imported supplies. A national effort to reduce dependency directed by MITI and other governmental agencies promoted conservation and the shift to new and higher technology for value-added production. One result was a decline in the position of manufacturing within Japan's economy and the advancement of the tertiary sectors. Statistically, distribution services, finance and insurance, transport and telecommunications, electricity, gas, water supply, and other branches of the tertiary sector rose from 51 percent of the GDP in 1970 to 61.9 percent in 1993; the corresponding share of the employed population expanded from 47.4 percent in 1970 to 59.9 percent in 1993. The change was especially dramatic in the areas of distribution and services, which, by 1993, made up 12.1 percent and 15.8 percent of GDP, respectively, employing 22.4 percent and 23.5 percent of its workforce.

The oil shocks had a powerful impact, rippling through the distribution system. During the 1950s and 1960s Japan had been transformed into a consumer society, mass-produced goods, sales, and consumption forming a part of everyday life. At the retail level, department stores, supermarkets, and specialty shops began to replace neighborhood family shops. Contraction of the economy in the face of the oil shocks deflated consumer enthusiasm for endless acquisition; peoples' tastes changed and diversified. Manufacturers responded with more variety and smaller production runs; flexible manufacturing of smaller quantities spurred innovative technology. The Japanese have become masters of rapid innovation in the twenty-first century when cell phones, for example, have a four-month shelf life, and a new model car is outdated within a year of its release. Merchants, too, have had to change, spurring innovative marketing and advertising thus transforming the retail industry, contracting the number of stores from 6.6 percent between 1991 and 1994 down to 1.5 million, while small family shops declined by 10.9 percent during the same period. These contractions happened while annual sales rose by 0.7 percent to 143 trillion yen. A similar phenomenon affected eating and drinking establishments, reducing their numbers by 7 percent between 1986 and 1992 to 474,000 while sales increased (despite the bursting bubble in 1989) by 35 percent to 13.1 trillion yen.

EXPORTS—AUTOMOBILES

The most visible item in the surge of Japanese exports has for some years been the automobile. From 1955 onward Germany's Volkswagen had been the firm selling the highest number of cars imported into the United States. The Japanese Datsun began selling in the United States in 1960, and by 1975 it had replaced Volkswagen as the leader in sales. In 1976 Japan's export of cars to all markets was the highest in the world, followed far behind by France. Of the imported cars purchased in the United States that year, 62 percent were made in Japan. The U.S. Department of Commerce attributed the popularity of Japanese cars to their "competitive prices, reputation for quality, and efficient sales networks." At this point the U.S. production of automobiles was greater than that of Japan, but by the middle of 1980 Japan became the largest producer of cars and trucks in the world. The United States, which had dominated world auto production in the post–World War II period, was the world's largest market for autos and still considered itself auto-central of the universe.

The United States, not surprisingly, reacted. Douglas Fraser, president of the United Automobile Workers, called the conduct of Toyota and Nissan "outrageous—exporting not just cars but unemployment to the United States." Two hundred thousand American auto workers were unemployed in 1980. Fraser said that Japanese car manufacturers should be compelled by law to build cars in the United States. He visited Japan to persuade firms there to set up production in the United States or limit the number of cars exported, at the same time warning them that they risked future barriers of protectionist legislation. Honda announced plans to build an assembly plant in Ohio; Nissan and Toyota contemplated similar moves. To stave off American legislation, the Japanese government announced in June 1981 that it would place voluntary limits on car exports to the United States.

It is worthy of note that both of Fraser's remedies—the building of factories in the United States and limits on auto exports—found support in Japan. On the other hand, the union leader was typically American in looking to law in addition to management policy for answers, while the Japanese preferred voluntary action and consensus. Japanese factories were built in the United States, and voluntary limits on car and truck exports from Japan to the United States were adopted, which continue to the present day. The "voluntary" quotas for each Japanese exporting firm were set by MITI, a new role for this ministry but not untypical of the Japanese amalgamation of public and private policy.

A U.S. government study of the whole question released in July 1982 indicated that American auto production was weakened by a management style that was basically adversarial and control-oriented, "which . . . inspires no loyalty or commitment." Japan's success in capturing so much of the U.S. car market was "due less to superior technology and more to better management." The debate on this point continues. The part played by American workers has also been a matter of debate. The Speaker of the Japanese House of Representatives criticized them as being "too lazy" and further remarked that a third of them "cannot even read." But a Japan Labor Ministry study, issued in February 1992, found that, when the value of their work is calculated by purchasing power, American workers produce 1.62 times more than their Japanese counterparts.

Plans for joint ventures in automobile manufacture became realities, as the following partial list of factories indicates:

1982	Isuzu/General Motors	in Japan
1983	Toyota/General Motors	in California
1985	Mitsubishi/Chrysler	in Illinois
1988	Nissan/Ford	in Ohio

In a number of the joint-venture plants nonunion labor was hired, as preferred by the Japanese management. But in the Toyota/General Motors factory the first labor pact with the United Automobile Workers was signed. It included some significant provisions: the wage scale was slightly higher than that prevailing in General Motors; the union would have a say in the pace of work required (responding to the workers' fear of Japan's "driving" demands); and job classifications were reduced from the confusing dozens of classifications common at the Big Three U.S. auto firms to four, to make teamwork and negotiation easier for the incoming Japanese managers.

Cooperation in the economic field had to take place between Japan and the United States; it was so obviously in the interest of both governments and both manufacturing and merchant communities. But no one will imagine for a moment that the joint-venture road was without its awkward turns, to say nothing of periodic total roadblocks. Among these obstacles were problems of union versus nonunion labor, of stockholding, of taxation, and of expansion. There were also the difficulties caused by settling of Japanese nationals in local American communities. One big problem was "domestic content," that is, the proportion of American-made to foreign-made parts incorporated in the final product. Even the European Commission urged that antidumping duties be imposed upon "screwdriver plants" set up in Europe to assemble photocopiers, of which 70 to 98 percent of the parts were made in Japan.

American managers working for Japanese firms or for joint ventures in the United States have had varied reactions. Some have been enthusiastic at the success of new methods; some have been reasonably contented; and others have become resentful at the "glass ceiling" phenomenon, discovering that, after reaching some previously unmentioned level, they could not rise on the corporate ladder. Senior positions involving policy were reserved for Japanese executives in the United States; or policy matters were invariably referred to the headquarters of the firm in Japan. A variant of this practice, which seemed natural to the Japanese but not to the Americans, was the colleague-or-boss puzzle. A Japanese executive paired with an American was a great help in showing the latter the ropes at the beginning; yet at a certain point the American discovered that all decisions of any weight were being channeled through the Japanese colleague, while the American had to help in carrying them out. However, in a parallel situation, say in the Philippines, American control would probably have seemed quite natural to an American. Business is now truly global, and the consequences are only slowly being worked out.

As Japan edged closer to the twenty-first century, its eleven auto manu-facturers and thousands of parts producers contributed 42 trillion yen to the economy, constituting 13.4 percent of all Japanese manufacturing. They em-ploy 7.2 million workers from manufacturing to sales,which amounts to 11 percent of Japan's working population (as of 1993). During 2002 Toyota sur-passed the U.S. top three companies in market share within the United States. Honda and Nissan also threaten to surpass their American competitors. Econ-omy, reliability, the latest technology, and the ability of the Japanese compa-nies to speedily bring new models to production helps them increase market share not only in the United States, but throughout the world, even in the European Union. At the same time, European and American companies are expanding into the Japanese market, not by exporting, but by taking advan-tage of postbubble restructuring and the opening of Japanese industries and markets to foreign ownership and management. All three American compa-nies are invested in Japanese firms: GM with Toyota and Fuji Heavy (Su-baru), Ford with Mazda, and DaimlerChrysler with Isuzu. The French com-pany Renault purchased a controlling interest in Japan's second largest auto firm, Nissan, in 2000, dispatching Carlos Ghosn to take over management. Ghosn, applying a liberal amount of French capital and European manage-ment, has been able to engineer a remarkable turnaround as Japan's econ-omy moves rapidly into the global web of the twenty-first century.

EXPORTS—ELECTRONICS

Previous sections touched on the centrality of technology in Japan's postwar Miracle Economy. As MITI presided over the formation of new cartels in the 1950s, national policy made Japanese world superiority in technology its cen-tral concern; electronics formed the center of the center. From the 1950s through the 1970s Japan took advantage of the American electronics indus-try, which sold Japan, often at absurdly low cost, around 30,000 license and patent agreements. Western Electric's sale of patent rights to the transistor to what would become the Sony Corporation for the paltry sum of $25,000, epitomizes these transactions. Electronics were nurtured in the MITI-in-vented *Ikusei*, or "greenhouse program," which sheltered the electronics firms from foreign competition. By the 1980s, having perfected mass pro-duction and quality control systems, Japan came to dominate mass-market electronics. It remains on the cutting edge of such products, without serious competition.

Japan's unassailable dominance of market electronics, the result of man-ufacturing genius, prompted a shift during the 1980s in MITI targeting from technology to pure research and experimental science. Examples of this change can be seen in support for the Fifth Generation Project (computers capable of thinking) and HDTV (high-definition TV). Significantly, neither of these heavily invested efforts produced the expected results. The Fifth Gen-eration artificial intelligence project was scuttled in 1992 after 10 years. While it did train hundreds of Japanese engineers in advanced computer science and did demonstrate the potential of parallel processing (running 1,000 processors in parallel), cost and limited results discouraged continuing the effort. The HDTV project based on analogue technology was also set aside as global markets seemed to favor digital formatting promoted by U.S. and EU companies. Japan's efforts in these research areas triggered responses in the United States. Consortia of companies within the military industrial complex combined resources to compete with the Japanese on artificial intelligence work. In 1990 the Bush administration budgeted $30 million in federal research funds for an HDTV project to compete with the Japanese who had invested $1 billion.

Recent global changes are influencing Japan's role in the high-tech electronics industries. The rise of the NIEs (Newly Industrializing Economies) including Korea, Taiwan, and the countries of Southeast Asia and China generated new markets and new competition. Japanese companies continue offshoring the production and assembly of mass-market electronics. As a result, Japan has lost dominance in various sectors. For example, South Korea has become the main producer of DRAM electronic chips. Japan controlled 90 percent of world market share for these chips in 1990, and just 40 percent in 1996. Weaker domestic producers are being allowed to die out as the "convoy system" of intracorporate support wanes. Of course, powerful global auto and electronics companies like Toyota, Honda, Sony, and Matsushita continue to be dynamic and profitable, and Japan remains the leader in the very high-technology sectors of design and production of goods, machinery, and precision computer-generated molding and modeling. Japan invests heavily in the merging of electronics with biotech, new machinery, software, artificial intelligence, and robotics. Japanese investment in high-tech research and development continued to increase, even in the face of the lingering recession of the 1990s reaching 4.7 percent of GDP in 1997.

Most of the triumphs and some of the difficulties of Japanese industry in the twentieth century are given a human face and reflected in the life of a remarkable man, Matsushita Konosuke,[5] who died on April 27, 1989, at the age of ninety-four. He was the founder of the Matsushita Electric Industrial Company, now the largest firm in the world supplying electric and electronic consumer goods. Matsushita started in 1918 by selling a new type of electric light socket; his firm now sells everything from rice cookers to videocassette recorders (VCRs) and DVDs. By 1980 the sales—many of the items under the name Panasonic—were in the region of $41 billion.

Matsushita was a self-made man, a supersalesman, and a hard driver. His motto seems to have been "We protect our family and care little about outsiders." When his firm first expanded overseas, he purchased Quasar TV, an American business. The product was improved; soon almost no repairs were

---

[5] Again, the reader should note that throughout this book, surnames are placed first and given names second. See Preface.

required. However, one of his Japanese managers in the United States was forbidden to fraternize with his American colleagues because he was becoming "too American." Then Quasar's American technical and engineering staff was phased out. No Japanese were fired; their salaries were even raised. Japanese suppliers in Japan were used to furnish the components for the plants in the United States, even though their prices were higher. Matsushita erected over foreigners not a glass but an armor-plated ceiling.

All this took place in the early days of Japanese-American industrial interchange; relations have improved since then. But one cannot understand Matsushita Konosuke and his mindset until one looks more deeply into the history of modern Japan. Consider what Matsushita passed through in experience and memory. He was born in 1895, the last year of the Sino-Japanese War, just when both nations were emerging into the modern world from a rich but isolated past. Ten years later Japan defeated Russia and amazed everyone. By the time Matsushita had established his small business at the end of World War I, his country was entering a short period of openness and liberalism. But this was immediately succeeded by the heyday of the militarists. At that time a young man of twenty-three would easily acquire an immense sense of pride and a feeling of superiority to other nations. It was a time of confident expansion to be followed in turn by the humiliation of utter defeat in 1945, the first time a conqueror had ever set foot on the sacred soil of Japan. Matsushita was then fifty years old, ready and fully charged, like one of his batteries, to go out and conquer in turn—this time economically. He was going to do it by his own rules, yielding to international rules where it was absolutely necessary, keeping his own counsel, and never ceasing in his determination to succeed, by energy, ingenuity, pride, and self-assertion. His story is in many ways the story of the Japan of this age.

In amassing his firm's and his own wealth, Matsushita-san was known to operate in the gray area, if not in the black of illegality. To capture a larger market share of a particular product such as VCRs in the United States, he would sell them there at a lower price than that on the domestic Japanese market, a practice known as "dumping." He cut the U.S. distributors into the deal in the following manner. The customs import declaration would state a price near the current U.S. market price. The dealer would then add his markup; but in addition Matsushita would make a secret refund to the dealer through a Swiss bank account. He would lose money temporarily but gain an important share of American sales.

The eagerness for market share naturally worked both ways. In the spring of 1987 the Reagan administration planned a 100 percent retaliatory tariff against Japanese electronics goods, charging, among other things, that the Japanese were dumping computer chips through third world countries, such as Malaysia, for re-export to the United States, thereby undercutting the American manufacturers. At the end of April, Premier Nakasone visited Washington to try to allay the discontent of both the United States and the European Community over a record Japanese trade surplus of $101 billion in the previous year. President Reagan promised to review the 100 percent tariff; but the very next day the U.S. House of Representatives passed a bill requiring the president to order retaliation against any trade partners that did not open their markets to U.S. products. By the end of the 1980s the Japanese bubble burst, sending the economy into a prolonged recessionary cycle. During these years of Japanese recession, the U.S. economy entered its own expansionary phase. Extolled as the "new economy," U.S. expansion was driven by its information technology and finance sectors. In response, the Japanese had to globalize, offshoring factories for the production of autos and electronics. These processes allowed foreign companies to finally penetrate Japan's domestic economy. The once monolithic "Japan Inc." came to build most of its autos in the United States or other markets. Japanese industries were forced to restructure. Even global giants like Matsushita have recently announced cuts of more than a thousand jobs, the closing of domestic plants, and the relocation of primary electric motor manufacturing to China. By 1990 Japan was exporting more to Asia than to the U.S. market. By 2004 a restructured, global Japanese market appears to be slowly improving.

OTHER EXPORTS

In addition to exports in the automotive and electronic fields already mentioned, Japan sells abroad such important items as steel, machine tools, ceramics, and textiles. Japan has been a leader in machine tools of extreme sophistication. Toshiba, for example, found itself in trouble for illegally exporting to the former U.S.S.R. computer software to control a machine tool for honing submarine propeller blades. This tool finished them to such a fine tolerance as to make them scarcely audible to enemy sonar tracking. Items which the West used to connect with Japan, such as shoes, clothes, and toys, have long ago passed to the newly industrialized countries (NICs)— Hong Kong, Taiwan, Singapore, South Korea, Indonesia, and the Philippines. Japan has progressed to couture and high fashion, in which it has recently become successful.

FOREIGN IMPORTS

Throughout the first fifteen years following the end of World War II, Japan's industrial output was swallowed up by its domestic economy. Rebuilding and development in all sectors drew in imports, especially from the United States, which was the only industrialized nation to escape the devastation of war. By the late 1950s, however, a revitalizing Europe along with the United States had already begun to worry about a Japanese competitive edge. Building rapidly on its immense, highly sophisticated prewar industrial and human resources, guided by national policy, and protected behind a labyrinthine system of tariff, structural, legal, and other barriers, the Japanese were shifted to competitive mode. At the same time they closed off their markets to foreign imports. The United States and many other countries were frustrated by the Japanese unwillingness to open up their markets to foreign imports. In 1983, after the U.S. electronic industry complained of Japanese government loans, tax breaks, and support for research to their companies, the Japanese authorities agreed to open certain high-technology markets, in particular the lucrative sources in the national Nippon Telephone and Telegraph (NTT). The United States also gained some access to Japan in drugs and medical equipment by an agreement in 1985.

But one Japanese market, agriculture, is particularly difficult to crack open. The farm lobby is very strong, had close ties with the then ruling Liberal Democratic Party (LDP), and makes campaign contributions to many politicians. Rice is a special case in Japanese agriculture. The rice farmer has been from ancient times a traditional figure, honored as the foundation of the state. Rice growers in California and the southern United States could export huge quantities of rice from their large, flat, efficiently cultivated tracts. But Japan has imposed a ban on the import of all foreign rice. The farmers in Japan grow only a fixed quota of rice. They have to sell all their crop to the government, which determines the price and then sells the rice to the consumer at four or five times the world market rate. As with industry, so farming interests have often tied the hands of Japanese officials.

In early 1983, the United States was bringing pressure to bear on Japan for the removal of quotas on imports of beef and citrus products. A week before Premier Nakasone's conference with President Reagan began, Nakasone received a petition with 9 million signatures urging that he reject the American demands. Five years later the two nations finally signed a pact eliminating these quotas. It was estimated that this would double the amounts of American beef and citrus products exported to Japan. However, although quotas had been eliminated, they were replaced by a customs duty of 70 percent on beef, declining later to 50 percent.

Despite these barriers, Japan's main imports in foodstuffs come from the United States, 33.2 percent in 1989. And to the surprise of everyone, a rice shortage surfaced in mid-1992, affecting not so much the regular consumers as the manufacturers of rice products, such as sake and rice cakes. Unwilling to alter the ban on imported rice, the Japanese government released 30,000 tons from its reserve specifically to these manufacturers until the 1992 harvest came in.

As of 2003 the Japanese still produce 74 percent of their agricultural needs in a highly subsidized agricultural system. Most of the 26 percent of imports come from the United States.

By the mid-1980s, faced with hostility from both the United States and the European Union over trade imbalances and forced to restructure by globalization, the prime minister, Nakasone Yasuhiro, formed an Advisory Group on Economic Structural Adjustment for International Harmony. The Advisory Group was headed by former Bank of Japan governor, Maekawa Haruo.

Trade Crises between Japan and the West.

SOURCE: Jean-Marie Bouissou, *Japan: The Burden of Success* (Boulder, CO: Lynne Rienner Publishers, 2002), p. 231.

The group produced the Maekawa Report followed by the New Maekawa Report of the Economic Council, promulgated in May of 1987. These documents signaled Japan's intention to embark on major restructuring of its economy, turning from an export-directed model to growth based on stimulating domestic demand. The reports were comprehensive, and they opened Japan to all types of products and services. Tariffs and legal, market, and structural barriers fell throughout the 1990s. Corporations accelerated the offshoring of industrial production. Japan's markets from IT to banking, financial and insurance services, retailing, advertising, industrial products and services, and even agricultural products, including rice, have been opened. Now, at the beginning of the twenty-first century, there is some reduction in Japan's trade surpluses. Competitors agree that there is a more equitable playing field.

U.S.-JAPAN TRADE NEGOTIATIONS

American negotiators, although constantly pressed by industry to be tough on the Japanese, have been strictly limited in the demands they can make because of the enormous size of the U.S. national debt. If they offend Japanese business, there is always the danger that Japanese financiers will withdraw their funds from Treasury bonds which are essential to the financing of the debt. A useful mechanism in U.S.-Japan trade negotiations was the Structural Impediments Initiative, setting up a continuing process in which representatives of Japan and the United States make concrete suggestions to each other on how to reform their economies. In some disputes it may have a positive effect; but it is a controversial meeting point of two different lifestyles reflecting two different cultures.

GOVERNMENT CONTROL VERSUS PRIVATIZATION

It is by now clear that the government of Japan exercises strong control over its businesses and its citizens. For example, in the stock market crisis of 1987 the government brought pressure to bear upon the top banks, and they ceased to issue loans for speculation in real estate. This was an attempt to control a sharp rise in the value of land; an average family home in the city then cost $500,000 or more. Business, on the other hand, had its own way of influencing, if not controlling, the government through campaign contributions to the ruling Liberal Democratic Party members. There is, however, a new trend lessening government control by privatization and deregulation.

In the spirit of the Maekawa Report, during 1985 Nippon Telephone and Telegraph was denationalized, ending the huge monopoly on telecommunication. Up to two-thirds of the government-owned stock was to be gradually sold off to private individuals and companies. Two years later, in 1987, Japan National Railways was privatized after 115 years of existence. A number of smaller feeder lines had been privately owned from the beginning, but the national railway was by far the largest. The system had made no profit for twenty-two years; it had a drastic loss in 1985, involving the government in a debt of $250 billion. But the service was safe, speedy, and generally reliable, known best for the famous *shinkansen*, "bullet trains," among the first in the world to run regularly at 125 miles per hour. Before the announcement of privatization there had been serious strikes and stoppages, some involving violence. Premier Nakasone succeeded in pushing the new plan through the Diet. Management would endeavor to find other jobs for the 91,000 employees expected to be fired. The new company would form the Japan Railways Group, divided into six regional groups, a freight group, and four auxiliary groups for research, maintenance, and so forth.

Privatization efforts were extended to other money losing sectors. The tobacco monopoly, National Theater, and Japan Airlines were turned over to the private investors. In June 2003, the government decided that the Japan National Oil Corporation, with debts of almost $40 billion, would be dissolved by March 31, 2005. Privatization is one part of the government's efforts to transform the economy. Other changes include deregulation, development of global markets, and the opening of Japan's financial and capital markets. There have also been programs to stimulate domestic demand and reform the state welfare system. All these changes had been formulated in the mid-1890s by the government of Prime Minister Hosokawa Morihiro. His Advisory Group for Structural Reform under Hiraiwa Gaishi, then chairman of the Keidanren (Japan Federation of Economic Organizations) had included these initiatives in its road map for change. In all of these initiatives the Japanese are making significant structural changes.

THE BUBBLE AND BEYOND

By the 1980s, Japan had reached the pinnacle of economic success, power, and influence. It was respected and emulated as part of the global economy. In 1988 seven of the top ten world banks and six of the top ten richest men in the world were Japanese. Using apparently inexhaustible resources, Japanese banks and investors gobbled up high-profile landmarks around the world. For example, Sony purchased CBS in 1987, Rockefeller Center in the middle of Manhattan, along with numerous office towers, condominiums, and stores. By the late 1980s Japanese interests controlled one percent of total U.S. property values, approximately $32.5 billion worth. Without question, Japan had achieved its postwar objective of catching up with and, in some areas, surpassing the West.

The cost, however, was that as part of a global economic system Japan's long-cherished dream of autarchy had become impossible. Japan's destiny was tied to the global economy, especially that of its postwar mentor and prime partner, the United States. While, as a major trading nation, Japan had regularly experienced jolts through the global system (the oil shocks of 1973 and 1979, for example), black October of 1987 was an unprecedented event. As markets in New York and London collapsed, Japan was pulled into the vortex. On October 20 the Nikkei average showed that 5.4 trillion yen ($400 billion) in value had been wiped out in a single day. Though the markets stabilized within a week and there was some economic improvement with GNP growth for that year at 5.7 percent, up from 4.0 of the previous year, clearly, Japan's vulnerability quotient had risen with its success. At the time, most Japanese were unaware that their economy was about to enter a major prolonged recessionary spiral. The lost decade of the 1990s began with the ominous sound of the bursting asset bubble, the collapsing of the iron triangle of business, bureaucracy, and political party, and the shaking confidence of people accustomed to an ever improving quality of life.

In fact, the disaster of the 1990s can be understood as the convergence of two storms, the pounding waves of global economic change, suggested above, and the deep undertow caused by the disintegration of Japan's postwar economic model. In the early 1990s the full significance of Japan's domestic economic crisis was not immediately evident. Pundits and scholars in the United States and Europe regularly imagined a Japanese conquest of the world. French Prime Minister Edith Cresson worried about Europe's ability to fend off Japanese economic power. Writers like James Fallows seriously discussed "the coming war with Japan." Yet as Japan was perceived as a threat, economist Shimada Haruo wrote in August 1989 of feelings of unease in the face of Japan's booming economy.

Shimada's unease was well founded. He went on to explain his concern for what he called "investment alchemy using fictitious values." For example: "The price of Japanese land is simply beyond belief. Its total value of 1.6 quadrillion yen in 1987 was enough to purchase all the land in the U.S. four times over, in other words it is valued at 100 times the unit value of that in the U.S."[6] Stock shares, too, had become absurdly inflated. An even greater danger was that the Japanese were dazzled by their own "investment alchemy" so that they indulged in a "euphoric confidence that Japan's economic prosperity and its position as the world's mightiest financial power would last forever."[7] Ushio Jiro, founder and chairman of the electronics company, Ushio Inc., and chairman of Keizai Doyukai (Japan Association of Corporate Executive) noted a structural change in the global capitalist system which was forcing change in what he characterized as the extreme arrogance of the 1980s.

In time Japanese banks accounted for a full quarter of the total assets of banks in London; they were also responsible for 20 percent of the total corporate lending in New York. The pumping up of Japan's asset bubble, the hyper-valuation of real estate, stocks, and overseas investments benefited from the distinctive qualities of Japan's modernization and postwar reconstruction models. To summarize the insights of Gyohten Toyoo, economist and former vice-minister of finance until the early 1990s, economic life in Japan was guided by "the 1880 legacy." Japan's earliest modernization and industrialization began in the 1860s during the Meiji period. From this time the Japanese reached a consensus on national purpose to catch up with and surpass the West; this consensus assumed that failure would threaten national survival. Under these circumstances, driven by a sense of urgency and shaped by inherited cultural norms, it was accepted that Japan's modernization would incorporate a form of state capitalism along with central planning. Market forces were accepted, but a critical state role was never questioned.

In this context, the origins of Japan's financial industry differed from that of the West. The banking system was specifically set up to facilitate modernization and industrialization by gathering the savings of the people for investment and to handle foreign exchange. In Gyohten's words: "The authorities took the lead, viewing banks as a tool for the strategic apportionment of funds to power economic development." Thus banks never grew spontaneously; rather they were seen by the people "virtually as a public utility . . . to receive deposits from the general public and distribute them among industries supporting the nation." Playing a critical role in the struggle for national survival, banks could not be allowed to fail. Depositors were protected by the government's backing of banks and the use of what is called the "convoy system" in which no industry was allowed to fall behind. To insure this

---

[6] Haruo Shimada, "Asset Inflation and the Strained Social Fabric," in Masuzoe Yoichi, *Years of Trial: Japan in the 1990s* (Tokyo: Japan Echo, 2000), p. 133.
[7] Ibid.

system, the Ministry of Finance and the Bank of Japan established strict regulations and critical supervision of the banks.

A result of this fiscal system was that Japanese industries relied heavily on bank loans for financing rather than on equities markets as is done in the West. It also helped to forge the iron triangle of bureaucracy, business, and government in which each corner had a vested interest in the destiny of the others, and an inevitable closed system conducive to corruption took shape. There were, however, great strengths in the system as well. For example, the efficient coordination of bureaucratic expertise, economic resources, and political will helped to propel Japan from its agrarian condition to an industrial power by 1900 and onto the world stage by the middle of the twentieth century. This same system managed Japan's reconstruction with dramatic success through the remainder of the century.

Unquestionably the Japanese national economy, supported by the iron triangle, served the country well through most of the twentieth century. Success, however, produced overconfidence and disdain for competitors who increasingly felt that the Japanese were "playing by their own rules" and had unfair advantages. The structural changes in the global economy that were transforming economic life were often ignored by Japan. In 1985, the Plaza Accord, which changed international exchange rates from postwar "fixed" to floating, caused a dramatic increase in the value of the yen from the fixed $360 to $120, an increase of three times the 1985 rate. This change, initiated by the United States, had an immediate and dramatic impact on exports. To counter the negative effect, the government reduced interest rates. This policy of easy money left the banks "awash in liquidity." Subsequent massive investment in stocks and real estate rapidly propelled these assets to unprecedented and unreal heights as discussed above.

Further value inflation was fueled by the government's efforts to deregulate the financial sector. Specifically, the opening of bond and capital markets to foreign investors provided Japanese industry with new huge sources of investment funds, which were irresistible. Thus corporate Japan began to separate from its traditional link to bank loan capital and globalized its funding source. That is to say, the globalization of the Japanese economy and its convergence into what would be called the "new economy" had begun with the concurrent loss of control and autonomy.

There were other, more ominous effects of these changes that were not at first apparent. The economist Ozawa Terutomo notes that as corporations dipped into their own wealth and the new overseas capital sources, small and medium-sized manufacturers, housing-loan companies, real estate firms, and construction companies replaced them as the bank's major borrowers. While these new borrowers leveraged the rising value of their assets to borrow ever more, their lenders, operating in a new environment, were unprepared and unable to regulate the process. As a result, an uncontrollable rise in lending for speculative investments became possible. Sooner rather than later the spiraling asset bubble was brought down by its own weight. The catalyst was provided by the bureaucracy which, concerned about the unrealistic inflation of values, tried to cool the economy by increasing the discount rate in early 1990.

The rapid collapse of the banking system and stock values has been mentioned. Strapped with hundreds of billions of yen on nonperforming loans, worthless properties, industrial overcapacity, and a plummeting stock market which had lost 38 percent of its value, or $2.07 trillion, Japan entered the 1990s. The bursting of the bubble did not immediately change life for most Japanese; it did, however, expose the fragmenting base of the 1880's legacy, and it led to changes in the iron triangle, politics, and society.

Japanese government and corporations responded by embracing globalization. They began to restructure industries. The government started to deregulate all sectors of the economy. Domestic industries, which had been closed to foreign investors, were finally opened. The lopsided flow of Japanese capital to foreign markets could now be brought into better balance. New capital began to arrive, helping stimulate the economy. By 2001 more than $32 billion was invested, growing from a mere $5 billion in 1990. During the past several years direct foreign investment has continued to expand with new competitors, including even the People's Republic of China.

Along with opening markets to foreign capital, the Japanese allowed changes in management, ownership, and new financial instruments like mergers and acquisitions. American companies including Goldman Sachs, Merrill Lynch, and Morgan Stanley Dean Witter have become important deal makers, buying up and consolidating failing or bankrupt Japanese companies. In August 2003, Ripplewood Holdings L.L.C. spent $4 billion taking over Japan Telecom Holdings fixed-line assets. It now has a foothold in Japan's high end information technology sector. Foreign investors are also moving into the Japanese insurance industry and recently took over six of its major companies.

Similar changes are taking place in manufacturing and retailing. American and European companies are heavily invested in the Japanese auto industry controlling Fuji Heavy Industry's Subaru brand, Mazda, Mitsubishi, and even Nissan, Japan's second largest company now owned by Renault of France. American retail giants like Wal-Mart and fast food chains like McDonald's are speeding a restructuring of the retail and food markets, destroying the traditional mom and pop neighborhood stores and the old sense of community as well.

Finally, Western services industries are moving into Japan. For example, American Selectron, the world's largest electronics manufacturing services (EMS) industry, took control of Sony's giant research facility in Nakanitta in 1999. This facility contains much of Sony's most advanced research capital; its control by a foreign company is very significant.

This new opening of Japan is qualitatively different from other openings in the past. It is the first time in Japan's history that foreign direct investment, managerial control, and ownership of significant financial and industrial assets have been embraced as a national policy. On November 11, 2003, Prime Minister Koizumi Junichiro was reelected for a second term on a platform committed to continuing the new global economic policies. His reappointment of Heizo Takenaka, 52, to concurrent positions in economics and banking is a signal that reform will continue and expand. These reforms constitute an end to the Japanese model of the past, with its parochial Japan-centered orientation. The admirable qualities of that model, lifetime employment, seniority-based salary increases, harmonic company-based unions, and positive worker-management relations including relatively egalitarian income scales are all weakening. The Japanese remain unwilling, however, to completely abandon their "companyism" (the corporate equivalent of "familism") in favor of a Western model, which considers only the interests of shareholders. They are looking for a compromise that can soften the blows of hardball capitalism in favor of familiar ideals of the past.

17

JAPAN TODAY—FOREIGN AFFAIRS AND POLITICAL LIFE

FOREIGN AFFAIRS

Japan began its modern diplomatic history in the 1850s when the United States used threats of military action to force the country out of more than 200 years of isolation. In these early years of the third millennium, the United States remains the most important single star in Japan's foreign affairs universe. Japan's foreign relations have always been intimately bound up with the economic concerns, which are discussed above, but there have been purely diplomatic aspects as well. Following World War II as Japan struggled to rebuild, regulated by the "peace constitution" imposed by the United States, its diplomatic options were limited and leaders correctly maintained a "low posture." Japan willingly and successfully served as a base for U.S. military actions during the years of the cold war from the 1940s through 1989, and most importantly during the Korean War, 1950–1953, and the Vietnam War, 1963–1975. Subsequently, through the end of the cold war with the fall of the Soviet regime in 1989, Japan remained a solid anchor and ally of the United States in East Asia, this, in spite of trade and economic tensions during these years. As the new millennium unfolds and the international community reconfigures in the aftermath of the cold war, the 9/11/01 terrorist attack on the United States, and the U.S.-led wars in Afghanistan and Iraq, Japan remains firmly committed to its close ties with the United States and takes these ties as the key links in its international position.

In autumn 2003, Japan's English-speaking prime minister, Koizumi Junichiro, building on his reputed "friendship" with U.S. president George W. Bush, strongly reaffirmed the centrality of the U.S. link in Japan's foreign policy. Aside from economic issues and Japan's limited military options (see below), the ascending power of China, the unpredictable behavior of North

231

Korea, and frictions with Russia all foster the American option. The general sense is that never, in recent years, has the Japan-U.S. relationship been better. This has not always been the case.

Throughout the postwar years, the shadow of defeat at the hands of the United States lay over official and popular sentiment regarding America. The need to rely on U.S. military power and its nuclear shield, as well as the presence of U.S. forces on Japanese soil, weighed heavily on the Japanese. There has been a tension between necessity and the desire for independence. Throughout the 1960s and 1970s the U.S.-Japan security treaty came to symbolize this tension. The decennial question of renewal inevitably triggered suppressed shame in the government and mass protests and demonstrations among the people. When the treaty was automatically extended in 1970, for example, nine days of large-scale and violent demonstrations were unleashed across Japan involving 750,000 people; 600 arrests were made. Conditions in Okinawa, which the United States had turned into a base for dozens of military installations, fueled much of the popular anti-American sentiment. When governance of Okinawa was returned to Japan in 1972, although many bases remained, a major cause of resentment was removed.

Aside from specific problems like Okinawa, there was the deeper issue of U.S. treatment of Japan. The American tendency to ignore or dismiss Japanese sensitivities continued to incite anti-American sentiment. For example, President Nixon's surprise rapprochement with the People's Republic of China in 1972 caught the Japanese completely off guard. Then Prime Minister Sato learned of the visit from a television broadcast. His comment at the time: "It must be an historic event, since he himself says so." This pattern of neglect and noblesse oblige strained U.S.-Japan relations throughout subsequent years. Aside from friction over trade issues, the Japanese continued to support U.S. policies with funds, as in the first Gulf War in the fall of 1991. With increasing U.S. concerns about Korea in the 1990s and a shift to a positive China policy under President Clinton, the Japanese felt increasingly marginalized and exploited. For example, when Clinton flew to China in 1998 for meetings with Jiang Zemin, he did not even stop in Japan. Subsequent U.S. discussions with Korea over the firing of rockets near the Japanese archipelago (the Taepodong Incident), while done in consultation with China, ignored Japan completely.

The scene shifted, however, bringing Japan and the United States closer together. The 9/11 terrorist attacks on the New York World Trade Center and the Pentagon, followed by the wars in Afghanistan and Iraq, brought swift support from Prime Minister Koizumi and promises to deploy Japan Self-Defense Force (SDF) units. Even prior to the events of the past few years, with Japanese economic reform and restructuring and a new, more balanced global financial setting, the two nations have been trying to adjust their relationship. As early as 1992 Clinton and Hashimoto signed the Alliance for the Twenty-First Century. Described by Bouissou as a "fundamental change" in the relationship, the alliance was a major step in transforming the military cooperation of the two countries in East Asia. In the economic sphere, Japan's wealth continues as a source of leverage. A key player in all the significant agencies of global economic cooperation, Japan was a founding member of the WTO in January 1995. As the two largest economies in the industrialized world, Japan and the United States will be key allies in the foreseeable future.

RELATIONS WITH CHINA

From a literary standpoint one might say that Japan's history began with China. Along with borrowing the Chinese orthography in the fourth and fifth centuries, Japan embraced much of Chinese culture, values, and institutions. During the ebb and flow of their long and intimate relationship, Japan reached across the China Sea time and again only to close inward for periods of assimilation and search for self-identity. Through this process the Japanese retained a deep respect and even gratitude for their neighbors to the west. At the time of Japan's modernization during the nineteenth century, the great Qing dynasty, last of the imperial Chinese states, was showing signs of decay. Assaulted by civil war and foreign economic and military power, China fell into a phase of revolution and unimaginable violence, which was accelerated by Japan's own military during the Sino-Japanese War of 1894–1895. These nineteenth century attacks were but a prelude to the massive Sino-Japanese wars of the twentieth century, which some demographers claim cost the Chinese 30 million casualties. Broken and torn by continuous civil war until 1949, China had to endure another fifty years of civil war and reconstruction under a communist authoritarian system. Only since the late 1970s did China begin its rise to renewed power and influence.

In this context, Japan's relationship with China during the last decades of the twentieth century is woven tightly with threads of history, the memory of twentieth century violence, and the retarded yet dramatic ascent of China during the 1990s. For the first time in close to 200 years China is once again emerging as a colossal economic, military, and cultural presence in Japan's backyard. Japan's immense global economic power and limited offensive military resources have conditioned this relationship; shifts in economic and military resources continue to shape Sino-Japanese dialogue in the twenty-first century.

Prior to the the early 1970s when Nixon went to China without consulting the Japanese, the Japanese simply followed the U.S. cold war policy of isolation and embargo of the People's Republic of China (PRC). Official relations were maintained with Taiwan. Nixon's disregard for Japanese sensitivities caused a shift. Japan began to build its own East Asian foreign policy centered on the recognition of the PRC. Mao Zedong's death in September 1976, followed by the ascent of revisionists under the leadership of Deng Xiaoping by 1979 during the 11th CCP (Chinese Communist Party) Congress, transformed China's leadership. For the first time since the 1950s,

China opened itself to the outside world. Though deep suspicions and buried anger had to be sublimated, the Chinese welcomed Japan along with other capitalist economies to participate in the development of new economic initiatives.

Japan, for its part, moved with some caution but could not resist the China fever, which swept the world as doors were opened. More than one billion potential customers and the Japanese understanding of the need to get in on the ground floor and build networks for long-term growth stirred the government and corporations to action. The 1980s saw frequent visits by Japanese prime ministers to the PRC. The old ties to Taiwan were downgraded to unofficial status though, unlike the United States, Japan continued investment and trade with the island. Prime Ministers Suzuki and Nakasone both visited China. In 1982 Nakasone took along $2.8 billion in low-interest loans, the largest amount of foreign aid ever given by Japan up to that time. The money, for distribution over seven years, was for critical infrastructure development. By 1986 Japan already had a trade surplus of $4 billion with China, which led to friction in the young relationship.

Aside from trade frictions, which continued into the 1990s, there were other issues unsettling the Japan-China relationship. Both sides tried to ignore the opened wounds of World War II, but it was impossible. Historical memory could also be enlisted in domestic as well as international political struggles. For example, the Japanese have been unable to express a suitable "apology" for the immense suffering their war policy caused the Chinese. They have been unable to settle their own collective memory of the war as evident in the "textbook controversy" of the 1990s in which officially approved school textbooks ignored the significance of the war and used neutral terminology to describe Japan's policies. In spite of strong protests from China, Korea, and other targets of Japanese aggression, the books were allowed to stand. Even more hurtful to the Chinese and Koreans were the visitations of Japanese government officials to the Yasukuni Shrine in Tokyo. This shrine, a remnant of State Shinto from the Meiji and war years, had been specifically built to house the souls of Japanese war dead from overseas campaigns. The shrine provides not only a home for these souls, but also a place for their deification as *Kami* or "gods," in the Shinto tradition. Visitation implies a ritual honoring of these souls and recognition of their sacrifice on behalf of the Japanese emperor and nation. That is to say, it implies a vindication of the war. In 1985, Nakasone became the first Japanese prime minister to make an official visit to the shrine since the war; while protests from China and Korea temporarily put a halt to such official visits, cabinet members and prime ministers resumed the practice in the 1990s. In 2003 Prime Minister Koizumi regularly visited Yasukuni along with other government and party officials. While still a bone of contention, the new openness fits well with Japan's remilitarization. China, busy absorbing huge Japanese ODA (overseas development assistance) and direct business investment and expanding her own military power, appears somewhat less concerned with rituals related to history.

Finally, the 1990s witnessed the spectacular rise of China as a regional and global power. China's resurgence encompasses the full spectrum of human concerns from economic success, with consistent 8–10 percent annual growth statistics, through military and high-tech achievements. The latter include China's invitation to cooperate with the European Union in establishing the Navistar global navigation system, to be completed in 2008, in competition with the United States and the launch of its first manned orbiter in the fall of 2003. In contrast, for Japan the 1990s have been "the lost decade," symbolized by chronic economic problems notwithstanding improvements in the latter half of 2003. The contrast between China's successes and Japan's seemingly intractable problems is reflected in the growing ascendancy of China as a new center of East Asian regional dynamics. For example, in recent regional economic, military, and diplomatic forums, such as the Jakarta meeting of ASEAN (Association of Southeast Asian Nations), October 2003, China was clearly the dominant influence. Of course, Japan's economic power is never forgotten, but that power is becoming less decisive as China returns to a central roll. Both countries have also been part of the East Asian arms race of the 1990s; the nature of the balance between them is still taking shape in the post–cold war transition.

RELATIONS WITH KOREA

Two conditions continue to dominate Japan's relationship with Korea: the prolonged, abusive treatment of Koreans by Japanese beginning during the Meiji period through colonization and World War II, and the cold war political division of the Korean peninsula into Northern and Southern states. The latter has engendered a unique and problematical trilateral relationship that has intensified during the post-cold war decade of the 1990s. The former runs as a leitmotif through every dimension of Japan's relationship with the two Koreas.

From earliest times Japan has been intimately linked to Korea, which served as a conduit to the great culture of the mainland and provided Japan with a steady stream of artisans, craftsmen, monks, intellectuals, and populations at the elite and mass level. Japan maintained economic and military colonies in southern Korea and waged wars there, including Hideyoshi Toyotomi's attempt to conquer the peninsula in the sixteenth century, interestingly, on his way to conquering China and the entire world. This dynamic changed rapidly with Japan's successful Meiji modernization when, as with the China connection, traditional respect changed to a critical condescending attitude. The conquest and annexation of Korea in 1910 was a logical development of Japan's efforts to emulate and surpass the West, including the acquisition of an empire. The Japanese opinion of Koreans during this period was expressed well by Japan's first resident-general of Korea, Ito Hirobumi,[1] who on his deathbed, following an attack by a Korean nationalist, used his last breath to call, "Damned fool [*baka, na yatsu*]."[2] Sadly this attitude of disdain informed much of Japan's treatment of Koreans throughout the years of the empire. For example, the Korean language was banned in favor of education in Japanese, and Koreans were even obliged to take Japanese surnames; these cultural assaults came on top of a general brutalization and militarization of society, engendering a deep legacy of distrust and even hatred of the Japanese.

The atmosphere of distrust has not been entirely dissipated, yet there have been important changes, especially in Japan's relationship with the Republic of Korea (south). While there have been formal apologies, including that of Emperor Akihito in 1990, issues remain, like the Japanese unwillingness to deal forthrightly with war time "comfort women" (Korean, southeast Asian, Chinese, and even Japanese women forced to provide sexual favors to soldiers in field brothels). The Chinese have never felt completely satisfied. Needless to say Korea, like China, was incensed over the textbook controversy and continues to cast a wary eye on Japan's recent military transformation. There are, however, changes, including the south's emergence as a significant economic competitor. In steel, autos, shipbuilding, high-tech electronics, and certain agricultural areas as well, Korea has superseded Japan. For example, Korea now leads in shipbuilding and Dram production. The two countries are bound by trade, Japan providing Korea with almost 20 percent of its imports and absorbing about 12 percent of its exports, which is second only to the United States. This makes Korea the third most important source and destination for Japan's imports and exports. More recently, Japan and Korea have, for the first time, engaged in joint naval exercises and have expanded cultural ties, cosponsoring the international soccer championships in 2002. Japanese popular culture from music to anime, once banned in Korea, has captured the heart of the youth scene there.

In Japan citizens of Korean ancestry, many with multigenerational roots in the islands, had been treated shabbily, denied citizenship, the right to vote, and certain educational jobs. They have even been required to submit to finger printing periodically. In recent years, these humiliations have been largely lifted as Japan embraces a more tolerant social ideal. The new climate has also contributed to better cross-straits relations.

Japan and South Korea share one additional common concern: the unpredictable and intransigent North. A relic of the cold war, the Stalinist government in the North remains a flash point in East Asia, especially since the collapse of its Soviet mentor in 1990. Both North and South Korea made sporadic attempts to discuss reunification during the 1990s, without success.

---

[1] Ito Hirobumi (1841–1909), regarded by some as the most important statesman of the Meiji period, drafted Japan's first constitution and served as the first prime minister among many other accomplishments.

[2] Donald Keene, *Emperor of Japan: Meiji and His World* (New York: Columbia University Press, 2002), p. 662.

The North's on-again/off-again nuclear weapons program has been restarted (fall 2003) along with its successful testing of medium- and long-range missiles. In fact, the North now possesses missiles capable of striking any location within Japan; it also claims to have operational nuclear weapons. Understandably Japan takes the North as a serious threat to its survival and is taking countersteps, including revision of its treaties with the United States to include first-strike provisions, participation in a regional antimissile defense system, RMA (revolution in military affairs, i.e., the substitution of technology for human resources), upgrading of its air and naval systems, and placement of an autonomous satellite surveillance system.

Japan's relationship with North Korea is further complicated by the North's admission that Japanese citizens had been kidnapped and forced to live in the North during the 1970s and 1980s. While some have been allowed to return to Japan with their families, others are unaccounted for and the North continues to be less than forthright about these cases. The fear of unpredictable actions by the North, as well as disturbing human rights issues, do not suggest a harmonious relationship in the near future.

RELATIONS WITH SOUTHEAST ASIA

Japan's links to Southeast Asia are as varied as the cultures and nations that constitute the region. Wartime relationships were not necessarily all negative; for example, the cooperation between Imperial Japan and Sukarno's Indonesia reflected a shared hatred of Western imperialism. Along with China, the nations of Southeast Asia continue to be major recipients of Japanese ODA (Overseas Development Assistance) and Japan is committed to building regional military and trading blocks organized primarily out of the ASEAN nations. It is significant that these nations, especially Thailand, Indonesia, and Malaysia, appreciate Japan's distinct national interests and are grateful for its aid and investment. They are also grateful for its role as the economic engine of the region, which has helped create a quality of life for its 500 million citizens. Most recently Japan stepped in with huge loans to bail the ASEAN nations out of the financial crisis of 1997. This help has not been taken for granted.

While Japan remains bound to its relationships with the West and has not embraced the Asian Values alternative championed by nations like Singapore and Malaysia, there is a neonationalist fringe including Hashimoto, Ozawa, and Ishihara. These neonationalists imagine a Southeast Asian emphasis as a valuable component of regional solidarity under a Japanese hegemony, i.e., an Asian block to counter the European Union and the United States. The ascent of China into the regional mix complicates Japan's position. In the economic sphere, Japan has been transferring production to China from Southeast Asia. China's rising military power is also shifting the balance, as the People's Republic acquires the ability to project power beyond its borders. (China already possesses missiles and warheads that cover the entire region and is slowly building an arsenal of RMA conventional weapons.) Critical in this mix is China's will to lead in contrast to Japan's customary role as a happy number two. For example, during the recent ASEAN "plus two" (China and Japan) regional conference in Indonesia, China took the initiative, suggesting the formation of a regional economic block by 2005.

RELATIONS WITH RUSSIA

Japan has never had a comfortable relationship with the U.S.S.R. or with Russia for that matter. As early as the Meiji period its oligarchs distrusted Russian power and ambitions. Following the Japanese defeat of China in 1895, Russian intervention together with Germany and France (the Tripartite Intervention) denied Japan territory on the Asian mainland. The two nations subsequently fought an extraordinarily brutal war (1904–1905). Japan's "victory" on land and sea once again did not yield the hoped-for rewards. The Japanese harbored a simmering dislike for the Czarist empire. Success of the Bolsheviks in 1917 added an ideological gulf between the two countries. During World War II they held to a pragmatic "nonaggression" treaty. Throughout the cold war years Japan remained solidly on the side the United States, benefiting from the stasis of nuclear balance and the opportunities of the free market. Since the collapse of the Soviet Union, instability there has limited Japanese investment interests. Efforts to tap into Russian oil supplies have not been successful. and the issue of the contested islands to Japan's north is still unresolved. While there are no threatening issues, this is still an unsettled relationship and Russia remains an unfriendly neighbor in the popular consciousness, distrusted more than any other nation after North Korea.

JAPANESE ARMED FORCES

In the early 1950s, during the Korean War, the United States had encouraged Japan to take part in the common defense, despite the provisions of Peace Article 9 of the Japanese Constitution of 1947. The National Safety Force was formed in 1951 and was transformed into the Self-Defense Forces in 1953. The budget for the Self-Defense Forces has risen slowly but steadily since that time.

Nakasone Yasuhiro, during his long tenure as prime minister that began in 1982, sought to strengthen self-defense further. A number of factors were involved. He was concerned by overflights of Russian Backfire bombers and by the basing of over one-third of the nuclear and conventional forces of the U.S.S.R. in the East Asia region opposite Japan. The United States was anxious to have Japan undertake responsibility for the naval defense of the sea-lanes for 1,000 miles off the Japanese coast, lanes essential for the importation of oil. The U.S.S.R., moreover, objected to Japan's constant raising of its claim for the return of four islets in the southern Kurile Islands northeast of Hokkaido. (These are called in Japan the Northern Territories.) Nakasone's efforts were successful; the defense budget rose from $11.4 billion in 1983 to $13 billion in 1984 and then, under a five-year plan, by about $15 billion annually. A group of prominent leaders in government and academic circles proposed to do much more for their country's defense, saying it was a stain on the national honor to rely on the United States to such a degree while the U.S.S.R. was spending 15 percent of its GNP on its defense.

But Nakasone had to move with great caution. The Japanese people had no wish to return to any kind of military posture. For years it had been an unwritten rule that the defense budget should not exceed 1 percent of the country's GNP. That barrier was broken in 1986, but only by a narrow margin. By the next year the barrier was abandoned, and the defense budget, settled under a five-year plan, bore no relation henceforth to the GNP.

Since the 1980s Japanese society has been endeavoring, with considerable anguish, to come to terms, first, with World War II and the part played by the Japanese Army and, second, with a wholly new problem raised by the use of United Nations peacekeeping forces and Japan's proper part therein.

During these years, with the maturing of postwar generations, the Japanese took a new interest in World War II, sometimes called the "Fifteen Years' War" dating from the Imperial Army takeover of Manchuria in 1931. This could be seen in popular morning television 15-minute serial dramas. These shows often dealt with the war and its effects on the lives of ordinary people. While the government and the ruling Liberal Democratic Party did not necessarily want a popular review of the war in prime time, these breakfast dramas had a large following on the NHK government-sponsored station.

On another level, some sinister events that took place during the war have come to light. The government itself reported to the Diet in April 1982 that germ warfare experiments had been conducted on 3,000 Chinese, Korean, Russian, and American prisoners of war. In these experiments, the prisoners were injected with plague, cholera, and typhoid germs, and the bodies were dissected after death to determine the results. Also, the Bulletin of Atomic Scientists reported in 1988 the use of chemical weapons during the war by the Japanese Army against Chinese.

Prime Minister Takeshita became involved in the discussion of Japan's culpability at one point. He said that there were various arguments as to whether the war came about by accident or in self-defense. It was the task of the historian to determine whether or not it was a war of aggression. This provoked indignation abroad, especially in China, South Korea, and the former U.S.S.R.

This incident came just before the funeral of Emperor Hirohito, and in some embarrassment Takeshita was compelled to admit in a speech to the Diet that "there was aggression by militarism." This was in reply to a statement by a member of the cabinet, Okuno Seisuke, provincial wartime director of the Kempeitai secret police, who had said, "The white race turned Asia into a colony. Japan was by no means a nation of aggression. It is regrettable that Japan has been accused of being the aggressor. The war in China erupted

accidentally." There was an angry outcry in Chinese and South Korean newspapers, and the Japanese Foreign Ministry acknowledged "quite severe damage" to relations with Asian nations.

On the other side, Japanese Americans who were interned in World War
II received in 1987 a belated apology from the U.S. House of Representatives and the promise of $1.2 billion in reparations. The House spoke of "a
grave injustice, caused by racial prejudice and war hysteria." An earlier con-
gressional commission report said that there was "not a single documented
act of espionage, sabotage or fifth column activity" by any Japanese American on the West Coast. The commission also stated that the Roosevelt administration had ignored reports from the FBI and Naval Intelligence that
no internment program was necessary. Of the 120,000 interned, 66,000 were
still alive in 1987. Later news accounts reported a delay in making the payments, and more have meanwhile died without receiving reimbursement.

Germany faced up earlier to the facts of its past, but it has been extraordinarily difficult for the Japanese to do the same. Strict hierarchy and control
from above inevitably carry with them secrecy, and the Japanese public has
remained largely ignorant of the conduct of its military. The awakening is
painful. Three Korean women brought suit against the Japanese government
in December 1991 for their mistreatment during the war as "comfort
women" for Japanese troops. Moved by the courage of these women, a Japanese professor of history, Yoshimi Yoshiaki,[3] uncovered documents in the
archives of the Japan Self-Defense Agency showing clearly that the wartime
government had been directly implicated through the Army Command in recruiting tens of thousands of women, mostly Korean, but also Chinese, In-
donesian, and Philippine, and even Japanese, to serve in brothels for the
Japanese troops. Many were teenagers, kept in filthy conditions and compelled to service twenty or thirty, even fifty soldiers a day. The number of
women involved is unknown, but estimates range from 100,000 to double
that number. Many of them died during the period they were forced to act
as prostitutes. The question of compensation to the survivors is still outstanding.

At the same time as they looked at the military past, the Japanese people
had of necessity to consider the future. One momentous question was that
of sending Japanese troops to serve abroad. The problem first arose during
the Persian Gulf War. In October 1987 two Japanese-operated oil tankers
were attacked by Iranian gunboats in the Strait of Hormuz. The Persian Gulf
countries were the source of 55 percent of Japan's oil, and the U.S. government criticized the Japanese for not offering more help to the international
effort to control the region. The Japanese thereupon offered technical aid
and more funds to finance the U.S. forces stationed in Japan.

Then came the Gulf War and Operation Desert Storm. The U.S. ambassador informed the Japanese press that Americans were "bewildered and

---

[3] "Japan Battles Its Memories," *New York Times*, Mar. 11, 1992.

exasperated" at Japanese delay in providing help for the common effort of the allies. But the Japanese were themselves bewildered, discussing in the government and in the streets whether they should send Japanese troops abroad for the first time since World War II. The decision in August 1990 was to send no combat troops but to give grants and loans of funds to Egypt, Jordan, and Turkey, which were suffering from the embargo on Iraq, to provide transportation and equipment to the allied forces led by the United States, and to send in a medical team to assist with the wounded. The medical team was not sent; not enough doctors were willing to go. An effort by Prime Minister Kaifu in November to send 1,000 noncombat troops to the Persian Gulf failed. The decision to contribute cash but not troops was characterized as "cashbook diplomacy" and seemed to be a reflection on Japanese honor.

This emotional issue reappeared for the third time in connection with the United Nations presence in Cambodia. Akashi Yasushi, the head of the U.N. peacekeeping operation there and himself a Japanese, told government leaders in Japan that their country would be expected to bear at least one-third of the cost of maintaining the U.N. force in Cambodia and that civilians should be sent to aid the effort if military personnel were not permitted to go.

Prime Minister Miyazawa fought hard for the proposal to allow Japanese self-defense forces to operate in Cambodia under the command of the United Nations. This inevitably raised the prickly question of the bad image left over in Asia from the conduct of the Japanese Army in World War II. But Miyazawa persisted, and a bill was introduced creating a unit of 2,000 troops which could be used under U.N. leadership for limited purposes, such as building hospitals, providing communications, and bringing in food. They were not to monitor cease-fire arrangements, disarm fighting troops, or even remove land mines without specific approval from the Diet. The troops were to be allowed to carry arms but to fire them only in self-defense.

Each of these stringent conditions was argued over a period of two years. Before the final debate the Socialist Party leaders attempted to secure a mass resignation of all their members. They were unsuccessful, and in June 1992 the measure passed by 329 votes to 17. However, to get the bill approved, the government had to accept an important compromise: a freeze on deployment of such a force for an indefinite period and agreement that the two houses of the Diet would vote separately on each dispatch of troops. The enactment of this bill was a triumph for Miyazawa and one welcomed by many Japanese, despite their regret at the surrender of the full force of Article 9 of the constitution: "the Japanese people, forever, renounce war as a sovereign right . . . or use of force as a means of settling disputes with other nations."

A contingent of Japanese troops arrived in Cambodia in September 1992. In the spring of 1993 two of its soldiers were killed. The Japanese commander wanted to withdraw his contingent but was told that the force as a whole was under U.N. command.

Throughout the rest of the 1990s and beyond, Japan's armed forces and military posture have evolved in significant and critical ways. The end of the cold war, changes in the U.S. commitment to East Asia, the rise of China as an economic and military power able to project force beyond its borders, and an unpredictable North Korea armed with nuclear weapons and missiles capable of hitting any place in Japan within 10 minutes all affect Japan's defense policy. The speed of these changes, coupled with the RMA, have changed the nature of warfare in the twenty-first century.

Japan's response has been to join the recent East Asian arms race with the full commitment of its wealth and technology. Japan remains the world's largest spender on the military after the United States, committing $41 billion (2003) or approximately 0.1 percent of its GDP to defense. In addition Japan spends roughly $5 billion per year to help pay the cost of 50,000 U.S. troops stationed on Japanese soil. These investments sustain a force level of approximately 237,000 regulars and 50,000 reservists, not large compared with China's combined 3,410,000 or even Indonesia's close to 700,000-man force level. However, Van Vranken Hickey suggests the real value of Japan's armed forces:

> With over 1,000 tanks, 330 warplanes, 16 submarines, and 55 warships, Japan's SDF (Self-Defense Force) is one of the most powerful militaries in the world. As Adm. Robert J. Kelly, then commander of the U.S. Pacific Fleet, observed, "Japan has the capability to defend itself against all but perhaps a resurgence of the Soviet Union. They have invested a lot of money to build a very capable self-defense force. However, the SDF differs from other modern militaries in one critical respect—it lacks the ability to project power."[4]

Article 9 of the Japanese Constitution and the legacy of World War II have been legal and psychological reasons for limiting the military to a defensive force. Recently, however, Japan has been changing. There is a growing sentiment, not only among political conservatives and some nostalgic old warriors, but among postwar generations and the young as well, to make Japan a "normal country," that is, "armed and able to fight wars." Many people are tired of dependence on an uncertain alliance with the United States. They are also embarrassed by a reputation limited to that of banker for other countries' wars.

In recent years more Japanese have embraced a positive view of the military. At the official level, in 1996 U.S. President Clinton and Japanese Prime Minster Hashimoto set a revised framework for military cooperation in which Japan agreed to play a more active and expansive role in defense even beyond its borders within East Asia. After the 9/11 terrorist attacks, the Japanese government became committed to the global war against terrorism, most dramatically with a promise of ground forces even without U.N. sanction to the

---

[4] Denis Van Vranken Hickey, *The Armies of East Asia: China, Taiwan, Japan, and the Koreas* (Boulder, CO: Lynn Rienner, 2001), p. 51.

U.S.-led effort in Iraq. Though the 10,000 promised troops have yet to be dispatched as of January 2004, Japanese Prime Minster Koizumi did commit $1.5 billion to the reconstruction effort and agree to forgive billions of dollars of Iraqi loans. The LDP and the Koizumi government are clearly determined to revise Article 9 so that Japan might become a "normal country." A poll published by the *Mainichi Shimbun Daily* newspaper in the spring of 2004 claimed that 78 percent of Japanese lawmakers and 53 percent of the citizens feel revisions to the constitution are necessary.

More ominously, the Japanese remain unable to resolve the issue of their behavior during World War II. The question of apologies is still not settled. In fact, as in Germany, revisionist historians continue to deny atrocities. There is a movement to renew public awareness of the horrific fatalities suffered by the Japanese in the atomic bombings and fire bombings of cities in the last days of the war. That is to say, there is an effort to shift war-guilt from Japan to the United States.

Finally, while most analysts doubt that Japan will revert to its prewar militarism, there is the shadow of nuclear armaments. As the only nation ever to suffer the terror of nuclear attack, the Japanese have embraced an almost religious opposition to these weapons. Yet, as one of the most technologically advanced nations in possession of all necessary human and material resources to produce nuclear weapons and delivery systems, it would be relatively easy for Japan to quickly arm itself with such weapons. The war against terrorism, China's ascendancy, and the problem of North Korea have helped to trigger a debate among officials and the public over the possibility of a Japanese nuclear deterrent. What had once been a topic discussed on the radical fringe is now in the mainstream. The "unspeakable" is frequently discussed in the print media and on television. A recent poll found that 53 percent of Japanese thought that it would be acceptable for Japan to build nuclear weapons. Though it is unlikely that Japan will take the nuclear road in the foreseeable future and since Koizumi and the LDP seem to oppose the idea, the discussion itself suggests that Japan's military future is in transition.

POLITICS

Prime Minister Nakasone Yasuhiro, when elected in 1982, announced his policy "to foster ties with the United States" and "to strengthen national defense." If these two aims were to be combined with a third, namely, the emphasis of early postwar prime ministers on building up economic strength and increasing the GNP, they would sum up the main objectives of the ruling Liberal Democratic Party over the years. These goals have enjoyed sufficient support from the people of Japan to have kept the LDP in control from its founding in 1955 until the summer of 1993.

The turn after World War II toward a general agreement with the United States and the free enterprise system follows logically from Japan's recent past. Once again it is evident that history determines politics, even though the par-

ticipants—the people and their leaders—may be scarcely aware of what is going on. Japan at the very end of the sixteenth century, with civil war threatening ruin to the economy, submitted finally to the Tokugawa regime, which
brought peace at the price of severe standardization and control over a period of two and a half centuries. Japan thus had a chance to recover and build
inner reserves of strength and leadership. Isolated from the rest of the world
by deliberate government policy, the people fell behind in technology but
gained in cohesiveness and a sense of their national uniqueness.

When contact with the West began afresh in the mid-nineteenth century
and modernization was adopted, again as a deliberate government policy,
Japan was ready, somehow refreshed, and able to devote full energy to certain chosen goals. These goals were not dissimilar from the objectives of the
later Liberal Democratic Party. They included cordial relations with Western
powers, at first European powers—relations entered into frankly in order to
be able to catch up and "join the club." They certainly included strengthening national defense. And a main objective, then as now, was to build up an
economic power base.

At this time of the Meiji Restoration there was already a trend toward
commercial development and capital formation (see pp. 157–160). Even in
the militaristic period of the 1930s and 1940s, which so confused and an-
gered the West, a search for raw materials, new markets, and commercial opportunities was a part of the drive for empire. Once peace was restored in
1945 and the economy rebuilt with some help from the United States, it was
highly likely that Japan would continue, as it did, on the path of modernization and economic growth, and thereby almost automatically toward alliance
with the Western democratic nations. The development of Japan from 1600
on has not been a straight line or an inevitable one, but in hindsight one can
discern a certain logic leading to the prominent position the nation has now
attained. Japan's postmodern cycle of development begun in the decade of
the 1990s has added some new twists to the process of political evolution.

POLITICAL PARTIES

Japan's postwar, national politics have been dominated by parties. Distinctive products of Japan's modern history, national-level parties were able to
flourish in the open climate established during the American-led occupation.
In 1955 various conservative nationalist groups formed into the Liberal Democratic Party which, one eye on the past with another on the future, embraced the ideal of restoring Japan to its prewar glory through national reconstruction in cooperation with the United States. Its ideals, policies,
leadership, and organization suited Japan's needs during the decades of great
sacrifice and struggle. It successfully moderated divisiveness and formed a new
national consciousness. As the institutional political leg of the iron triangle
(politicians, business, and bureaucracy), the LDP remained in power for the
succeeding 38 years until 1993 when it lost the majority in the lower house

of the Diet and was forced into a coalition government. The most viable opposition to the LDP was the Japan Socialist Party (JSP), which, in contrast to the LDP's tight links with business and industry, had its base in the labor union movements, looked to the future rather than at the past, and rejected Japan's dependence on the United States for security. While there were many other parties formed around personalities and issues, the only other significant forces, prior to the middle 1990s, were the Communists in the Japan Communist Party (JCP) and the Komeito, or Clean Government Party, a Buddhist organization affiliated with the Sokkagakai.

The LDP retained national power by electing a majority to the Diet, which had to approve the party's choice of prime minister. Over the years it has worked out alliances, cooperated, and clashed with its rivals. In 1973 opposition members boycotted sessions of the Diet, forcing the resignation of two members of the government. In 1980 the LDP was defeated in a confidence motion in the lower house for failing to deal with inflation and government corruption. During the early 1980s, violent antigovernment protests were led by farmers and students over the expropriation of land for the building of the new Narita Airport outside Tokyo. Demonstrators built a concrete redoubt and a steel tower on the runway and engaged in pitched battles with the police, actions reminiscent of the 1960s. There were 5,000 on each side, and they used clubs, shields, stones, spears, and bottles of gasoline, which resulted in heavy casualties. The elections of 1983 registered another loss for the LDP, which, in order to remain in power, required help from small, splinter conservative groups and some independents. The end of the cold war in 1990 along with the bursting of the economic bubble and the descent of Japan's economy into the lost decade of the 1990s ended the image of LDP invulnerability; corruption, incompetence, and criminality, results of cozy inbreeding within the iron triangle, stirred the Japanese public to action. While many opted for apathy, others joined the struggle, beginning a grass roots, local movement against the inbred political elite. In 1993 the LDP lost its mandate and coalition government seemed to break the "autocracy ruled by bureaucrats." Though the LDP began its return to power in 1996, a new style of politics signaled by the Koizumi premiership is emerging.

In addition to interparty rivalry, Japanese politics are marked by a distinctive, intense intraparty factional struggle. In part this form of struggle is characteristic of the highly personal nature of political life in Japan over all. That is to say, factions have traditionally been organized around individual power brokers and patronage systems more so than around policy issues. Strong bonds of personal loyalty and historic ties unified individuals for the common struggle. The erosion of these bonds and traditional concepts of personal loyalty help to explain the failure of the "1955 System" in 1993 and the appearance of numerous breakaway factions forming new, discrete parties. Of course, traditional politics, though weakened, still influence behavior, as the various breakaway organizations retain a central person who serves as the nucleus of a loyalty network.

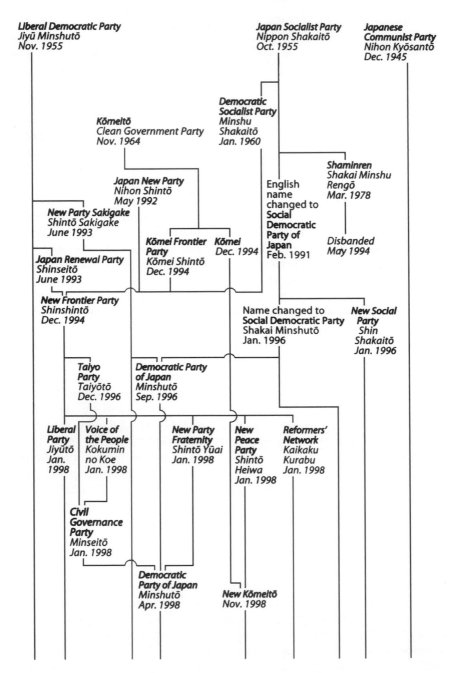

Major Political Parties Since 1955.

SOURCE: Masuzoe Yoichi, *Years of Trial: Japan in the 1990s* (Tokyo: Japan Echo, 2000), p. 88.

Though there has been a popular movement for the national election of the prime minister on the Israeli model, Japan's prime ministers, though subject to the approval of the Diet, have been the president of the reigning faction within the dominant party. Until recently LDP presidents had been chosen in smoke-filled rooms behind closed doors; now a national vote of party members is factored into the decision process, something like a party primary in the United States. In April 2001 the LDP's rank-and-file voters chose Koizumi for his first term, electing a "lone wolf" candidate against the wishes of party power brokers. For some, this new phenomenon signals the start of a "new political equilibrium" and the rise of local and civil society in contemporary Japan moderating the postwar influence of national, self-appointed elite.

PRIME MINISTERS

The brokerage of power goes on in Japan, as it does everywhere in one form or another. In Japan, although the LDP continued as the dominant party, power groups within it rose in turn to the surface, headed by eminent political figures, each with his loyal following. Relationships can be close within the network of *giri*, or "mutual duties owed," in a manner not unlike that of the political figures and their "clients" in ancient Rome. The leaders include men such as Sato Eisaku (the postwar prime minister with the longest continuous service, 1965–1969), Fukuda Takeo (prime minister 1976–1978), and Ohira Masayoshi (prime minister 1978–1980) allied with Suzuki Zenko (prime minister 1980–1982).

One of the most powerful political figures was Tanaka Kakuei (prime minister, July 1972–1974). A self-made man from a poor family, he founded a construction company and then entered politics, where he rose rapidly in the ranks of the Liberal Democratic Party. His most notable achievement as prime minister was in Japan-China relations. The People's Republic of China had been admitted to membership in the United Nations in October 1971. In February 1972 President Nixon visited Beijing and began the process of establishing diplomatic relations between the United States and China. The Japanese were surprised and offended that they had not been informed beforehand of this important move.

But in August 1972 Tanaka, now prime minister, had a consultation with President Nixon in Hawaii. By September he was ready to go ahead with a historic visit to Beijing. He met Zhou Enlai and agreed that Japan would establish full diplomatic relations with the People's Republic of China and acknowledge it as the only legal government of the whole country including Taiwan. While Tanaka was beginning the diplomatic process of reestablishing Japan's political links to China, at home his administration was shaken by scandal. As has been noted, the iron triangle of politicians, business, and bureaucracy was a closed network conducive to cronyism and corruption. In

Tanaka's case, a foreign corporation, the U.S. aircraft manufacturer, Lockheed, became involved. Ultimately, he was indicted and found guilty. Tanaka's daughter, Makiko, inherited her father's Niigata seat and served for nine months in 2001 as Japan's first female foreign minister. She subsequently left politics only to return, running for her old Diet seat in 2003.

This Lockheed scandal erupted in 1976 but concerned transactions made earlier. Apparently Kodama Yoshio, a right-wing lobbyist and incidentally a former war criminal, had funneled from the Lockheed Corporation some $7 million to various business and political figures. The objective was to void a McDonnell Douglas option for the sale of civilian aircraft to Japan and to secure the contract for Lockheed Tristar planes. Prime Minister Miki (1974–1976) had to resign over the scandal, though not himself involved. Trials dragged on until 1983, when Tanaka, still protesting his innocence, was convicted of taking bribes from Lockheed. He appealed and was released on $1.3 million bail. The judge said that Tanaka had "seriously impaired the Japanese people's confidence" in government and that the ill effect was "immeasurable." However, in "consideration of the defendant's achievement as a cabinet minister and a premier," the judge sentenced him to four years' imprisonment, instead of the maximum of five, and fined him $2.1 million. That was not the end of the story. But Tanaka used patronage skillfully and had bluff qualities of courage, stubbornness, and braggadocio that appealed to his followers and constituency. In 1987 the voters returned him to his Diet seat in spite of his conviction and a subsequent stroke. Later that year the Tokyo High Court upheld his conviction. He appealed to the Supreme Court but died before the judgment was handed down.

The Japanese government took the problem of the Lockheed scandal seriously; they tried and convicted top political and business figures. This fact should be taken into account if we are to assess correctly the patronizing and cynical stance of the Lockheed Corporation, which insisted that bribery was necessary in dealing with foreign countries like Japan.

A notable prime minister of a different stamp from Tanaka was Nakasone Yasuhiro, who held the office twice, from 1982 to 1984 and from 1986 to 1988. Nakasone presided over a government and economy dominated by a confident and stable LDP. His tenure also witnessed a new level of neonationalism and conservatism, revealing the hidden agenda of the LDP right wing. From the beginning he sought to maintain close ties with the United States and to increase the budget for the Self-Defense Forces of Japan. During his second term he succeeded in raising defense expenditure beyond the 1 percent of GNP, which had become customary, and then in having the defense ceiling of 1 percent abandoned. The raises were very moderate, for Nakasone had to face strong opposition to any sign of forsaking the spirit of Peace Article 9 in the constitution.

Nakasone was generally popular and was known worldwide as a vigorous but usually tactful spokesperson for Japan. While prime minister he traveled widely, to South Korea and Indonesia in 1983, to Canada and China in 1986, and several times to Washington, D.C.

A high point during Nakasone's tenure was the celebration in April 1986 of the sixty-year reign of Emperor Hirohito, coinciding with the emperor's eighty-fifth birthday. It was the longest life and the longest reign of any emperor in the history of Japan. Immediately following this event Nakasone was host to the seven-nation economic summit meeting in Tokyo. (At this meeting two new nations—Canada and Italy—were added to the original five: the United States, the United Kingdom, Germany, France, and Japan.) The main results of this meeting were decisions to pursue prudent free-market policies with increasing economic cooperation and to adopt a tough statement on terrorism, with agreed-upon measures to combat it. It was unfortunate, in view of the latter statement, that just prior to both events militant leftists launched an attack with five homemade rockets on the Akasaka Palace, where the foreign delegates were staying. The rockets passed over the palace and exploded in the street without much effect.

The elections to both houses of the Diet in 1986 produced landslide victories for the LDP, which gave the party a straight majority and recouped the losses it had suffered in 1983. Nakasone called it "a gift from Heaven." The elections, disastrous for the Japan Socialist Party, led to the resignation of its chairman. He was replaced by Doi Takako, aged fifty-seven, who received 83 percent of the members' votes and was the first woman ever to hold such a senior position. She was at that time one of only 29 women among the 764 members of the Diet. Of these 29, only 7 were in the more powerful lower house, the House of Representatives.

Although Prime Minister Nakasone was generally successful, he ran into a stone wall on a question of taxes. Early in 1987, the government had proposed a 5 percent sales tax, and the opposition in protest boycotted the Diet session for almost a month, making the transaction of business impossible. Nakasone suffered considerable political damage. Many members of the LDP joined the protest, to which Nakasone replied by warning that the action of the rebels would be remembered when the moment came for considering appointments to party positions. A month later, however, the new tax proposal was dropped, and the budget was passed. There were scenes of disorder in the chamber, and some used the tactic of the "ox walk," a slowdown in which a member takes thirty minutes to cross the Diet floor to cast his or her vote. In 1988 large cuts were made in personal income and corporate taxes, in exchange for a 3 percent "consumption tax" on all goods and services and new taxes for capital gains on stocks and bonds.

The period of Nakasone Yasuhiro's premiership exhibits in summary most of the features which have marked the politics of Japan from the 1970s to the early 1990s, such as the good and bad aspects of relations with the United States, increased concern about Japan's share in the common defense, tax problems, the rise and decline of opposition in the Diet, and the problem of where to draw the line on moral conduct in business and politics.

When Nakasone's period of office ended in 1988, Takeshita Noboru, whom Nakasone had favored, was elected as prime minister. Takeshita had trained as a pilot in World War II but was never in combat. He was elected to the Diet in 1958 at the age of thirty-four and served later as Minister for Construction and more than once as Finance Minister. In 1986 he was made Secretary-General of the LDP. His term as prime minister was overshadowed by another scandal. The Recruit Company, a real estate conglomerate, had given gifts of unlisted stock to a wide range of politicians and others before the stocks went on sale to the public. After the public sale the value of the stocks shot up, and the recipients were able to sell at a huge profit.

The Recruit scandal broke in the press in the summer of 1988, and by the beginning of 1989 it had assumed serious proportions. Three cabinet ministers were forced to resign—Miyazawa Kiichi (Finance), Hasegawa Takashi (Justice), and Harada Ken (Director-General of Economic Planning)—all on the grounds of unethical practice. In April Prime Minister Takeshita, answering charges in the Diet, admitted to receiving large political donations but refused to dissolve the Diet or to resign. Six prominent businesspeople were arrested, the most notable being a former chairman of the giant Nippon Telephone and Telegraph Company.

Then after further revelations by the newspaper *Asahi Shimbun*, Takeshita at the end of April announced he would resign "to take responsibility for the public distrust caused by his involvement." Now began a rather desperate search for a new prime minister untainted by the Recruit scandal. At the beginning of June a comparative unknown, Uno Sousuke, was chosen; but his tenure was destined to be short-lived. A magazine ran a story implicating Uno in relations with several geisha. Such relationships of politicians are usually known but not published; but at this point the Japanese people were offended and alienated by a sex scandal on top of a money scandal.

Prime Minister Uno was forced to resign after only sixty-nine days in office. Even former Prime Minister Nakasone, after some months under pressure, agreed to testify about his part in the Recruit affair in order to "normalize parliamentary business." This was a reference in part to the fact that during the chaos the LDP had forced a budget through the Diet without debate. The chairman of Recruit, at the nub of the whole affair, was indicted.

The punishments meted out were very light, in spite of the known involvement in the scandal of two prime ministers and a future prime minister, Miyazawa, as well as leading businesspeople. In the end, only four low-level aides to three cabinet ministers were actually convicted, given small fines, and released. Two leading Diet members were indicted but not arrested, under the plea of parliamentary privilege, while the Diet was in session. Not surprisingly, politicians of the opposition and the press, representing public opinion, were enraged on learning that no high-ranking LDP officials were convicted or even charged. What had been done here in the Recruit scandal was, in Japanese terms, unethical but not illegal. Actual bribery in the Lockheed affair was illegal, and so top figures were indicted and convicted. This scandal revealed the depth and breadth of corruption within the iron triangle.

POLITICS OF THE 1990s

In response to public opinion Prime Minister Takeshita had, before his resignation, already appointed a commission (April 1989) to recommend political reforms. The commission's report included such items as cabinet ministers being barred from dealing in stocks, all candidates for office disclosing income and assets, and politicians no longer being expected to give cash gifts to constituents at funerals and weddings. These proposed reforms were criticized as being both insufficient and unenforceable. Neither Takeshita nor subsequent prime ministers were able to get any meaningful package of reforms through the Diet.

The LDP suffered a severe defeat in the elections for the House of Councillors, the upper house, in July 1989 and lost its majority there to the Socialists for the first time since 1955. Socialist Doi Takako, the first woman elected as leader of a major political party, used a "madonna strategy," putting forward large numbers of women candidates and stressing issues of importance to women—for example, the sales tax, sex scandals, and the sexist attitudes discerned in the LDP leaders. In municipal elections this strategy was notably successful; twelve out of thirteen Socialist women candidates won seats, and a record seventeen out of thirty-threee female candidates of all parties were elected.

Upon the resignation of Prime Minister Uno, Kaifu Toshiki, aged fifty-eight, a former Minister of Education, was elected to the office. He belonged to the first generation which had had no experience of service in World War II. For the first time in several decades the upper and lower houses in the Diet voted for different candidates for prime minister. The upper house, dominated by the Socialists, put forward Doi Takako, but Kaifu Toshiki, given preference by the constitution as the candidate of the lower house, was elected.

Political memories often seem to be as short in Japan as elsewhere. By the time of the lower house elections, February 1990, the fortunes of the LDP were on the rise again. The opposition was still divided and did not command either the patronage or the war chest of the LDP. Perhaps the Japanese people were also too anxious about the future to risk entrusting an untried party or coalition with the helm of the ship. The LDP, plus a small number of allies, now held 286 seats (compared with 295 in the previous lower house). The Socialists increased representation to 139 (formerly 83).

This was an important gain, but it was achieved for the most part by the capture of seats from parties other than the LDP. For example, the Komeito declined from fifty-four to forty-six seats, and the Communist Party from twenty-six to sixteen. Doi Takako was reelected, but the trend of success for women in the Tokyo municipal elections was not reflected in the House of Representatives, where few women gained seats.

Prime Minister Kaifu had taken to heart the lesson of political corruption and appointed to his "clean politics cabinet' only those free of association with the Lockheed and Recruit scandals. He thus offended some of the entrenched political bosses; nevertheless he wielded an increased measure of power by virtue of the LDP success in the recent elections. Kaifu's Japan was fundamentally influenced by earth shaking global transformation with the collapse of the Soviet Union in 1990 and the consolidation of Communist autocracy in the People's Republic of China during the summer of 1989. On the domestic front Japan was about to experience the bursting of the asset bubble and the start of the Lost Decade of the 1990s during which prosperity and its underlying assumptions spun wildly down and out of control. In early 1990 Kaifu made a rapid tour of Eastern Europe and announced aid for Poland and Hungary. "Japan, as a leading member of the industrialized democracies," he said, "expects to play a leading role, not only economically but politically. . . . Japan is ready to support the democratization of Eastern Europe and help bring about a new world order." The Suzuki automobile manufacturing firm followed up by investing in a plant in Hungary, the first for Japan in Eastern Europe.

At the end of 1991 near the close of Kaifu's prime ministry, a commission of business, union, and academic leaders was appointed to propose reforms for the securities market. Over twenty securities brokerage firms had admitted to paying more than $1.5 billion in improper compensation to important customers for losses they had suffered in order to retain them as clients. Strictly speaking, the law requires only that promises to reimburse should not be made and does not forbid the act of reimbursement. But public opinion clearly felt that this was a loophole which must be closed. The commission recommended that a new enforcement agency be created to oversee and deal with abuses in the securities industry, that stock commission rates be deregulated, that the securities business become more competitive, and particularly that the whole market be purged of the *yakuza*, "organized crime syndicates."

Public anger, aroused during the past months of scandals, was in this case directed especially against the Ministry of Finance. The ministry insisted that the new enforcement body not be independent but subject to its jurisdiction, and that the ministry, not the new body, have the right to punish wrongdoers. It was public knowledge that the ministry had been well aware of illegal actions of one of the largest firms, Nomura Securities, and had looked the other way. Nomura had used excessive pressure on its customers to buy certain stocks and thus raise their value. These were the stocks held by organized crime figures. The ministry had to reopen the investigation after two years' delay and found Nomura to be in violation. A trade union member of the 1991 commission claimed that provisions in the report concerning the all-important penalties had been taken out of the final version by one of the Finance Ministry staff. Once more the cozy inner ring of regulators and regulated had proved able to maintain something close to the status quo. A leading daily, the *Yomiuri Shimbun*, commented, "It is sad to admit that Japan is a country by bureaucrats, of bureaucrats and for bureaucrats."

It might appear from the frequent mention of scandals in even a brief account of Japanese politics that scandals are the rule and not the exception. This is, of course, not the case. Ordinary life goes on, in Japan as elsewhere, with the vast majority doing an honest day's work for a day's pay. The exposure of scandals and the fact that high officials feel compelled to resign in the wake of them are signs of the new awareness and readjustment in contemporary Japan.

When Kaifu's term in office ended in the fall of 1991, his place was taken, after some rivalry and backroom maneuvering, by Miyazawa Kiichi. Miyazawa appears as a polished personality, fluent in English, a skill which helped him abroad but which curiously has been viewed as a slightly suspicious qualification by some conservative Japanese who think it might render him more subject to pressure by foreigners. There was no doubt about his political and administrative experience, since he had been in turn finance minister, foreign minister, and the head of MITI. As to political power, both Kaifu and Miyazawa have been regarded as dependent for their position on bosses in the background; yet both have made real contributions while in office, though unable to put through all the reforms they desired.

Miyazawa ran into a problem at the very beginning of his tenure with the fiftieth anniversary of Pearl Harbor on December 7, 1991. The Socialists attacked him for not offering a sincere apology for the aggression of Japan in World War II. Official statements went so far as to express "deep reflection" over the "unbearable suffering" caused by the war. The word *hansei*, usually understood as "reflection," was translated by the Foreign Ministry on an earlier occasion as "contrition" and this time as "remorse." There was conservative opposition in Japan to any expression of regret; it supported this position by pointing out that President Bush had refused to apologize for the atom bomb attacks on Japan at the end of the war.

The visit of President Bush to Tokyo in the opening days of 1992 was also something of a problem; but it turned out to the benefit of Miyazawa's popularity when he was so attentive to Bush during the president's illness at a banquet. The U.S. administration's planning of the whole visit was ill-advised. What was originally to be a formal state visit was first postponed because of pressing concerns in the United States and then turned into a trade visit by the inclusion in the presidential entourage of no less than twenty-one chief executive officers of U.S. firms. This showed no understanding whatever of Japanese feelings, particularly when the top representatives of the Big Three U.S. automotive companies voiced their complaints. The fact that manufacturing plants had just been closed and thousands thrown out of work in the United States, while the executives drew down salaries and benefits several times the amount of those customary in wealthy Japan, was not lost on the Japanese or the American public. Some American businesspeople made successful deals with their Japanese counterparts, but the visit as a whole was a failure of more than usual proportions.

When Miyazawa opened the Diet session in January 1992, he engaged to cooperate with the United States to solve outstanding economic problems and to overcome the difficulties of a sluggish economy at home (growth projection was down to 3 percent). He also vowed to carry out reforms to control the effect of money contributions on politics—a vexing question not likely to be soon answered, in Japan or in the rest of the world.

A surprising political development in the summer of 1992 was the emergence of the "Japan New Party," founded by Hosokawa Morihiro. Hosokawa, aged fifty-four, was the former governor of Kumamoto, the area of the earlier fief belonging to the Hosokawa *daimyo*. He was friendly with Takeshita Noboru, leader of a powerful LDP faction, but he split off from the LDP. His aim was to decrease the centralized grip of "modern day shoguns" in Tokyo over the rest of Japan. He attacked the "structural conspiracy" between business, politicians, and permanent bureaucrats. The attitude of many Japanese toward their government in recent years would indicate considerable support for this view.

Elections to the upper house on July 26, 1992, yielded a moderate victory for the LDP. It won 68 seats of the 127 up for election, a sizable gain over the 39 it won in 1989. The Social Democratic Party of Japan secured only 22 seats, down by a half from the last election. Hosokawa's hopes were somewhat justified, for the New Party won a respectable 5 seats on its first try. The signal from the people seems an uncertain one, possibly derived from anxiety about the future, the fall in the stock market, the disillusionment concerning government, to which Hosokawa pointed, or simply apathy. The voter turnout was 47 percent, the lowest since World War II.

It was becoming clear, however, that there were serious problems within the LDP. Massive corruption plaguing the party, bureaucracy, and corporate triangle could no longer be contained; economic decline with no hope for a turnaround suggested that the LDP was unable to heal itself or the nation. Members of the LDP, however, started to bolt from their party and to form new parties, such as the Renewal Party under Hata Tsutomu and Ozawa Ichiro, and the Harbinger Party under Takemura Masayoshi. An earlier breakaway, mentioned above, had taken place in the Japan New Party formed by an ex-LDP member, Hosokawa Morihiro.

The tension began to mount, heightened by the fact that Japan was host to the Summit Meeting of the seven industrial nations, which took place between the vote of no confidence and the election.

On July 18, 1993, the election of members to the lower house proved to be a dramatic and unprecedented event in Japanese political history. The LDP, though still the largest single party, lost its majority in the Diet for the first time in thirty-eight years.

The results of the election were as follows:

LOWER HOUSE	1993*	1990*
LDP	223	275
Socialists	70	136
Japan Renewal	55	—
Clean Government (Komeito)	51	45
Japan New	35	—
Harbinger	13	—
Independents	30	22
Others	34	34

*Of 511 seats.

Indignation against the LDP was increased on July 22 by disclosures made at the beginning of the trial of Kanemaru Shin, so-called kingmaker of the LDP. He was being tried for evading almost $10 million in taxes. On that same day Miyazawa resigned as leader of the LDP, although he remained as acting prime minister for the statutory limit of thirty days after the election.

The disastrous loss of almost half its seats by the Socialist Party, and the fact that the new parties were all to a greater or lesser extent conservative, meant that the new political scene would not reflect any marked shift to the left. Events moved rapidly, driven by the thirty-day rule for filling the prime minister's position. On July 29 a coalition of seven parties, excluding the LDP, was cobbled together and agreed to nominate Hosokawa Morihiro for the post. The seven parties involved were the Japan New Party, supported by the Harbinger Party, the Socialist Party, the Clean Government Party (Komeito), and two smaller groups, the Democratic Socialist Party and the United Social Democratic Party.

Hosokawa Morihiro received the nomination because he enjoyed the advantage of a courageous decision. He had been the first to quit the LDP and join the Japan New Party eighteen months before the election. On the other hand, Hata and Ozawa of the Renewal Party were somewhat tainted by their recent association with the Tanaka/Kanemaru faction of the LDP.

Hosokawa's grandfather, Konoe Fumimaro, had been a prime minister of Japan during World War II. Called by some a conservative populist, Hosokawa favored a more open economy, thorough political and electoral reform, greater support for consumers as opposed to producers, and a more active role for Japan in international affairs.

The LDP responded by electing as its new chairman Kono Yohei. He was young at fifty-six and one of the very few members of the party untainted by the scandals which had given rise to the surge of public anger. In this it seemed that the LDP, still holding more Diet seats than any other single party, was nursing the hope of a political comeback. The members endeavored to have one of their own number made speaker of the lower house and demanded that the special session of the Diet then meeting be extended from a few days to three weeks, a patent effort to delay and embarrass the new government.

However, on August 6, after two days of disagreement and delay, Hosokawa, at fifty-five, was elected the youngest prime minister since World War II with 262 votes in the lower house. Kono Yohei of the LDP won 224 votes, and two other candidates shared the rest of the votes for the 511 seats. It was a double victory for the new coalition, since the symbolically important post of speaker went to its candidate, Doi Takako of the Socialist Party. She became the first woman to be chosen for the position. Hosokawa said, "A new age has just started." The way ahead for the coalition might be a rocky one, but there was no doubt that the LDP was discredited and that Japanese politics had altered direction, probably for the better. Hosokawa was able to put through only part of the electoral section of his reforms before his surprise resignation as prime minister in late March 1994. Although hints of scandal in his own background provided fuel for his enemies, the main reason for his resignation was the inability of his seven-party coalition to hold together. As noted, the formation of new breakaway parties signaled both serious ruptures in the factional alignments within the LDP and vitalization of regional political interests. Leaders like Hosokawa were forging new institutional structures to support the anger, frustration, and alienation of those long excluded from the elite club of Tokyo power holders. Between 1993 and 1994 the LDP lost its effective control over parliament. For the first time since 1955, it would have to enter into a coalition with other parties.

In April 2001 Koizumi Junichiro became head of the LDP and Japan's new prime minister. Koizumi had not been the choice of LDP power brokers. They had preferred the return of Hashimoto Ryutaro who had served as prime minister during two terms from January 1996 through July 1998, following the return of the LDP to power. Koizumi's ascent to the top party and national position was the result of grass-roots support through the revived system of primaries. His choice was a slap in the face to the capital power brokers, signaling the rising influence and dissatisfaction of the local political constituencies. In addition, Koizumi did not quite fit the profile of the typical postwar party or national leader. He is considered a "lone wolf" in a society of conformists. Divorced, and recognized by his unconventional "leonine" hair style, Koizumi had been fearless in attacking his party's establishment. He is sometimes considered to be the archetype of a new style Japanese politician capable of attracting votes on the strength of his individual appeal, autonomy, and perhaps even some charisma. These qualities, com-

Prime Minister Koizumi
Junichiro.

Japan Information Center

monplace in other parts of the world, signal an important shift in the political winds in Japan where individualism remains a questionable ideal.

Koizumi retained his leadership of the LDP and his position as prime minister as of January 2004. This suggests a return of the LDP in the immediate future. The five years or so between Koizumi and the LDP's return were a period of extremely complex mutation in Japanese national-level politics. To a certain extent this mutation was born in the widespread popular anger and frustration with the ruling elite in the LDP and its inability to stop corruption and economic decline. Such sentiments penetrated the party organization, which was unable to contain or deal with the new situation. The party ruptured, expelling its critics who formed new parties, and was still centered on individuals and factions, but now, by choice, outside of the mother party. Hosokawa's New Party, Ozawa's Japan Renew Party, and Takemura's Harbinger (Sakigake) Party formed in 1993 began the proliferation of new parties.

These same new parties and factions engaged in an ongoing, opportunistic dance of alliances as they struggled for power in the national arena. In perhaps the most significant of these alliances, the LDP itself joined forces with the Japan Socialist Party and the Sakigake on June 30, 1994. Murayama

Tomiichi, head of the Socialists, then served as coalition prime minister from June 1994 to January 1996 when he was replaced by Hashimoto of the LDP. Murayama's tenure was unexpectedly long because of two disasters that struck Japan during 1995. The Hanshin earthquake struck Kobe in January causing massive and unexpected destruction of infrastructure. Close to 300,000 homes and apartments were destroyed; "earthquake proof" roads and rails were toppled with more than 30,000 casualties including 5,478 dead. On March 20, the Aum Shinrykio sect perpetrated a human tragedy in the subways of Tokyo. Members released the deadly gas, sarin, killing a dozen and poisoning close to 6,000. Many suffered permanent debilitating effects.

The sarin attacks and earthquake kept Murayama in office out of necessity, and the government's slowness to respond to these disasters further troubled and alienated many Japanese. Angry Kobe citizens took things into their own hands. There was a massive, unprecedented outpouring of popular volunteerism as thousands of ordinary people rushed to help or bring materials. The sarin attacks triggered a profound national soul searching as the Japanese tried to understand how the perpetrators of the attacks, many graduates of top universities, could engage in such acts of terrorism against their own people. Others questioned the national system of education and values of the society as a whole. These events heightened alienation from national politics. People began to turn away from the establishment political machines and consider their own resources.

In January of 1996 Murayama gave up the prime minister slot, which returned to the LDP under Hashimoto Ryutaro. Hashimoto represented the resurfacing of conservatism and nationalism within the LDP. In fact, the core of the party had never abandoned its dream of rebuilding Japan to its prewar glory. During Hashimoto's two years in office the party roller-coaster ride continued. Having "sold out" by cooperating with the LDP, the Socialist Party, renamed the Social Democratic Party of Japan, came close to disappearing from the political scene. Other new parties like the Democratic Party founded by Hatoyama Yukio and Kan Naoto in 1996 and Ozawa Ichiro's New Frontier Party, which he had organized in December of 1994, entered the scene. The latter, dominated by Ozawa, became the second largest party in the lower house, only to collapse in 1997 into five splinter parties including the Reform Club and the New Party of Harmony. Needless to say, the rise and fall of parties and factions generated confusion and alienation among the electorate, which absented itself from national elections in unprecedented numbers. Many completely lost trust in politicians, and more than half abandoned their party affiliations.

Under these fluid circumstances of intense political opportunism the LDP remained anchored in its conservative past. The end of the cold war and the start of the "war against terrorism" following September 11, 2001, found Japan in an unstable international environment. The seemingly endless downward spiral of the domestic economy, massive debts, and intractable problems in the financial sectors, including negative growth and deflation, cast a dark shadow of concern over Japan's aging population. In 1998 Hashimoto passed the prime minister position to Obuchi Keizo. Derided as a rather bland personality, he was able to pull together the tattered LDP and build a coalition with outside parties, thereby restoring LDP dominance in the parliament. Prior to his untimely death from the rupture of a brain aneurysm in April 2000, Obuchi put in place policies to deal with the stubborn banking problems. He also presided over the LDP resurgence of nationalism symbolized by the official recognition of the Hinomaru as the flag of Japan and the Kimigayo as the national anthem. Both have deep associations with Japan's imperialist expansion and extreme nationalism of World War II.

Obuchi was followed by Yoshiro Mori, who lasted for one year (April 2000–April 2001) as prime minister. He continued the Hashimoto and Obuchi policies, but carried his nationalism too far with positive references to Japan's imperial age and divine ancestry. His extremism shocked most Japanese who may be searching for a new twenty-first century Japanese identity, but are unwilling to repeat the mistakes of the past.

As noted at the start of this section, Mori was succeeded by Koizumi, who was chosen not in the back rooms but from the grass roots. One of his serious rivals had been Tanaka Makiko, daughter of Tanaka Kakuei, prime minister in the 1970s whose grandiose plans for remaking Japan collapsed in corruption and his own involvement in the Lockheed scandal. Koizumi did give Makiko the Ministry of Foreign Affairs, making her Japan's first female foreign minister in what was to be a salvo in his attack on vested bureaucratic interests. She lasted only nine months before Koizumi fired her on the demand of the conservative old guard in the Foreign Ministry.

Still, Koizumi has had his successes and continues to be popular among the Japanese electorate. His administration has undertaken major structural reforms in the banking and finance areas, assuming responsibility for nonperforming loans and corporate restructuring. His aggressive and respected finance minister, Takenaka Heizo, remains in office despite the misgivings of conservative insiders. Attractive to independent urban voters, he also remains connected to the LDP's traditional constituencies, traveling to the countryside, for example, to nail down the critical rural vote.

In foreign policy, the Koizumi government has taken a strong stand in the continuing showdown with North Korea over nuclear weapons. It has also taken a solid stand with the United States in its war against terrorism, most specifically in the recent war in Iraq; to this end it has supported expansion of the National Defense Forces and revision of the constitution, including Article 9, which prohibits Japan from having armed forces, let alone sending them outside the country.

Most recently in the spring of 2004 after a decade of negative growth and deflation, Japan's economy is showing signs of improvement. The lone wolf and the LDP appear to be presiding over a period of growth and national pride. With no serious competition, there is little likelihood of significant political change in the immediate future.

18

CONTEMPORARY JAPANESE SOCIETY

During the enthronement of the Emperor Akihito in the fall of 1990 there was a moment at which Prime Minister Kaifu stood on a dais at the same level as the emperor, dressed in an ordinary formal jacket and trousers, not in the traditional dress of a vassal. To a Western observer this might be scarcely noticeable; but in 1926, when Akihito's father, Emperor Hirohito, was enthroned, such signs of democratic equality would have been quite unthinkable. There was another moment even more disturbing to Japanese tradition. At a state banquet in Tokyo for South Korean Prime Minister Roh Tae Woo, Emperor Akihito publicly apologized for the occupation of Korea from 1910 to 1945, expressing "deepest regret for the occupation brought about by my country." The Japanese government had offered an apology by the prime minister; but this did not satisfy the Koreans. The occupation had taken place in the name of an emperor, and an emperor must apologize.

Japan has vastly changed since 1945, in its view of the emperor, in its view of other nations, in the way its children are educated and socialized, in its attitude toward women, in its feeling about the environment, and in the forms of its culture. Let us begin with the children.

EDUCATION

During the Meiji period the modernizing Japanese state made a commitment to universal education and literacy. With its new secular and open system, building on the impressive urban literacy of the Tokugawa (with an estimated male literacy rate as high as 80 percent), the government sought to prepare all Japanese for new roles as citizens and participants in a modern, industrial economy. The purpose was to strengthen the nation. Expansion of national, public education during the Meiji period resulted in universal,

261

A modern primary school on sports day.

Japan Information Center

free, public, primary education by 1904 and an astonishing literacy rate of about 90 percent. In 2003, Japan could claim near universal literacy. Following World War II, the rigid and doctrinaire curriculum gave way to an American-occupation-directed program designed to replace the old values with new, individualistic alternatives. This resulted, as described by Edwin Reischauer, "in a new breed of young Japanese, more direct, casual and undisciplined than their prewar predecessors, but at the same time more independent, spontaneous and lively."[1] If today's Japanese students are considered to any degree to be undisciplined, it is only in comparison with the state of discipline in the past, and educational standards have remained high. Today all children attend six years of elementary school, beginning at age six, and three years of lower secondary school (or junior high school) at ages twelve to fifteen. Further education is voluntary; but the percentage of students going on to upper secondary school, public and private, has increased rapidly since the 1960s. It was 97 percent in 1995, which is a ratio similar to that of the United States. And 45 percent of all secondary school graduates continue on to college, a ratio somewhat lower than in the United States, but better than that of the European Union countries. Other students continue on to vocational schools or attend universities in foreign countries (151,000 in 1994). Others take courses through The University of the Air, which began operations in 1984.

---

[1] Edwin O. Reischauer, *Japan—The Story of a Nation* (New York: Alfred A. Knopf, 1974), p. 233.

Number of Schools, Students, and Teachers, May 1995

	Schools	Students	Teachers	Student-Teacher Ratio
Kindergartens	14,856	1,808,432	111,789	16.2
Elementary schools	24,548	8,370,246	436,665	19.2
Lower secondary schools	11,274	4,570,390	292,312	15.6
Upper secondary schools	5,501	4,724,945	342,672	13.8
Schools for the blind	70	4,611	3,857	1.2
Schools for the deaf	107	7,257	5,124	1.4
Schools for the handicapped	790	74,966	44,623	1.7
Higher technical schools	62	56,234	6,808	8.3
Junior colleges	596	498,516	58,947	8.5
Universities	565	2,546,649	250,132	10.2
Technical schools	3,476	813,347	141,785	5.7
Miscellaneous schools	2,821	321,105	37,135	8.6

Source: Ministry of Education.

Aside from the influence of Japan's traditional obsession with education, economic issues also propel the national emphasis on academic achievement. A good job in any sector of the modern economy demands graduation from the best possible schools; contraction of agricultural and industrial positions has made a good education ever more essential. Families and the state demand intense, focused concentration on education from the young. There is fierce competition for slots even in preschool and kindergartens where the youngest begin to learn socialization and subject matter. Children begin homework in first grade and may end up in later grades with four or five hours of it a night. The school day is longer in Japan than in the United States. The week includes a half-day on Saturday, and the school year lasts for 240 days (compared with 180 in the United States). (In the fall of 1992 the Ministry of Education passed a regulation requiring one free Saturday per month. In the new millennium there is a movement to eliminate all Saturday classes. Some students apparently find it hard to cope with all this free time.) The quality and status of teachers are high, and they remain among the best paid of civil servants. For these perks they are expected to give totally to their students and schools, visiting with families and being involved in extracurricular activities. While Japanese students emerge from their mandatory schooling with a well-rounded education, they have consistently done especially well in science and mathematics and still rank at the top of the world order in these subjects along with their close competitors, China, Korea, and Taiwan. Language study in their native tongue takes up a good part of their humanities training, and though they begin to study English in junior high school (the Ministry of Education is working toward a bilingual system), overall, the Japanese continue to perform poorly in foreign languages, especially in spoken languages.

Such a record in the schools is clearly of great benefit to the nation, since it makes available not only leaders capable of being trained at higher levels but also an educated labor pool, able to supply the requirements of the present postindustrial world for work which is knowledge-intensive. Without a solid record in science education Japan's entry into the arena of space exploration would not have been possible. Already in 1985 Japan had entered into an agreement with the United States to become a major partner in the $30 billion space station program; and by September 1992 the first Japanese astronaut, a physicist, Dr. Mohri Manoru, joined the crew of the shuttle Endeavor for the mission Spacelab-J (for Japan). The National Space Development Agency of Japan contributed $90 million of the $300 million cost of the mission, which was designed to determine the effects of near weightlessness on biological organisms. In 1986 Japan sent up an unmanned spacecraft to examine Halley's comet, and in the same year it launched a rocket whose second stage and inertial guidance system were made in Japan and not in the United States.

While Japan continues to occupy a position at the cutting edge of advanced science, supported by its scientific, mathematical, and technological education system, the 1990s brought a succession of technological failures, including several aborted launches in its space program, tunnel collapses and accidents along its famous bullet train routes, the first serious accident in its nuclear program (the Tokaimura accident), and engineering failures during the Kobe earthquake in 1995. These disasters, coming in the face of the Aum sarin attack in Tokyo (1995) perpetrated by science graduates of some of Japan's most prestigious universities, has resulted in a reassessment of education and a search for better ways to train children for the twenty-first century.

Japanese schools have always been given a heavy responsibility for character formation. Socialization, propriety, and ethical values are main concerns beginning at the preschool level where it is assumed that schools will reinforce familial and national values. While the primary mission of the Japanese schools, set by the Ministry of Education, is "to produce self-reliant citizens of a peaceful and democratic nation who respect human rights and love truth and peace," they also teach the importance of traditional, Confucian, family values and nationalism. In 1957 ethics classes were reintroduced to the social studies curriculum (they had been banned after the war). Following 1999, the Hinomaru (Rising Sun Flag) and the Kimigayo (the national anthem), both prewar and closely associated with imperial Japan, returned to public school ceremonies. This resurgence of nationalism tinged with prewar elements is a marked change in recent years.

While the Japanese are justifiably proud of their educational system, there are serious problems and concerns. The public, the Ministry of Education (renamed The Ministry of Education, Culture, Sports, Science, and Technology in 2000), the National Council on Educational Reform (an advisory panel to the prime minister), the National University Association, teachers unions, and other organizations have continued an ongoing dialogue in search of solutions for what some consider to be a crisis in Japanese education. At all levels of the public school system educators are alarmed by a quantifiable and drastic decrease in scholastic ability. The declining ability of students to perform on standard exams is complicated by Japan's demographic time bomb characterized by a decline in the number of students at all levels, reducing competition along with standards. Japan's "new children" are listless and uninterested in learning, not infrequently turning classrooms into chaos, attacking teachers and other students, or refusing to go to school where they are bored or persecuted by classmates (*ijime*). These latter unfortunates have necessitated the coining of a new term, *hikikomori*, to describe more than a million young people who live as recluses, refusing to leave their rooms or even to associate with family members. At school, *ijime* has proliferated in shocking cases of torture, murder, and even decapitations; outside the classroom, the young are involved in a disproportionate number of murders and violent crimes. Parents are often at a loss as to how to deal with their own children, or worse yet, blame the schools alone while they preside over families in which the members are alienated from one another.

To a certain extent these serious problems do reflect the social transformations and breakdowns associated with globalization and a shift to postmodern societies. Japan still suffers, however, from its own weakness, declining job opportunities in the best positions, which heightens competition to a fevered pitch. The examination hell separating students from the best senior high schools and universities becomes more terrifying rather than less; failure and exhaustion, family sacrifice, and expectation drive hundreds to suicide each year. At home the proverbial *kyoiku mama* or "education mom" has been known to drive her children brutally in the struggle for success. Of course, the family effort is done for "the good of the child," whose failure to succeed would close all doors to a comfortable and secure future.

The strain of school is expressed in the phrase "examination hell," referring to the examination to gain entrance to the university. "Four hours sleep, you pass. Five hours, you fail." In addition to the psychological, not to say physical, damage to the students, there are also harmful side effects on the curriculum. Although study of English, for example, starts early, the stress on fine points of grammar required by the examination means that thorough reading in the English language is neglected, and fluency in speaking, even the comprehension of spoken English, is often extremely poor. (How many Westerners, on the other hand, even attempt to study Japanese?) It is not unknown to find a Japanese student learning the contents of a small dictionary by heart. More serious is the fact that stress on standardized material and memorization by rote means that creativity, imagination, critical thinking, and the ability to enter into independent discussion tend to be sacrificed. The gradual acquisition of a love of learning, on which civilization is built, is an early casualty; but that problem is not confined to Japan. Memorization by rote was the way the Chinese classics were taught and learned from at least the Han dynasty (206 B.C.) on, and such has been the rule in most of East Asia in the past.

Once a student has gained access to the university on a first, second, or third try, he or she tends, understandably, to relax, study little, turn to sports (which were prohibited in the last year of high school as time is needed for exam preparation), or simply enjoy time with friends in the critical practice of networking. As for political activism, a coming of age ritual during the 1960s, especially with the decline of the socialists and communists since the late 1990s, it is all but moribund. That is not to say that the average Japanese college student studying the liberal arts spends much time in the library. Though each professor collects a circle of promising students to take under his or her wing, most manage to find plenty of time for recreation. In part it has to do with expectations. Poor class attendance is attributed by many to the lack of intellectual stimulation in the university. A trenchant criticism of the system came from the writer Eto Jun, who said, "The contemporary Japanese university . . . is a dry, sterile world where true education is seldom dispensed or desired."[2] This is doubtless an extreme view, and the level of preparation of most students is high. But the four years of college are often not fully utilized, although students rarely drop out.

National universities and professional schools remain the top choice for all Japanese students because of their low subsidized tuitions and high prestige. They are extremely hard to get into so that most of Japan's college students (more than 70 percent) study at private institutions where they end up paying, on average, $35,000 for their tuition. While there are a number of well-endowed, prestigious, private universities including Keio and Waseda in Tokyo, budgetary problems are severe in most, which depend largely on student tuition and entrance examination fees. Japan has lacked, up to now, a tradition of large private contributions; therefore, pressure on private universities is excessive and getting worse as the student population declines. It is not unusual these days for private institutions to use the American method of recruiting students from overseas, with the main source coming from China and Taiwan, which share a character-based orthography with the Japanese. Sadly these foreign students have not always proven to be a reliable source of revenues as many disappear into the Japanese job market never to be seen again.

Finally, we can glimpse a tension within Japanese academia over the unending "textbook controversy." The Japanese remain unable to reach a consensus on the historical memory they should attach to World War II. In 1989–1990 a controversy arose over statements in school textbooks concerning World War II. Many older persons remembered the war as a "black nightmare"; others took pride in the imperial forces. The question has importance for the society as a whole, since new generations are growing up with no personal recollection of the war and little idea of how the Japanese

[2] *Journal of Social and Political Ideas in Japan*, 1967, p. 179f.

Army was regarded on the continent of Asia. The controversy concerned a social studies textbook, approved by the Ministry of Education, that used such words as "the advance into" instead of "the invasion of" China, played down atrocities committed by the Japanese Army such as the rape of Nanjing, and praised the nation's imperial tradition. China accused Japan of breaking a promise given in 1982 to amend the texts which offended Japan's neighbors. The Japanese government had temporized on the matter for some time; but when this new complaint from China arrived, followed by similar angry words from North and South Korea, Singapore, Thailand, and the Philippines, the Education Ministry revised the textbooks, removing some of the most controversial material.

The person mainly instrumental in forcing the conservative Ministry of Education to make at least some changes in the official history textbooks was Ienaga Saburo, a history teacher who died on December 9, 2002, at the age of eighty-nine. For twenty-eight years he sued the government for compelling him to delete uncomfortable passages in the World War II period of a history book he wrote. In March 1993 he finally lost his case in the Supreme Court of Japan. This was his comment: "In the end, almost no one wins a lawsuit in Japan against the Government. But for more than twenty years I think I have proved a great deal. Even if I couldn't win in court, in the court of history I think I have been victorious."

As the Ienaga case suggests, the Japanese remain unable to settle the issue of their imperial past. The recent ascent of conservative power within the LDP, the frequent public visits of politicians to Yasukuni Shrine, reinstatement of the Kimigayo and the Hinomaru flag are visual signs of a strong push to rewrite the history of Japan's imperial wars. Recently these efforts have reached the schools with a strong effort to rewrite the old 1947 law concerning the basic aims of education to include a heavy patriotic content including "respect for Japanese tradition" and "love of country and hometown" into text and curriculum. Along with the new militarism and the push to revise Article 9, it seems that education must be harnessed for new nationalist purposes.

POPULATION

These census figures show the population growth of Japan since World War II, in round figures:

75,750,000	1946
99,036,000	1966
117,660,000	1981
123,612,000	1990
127,100,000	2003

However, the rate of population growth in the years 1980–1985 was only 3.4 percent, and in 1985–1990, only 2.1 percent, plunging further in 2003 to only 1.3 percent. Demographers predict that Japan's population will peak

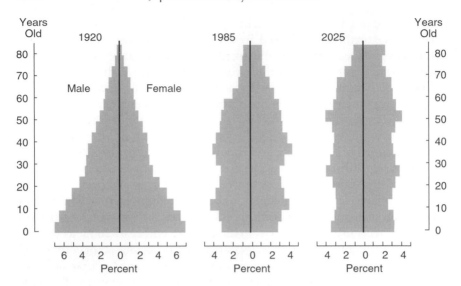

Japan's Population Pyramid, 1920–2025.

Source: Institute of Population Problems, Ministry of Health and Welfare.

in 2010 at 130,400,000 to be followed by a drastic and ultimately cata-strophic decline. If the predictions hold true, there will be a mere 100 mil-lion Japanese by 2050 and about 67 million by the year 3000. The flip side of population decline is the "graying of Japan," an increase in the number of people above age sixty who are no longer in the work force. It appears that the world-record longevity of the Japanese (men live to age 77.8 and women to age 85 in 2003, with more than 20,000 people over the age of 100) might propel Japan into a demographic crisis with a declining and unwilling num-ber of working-age people to tend an ever-increasing population of the aged whose needs can only increase. Population decline is not exclusive to Japan; rather it is characteristic of rich, postindustrial nations overall. Outside of Japan, immigration is used to help compensate for declining fertility rates. The Japanese would need an estimated 600,000 immigrant workers per year to compensate for declining fertility; however, they are unwilling to open their doors to outsiders. Not that Japan has completely closed its doors, as more than 1,200,000 residents in Japan are foreigners, mostly Koreans, Chi-nese, and Brazilians of Japanese ancestry. Proud of their ethnic homogene-ity, it will be difficult for the Japanese to increase immigration significantly. The immigrants, even Japanese from overseas, find it very difficult to assim-ilate or be accepted into the larger population. Population decline has already begun to have an impact on schools; smaller factories at the base of the *keiretsu* system are being forced to offshore production, and strains are be-ing felt in the welfare, pensions, and insurance systems. Demographics are bound to play a major role in Japan's future.

HOUSING

In traditional Japan three-generational families were common under one roof, with grandparent(s) living in the same house as one married son, usually the eldest, or with a married daughter. Aging and the declining number of offspring are having an effect on this tradition. Three-generational families have declined to 29.7 percent from the 55.8 percent in 1972, and 46 percent of households in 1999 had people over sixty-five living on their own. Some of them do live in separate attached residences (*hanare*) connected to those of their children, yet they maintain independence.

In spite of the bursting of the real estate bubble in the early 1990s, the cost of housing remains extremely expensive in Japan. To buy a plot of land in a Tokyo suburb costs twice as much as the construction of the house on the site, according to Japanese government figures. Houses, therefore, tend to be very small, perhaps 800 square feet in area as contrasted with 1,700 square feet for a corresponding dwelling in the United States. A house of average size in Tokyo may be priced as high as $500,000. Housing generally is not of good quality, with the exception of homes of the wealthy. This fact, along with small size, led a Japanese politician in an election speech pressing for a better quality of life to refer to Japanese houses as "rabbit hutches."

The spread of cities and suburbs has led to inordinate expenditure of time and energy getting to and from work, a problem common to many modern societies. In Japan daily commuting times extend to two, three, four, and

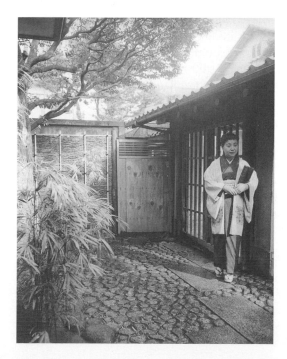

Japanese house with a typical Japanese-style gate.

Japan Information Center

A contemporary Japanese family at home.
The furnishings are part modern, part traditional.

Japan Information Center

even more hours. Conurbation, the joining of city to city, has reached such a point that from northern Kyushu, through the Kyoto-Kobe-Osaka area, right up to Tokyo and Yokohama, some 600 miles, buildings run more or less continuously with occasional patches of farmland.

TRANSPORTATION

Small ships plying the Japanese coast have for centuries kept supplies—and ideas—flowing from one part of the country to another. The rugged coastline and interior mountain ranges have made land transportation difficult; but roads and railways, with innumerable tunnels, bridges, and cuttings, have in the course of time been driven through. Now there is an internal air network to the chief cities, and world connections are maintained by Japan Air Lines. By rail the "bullet train" expresses have been running for some time from Tokyo to northern Kyushu with a tunnel under the straits at Shimonoseki. The fast express line has now been extended northward to Niigata. In 1988 a train tunnel was opened from the main island, Honshu, to the northern island, Hokkaido, to enlarge the system further. The world's longest train tunnel to date, it runs under the sea for a total length of 33 miles. In the same year the Seto Ohashi road and rail bridge were opened, connecting Honshu

Bullet train.
Tokyo-Osaka super-express passing Mt. Fuji.

Japan Information Center

with Shikoku; for the first time the four main islands of the country are joined by land transportation. This will further unify a people whose links are already close and should strengthen the internal economy. Aside from having built one of the most advanced, efficient, and convenient systems of intra- and inter-urban public transportation, the Japanese have been bitten by the private automobile bug. Alongside rail and air systems they have a superadvanced national highway system as well as many congested urban and rural roads. More than 80 percent of Japanese families own automobiles. Whether a leveling down process will take place, diminishing the riches of regional individuality and culture, remains to be seen.

WOMEN

The traditional Confucian values, which cast women in the three dependencies, to father, husband, and son, were strengthened during Japan's modernization period and reinforced in the decades of war and imperial expansion. Social momentum carried these values into the early postwar years, and they still have a tremendous residual influence, defining a family-based society in which the woman serves as the center of family life. However, the re-

Moon viewing in the peace of the family.
The moon-cakes are set out as an offering.

Japanese National Tourist Organization

ality is undergoing a slow but dramatic transformation as Japanese women are changing their roles in society and the world. The traditional role meant marriage, home, children, and total devotion to family and spouse. Husbands worked outside the home, and the single salary was supposed to support wife, children, and other dependents. Familial responsibilities, from cooking to child rearing to education, as well as fixing a leaking water tap, all fell to the woman, who also had responsibility for parental in-laws until their deaths. This role left little time for activities outside of the family (though, of course, in rural households women worked alongside their men in the fields) and consumed most of a woman's life.

In the past few decades, Japanese women have found more time, and less need to be consumed by household work. Many are postponing marriage or even opting for a single life. More in control of their reproductive lives, they are having fewer children, as noted above, and one-child families are becoming the norm. Abortions have been legal in Japan since 1948 and are readily available. Official family planning favors the use of condoms and takes a lenient view of abortions. Although the pill is now available to Japanese women, condoms are still promoted as a defense against HIV/AIDS. Japan does have one of the lowest AIDS-related death rates among the industrialized nations with 150 recorded in 2003, most of these related to blood transfusions.

One practice, perhaps significant, has become more common since the 1960s. Miscarriages, abortions, and stillbirths are often commemorated in a ceremony where a Buddha name is given, offerings are made, and a small statue is set up, usually of Jizo, protector of children and travelers. The custom has been criticized as being promoted by monks for the fee involved. But it has also been defended as a comfort to women who feel grief or guilt. It is commonplace to see row upon row of Jizo, dressed in baby clothes and provided with toys and food, on the grounds of Buddhist temples being visited by young women. Clearly they remain directed by Buddhist ideas of karma, retribution, and the sacredness of all life.

A second factor contributing to new freedom for women is the availability of labor-saving appliances. A small house or apartment so equipped takes little time to clean and maintain. When the last child goes off to school, there is a long day until the husband comes home from work, and many wives would like to do something meaningful. Some find an outlet in helping with the parent-teacher association or in attending a cooking school. The typical housewife also has more money to spend on shopping in today's consumer society. Aware of this fact, the merchants are now targeting women and young people for the sale of clothing, luxury and sports goods, cars, and trips abroad. Many women are now able to find additional personal time by taking advantage of Japan's abundance of instant or prepared foods. These convenient alternatives to the tedious work of cooking from scratch are available in supermarkets and the ubiquitous *kombini* or "convenience stores," which seem to be on every block. Finally, Japan must have the world's greatest concentration of take-out/home-delivery restaurants in the world. If time is limited, a tasty and inexpensive meal is just a telephone call away.

As the material environment has changed during the past several decades, attitudes and institutions have been profoundly effected. On the one hand, Japanese women are emerging as educational equals of their male counterparts. Of enrollees in junior colleges, 90 percent are women, and they are gaining on men in four-year colleges as well, at 37 percent in 2001. Many others are making the choice to study abroad. Even those who do choose the preferred path of motherhood are probably among the highest qualified in the world. Certainly formal education expands and changes the horizons of Japanese women. They are also constantly exposed to the themes of popular culture from the print media, film, theater, and television, which present a full range of postmodern and globally inspired alternatives to traditional Japanese ideals of female behavior. Importantly, consumerism and the dominant theme of individualism and self-fulfillment corrode the old social imperative, which supports the family and women's role within it.

As mentioned above, young women often postpone marriage (the average marriage age is now twenty-seven) to pursue their personal interests and careers. Once married, they are more likely to want their husbands to act as partners in family matters, including the rearing and educating of children. Once expected as a matter of course, the role of *yome* or the "good daughter-in-law" who assumes responsibility for parents, either her own or those of her husband, can no longer be taken for granted; the shifting role of wife to outside work is forcing the state to step in with welfare programs for the aged to take the place of services traditionally provided by the good daughter-in-law. Finally, divorce is soaring in Japan (289,836 couples divorced in 2002), especially among women in their fifties and sixties who are no longer willing to embrace the Japanese ideal of *gamman* or "enduring the unendurable" for the sake of family survival. Divorce for the middle-aged has risen 300 percent in the past ten years as women opt for a chance at their own fulfillment. As a somewhat symbolic phenomenon, women who have endured unhappy marriages without love or consideration are opting to be buried separately from their deceased partners—a final assertion of themselves into eternity.

Beyond the family, women are advancing in politics and social activism at the local and national level. They have launched movements at the grass-roots and national levels promoting consumer interests, environmental concerns, and welfare interests, by both direct action and political action. As early as the 1970s they helped elect the reformist Minobe Ryokichi governor of the Tokyo District. By the mid-1990s they were active supporters of reform and of maverick candidates who challenged the establishment, including eccentrics like Yukio Aoshima in Tokyo and Knock Yokoyama in Osaka; both won their respective campaigns. And they continue to make progress at all levels of the political system.

In the business and financial world, Japanese women are also seeing changes, albeit slowly. To be sure, many still serve as "office ladies," serving tea and receiving visitors, biding their time until marriage and family. It is also true that the Japanese corporations remain in the hands of a male-dominated hierarchy in which seniority continues to play an important role. In spite of a 1985 Equal Employment Opportunity Law and the fact that close to 50 percent of the labor force is now female, many obstacles impede women's ascent up the corporate ladder. For example, in most firms there is a two-track system, overt or latent, namely, the general/clerical track and the elite managerial track. Few women are permitted to interview for the managerial track; if and when they do and they are hired, they are compelled, like the men, to accept long hours at work and compulsory transfers to other sites. This may mean a delayed marriage or no marriage. The equal employment law might seem to offer women some protection against discrimination; but a court of law refused to recognize the two-track system as being discriminatory and hence illegal.[3] With the two-track system firmly in place, women must often make hard choices—about marriage, about their working careers—that may demand of them too little or too much. And many women see the long hours and stringent conditions under which their husbands work and do not want to enter upon the same wearying path. Few industrialized countries, Japan included, are yet prepared to recognize that what is wrong for women may also be wrong for men, if family life is to remain as a strong

---

[3] See Joyce Gelb, "Tradition and Change in Japan, the Case of Equal Opportunity Law," *U.S.-Japan Women's Journal*, English Supplement no. 1, 1991.

FOR THE RECORD

HOW WOMEN FARE

A comparison of professional women in Japan to those in other industrialized countries.

Women as a percentage of . . .

	ALL WORKERS	MANAGERIAL WORKERS	CIVIL SERVICE WORKERS GENERAL	MANAGERIAL	NATIONAL PARLIAMENT/ CONGRESS
Japan	41.0%	8.9%	20.2%	1.4%	7.3%
United States	46.6	46.0	49.3	23.1	14.3
Sweden	48.0	30.5	43.0	51.0	45.3
Germany	44.0	26.9	39.0	9.5	32.2
Britain	44.9	30.0	49.1	17.2	17.9

SOURCES: The Cabinet Office of Japan; International Labor Organization; Inter-Parliamentary Union; Howard French: "Japan's Neglected Resource: Female Workers": *NY Times*, July 23, 2003.

foundation of national well-being. For those Japanese women who do want to remain in the corporate world, the globalization of Japan's economy during the 1990s provided an entirely new range of opportunities—working for foreign corporations either in Japan or abroad. These firms are extremely welcoming to talented women, snapping up the best in global recruitment programs, even luring talent from Japan's top companies such as Toyota, Fujitsu Ltd., and NTT DoCoMo Inc. Global corporations offer women open opportunities for advancement based on merit rather than on seniority or gender; they also cultivate a looser, freer working environment, with space for personal time and family life. The loss of talent to these new foreign competitors has been forcing Japanese companies to rethink their corporate cultures vis-à-vis their female employees and perhaps their male employees as well. Toyota's Miyadai Haruyuki, group manager of the global human resources division, while not overly concerned about the loss of female employees to foreign firms admitted that it was necessary to strike some balance between new social trends and the old core value.

Finally, while the progress of Japanese women has been rather slow compared to that of other industrial nations, there has been considerable change. Clearly, laws alone cannot transform social values. In fact it is likely that most Japanese women prefer their mix of traditional family values and modernity. However, with changing demographics and the aging of its population, Japan will have to find ways to use the vast talents of this underutilized human resource.

YOUTH

Trends among today's young people are determined by several factors. World War II took place more than fifty years ago, so that no young person today has any direct experience of the "black nightmare." Nor does he or she have any memory of the shortages, want, fear, shame, and distress of the immediate postwar years. In fact quite the opposite is true. Until the economic decline of the 1990s, members of the younger generation lived in a time of unprecedented domestic peace and prosperity during which they could look with pride, and perhaps even a bit of arrogance, at the achievements of Japan. They have surely been creatures of comfort, the new Japanese youth. They have also had instant access to the world through television, high-pressure Japanese and international advertising, and the Internet. Barriers of distance, language, and even culture have been overcome as never before. They are fully aware of their world and the thoughts and aspirations of people in other countries, especially the United States. In recent years they have also had to confront Japan's "lost decade" of economic decline, identity crisis, and shaken confidence; they have seen unprecedented unemployment (5.6 percent in 2003) and suicides among the salarymen who have lost their jobs; they have been exposed to the collapse of great banks and companies, bankruptcies of small factories, and revelations of corruption reaching all levels of government. It is fair to say that while they continue to live in a comfortable world, that world is tarnished and filled with uncertainties. On top of it all, they are challenged by the same problems confronting all postmodern nations, those of abstract detachment from reality and existential malaise.

These challenges have produced many troubling symptoms in Japanese youths. Of course, most struggle along the path set for them by their elders, but the elders too are shaken by uncertainties. Many young people are alienated from their families and the institutions of society and have retreated into themselves or, tragically, into destructive, even violent, behavior. We have already spoken of declining achievement, disorder, *ijime*, and crime perpetrated by alienated youths. Brutal murders, such as the case of a twelve-year-old killing a kindergarten student, have become more common. Most disturbing in these cases is the fact that the perpetrators come from apparently normal and happy families. In fact, the more spectacular cases are the tip of an iceberg in which most violent crimes in Japan are committed by children nineteen and under, and these crimes have been increasing on a yearly basis.

Aside from violent criminality there are other problems. The sad reality of extensive teenage prostitution by school girls *enjo kosai* or "dating for assistance" is difficult for the Japanese to explain. Most of the child prostitutes have no need for the money, nor do they have any sense of shame or guilt. They do it to purchase luxury items or entertainment. Other youths join "motorcycle gangs" or *bosozoku*, rejecting all social mores. Less destructive, but equally disturbing, are the million or so *hikikomori* or "urban recluses" mentioned previously. Even the so-called *freeters*, or "college-educated youths who opt out of the conventional job market, live with their parents, and do part-time work to finance a Bohemian lifestyle," reflect a widespread and destructive form of behavior. It is estimated that there are more than 4 million *freeters* today.

Clearly, Japanese young people are caught in the cross currents of a changing world, and the full force and direction of those changes are not clear. Crime, violence, deviance, and just opting out affect a small minority of the hard-working and diligent Japanese youth, yet their growing numbers are worrisome to their elders. They are the topic of endless discussion throughout society and the government, and the truth is that the Japanese do not have answers as yet, though psychologist Iwao Sumiko offers the following ideas as to causality:

> I feel the single greatest cause for the wave of juvenile crime has been our failure to instill the basic consciousness in children that tells them what they may and may not do. This is why young people are not troubled at the prospect of committing a criminal act, and why they feel no remorse after the fact . . . a gulf exists between three groups: parents, teachers, and children. I believe this alarming distrust lies at the heart of the increase in juvenile crime.
>
> Moreover, human relations—be they between husband and wife, parent and child, teacher and student, fellow teachers, or among children—have grown shallow. A fear of treading on another person's human rights has led to a weakening of personal commitments. As a result, children sense that neither parents nor teachers are truly seeing them for who they are.[4]

THE ENVIRONMENT

In the Nara period, during the eighth century, Japan's emperors and poets sang of the natural beauty and abundance of their precious land. Throughout the ensuing history, farmers nurtured a symbiotic relationship with this land. Nature remained at the center of poetry and art, the source of Japan's aesthetic tradition. The industrial revolution changed this relationship, but never as destructively or intensively as during the postwar years. In their rush to rebuild and catch and overtake their conquerors, Japanese politicians and industrialists decided to cast aside any thoughts about the environmental impact of what they were doing. By the 1960s industrial poisons were killing nature and people; thousands were deformed or deprived of full life spans. At first from the grass roots desperate citizens struggled against the great power of corporation, government, and bureaucracy. In the so-called "pollution Diet" of 1970, a bill was passed making "the emission of materials harmful to human life" a crime for the first time and punishable by up to three years in prison. Two notorious cases followed. In one, seven persons died and seventy more were affected by mercury poisoning from eating tainted fish. This resulted in a fine of $800,000 for a leading chemical firm. In a second, even worse case, the Chisso Corporation was ordered to pay $3.6 million to victims of mercury poisoning. It was discovered that 67 persons had died and 330 had become permanently disabled in the six years pre-

---

[4] Iwao Sumiko, "Problems Among Japan's Young," in Yoichi Masuzoe, *Years of Trial: Japan in the 1990s* (Tokyo: Japan Echo, 2000), pp. 256–260.

ceding 1973, the date of the case. *Kogai*, "environmental disruption," has come to the forefront as a political issue; Japanese women were the first to see it clearly. Of what value was a constantly rising GNP, they argued, if they and their families were not receiving benefits in the same proportion? As a result, all Japan is gradually realizing that a new concept of "net national welfare" must replace "growth of GNP" as a national goal.

In recent years Japan has had a better record in cleaning up the environment than many other countries, notably in greatly reducing auto emissions and in conserving energy. A directorate for global environmental affairs has been set up within the Ministry of International Trade and Industry (MITI). But Japan's past record abroad has often come in for serious criticism. A ban on the killing of certain whale species was promulgated in 1986 by the International Whaling Commission. Since this body has no enforcement powers, the United States applied its international fishing sanctions to violators. In June 1987 Japan was accused of having killed 2,769 whales since January 1, 1986. Some whale killing was allowed for experimental purposes; but the charge was that Japan was actually engaging in commercial killing, using large ships in which slaughter and immediate processing were combined. Charges of varying gravity were also leveled against the former Soviet Union, South Korea, Norway, and Iceland. The Japanese representative on the Whaling Commission resigned in protest at the constant criticism of Japan. There has probably been some recovery in the number of minke whales, one of the main species in dispute, along with sperm whales; but numbers are hard to establish. In July 1992 Norway announced that it would begin hunting minkes again, and this meant the virtual collapse of the ban.

A parallel issue is that of drift-net fishing. Ships lay out immense nets, thirty or more miles long, enough, for example, to encircle Manhattan. When drawn in, the nets enclose vast quantities of fish and the squid popular in Japan; but they also enclose and kill sea mammals, such as dolphins, in large numbers. Again, other nations besides Japan are involved. The U.N. General Assembly agreed in 1987 that the use of drift nets of this type should be brought to an end. The United States and New Zealand requested an immediate date, but Japan, a few days before the final ruling, gained extra time by announcing that it would cease the practice in 1992. The General Assembly set the date at June 1992.

There is no doubt that the Japanese government, driven by world opinion and pressure at home, is alive to the importance of caring for the overall environment. Before the International Conference on Global Warming in Geneva in 1990, Japan announced a national plan to stabilize emissions of carbon dioxide by the year 2000. (The United States, by contrast, led the opposition to setting firm dates by which elimination or reduction of a main cause of global warming was to be achieved.) And at the Earth Summit held at Rio de Janeiro in 1992 the Japanese government pledged $7 billion in aid to clean up the environment. In 1997 Japan hosted the U.N. Kyoto summit on the environment, which decided on sweeping guidelines and deadlines for dealing with carbon pollution of the atmosphere by the industrial nations. Unfortunately the United States refused to sign the treaty; since the United States is the greatest global polluter, its nonparticipation signaled the failure of this effort. On the home front, national and local governments continue to write laws and bylaws mandating levels of pollutants including noise and vibrations. All forty-seven of Japan's prefectures have environmental laws that supplement and compensate for nonaction at the national level. Thus, local-level activism remains a driving force in protecting the environment. Significantly, women have taken the lead in these grassroots movements.

Japanese conservationists are concerned that overbuilding in Japan poses a threat to the environment. For example, the Kyoto Buddhist Association, a group of 1,000 Buddhist temples, printed a full-page advertisement in the *New York Times* headed by the following statement:

> Kyoto, a sacred Buddhist site and center of Japanese culture, has recently become in danger of losing its unique character and appearance. The construction of high-rise buildings by large Japanese enterprises who are only interested in realizing higher profits on their land investments is rapidly spoiling Kyoto. The Kyoto Buddhist Association is very much in opposition to such plans and has decided to protect this historical city.[5]

To make public such a concern outside Japan is an unusual action. It is a signal of the level of anxiety about the ancient capital, spared by the bombers of World War II but now under another form of attack.

RELIGION

The Japanese people today seem to be basically of a pragmatic, rational, or scientific turn of mind. Less than one-third profess a personal religious faith; yet most think, paradoxically, that a religious attitude is important. Shinto, the original native religion, worships the powers of nature, and its principal deity is Amaterasu, the Sun Goddess (see Chapter 1). Shinto imparts to the Japanese ethos a happy if not profound or moral tone. Morality derives to some extent from Buddhism, but more from the Confucian element in Japan's past and from the group responsibility which it fosters. State Shinto, which had been exploited by the military in the 1930s for extreme patriotic purposes, was separated from the private practice of Shinto by decree of the 1947 Constitution. Shinto festivals punctuate the year with holidays that correspond to the cycle of nature. Buddhism, whose importance is abundantly illustrated in Japanese history, today accounts for 84 percent of the population of 127 million, but not all these can be reckoned as devout. Shinto overlaps with Buddhism, so no numbers of Shinto believers can be given with any accuracy. Japanese may employ Shinto rites when they marry and Buddhist

---

[5] *New York Times*, Feb. 23, 1992.

funeral rites when they die. Or a family may, with no feeling of contradiction, go to the Shinto shrine in Kyoto at midnight of the New Year to receive a light for their hearth and go on the same night to the Buddhist temple to hear the boom of the great bell which drives away the 108 evil passions.

Christians, divided approximately equally between Protestants and Catholics, number only 0.7 percent of the population or more than 1 million, a slight decline. But they probably exert a greater influence upon society than their small number would indicate. Many leaders in public life have imbibed Christian ideas, particularly with regard to education and social welfare. Christians, for example, were the pioneers in opening schools for girls. And in the 1920s, in the early days of the labor movement, Christians and Socialists combined their efforts led by activists such as Kagawa and Suzuki. The Christian church in Japan today is still much involved with issues of social justice. Sophia University (Roman Catholic) and International Christian University (Protestant) both play a role as intermediaries of foreign thought in Japan. Christians also tend to play important social roles, quietly and unobtrusively, often concealing their faith. They help in suicide hotline counseling and community welfare projects. Christianity retains an appeal to marginal groups including *burakumin* or "outcasts, prostitutes, and the homeless."

A postwar phenomenon has been the rapid growth of the "new religions." There may be several reasons for this, but one is almost certainly the disillusion and malaise following the defeat of World War II. The sects were so numerous that a book describing them was entitled *The Rush Hour of the Gods.* The phenomenon seems proof of a deeply felt need. Most of these new religions were founded in the nineteenth or early twentieth century but showed a great increase after 1946. As the turn of the millennium approached there was a further blossoming of religion, sometimes named "the new new religions." The combined adherents of these religions include approximately 14 percent of the population or about 17 million adherents.

Two of the more popular religions are Tenrikyo and Soka Gakkai. Tenrikyo, the Religion of the Heavenly Principle, generally Buddhist in background, was founded by a housewife; it stresses simple and joyful service and cleanliness. Believers run spotlessly clean work camps and, as an act of service, join in large numbers in front of the emperor's palace to clear the whole area of litter, as a physical symbol of spiritual cleanliness. To Westerners this emphasis on keeping clean may seem superficial, but for the Japanese the notion of ritual purity extends far back in history. Shinto worshippers rinse hands and mouth before approaching the shrine; even Buddhists ritually cleanse themselves with incense smoke prior to entering a temple; and everyone who visits Japan comments on the constant bathing and personal cleanliness of the people.

The religious movement that has shown the most rapid growth of all has been the Soka Gakkai, "Value-Creating Society." This is a militant Buddhist group, founded by a schoolteacher, which draws its inspiration from the Buddhist patriot saint of the thirteenth century, Nichiren. Intolerant of other religions and of other Buddhist sects, it promises health and well-being to all who will embrace its tenets and work actively for its extension. The movement makes a special appeal to youth between ages twenty and thirty, and to small business owners, many of whom have found their capital insufficient and have gone bankrupt in the competition of modern commerce. It also appeals to the downtrodden and to those in the lower classes seeking security, such as domestic servants from the countryside, who feel alienated in the cities and cannot claim membership in a labor union or other similar group. The movement owes much of its success and expansion to a large selection of popular literature, actively promoted for sale by members. Soka Gakkai makes use of paramilitary methods to incite mass enthusiasm through parades, marching bands, and sports. It has been accused of using brainwashing and strong-arm methods, including entering homes and chanting Buddhist services for endless hours in order to gain converts. The political arm of Soka Gakkai is called Komeito, or Clean Government Party.

The main component of these two religions is Buddhist. For an example of a religion with a base in Shinto, one may cite Kurozumikyo, or the Religion of Kurozumi.[6] This faith is worthy of consideration, since it combines Shinto with Confucian elements and has moral and egalitarian features. The founder, Kurozumi Munetada, was born in 1780 to the family of a Shinto priest of low samurai rank. He also became a Shinto priest and determined at the age of nineteen to become a *kami* in this life as a sign of honor to his parents. By using the term *kami*, he was pointing, in Shinto terms, to the ideal of the sage found in Neo-Confucianism. While worshipping the sun on his thirty-fifth birthday, Kurozumi had a mystical experience of becoming one with the sun, which he called the Direct Receipt of the Heavenly Mission.

Soon after his vision Kurozumi began to preach. It is significant that his first converts joined him as the result of faith healing, carried out by the laying on of hands and the recital of the Great Purification Prayer. This prayer embodies phrases from the earliest records of Shinto:

> The heavenly deities will push open the heavenly rock door . . . and pushing aside the mists of the high mountains and the low mountains . . . then . . . in the lands of the four quarters under the heavens, each and every sin will be gone. . . . Beginning from today, each and every sin will be gone. Cleanse and purify! Cleanse and purify!

The founder's writings are used by the sect as holy writ. The main moral principles are family solidarity, respect for the authority of older persons, and an exact division of labor between the sexes. Although women do not preach, they have an important role in the ongoing work of the church. The founder preached equality and "mutual reverence" among members; he even regarded

---

[6] See Helen Hardacre, *Kurozumikyo and the New Religions of Japan* (Princeton University Press, 1988).

his wife as a *kami*, or "divine being." At meetings there was no observance of rank; even with samurai present, poor women and children might be given the best places.

  In fact, in the new religions as a whole, women find conspicuously better treatment than they do elsewhere. Their daily work is usually the most restricted, the least interesting, and the most poorly paid. In the new churches they can occupy positions which bring some prestige, and they can find outlets for their energy and creative talents. Restrictions tied to old ideas of pollution often hamper women in the established religions, but in the new religions these restrictions rarely apply. Even the division of labor between the sexes is relaxed. It is no wonder that women join the new churches in considerable numbers and contribute unusual energy to their expansion. In the spring of 1995, following the devastation of the Great Hanshin earthquake in Kobe, on March 20, Tokyo citizens awoke to news of a deadly sarin attack in the maze of subway stations beneath their city. More than a dozen died and thousands were hospitalized, many with serious and lasting side effects. The perpetrators, members of Asahara Shoko's Aum Shinrikyo had hoped for many more deaths and the collapse of society. One of the new new religions, Aum attracted intelligent and highly educated members, people, sadly, who had been alienated from conventional society. They had come to search for meaning in a bizarre doomsday cult built on the remnants of traditional religions and led by a charismatic, blind fanatic. In 2003 Yuko Chino's Panawave Laboratory, a group of alienated marginals, drove around Japan in a caravan of white vehicles in their efforts to save *Tamachan* (the bearded seal) while promoting nonbathing, avoidance of electromagnetic waves, and a diet limited to instant noodles. While these religious phenomena suggest the level of alienation and spiritual malaise in contemporary Japan, they also expose a frightening loss of human awareness and meaning. Yamaori Tetsuo calls these tragic happenings symptoms of the "death of religion" in Japan.[7]

CULTURE

The Japanese, who can be withdrawn and meditative as well as outgoing and energetic, are nourished and sustained by a sense of their own past to a degree not found elsewhere. They go out to seek the new and the latest, in style and taste, yet know the value of ancient forms in art and have sedulously conserved them. This fertilizing effect of traditional forms upon modern art and design is not easily explained but must be felt and experienced through a study of Japan's cultural past. Nevertheless, such is its intrinsic appeal that Japanese design in furniture, graphics, gardens, and architecture is having an

[7] Yamaori Tetsuo, "Aum Shinrikyo Sounds The Death Knell of Japanese Religion," *Japan Echo*, vol. 22, no. 3 (Autumn 1995) in Masuzoe Yoichi, *Years of Trial: Japan in the 1990s* (Tokyo: Japan Echo, 2000), p. 226.

increasing influence upon Western styles. The Japanese have long known the appeal of simplicity and clean lines, of the asymmetrical and the informal. They are adept at the use of materials which they allow to preserve their original nature—stone, clay, wood, bamboo, thatch—often untreated and unpainted. They value texture as much as shape and color; and in this respect particularly their architects and artisans have helped to raise the level of international taste.

ARCHITECTURE

The Japanese architect who is probably best known in the West is Tange Kenzo. One of the most noteworthy of his buildings is the Swimming Arena built for the 1964 Tokyo Olympics, which, when seen from above, exhibits swinging curves reminiscent of a leaf of a clam shell. His Hall Dedicated to Peace at Hiroshima has as a central feature a freestanding, widespreading arch, broader at the base. It has an ancient, vaguely Japanese shape. Is it a somber arch through which suffering souls must pass to find release? One does not know; but it bespeaks tragedy, of those no longer tortured but at peace.

Tange's mantle may be said to have passed to Maki Fumihiko. Maki's design of a modernist building on Tokyo's fashionable Aoyama Boulevard reflects, he says, the fragmented nature of the street. His buildings stress a pronounced center, but in the rest of the structure he prefers asymmetry. He makes bold use of natural shapes, such as an oyster, or traditional shapes, such as a samurai helmet.

Ito Toyo has a special regard for the city of Tokyo. He sees Paris, London, and Rome as museums, but Tokyo, impermanent, always changing, he compares to a theater. He seeks to make a house there lighter, more temporary in effect, with an atrium like a Bedouin tent. Ito has lived in Southeast Asia; and the hut, the basic dwelling of that region, has been one of his models for reproduction in modern, more permanent materials.

Arata Isazaki has made some remarkably successful experiments in combining elements of East and West. In an extensive clubhouse complex for a golf course, he set up a rectilinear, pagodalike tower, with projecting eaves at each story, as a focus visible from any part of the course. He offset that with a lower circular building at a suitable distance. Its circle form was emphasized with plain columns, without capitals but highly reminiscent of a small Greek temple. Careful attention to proportion and perspective make the scheme, with its low connecting structures, extremely pleasing.

Ando Takao, a young and successful architect, is perhaps unique today in never having had a formal architectural training. He had an education in crafts, then worked on building sites and traveled the world. He finds many very large buildings "meaningless." The larger the structure, the less the significance. He resists consumerism and retains a profound respect for nature. A small Roman Catholic chapel he designed on Mount Rokko, high above Kobe, is approached by a long, gentle, transparent tunnel or arcade on the hillside. The tunnel, open at both ends, frames a natural scene of hill and pines, in the spirit of Shinto. To enter the chapel, placed parallel to the tunnel, one turns left and comes into a peaceful, simple space, lit by a large window down one side and small light slots elsewhere—again asymmetry. The large, thin cross of metal is suspended against the chancel wall. The chapel is built of concrete, not very commonly used in Japan in such a context. Ando has developed a lightness of construction in which for a moment concrete looks like paper.

Japanese architects continue their contributions to domestic and international projects. The Japanese-American architect, Minoru Yamasaki, for example, designed Manhattan's ill-fated twin towers of the World Trade Center. Some, like Maki Fumihiko, enhance their global designs by incorporating the latest in technologies and materials. Others, like Shigeru Ban, seek to preserve and enhance the use of traditional materials while adapting them to cutting-edge design and social needs; consider, for example, his paper housing designed to meet the needs of victims of natural disaster and reflecting a certain social consciousness as an element of architectural concern. Other contemporaries of Shigeru Ban, like Yoshiharu Tsukamoto and Akira Nagae, all under fifty, are helping to transform domestic architecture. They are opening the closed spaces of typical Japanese housing, bringing in light and the outdoors in new and innovative ways. One might say there is a minirevolution in aspects of residential architecture.

FILM

The great days of Japanese filmmaking were in the 1950s with the work of such directors as the late Ozu Yasujiro (*Tokyo Story*, the conflict between the traditional and the modern within a family) and the late Mizoguchi Kenji (*Ugetsu*, a medieval love story in which the real and unreal merge). Both these directors were extremely prolific, beginning production in the 1920s and continuing uninterrupted to the end of their lives in the 1960s. They were followed by a group sometimes called the postwar humanists, which included the single Japanese director best known in the West, Kurosawa Akira. His films include *Rashomon, Ikiru (To Live)*, and *Seven Samurai*. The warlike samurai themes are shot through with constant, subtle reminders of enduring human values. Kurosawa uses the camera to show humans *within* nature and humans caught up in the inescapable flow of time.

Another in this group is Ichikawa Kon. His *Harp of Burma* depicts a young Japanese soldier in that country sent to convince a small group of his fellows up in the mountains that the war is over. He fails, and they are all killed. He can survive only by stealing a Buddhist monk's robes to use as a disguise. On his way back to base he comes upon piles of corpses. He is thus faced with the task of burying them, and in so doing begins to take on the character for which the robes were intended. He remains in Burma as the other troops sail for home. The story of the film *Conflagration* is taken from

Mishima Yukio's novel concerning a real incident, the destruction by arson of the beautiful *Kinkakuji* (Temple of the Golden Pavilion) in Kyoto. In 1965 he filmed *Tokyo Olympiad* of the actual games, but with more emphasis on human feelings than on the athletic performances themselves. The film asks, in effect, "What have they won? Even a gold medal provides no answer to the problem of living."

Oshima Nagisa has been credited with being the founder in 1959 of the New Wave in Japanese film. (These groups of directors all overlap chronologically.) *The Sun's Burial* (1960) has as background the discontent of Japanese youth with the Japan-U.S. Security Treaty and the riots which led to the cancellation of President Eisenhower's visit. The film deals with petty crime and low life in a slum, and a semidocumentary presentation of the life of a girl who is a seller of black-market blood by day and a prostitute by night. She has a father who is a militarist, using thieves he controls to steal and devoting the proceeds to a scheme to start the war all over again. The title of the film evidently refers to disillusionment about the state of the country.

Night and Fog in Japan, also by Oshima, is a strongly political film pointing out the errors of the student movement and issuing a call for action to a new Left. The assassination of a leader of the Socialist Party a few days after the release of the film led to its immediate withdrawal. Later turning away from politics, Oshima directed one of his best-known films, *The Ceremony*, in 1971. Weddings and funerals are the only times at which the members of a rich family meet one another—from the end of the war to the present. The complicated interrelationships, all dominated by a tyrannical grandfather, are seen through the eyes of a boy. He is a little different, for he was born in Manchuria and repatriated to Japan. The film hints at regret that Japan had to turn back from the adventure in Manchuria. It records the reactions of members of the family to such themes as the leftover elements of feudalism, militarism, and the disillusionment of the young. It was rated number one among the top ten in Japan at the time.

A contemporary of Oshima is Imamura Shohei, who was born into a home of the privileged class but whose attitudes, and hence his creative ideas, have come much closer to those of ordinary working people. In *The Insect Woman* (1963) (insect not by appearance but because she has to grub in the earth to stay alive and win out) he traces three generations of women, all illegitimate. They succeed somehow in spite of wars, poverty, the disapproval of society, and the constant presence of weak men who seek to exploit them. Imamura's humor and sharp social comment emerge in *Pigs and Battleships,* set in Yokosuka, long a naval base and at the time of the film used by the U.S. Seventh Fleet. Haruko, a prostitute, tries to keep the young man she loves from involvement with a gang selling pigs illegally, but fails. He is shot during a wild and wonderful stampede of the pigs. She is gang-raped by American soldiers but manages in the end to escape the sordid surroundings.

Not every Japanese film is a tragedy. Itami Juzo has had great success with *Tampopo*, a comedy about a noodle shop, and with *A Taxing Woman*

(1987). In the latter film, the heroine, who works hard, but lightheartedly and courageously, for the Tax Office, is shown in clear contrast to women who are victimized by men yet remain submissive. She will take no nonsense, stands up to the *yakuza* ("mafia-type") figure, and neatly and hilariously defeats him. The film is in the mainstream of cosmopolitan filmmaking and has little trace of distinctive Japanese values.

Although television cut deeply into the Japanese film audiences (120 million in 1996, only one-tenth of the 1958 audience) there were still 378 domestically produced films in that year. In the later 1990s Japanese nonanimation films continued to collect numerous awards overseas, from Kitano Takeshi's Golden Lion Award at the 54th Venice International Festival for his film, *Hana-Bi*, to Imamura Shohei's Cannes International Palme d'Or for his *Unagi* (*The Eel*) reflecting a reinvigorated Japanese film culture of the 1990s. Other directors of the new generation include Mitsuo Yamaguchi, Miyasaki Suo, and Japan's first important woman director, Naomi Kawase. A number of the nonanimation films, like Suo's *Shall We Dance*, the poetic story of a middle-aged salaryman and his attempt to grasp the fading of time struck a sympathetic cord among non-Japanese audiences; animated films by Hayao Miyazaki, *Mononoke Hime* (*Princess Mononoke*), *The End of Evangelion,* and *Nausica—of the Valley of Wind* were immense hits in Japan as well as overseas. These "*anime*" were derived from popular television series representing a cross-fertilization of popular cultural zones. The themes are highlighted by a cosmic drama of struggle between humans and nature, good and evil in a world of magic and the unknown.

LITERATURE

The sensitivity to nature and its moods seen in Kurosawa's films has from the dawn of literature been an integral part of the Japanese imagination. In ways reminiscent of the brief poems of the *Manyoshu* and scenes in *The Tale of Genji*, later writers at moments of great poignancy break off the narrative to speak of trees in the rain, the deer, the caprices of the wind, the clouds and their changing moods. Nature brings calming relief from unbearable tension.

Japanese novelists in the postwar period continue to share this sensitivity to the links between nature and the human spirit. There are brief scenes with skillful and minute observation of detail, then loose ends. Much space is left for the imagination, as space is intentionally left unfilled in Japanese painting. One seems to be left hanging; but a personality emerges, and the plot does resume. The method is particularly effective for delineating the compulsive, obsessive characters who fill the pages of such novels as Mishima's *The Temple of the Golden Pavilion*. In this work the main character is being visited in the temple by his mother, who despises him and whom he hates.

As Mother's frizzy locks touched my cheek, I noticed a dragon-fly resting its wings on the moss-grown stone basin in the dusky courtyard. The evening sky was reflected in the surface of the small, round patch of water in the basin. There was not a sound to be heard. . . . Finally I was able to look directly into Mother's face.

But writers also react violently against the tradition in their refusal to conform to the group and group mentality. They search and pursue the mind and the destiny of the individual, often the individual they know best, in the so-called I-novel. Here is a struggling spirit, alone by itself, isolated through heredity or through outward circumstances, often apparently trivial ones. The writer follows with minute care that person's joys and sorrows, purely interior ones, and often contrary to all "normal" expectation. The most powerful internal emotions concern love and death. These basic themes are common to all modern writing, but the way they are treated in Japanese literature leaves the impression of inherently Japanese roots.

In Japan a decisive factor in modern literature is, of course, "the war." By that is meant the long, slow, bleeding China Incident (1937–1941) followed by the great adventure of the war in the Pacific and its gruesome ending. The ending involved not only the atomic bombs but also the humiliation and suffering derived from the first experience in the whole of Japanese history of invasion and defeat on Japan's own sacred soil. This meant utter despair. But here and there in postwar writing beauty and ordinary human affection reassert themselves.

A few names and examples may be taken as illustrative of these varied themes. The late Tanizaki Junichiro was known as one of the "aesthetes," or "decadents." He wrote of the conflict between the past and the present in a psychologically involved tale, *The Makioka Sisters*, considered one of the best of the modern novels. Abe Kobo is concerned with, among other things, individualism versus conformity and the two faces of freedom. A man trapped in a sandpit (*The Woman in the Dunes*) longs to escape, yet is in no hurry to do so when the chance comes. So humankind longs to be free, yet is afraid of freedom. The late Kawabata Yasunari was the first Japanese to receive the Nobel Prize for Literature (1968). One of his best-known novels is *Snow Country*, published before the war. To say that it is the story of a sophisticate from Tokyo who goes to see a geisha he once knew, now at a hot springs resort in the high mountains, is to give no idea of its baffling imaginative power. Kawabata felt deeply the despair which followed the war. The title of one of his books, *Beauty and Sadness*, indicates his spirit and hints at the inspiration he found when he returned from an early preoccupation with the West to the old literary tradition of Japan.

Kawabata was a mentor to Mishima Yukio, a complex and intriguing writer, more influenced by foreign ideas than was Kawabata, but also one who turned back to his native roots. His *Confessions of a Mask* brought him fame as a young man; but he reacted against the confessional, egocentric tradition of the I-novel. He wrote on a variety of themes. The delightful *Sound of Waves* is a tale of young lovers in a fishing village. In *After the Banquet* he realistically portrayed an old-fashioned, aristocratic politician and a charmingly practical businesswoman who owned a restaurant. Mishima's return to his roots led to his conviction that the old military tradition must at all costs be revived. To this end he recruited a small private army. When an appeal to a regular military contingent failed, as he probably expected it would, he committed suicide, *seppuku* (popularly known as *harakiri*), in the traditional, formal manner. Two other modern writers also took their own lives; the romantic nihilist Dazai Osamu (at the fifth attempt) and Akutagawa Ryonosuke, author of the story behind the film *Rashomon*.

For contemporary Japanese writers, the war experience has not completely faded; rather it has merged with the alienation and disorientation of the electronic, global, postmodern age. In 1994 Oe Kenzaburo won Japan's second Nobel Prize in Literature for his collection of stories of the atomic aftermath, *The Crazy Iris (1985)*. His works, including *A Personal Matter* (1964) and *Silent Cry* (1967), address this profound alienation, not only of the Japanese, but all humans. The context and aesthetics might remain Japanese, but the concerns transcend time and place to address a collective human condition. Endo Shusaku, a rare Catholic author in Japan, has explored the spiritual malaise of modern people, the confluence and contradictions in Western and Japanese consciousness.

Murakami Haruki stands out as representative of the new generation. Many of his works have been translated into English (including *A Wild Sheep Chase, The Hard-Boiled Wonderland and the End of the World, Norwegian Wood,* and *Dance, Dance, Dance*), and he is a regular contributor to periodicals like *The New Yorker,* where his short stories draw a large audience. Fluent in English, world traveler, and Fulbright scholar, his work, laced with Japanese aesthetics and concerns, is addressed to a world audience. His characters live in the often surreal, abstract urban landscape of the contemporary postindustrial age, sharing the culture and concerns of the global society, merged and lost in the amorphous homogeneity, yet unwilling to lose the remaining fragments of identity. His contemporary writers, like the female authors Yoshimoto Banana and, more recently, the popular short story writer Tawada Yoko, write about similar concerns with an acute sensitivity drawing on Japanese tradition. Their characters, part of the "Banana Generation" (characterized in Yoshimoto Banana's works), live from day to day drawing beauty, poetry, and humor from the details of their strange yet familiar worlds.

Beyond the novel, Japan's literary culture is vibrant. Poetry remains a genre embraced by all. With 2,000 poetry magazines and newsletters, daily newspaper poetry features, and poetry books on the bestseller list, the Japanese embrace versification with a passion. The short forms of *haiku, tanka,* and s*enryu* are accessible to everyone; they remain an outlet for personal feelings in a society that values conformity.

Drama and theater are also important. In 1999, Imai Masayuki brought his play, *The Winds of Gods*, to New York City. With a specially trained cast speaking entirely in English, he made an effort to convey to Westerners the subconscious tensions hidden within contemporary Japanese life regarding the issue of World War II. The scenario involves two happy-go-lucky would-be comedians who are transported back to a *kamikaze* squad room in the final days of the war. Their meaningless lives are contrasted with the passionate devotion of previous incarnations in a reference to familiar Buddhist beliefs.

SPORTS

The Japanese remain avid sports participants and fans of spectator sports. Leisure sports span the global possibilities with participants and enthusiasts for everything from cricket to *kendo* (one of Japan's national sports, fighting with bamboo swords). National athletes regularly bring home medals from international competitions. (Japan has accumulated 388 Olympic medals through 2000, and 22 in the Winter Olympics.) Japanese regularly conquer Mount Everest on skies or on foot, and wherever they may be, they cannot resist golfing and are undaunted by astronomical greens fees. Baseball remains a favorite spectator sport, but soccer has captured the national interest rising to a threatening second. Sumo has been slipping in attendance at tournaments and television viewers declining. Still, with its Shinto/nationalistic overtones it remains a favorite.

In recent years Japanese sports have become inseparable from global integration. In sumo, for example, after years of resistance, foreign competitors have attained the highest rank of *Yokozuna*, or "grand champion." Mongolians like Asahoryu and the Hawaiian Musashihimaru are current grand champions. Other sumo "stables" include wrestlers from Russia, South Korea, the United States, and Brazil. Foreigners regularly play Japanese baseball and soccer, and overall, foreigners have become familiar faces on Japan's teams. Of course Japanese are also familiar faces on foreign teams as well, with Hideki "Godzilla" Matsui playing on the New York Yankees World Series team in 2003 and Ichiro Suzuki playing for the Seattle Mariners, a team, incidentally, which is owned by Japanese investors. Japanese fans regularly make the trip to cheer for their players in the United States. The internationalization of sports is a way of life for Japan.

COMIC BOOKS, ANIME, AND VIDEO GAMES

One branch of literature not usually taken seriously is the comic book. But since 1977 comic books have accounted for 20 percent of all book sales in Japan. In 1996 they had taken over 22 percent and 38.5 percent of all books and magazines sold, respectively. In fact, comic drawing has had a long history in Japan, with its origins in amusing self-portraits drawn by copyists as relaxation and found on the back of panels in the Horyuji Temple in Nara. The first cartoonist known by name was Abbot Toba (1053–1140), artist of the *Scroll of Frolicking Animals.* The wood-block printer Hokusai (1760–1849) was famous for his whimsical sketches on a wide range of subjects from animal life to pornography. In 1925 the *Asahi Shimbun* daily newspaper ran a comic series, *Shochan and the Squirrel,* which started a Shochan craze. After World War II, Osamu Tezuka started illustrating publications in comic format and created the modern genre of the "story *manga.*" The genre caught fire and continued in popularity, morphing and changing with the society.

Manga are written for all generations, from beginning readers to mature adults, and they may be gender-coded as well, with female-specific versions introduced in the 1960s with the appearance of women cartoonists. Subject matter can vary from humor to brutal violence and even pornography; fictional and nonfictional stories are told. The full blossom of *manga* fever first appeared in the late 1950s with the appearance of *Shonan Magazine* and *Shonan Sunday.* Both told popular stories geared to a young audience. In the 1980s *Shonan Jump* first appeared and eventually reached a weekly circulation of over 6 million, generating animation and video game spinoffs. *Manga* continue to merge with anime, video games, and trading card formats. Indeed, one might consider the present fusion of genres as a distinct Japanese creation of the IT age of the twentieth and twenty-first centuries. By the early 1980s Nintendo brought game animation into the Japanese household, creating a new addiction with a wide range of games and entertainment, from role-playing to action games.

Extended to the playground, Japan has spawned the "*Yu-Gi-Oh* mania." Generated from a TV animation program created by *manga* artist Takahashi Kazuki, the *Yu-Gi-Oh* game involves the collection of very expensive cards, beginning with a minimum of forty, and a mastery of complex rules, scenarios, and hidden secret codes. There is also a video game version. The phenomenon produced earnings of $2 billion in 2003. In Japan alone 3.5 billion trading cards have been sold. Konami, which sells *Yu-Gi-Oh,* has produced TV animations for an international audience and six video games for the major platforms, all built around the expensive cards. The game is currently sweeping Asia, Europe, and the United States. Konami is looking forward to substantial profits. One might say that Japan reigns supreme in the world of syncretic popular youth culture.

HANDCRAFTS

There is a small village in western Japan, looking out over tiny pine-clad islands in the Japan Sea toward Korea. It has a fishing harbor along a small river estuary and a miniature extinct volcano called Umbrella Mountain. This village is the home of a very famous potter who makes bowls of great refinement for the tea ceremony, bowls which are sold to wealthy persons all over Japan. Passing by the pond with gleaming red carp, he takes a visitor through the garden to his studio. Combined with the studio is a small museum which contains examples of pottery made by no less than thirteen generations of his ancestors, going back to his family origins in Korea. His work has been designated a National Treasure.

Some National Treasures on the Japanese list are not concrete art objects at all. There is, for example, the abbot of a temple on the sacred Buddhist mountain Koyasan. He is so famous for his beautiful, sonorous chanting of the Buddhist sutras that his voice has been declared an Intangible National Treasure.

Despite the rapid and increasing modernization of Japan, crafts of all kinds are greatly valued. It would not be possible to examine them here, scarcely even to list them all. Among these crafts are porcelain, lacquer, weaving (from silk brocade to common peasant textiles), sword making, and the carving of *netsuke* toggles. Generations of acquired and transmitted or inherited skills have probably equipped present-day Japanese for the construction of the miniature components needed for the instruments of high technology. However, handcrafted products are of value for their own sake—for beauty, functional fitness, charm, texture, and the refreshment of spirit they offer by simply being there. The Japanese know this, have always known it, and take steps today to see that the heritage and traditions are not lost.

MOOD AND THE OUTLOOK TODAY

The dawn of the twenty-first century finds a transformed Japan facing a landscape that did not exist one hundred years ago. Then, Japan was just beginning to sample the fruits of its own modernization. During the summer of 1900 the Imperial Army provided the main force that suppressed China's Boxer Rebellion. The Imperial Navy had defeated China and would soon sink Russia's supermodern Baltic fleet in the straits of Tsushima; during this period its command staff reached a consensus that some day it would have to engage the United States in a decisive battle for control of the Pacific Rim. It also began to make the shift from coal to oil as fuel for the boilers in its Japan-designed and built imperial fleet. From one point of view, the subsequent imperial expansion, which climaxed in the atomic bombings in August of 1945, might be considered as the unfolding of the Meiji dream to catch up with and surpass the industrial West. From the ashes of defeat through the second half of the twentieth century the Japanese did catch up and even, in some areas, surpass the West as an industrial, economic, and technological power. As a highly advanced postmodern economy it has immense economic resources, second only to the United States.

In 1900, Japan's economy, though turning the corner to an industrial, urban future, remained largely agrarian. Its farmers supplied much of the capital to sustain modernization, and its new city dwellers continued to maintain close ties to their *furusato*, or "home towns" which, while receding to the margins, became transformed into a kind of spiritual repository of purely Japanese values and lifestyle, a place where modern Japan could find the pure essence of traditional identity. Rice farmers, after all, embodied foundations of Shinto and familism in the daily practices of life while providing the sustenance for military and aristocratic elites throughout Japan's history. The ideals of agrarianism and a pure "Japaneseness" imbedded in the people and soil of the nation, with the help of official ideologists, managed to maintain fixed values for the Japanese well into the postwar period. From these roots, qualities of the national character including diligence (*gambatte*), perseverance (*gamman*), industriousness, and politeness continue to find their way into contemporary behavior. Until very recently the rural base also sustained the dominant, conservative political force of the LDP-built patron-client democracy throughout the postwar years.

Japan's twenty-first century world is the sum total of these and other transformational forces. By the 1980s the Japanese had achieved many of their postwar aspirations. Their economy was thriving. They were respected throughout Asia as the engine of regional prosperity, with Malaysia's Prime Minister Mohamad Mahathir calling on Japan to take the lead in an Asian alliance. American businesses were trying to adopt the "Japanese model," and the U.S. government relied on Japanese investors to sustain huge budget deficits. The Japanese even decided that they should cut the U.S. apron strings and say "no" to the world if they wanted to. Success bred a certain self-satisfaction and even hubris. In this regard, the Japanese had always felt snubbed by the United States. Beginning in the 1970s, they began to evolve an independent foreign policy vis-à-vis China and Southeast Asia. Throughout the 1980s, the Japanese consistently defended their economic policies against the United States and Europe, anticipating the advent of what Harvard professor Ezra Vogel called "Japan as Number One."

The 1990s, however, shattered the euphoria of success. The bursting of the bubble economy collapsed the real estate market, and stocks tumbled. Banks and businesses folded under the weight of "nonperforming loans" to the tune of perhaps $1 trillion. Sadly, success and prosperity had been purchased at the cost of corruption, which broke through into all levels of the iron triangle of politicians, bureaucracy, and businesses, pulling the Japanese into a spiral of recession, deflation, and collapsing dreams of the "Lost Decade" of the 1990's. The lost decade has taken a toll on the Japanese as they find their way into the new millennium. The years 2002 and 2003 seemed to hint at a turnaround for the economy with a shift from negative to positive stock market activity; ten years of decline have shaken confidence and triggered a new phase of introspection. The Japanese entered the twenty-first century doubting and in search of a new Japanese path to the future.

On the economic front, prodded by Prime Minister Koizumi's financial czar, Takenaka Heizo, long-awaited reforms and restructuring were beginning to have an effect by the summer of 2003. Banks were consolidated, nonperforming loans were cleaned up, and stocks began to show their first value increases in over ten years. (Tokyo's Stock Exchange key index rose some 30 percent in midsummer, the sharpest rise since 1952.) There was also a modest decline in bankruptcies, and structural reforms opened Japanese markets to impressive foreign investments, drawing $1.7 trillion in Japanese equities and assets purchases. The same restructuring which is drawing in investment capital and stimulating the economy has, however, been costly for the Japanese worker. The end of "lifetime employment" and the introduction of downsizing have yielded Japan's highest postwar unemployment rate of 5.6 percent. Offshoring of production throughout the Japanese industrial sector further erodes job security, while the aging of the population and the alienation of many youths from conventional career paths cloud the employment picture. Even in major, successful industrial and technological giants, like Toyota and NTT DoCoMo, the offshoring of production and the concentration on design and super-high-tech units suggest movement into untried terrain and resulting instability for the workforce. There are, of course, social implications.

Japanese youths have responded to the uncertainties of economic decline and the postmodern deterioration of conventional institutions and values. It may be true that the older generation does, in fact, not know what to teach the young. The technology-driven subculture of games and phones, the detachment of parents who care more about themselves than previous generations did, and the concern of the elderly who realize they must look out for their own interests as traditional family responsibility for the aged fades into an abstract system of social services leave young people with limited guideposts for behavior beyond the media. Classroom chaos, bizarre and violent crime, reclusion, and rejection of conventional job paths are on the fringe of an unstable core youth culture. At the same time, educational and political elites are seriously concerned about the new generations, which seem to be more interested in themselves than their families or the greater society.

During the years of postwar success as cities fused into DIDs (densely inhabited districts), vast, interconnected megalopolises took the place of farmlands just as the thriving industrial sector turned farmers into factory workers and urban dwellers. Today, the agricultural sector of the economy has dwindled to a mere 1.4 percent of GDP, the remainder going to industrial production and the services industries. Among those who remain on the farms, most are elderly or children, with many part-timers who supplement their income in the cities. The young do not want to stay, nor do the old feel it is right to ask them to remain. Villages are changing into bedroom communities, ghost towns, or the equivalent of dude ranches or recreational places. The source of traditional culture and political power is drying up; and the shift is to the urban centers where postmodern commercial culture, the type so well presented in Murakami Haruki's novels in which even individual names seem to disappear, prevails.

The diminishing significance of rural Japan has not only changed economic and cultural life, but it also affects political life as well. Until the elections in the fall of 2003, which returned LDP member Koizumi Junichiro to a second term as prime minister, that party's power base had been rooted in rural districts. While farmers' associations, now morphed into commercial enterprises, still retain considerable power and draw the energies of party candidates, urbanites are finally displacing their rural counterparts. Election reforms from the mid-1990s have improved opportunities for urban voters and weakened the iron grip of party machines. Restructuring of cabinet and bureaucratic offices offers an opportunity to rein in corruption, which has shaken public respect and confidence in the government. Elections in September 2003, however, contained mixed signals regarding the health of Japanese political institutions in the short term. Most newly elected parliamentarians are *seshuu gumi*, "second, third, and even fourth generations of politicians." Bureaucrats were also successful, winning 73 seats in the 480-member parliament. New candidates and women, in contrast, did poorly; and perhaps even more ominously, voter turnout was only about 59 percent of the electorate. This is among the lowest since World War II and a dramatic decline from the early 1990s when political change began. One positive outcome was the success of the Democratic Party, which has led some to suggest that Japan is slowly moving to a two party system. (The Japan Communist Party and Socialists are, at present, politically insignificant.) The Democratic Party, founded in 1998 by Kan Naoto, a former grassroots activist, won 177 seats, an increase of 40. While Kan relies on personal charisma and a populist reputation, most of his party members are old-line politicians and bureaucrats. In effect, this election suggests that change will continue in national politics but that a mood of uncertainty still grips the vast majority of the electorate. One might add that similar dynamics seem to operate in all the industrialized democracies as they move into the new millennium.

The Japanese, along with the rest of the inhabitants of planet Earth, are moving tentatively into the new post-cold-war global era. In a recent 2003 poll, among their greatest concerns for the new millennium, the Japanese shared the hope that humankind would work together for a peaceful and stable future. Indeed, since World War II the Japanese have enjoyed more than fifty years without war; they have gotten used to peace. It is hard at times to recall the overwhelming dominance of militarism and the modern mutation of the *samurai* spirit into violent imperialism during the war. However, the Japanese have not resolved the issue of the war; its memory haunts the hidden reaches of the national character and rises to influence relationships with other Asians who cannot forget the brutality of those years. Yasukuni Shrine still draws politicians and old-timers who come to visit the souls of war dead; veterans support war museums, memorials to their fallen comrades. One of the most difficult issues in contemporary Japan is the willingness to use force in the international arena. The astonishing and rapid rise of China, armed with rockets and nuclear weapons, and the uncertainty about a similarly equipped North Korea, have forced Japan to rethink its military posture in Asia. The end of the cold war, rise of the European Union, and outbreak of the American war against terrorism following the events of September 11, 2001, and recent wars in Afghanistan and Iraq increase pressure on Japan to deploy its formidable military in U.N. and other operations. At present, Koizumi and his conservative LDP continue to promote revision of the anti-war Article 9. Taking sides with U.S. President Bush in his unilateral invasion of Iraq, Koizumi hopes to rebuild Japan's military power in both regional and global arenas. Although some Japanese are openly discussing a nuclear option for their nation, public opinion, which had opposed support for American policy, remains firmly opposed to a remilitarization of Japanese society. Its preference is for a nation wielding economic and diplomatic influence.

Related to Japan's sense of its place in the world is the treatment of foreigners living in Japan. It is not easy for the Japanese, used to their homogeneous ethnicity, distinctive culture, and social mores, to open up to outsiders. Aging, low birth rates, and the specter of a drastically declining population after 2005 will force them to reach a new accommodation with an increasingly diverse population. Foreigners as well are more willing to accommodate themselves to Japanese life. From the popular Mongolian and Hawaiian sumo champions to black and Caucasian celebrities in the popular media, Japanese-speaking new citizens are helping to transform the exotic into the familiar. The government too is working to prepare foreigners for citizenship with language and cultural training, opening social services and education, and accelerating the process of becoming full, voting citizens of Japan. Perhaps there is a long way to go in this respect. Yet the Japanese travel widely, connect constantly to the world, and are true global customers and citizens; their stars in sports, popular culture, classical music, art, fashion, business, and technology are everywhere on the global scene.It should not be surprising that hopes for a tolerant and diverse society at home are an important part of Japanese hopes for their future.

GLOSSARY

anime	animated cartoon
ashigaru	foot soldier, light infantry
aware no mono	the sadness of things
bakufu	tent government, military rule
batsu	faction or in-group
be	corporation
biwa	lute
bosozoku	motorcycle gang
buke sho-hatto	ordinances for military houses
bunraku	puppet stage
burakumin	outcasts or social outsiders
bushido	the way of the warrior
bussangaku	science of production
butsu	Buddha
daikan	deputy
daikon	giant radish
daimyo	great name, territorial lord
dainagon	great councillor
dajo-daijin	chancellor
dajo-kan	state council, Department of State
enjokosai	"dating for assistance," teenage prostitution
fudai	hereditary vassals
fukoku-kyohei	rich country—strong army
fumi-e	treading picture, sacred emblem used to test Christians
furita	"freeter," a young person who prefers to live at home and work part time
gambatte	perseverance

gamman	endurance, to bear what is unbearable
genro	elder statesman
giri	right, obligation, duty
go	intricate Japanese board game
go-kenin	house men
gonin-gumi	five-man group
go-sanke	three houses of Tokugawa Ieyasu's sons
go-tairo	five (great) elders
haikai	chain poem
haikara	high collar, fashionable
haiku	poem of seventeen syllables
hanare	an attached but separate apartment, often for elderly parents
haniwa	clay funerary figures
hansei	reflection, remorse
harakiri or seppuku	formal suicide by slitting the belly
hatamoto	bannerman
hikikomori	student reclusion; refusal to attend school
hitatare	ceremonial robe
hyojosho	Judicial Council
ijime	brutal teasing by school mates, bullying
ikki	league, revolt promoted by a league
ikko	single-minded, name for Shinshu sect of Buddhism
ikusei	"green housing" government protection of new industries
insei	cloister government by a retired emperor
jidai	period, era in history
jingi-kan	department of worship
jito	steward
jizo	Buddhist statue associated with remorse for abortion, sorrow for the stillborn
juku	cram school (attended after school by students preparing for any entrance-level exams)
kabuki	a popular form of drama
kageyushi	Board of Audit
kaidan	ordination platform
kambun	written Chinese
kami	gods, those above
kamikaze	wind of the gods, typhoon during Mongol attack, suicide pilots in World War II
kampaku	regent after an emperor came of age; or civil dictator
kana	Japanese syllabary
karoshi	death from overwork

kebiishi-cho	Commissioners of Police
kega	wound, defilement
keiretsu	network of industrial companies
kempeitai	military police, secret police
kendo	Japanese fencing with bamboo staves
kirisute	to cut down and leave, the right to kill with impunity
koan	nonsense puzzle, used in Zen Buddhism
kokutai	national polity
kombini	local convenience store
kurando-dokoro	Bureau of Archivists
kyogen	mad words, farcical interlude, comedy
kyoiku mama	education mom
kyuba-no-michi	the way of the horse and the bow
mandokoro	Secretariat, Council
manga	illustrated comics
matsurigoto	religious affairs, government
metsuke	censors, secret police
mobo	modern boy
moga	modern girl
monchujo	Board of Inquiry
moningu	morning coat
monogatari	tale, story
narikin	extravagance of the newly rich
nihonjinron	debate on "Japaneseness"
Nippon no onna	idealized Japanese woman
no	classical Japanese drama
rangaku	Dutch learning, European knowledge
ritsu	disciplinary and penal regulations
roju	Council of Elders
ronin	wave men, masterless warriors
ryo	administrative and civil code
sadaijin	minister of the Left
sake	an alcoholic beverage made from rice
samurai	one who serves, retainer, warrior
samurai-dokoro	orderly room, Board of Retainers
sankin-kotai	alternate attendance (at the shogun's court)
sarariman	salaryman, company man
sarugaku	monkey music, comic performance
sebiro	Savile Row, business suit
sei-i tai-shogun	barbarian-subduing generalissimo
senryu	linked verse
sessho	regent during an emperor's minority
shibui	astringent, understated, minimalist
shiki	rights or shares in the produce of an estate

shikken	director, equivalent to regent for the shogun
shimpan	related or collateral fiefs
shinkansen	"bullet" express train
shinto or kami-no-michi	the way of the gods, native Japanese religion
shite	principal actor in a *No* play
shoen	tax-free manor
shogun	generalissimo, supreme military commander
shonagon	lesser councillor
shugo	protector (a Kamakura official)
sonno-joi	honor the emperor, expel the barbarians
tairo	Great Elder
tanka	poem of thirty-one syllables
terakoya	temple schools of the Tokugawa period
tokaido	the eastern sea road
tomo	attendant
tozama	outside lords, i.e., not Tokugawa vassals
tsuibushi	constable
tsumi	crime, sin
udaijin	minister of the Right
uji	clan
ukiyo-e	pictures of the floating world, of the transient scene
waki	second actor in *No* play
yakuza	organized crime syndicate
yamato-damashii	the spirit of Old Japan
yome	daughter-in-law, usually idealized
yu-gi-oh	contemporary children's card and video game
za	seat or pitch in a marketplace, guild
zaibatsu	financial clique, large industrial combine
zazen	sitting in meditation

CHRONOLOGY

YEAR	POLITICAL	MILITARY	CULTURAL
B.C.			
from 3000			Jomon culture
660	Traditional date of accession of first emperor, Jimmu		
300–100			Yayoi culture and Tomb culture
A.D.			
57	Envoy sent to Han court		
369		Japanese conquests at Mimana in Korea (held until 562)	
391			Scholars from Korea entered Japan, introducing writing
552			Buddhism officially introduced to Japan; image sent from the king of Paikche in Korea
586			Emperor Yomei supports Buddhism
587		Battle at Shigisen— Soga Umako against Mononobe over Buddhism	
592–628	Reign of Empress Suiko		

YEAR	POLITICAL	MILITARY	CULTURAL
593–622	Regency of Prince Shotoku—supporter of Buddhism and Chinese learning		
604	"Constitution" of Prince Shotoku		
607	Ono-no-Imoko on first official embassy of united Japan to China		Horyuji monastery built
630	Embassy to Tang China		
645	Taika Reform		
661–671	Reign of Emperor Tenchi—the former Prince Naka-no-Oye		
663		Defeat of Japanese army in Korea and destruction of ally Paikche by Silla and Tang	
669	Granting of surname Fujiwara to Nakatomi Kamatari before his death		
702	Taiho Law Code		
708	First issue of copper coinage		Horyuji monastery rebuilt
710	Location of capital fixed at Nara		

NARA PERIOD 710–794

YEAR	POLITICAL	MILITARY	CULTURAL
712			Compilation of *Kojiki*, "Record of Ancient Things"
720			Compilation of *Nihongi* or *Nihonshoki*, "Chronicles of Japan"
724–749	Reign of Emperor Shomu (d. 756)		
729–749			Tempyo period—great era of Buddhist statuary
738–756			Tachibana-no-Moroye compiles collection of poems, *Manyoshu*, "Collection of Myriad Leaves"
752			Dedication of Daibutsu (Great Buddha) at Todaiji Temple in Nara
781–806	Reign of Emperor Kammu		

YEAR	POLITICAL	MILITARY	CULTURAL
784	Move of capital to Nagaoka		
794	Heian capital established at Kyoto		

HEIAN PERIOD 794–1158
Early Heian Period 794–857

YEAR	POLITICAL	MILITARY	CULTURAL
800–803		Defeat of Ainu in northern Honshu by Sakanouye Tamura Maro—he receives title sei-i-tai-shogun, "barbarian-subduing generalissimo"	
805			Returning monk from China, Saicho, introduces Tendai sect with headquarters at Enryakuji on Mount Hiei
806			Monk Kukai, having studied in China, introduces Shingon sect, establishing center at Mount Koya
838	Last embassy to Tang China		

Late Heian or Fujiwara Period 858–1185

YEAR	POLITICAL	MILITARY	CULTURAL
858–872	Fujiwara Yoshifusa as first Regent not of the imperial family		
891	Sugawara Michizane in power		
899	Removal of Michizane to a post in Kyushu by Fujiwara Tokihira		
905			Compilation of Kokinshu by Ki-no-Tsurayuki and others
930–949	Fujiwara Tadahira as regent and chancellor		
935–940		Revolt and execution of Taira Masakado	
995–1027	Supremacy of Fujiwara Michinaga		
c. 1002			Writing of *Makura no Soshi* (Pillow Book) by Lady Sei Shonagon

YEAR	POLITICAL	MILITARY	CULTURAL
c. 1008–1020			Writing of *Genji Mono-gatari* (*Tale of Genji*) by Lady Murasaki Shikibu
1017–1068	Fujiwara Yorimichi as regent and chancellor		
1051–1062		Early Nine Years' War	
1053			Byodo-in (temple) erected by Fujiwara Yorimichi
1068–1072	Reign of Emperor Go-Sanjo (d. 1073)		
1072–1086	Reign of Emperor Shirakawa		
1083–1087		Later Three Years' War	
1086–1129	Shirakawa abdicates, but rules from the cloister, establishing custom of *insei*, "rule by a retired emperor"		
1107–1123	Reign of Emperor Toba		
1129–1156	Insei of Toba		
1156–1158		Hogen Insurrection led by Fujiwara Yorinaga	
1159–1160		Heiji War: destruction of Minamoto Yoshitomo and Fujiwara Nobuyori by Taira Kiyomori and his son Shigemori	
1167	Taira Kiyomori as prime minister		
1175			Founding of the Jodo (Pure Land) sect in Japan by Honen Shonin
1180–1185		Gempei Wars, between Minamoto and Taira forces	
		1180. Minamoto Yoritomo defeated at Ishibashiyama	
		Yoritomo successful at battle of River Fujikawa	
		1184. Battle of Ichi-no-tani—Minamoto victory	

YEAR	POLITICAL	MILITARY	CULTURAL
		1185. Yoshitsune victorious over Taira at Yashima. Battle at sea near Dan-no-ura, final Taira defeat, and death of child emperor Antoku	

KAMAKURA PERIOD 1185–1336

YEAR	POLITICAL	MILITARY	CULTURAL
1185	Constable and Steward system set up by Minamoto Yoritomo		
1189	Death of Minamoto Yoshitsune		
1191			Zen sect (Rinzai Branch) introduced from China by Eisai
1192	Yoritomo granted title of shogun by emperor		
1199	Death of Minamoto Yoritomo; power passes to Hojo family through wife Hojo Masako and father-in-law Hojo Tokimasa		
1203	Assumption of post of *shikken* (head of Council) by Tokimasa		
1221		Shokyu (Jokyu) disturbance—retired emperor Go-Toba tries to assume real power	
1224–1242	Hojo Yasutoki as *shikken*		
1224			Jodo Shinshu (True Pure Land) or Shin sect founded by Shinran
1227			Zen (Soto branch) introduced from China by Dogen
1232	Promulgation of Joei Shikimoku—Kamakura law code		
1246–1256	Hojo Tokiyori as *shikken* (d. 1263)		
1253			Founding of Nichiren sect by Nichiren
1274		First Mongol attack— Hakata Bay, northern Kyushu	

YEAR	POLITICAL	MILITARY	CULTURAL
1281		Second Mongol attack—*kamikaze*, "Wind of the Gods," saves the Japanese	
1297	Law of "virtuous administration"		
1318–1339	Reign of Emperor Go-Daigo		
1331–1336		Genko War	
1333		Ashikaga Takauji captures Kyoto in Go-Daigo's name	
1335		Destruction of Kama-kura by Nitta Yoshisada	
1335		Revolt of Takauji against Go-Daigo	
1336	Rival emperor placed on throne by Takauji; flight of Go-Daigo to Yoshino		

ASHIKAGA PERIOD 1336–1573

Nambokucho Period 1336–1392

(Southern Capital at Yoshino, Northern Capital at Kyoto)

YEAR	POLITICAL	MILITARY	CULTURAL
1338	Assumption of title of shogun by Takauji		
1339	Death of Go-Daigo		
1358–1367	Shogunate of Yoshiakira		
1365–1372		Battles on Kyushu be-tween rival forces of Prince Kanenaga and Imagawa Sadayo	
1368–1394	Shogunate of Yoshi-mitsu (d. 1408)		
1378			Building of Hana-no-Gosho
1384			Death of Kanami, who developed *Nō* drama

Muromachi Period 1392–1573

YEAR	POLITICAL	MILITARY	CULTURAL
1392	Regalia brought back to Kyoto; Southern Court to have alternate succession		
1394–1423	Shogunate of Yoshimochi (d. 1428)		
1397			Building of Kinkakuji by 3rd Shogun Yoshimitsu

YEAR	POLITICAL	MILITARY	CULTURAL
1404	Trade agreement with Ming China		
1429–1441	Shogunate of Yoshinori		
1443–1473	Shogunate of Yoshimasa (d. 1490)		
1444			Death of Zeami, who perfected *No* drama
1467–1477		Onin War—Ashikaga cease to be effective	
1483			Construction of Ginkakuji by 8th Shogun Yoshimasa
1485		Peasant uprisings in Yamashino Province	
1488		Members of Shin sect (Ikko-ikki) in control of Kaga and Echizen Provinces	
1506			Death of painter-monk Sesshu (b. 1420)

1534–1615 SENGOKU-JIDAI: PERIOD OF COUNTRY AT WAR
1534–1582 Oda Nobunaga

YEAR	POLITICAL	MILITARY	CULTURAL
1536–1598	Toyotomi Hideyoshi		
1543–1616	Tokugawa Ieyasu		
1542	Arrival of Portuguese at Tanegashima; firearms introduced		
1549			Arrival of the Jesuit St. Francis Xavier in Kyushu
1560		Battle of Okehazama; Oda Nobunaga's move on capital	
1568		Seizure of Kyoto by Nobunaga	
1571		Destruction by Nobunaga of Enryakuji	
1573	Imprisonment of last Shogun Yoshiaki; end of Ashikaga Shogunate		
1576–1579	Transfer of Nobunaga to his castle at Azuchi on Lake Biwa		
1579–1598			Azuchi-Momoyama "Peach Mountain" period in art
1580		Surrender of Osaka castle-monastery of Shin sect to Nobunaga	

YEAR	POLITICAL	MILITARY	CULTURAL
1582	Death of Nobunaga at the hands of Akechi Mitsuhide		
1583–1598	Land survey commissioned by Hideyoshi		
1587	Confiscation of arms of peasantry—the "Sword Hunt"		Promulgation of decree ordering expulsion of Christian missionaries
1590		Destruction of Hojo family of Odawara and installation of Tokugawa Ieyasu in Edo castle as master of Kanto	
1592		Hideyoshi invades Korea	
1593		Truce with Chinese armies in Korea and withdrawal of Japanese forces to extreme south	
1597		Resumption of Korean campaign; Hideyoshi orders death of 26 Christians near Nagasaki	
1598	Death of Hideyoshi and withdrawal of troops from Korea		
1600		Victory of Tokugawa Ieyasu at Battle of Sekigahara, last battle of civil war	
1603	Ieyasu granted title of shogun		
1605–1623	Shogunate of Hidetada (d. 1632)		
1614		Siege of Osaka castle by Ieyasu	Edict suppressing Christianity

TOKUGAWA PERIOD 1615–1867

YEAR	POLITICAL	MILITARY	CULTURAL
1615	Promulgation of *buke sho-hatto*, "ordinances for military houses"		
1622–1638			Period of greatest Christian persecutions
1623–1651	Shogunate of Iemitsu		
1636	Ban on Japanese travel abroad		

YEAR	POLITICAL	MILITARY	CULTURAL
1637–1638		Shimabara Rebellion	
1638	Expulsion of Portuguese traders		
1641	Dutch traders confined to Deshima island in Nagasaki harbor		
1651–1680	Shogunate of Ietsuna		
1657	Great Edo fire		Death of Hayashi Razan (Doshun), adviser to Ieyasu and proponent of Neo-Confucianism (b. 1583)
1680–1709	Shogunate of Tsunayoshi		
1688–1704			Genroku Era—new urban culture
1693			Death of Ihara Saikaku, novelist (b. 1642)
1694			Death of *haiku* poet Matsuo Basho (b. 1644)
1697	Dojima Rice Exchange founded in Osaka		
1701–1703			Chushingura incident (*Forty-Seven Ronin*)
1707	Last eruption of Mount Fuji		
1714			Death of Hishikawa Moronobu, first great *ukiyo-e* artist (b. 1638)
1716–1745	Shogunate of Yoshimune (d. 1751)		
1720			Ban lifted on importation of foreign books, on condition that they are not Christian
1724			Death of Chikamatsu Monzaemon, playwright (b. 1653)
1745–1760	Shogunate of Ieshige (d. 1761)		
1758			Aoki Konyo introduced sweet potato and published first Dutch–Japanese dictionary
1760–1786	Shogunate of Ieharu		

YEAR	POLITICAL	MILITARY	CULTURAL
1779			Death of Hiraga Gennai (b. 1728) who made contributions in botany, mining, electricity, and oil painting
1787–1837	Shogunate of Ienari (d. 1841)—instituted Kansei Reforms		
1793	Visit of Russian Lt. Adam Laxman to Hokkaido		
1798			Completion of commentary on *Kojiki* by Shinto scholar Motoori Norinaga (d. 1801)
1806			Death of Utamaro, wood-block artist
1808	British ship *Phaeton* arrives at Nagasaki		
1811			Translation bureau established for foreign books
1837	Rice riots in Osaka		
1837–1853	Shogunate of Ieyoshi		
1852	Visit of Russians to Shimoda		
1853	Commodore Matthew C. Perry arrives at Uraga		
1854	Treaty of Kanagawa with United States		
1857	Townsend Harris's visit to shogun's court		
1858	Commercial treaty with the United States		Death of wood-block artist Hiroshige
1858–1868	Rivalry between imperial court, shogunate, Choshu and Satsuma clans, and foreign powers		
1859	Foreign trading community established at Yokohama		Death of Yoshida Shoin (b. 1830), teacher of *samurai* and exponent of role of emperor

YEAR	POLITICAL	MILITARY	CULTURAL
1860	Exchange in Washington of treaty ratification by first embassy to U.S.		
1862	First Japanese embassy in Europe		
	Murder of Englishman Richardson at Namaugi by Satsuma *samurai*		
1863		Bombardment of foreign vessels by Choshu forts at Shimonoseki	
		Bombardment of Kagoshima, capital of Satsuma, by British	
		Expulsion of Choshu forces from Kyoto	
1864		Bombardment of Shimonoseki by British, French, Dutch, and American ships	
1866	Satsuma and Choshu clans agree to join against shogunate		
1866–1867	Shogunate of Yoshinobu (Keiki d. 1913)		
1867	Enthronement of Mutsuhito (Emperor Meiji)		
1868	JAN. 3. Proclamation of imperial restoration	JAN. 27. Capitulation of shogun's forces at Fushimi and Toba	

MEIJI PERIOD 1868–1912

1868	APR. 6. Emperor's Charter Oath		
	NOV. 26. Tokyo (Edo) established as new capital		
1869	MAR. 5. Return of lands by Satsuma, Choshu, Tosa, and Hizen to emperor		
	JULY. Appointment of *daimyo* as governors of their former fiefs		

YEAR	POLITICAL	MILITARY	CULTURAL
1871	NOV. 20. Departure of Iwakura Mission for America and Europe		SEPT. 2. Ministry of Education established. Postal service instituted. First daily newspaper published
1872	Railway opened between Tokyo and Yokohama		
1873	New land-tax system	Universal military service	OCT. End of ban on Christianity. Gregorian calendar adopted
	SEPT. Return of Iwakura mission		
	OCT. Peaceful policy toward Korea decided upon		
	Yamagata Aritomo becomes minister of army		
1874	Kobe-Osaka Railroad (1877 to Kyoto)	MAY. Victory of expeditionary force in Taiwan under Saigo Tsugumichi	
1875–1888	Civil legal code—final draft with German additions in 1896		
1876	MAR. 28. Prohibition of carrying swords by *samurai*		
	AUG. 5. Compulsory commutation of *samurai* pensions		
1877		FEB.–SEPT. Satsuma Rebellion and death of Saigo Takamori— last stand of *samurai*	
1878		Adoption of German General Staff organization in army	
1879	MAR. Beginning of elected prefectural assemblies		
1881	Emperor promises constitution by 1890		
	Political parties formed		
1882	Ito Hirobumi sent to Europe to study constitutional systems		

YEAR	POLITICAL	MILITARY	CULTURAL
1884	Creation of peerage		
1885	DEC. 22. Adoption of cabinet system with Ito as first premier		
1887	DEC. 26. Peace Preservation Ordinance		
1888	Creation of Privy Council		
1889	FEB. 11. Promulgation of Meiji Constitution		
1890	JULY 1. First election for Diet (convened Nov. 25)		OCT. 30. Imperial Rescript on Education
1892	Ito as premier (resigned Aug. 31, 1896)		
1894		JUNE 5. Uprising in Korea	
		AUG. 1. Declaration of war on China (Sino-Japanese War)	
		NOV. 21. Capture of Port Arthur	
1895		APR. 17. Treaty of Shimonoseki, concluding Sino-Japanese War	
		APR. 20. Japanese decision to return Liaodong Peninsula to China after interventions of Russia, France, and Germany	
1900		JUNE–AUG. Participation of Japanese forces in relief of Legation Quarter, Beijing, during Boxer uprising	
1902	Anglo-Japanese Alliance signed		
1904		FEB. 9. Attack on Russian Navy	
		FEB. 10. Declaration of war on Russia (Russo-Japanese War)	
		SEPT. 4. Liao-yang captured	
1905		JAN. 1. Port Arthur captured	
		MAR. 10. Mukden captured	

YEAR	POLITICAL	MILITARY	CULTURAL
		MAY 27–28. Destruction of Russian fleet at Battle of Tsushima Straits	
		SEPT. 5. Treaty of Portsmouth	
1906	MAR. Nationalization of railways		
	NOV. South Manchuria Railroad completed		
1909	OCT. 26. Assassination of Prince Ito in Harbin by a Korean		
1910	AUG. 22. Annexation of Korea by Japan		
1912	JULY 30. Death of Emperor Meiji, accession of son, Yoshihito		

PERIOD OF TAISHO EMPEROR 1912–1926

YEAR	POLITICAL	MILITARY	CULTURAL
1914		AUG. 23. Japanese declaration of war on Germany (World War I)	
		NOV. 7. Capture of Qingdao	
1915	JAN. 18. Twenty-One Demands on China presented to Yuan Shikai		
1917	NOV. 2. Lansing-Ishii exchange of notes with U.S., recognizing Japan's special interests in China		
1918	SEPT. 29. Hara Kei of Seiyukai party becomes premier, first commoner in post	APR. Japanese and British forces land at Vladivostok	
1920	JAN. 10. Peace concluded with Germany. Japanese given mandate over former German Pacific islands		
1921	NOV. 4. Assassination of Premier Hara		

YEAR	POLITICAL	MILITARY	CULTURAL
	NOV. 12. Washington Conference		
	Formation of Japanese Communist party		
1922	Nine Power Treaty and Open Door Policy		
	OCT. Withdrawal from Vladivostok		
	NOV. Return of Kiaochow (Qingdao) to China		
1923	SEPT. 1. Tokyo and Yokohama earthquake		
1925	MAR. Universal manhood suffrage and Peace Preservation Law		
1926	DEC. 25. Death of Emperor Taisho, accession of Emperor Hirohito		
1928	FEB. 20. First general election under universal manhood suffrage	JUNE 4. Bomb attack on Zhang Zuolin in Manchuria	
1930	APR. 22. London Naval Treaty		
1931		SEPT. 18. Manchurian Incident	
1932	FEB. 18. Creation of Manchukuo	JAN. 28–MAR. 3. Shanghai campaign	
1933	FEB. 24. Lytton Report on Manchuria adopted by League of Nations		
1935	NOV. East Hopei Autonomous Regime set up		
1936	NOV. 25 Anti-Comintern Pact	FEB. 26. Assassination of government ministers in Tokyo by troops of First Division	
1937		JULY. 7. Outbreak of war with China. Clash at Marco Polo Bridge, near Beijing	
		DEC. 13. Capture of Nanjing	

YEAR	POLITICAL	MILITARY	CULTURAL
1938	MAR. 24. National Mobilization Law	OCT. 21. Capture of Canton	
1939	JULY 27. Denunciation of 1911 Trade Treaty by U.S.	APR.–JULY. Fighting on Manchukuo-Outer Mongolia border	
	AUG. 23. German-Soviet non-aggression pact	SEPT. 1. Outbreak of war in Europe (World War II)	
1940	MAR. Wang Jingwei puppet regime set up in Nanjing	SEPT. 23. Entrance of Japanese troops into French Indo-China	
	JULY 6–AUG. 15. Dissolution of political parties		
	SEPT. 27. Tripartite Alliance of Japan with Germany and Italy		
	OCT. 12. Inauguration of Imperial Rule Assistance Association		
1941	MAR. 8. Cordell Hull and Ambassador Nomura Kichisaburo begin conversations	JULY 24. Occupation of southern Indo-China	
	APR. 13. Soviet-Japanese neutrality pact	DEC. 7. Attack on Pearl Harbor and start of Pacific War	
	OCT. 18. General Tojo as premier		
1942	NOV. 1. Greater East Asia Ministry set up	JUNE 3–5. Battle of Midway	
		AUG. 7–FEB. 9, 1943. Guadalcanal campaign	
1943	JAN. Casablanca Conference		
1944		JUNE 19–JULY 9. Saipan in Marianas falls to U.S. forces: Japan within bombing range	
		NOV. 24. B-29 bombings of Japan begin	
1945	JULY 26. Potsdam Proclamation	FEB. 5. Fall of Manila	
		APR. 1–JUNE 23. Okinawa campaign	

YEAR	POLITICAL	MILITARY	CULTURAL
		MAY 8. Germany surrenders	
		AUG. 6. Atomic bomb, Hiroshima	
		AUG. 8. U.S.S.R. enters the war	
		AUG. 9. Atomic bomb, Nagasaki	
	AUG. 14. Japan accepts terms of Potsdam Proclamation		
	SEPT. 2. Formal surrender received on U.S.S. *Missouri*		
	DEC. 15. Disestablishment of Shinto		
1946	JAN. 1. Emperor's denial of his own divinity		
	OCT. Land Reform Law enacted		
1947	MAY 3. New constitution		
1948	DEC. 23. Gen. Tojo and six others executed as war criminals		
1949	MAY 12. Announcement made of ending of removals for reparations and limitations on industry by Oct. 1.		
1950	AUG. 10. National Police Reserve created	JUNE 25. South Korea invaded by North Korea	
1951	APR. 11. Gen. MacArthur dismissed, Gen. Matthew Ridgway appointed Supreme Commander		
	SEPT. 8. Peace treaty signed with 48 nations		
	U.S.-Japan Security Pact signed		
1952	FEB. 28. Agreement regarding U.S. bases in Japan		
1953		JULY 27. Cease-fire in Korea	

YEAR	POLITICAL	MILITARY	CULTURAL
1955	DEC. U.S.S.R. veto on Japan's membership in UN		
1956	MAY 9. Japanese-Soviet fisheries agreement		
	DEC. 12. Japan admitted to U.N.		
1957	DEC. 6. Treaty of Commerce signed with U.S.S.R.		
1959	APR. 10. Crown prince and Shoda Michiko (commoner) married		
1960	JAN. 19. Treaty of Mutual Security and Cooperation with U.S.		
1964			Tokyo Olympiad
1965	Japan joins Asian Development Bank		Death of Tanizaki Junichiro, novelist (b. 1886)
1969	NOV. Premier Sato Eisaku visits Washington: negotiated return of Okinawa, effective 1972		JUNE. Final link of Tokyo-Kobe auto expressway opened
1970	Law passed in the Diet, making pollution a crime		MAR. 15. Expo '70 opened in Osaka
1972	SEPT. Peace treaty with China signed		Death of Mishima Yukio, novelist (b. 1925)
1973	Beginning of the oil crisis		Death of Kawabata Yasunari, novelist (b. 1899)
1976	Lockheed scandal		
1985	Nippon Telephone and Telegraph privatized		
	Equal Opportunity Law passed		
1986	APR. Sixty-year reign of Emperor Hirohito celebrated		
	Doi Takako (woman) elected leader of Socialist Party		
1987	Japan National Railways privatized		
	OCT. Stock market collapsed worldwide		

YEAR	POLITICAL	MILITARY	CULTURAL
1988	Recruit scandal began		
1989	JAN. Death of Emperor Hirohito		
1990	NOV. Enthronement of Emperor Akihito		
1991	Emperor Akihito visits China		DEC. Fiftieth anniversary of attack on Pearl Harbor
1992	JAN. U.S. President Bush's visit to Tokyo The Japan New Party formed	MAY. Law to permit troops overseas for U.N. purposes	SEPT. Mohri Manoru, first Japanese astronaut into space
1993	Liberal Democratic Party defeated. Hosokawa Morihiro of the New Party, Prime Minister		JUNE. Wedding of Prince Naruhito and Miss Owada Masako
1994	JUNE 29. Murayama Tomiichi, Chairman of the Social Democratic Party of Japan becomes prime minister		FEB. 4. Japan successfully launches its H-II rocket from Tanegashima Space Center. This rocket was completely developed in Japan OCT. 13. Oe Kenzaburo received the Nobel Prize in Literature
1995	AUG. 15. Prime Minister Murayama expresses "deep remorse" and "heartfelt apology" for Japan's role in WWII		JAN. 17. A massive earthquake strikes Kobe killing more than 6,300 and causing trillions of yen in damage MAR. 20. Members of the Aum Shinrikyo cult launch a sarin attack in the Tokyo subways killing 12 and injuring 5,500
1997			NOV. 24. Yamaichi Securities declares bankruptcy—the largest corporate failure ever in Japan
1998	OCT. 17. Emperor Akihito expresses "deep sorrow" for the suffering of Koreans during the years of Japanese occupation. Prime Minister Obuchi apologizes the next day		SEPT. 6. Film director Kurosawa Akira dies. He was the first Japanese to win an international film award 1999

YEAR	POLITICAL	MILITARY	CULTURAL
			AUG. 6. The Health and Welfare Ministry announces that as of 1998 the Japanese had an average life expectancy of 84 for women and 77 for men, making them the longest-lived people in the world

THE 21st CENTURY

2003			NOV. Toyota Motor Company displaces U.S. DaimlerChrysler as number three in the United States and nips at the heels of Ford and General Motors

PRIME MINISTERS

1972–1974	Tanaka Kakuei
1974–1976	Miki Takeo
1976–1978	Fukuda Takeo
1978–1980	Ohira Masayoshi
1980–1982	Suzuki Zenko
1982–1987	Nakasone Yasuhiro
1987 NOV.–1989 APR.	Takeshita Noboru
1989 JUNE–AUG.	Uno Sousuki
1989 AUG.–1991 SEPT.	Kaifu Toshiki
1991 SEPT.–1993 AUG.	Miyazawa Kiichi
1993 AUG.–1994 APR.	Hosokawa Morihiro
1994 APR.–1994 JUNE	Hata Tsutomu
1994 JUNE–1996 JAN.	Murayama Tomiichi
1996 JAN.–1998 JULY	Hashimoto Ryutaro
1998 JULY–2000 APR.	Obuchi Keizo
2000 APR.–2001 APR.	Mori Yoshihiro
2001 APR.–	Koizumi Junichiro

BIBLIOGRAPHY

Baba, Rensei. "The Rebirth of the Factory," *Japan Close Up,* March 2001.

Beasley, W.G. *The Modern History of Japan.* New York: Praeger, 1963.

Bock, Audie. *Japanese Film Directors.* New York: Kodansha International, 1978.

Bouissou, Jean-Marie. *Japan: The Burden of Success.* Boulder, CO: Lynne Rienner Publishers, 2002.

Burks, Ardath W. *Japan—A Postindustrial Power*, 3rd rev. ed. Boulder, CO: Westview Press, 1991.

Collingwood, Dean W. *Japan and the Pacific Rim.* Guilford, CT: McGraw-Hill/Dushkin Company, 2001.

Craig, Albert M., ed. *Japan, A Comparative View.* Princeton, NJ: Princeton University Press, 1979.

Dower, John W. *Embracing Defeat: Japan in the Wake of World War II.* New York: W.W. Norton, 1999.

Dower, John W. *War Without Mercy: Race and Power in the Pacific War.* New York: Pantheon Books, 1986.

Fairbank, John K., Edwin O. Reischauer, Albert M. Craig. *East Asia, Tradition and Transformation.* Boston: Houghton Mifflin, 1973.

Ghosn, Carlos. "Putting Nissan Back on Track," in Masuzoe Yoichi. *Years of Trial: Japan in the 1990s.* Tokyo: Japan Echo, 2000.

Gibney, Frank. *Japan—The Fragile Superpower.* New York: Norton, 1975.

Gluck, Carol. *Japan's Modern Myths: Ideology in the late Meiji Period.* Princeton, NJ: Princeton University Press, 1985.

Gordon, Andrew. *A Modern History of Japan from the Tokugawa to Present Times.* New York and Oxford: Oxford University Press, 2003.

Gyohten, Toyo. "Japan's Sheltered Banks Face the World," in Masuzoe Yoichi. *Years of Trial: Japan in the 1990s.* Tokyo: Japan Echo, 2000.

Hall, John Whitney. *Japan from Prehistory to Modern Times*. New York: Dell Publishing, 1970.

Hall, John Whitney, and Richard K. Beardsley. *Twelve Doors to Japan*. New York: McGraw-Hill, 1965.

Hardie, Robert. *The Burma-Siam Railway. The Secret Diary of Dr. Robert Hardie, 1942–1945*. London: The Imperial War Museum, 1983; Quadrant Books, 1984.[1]

Iwao, Sumiko. "Problems Among Japan's Young," in Masuzoe Yoichi. *Years of Trial: Japan in the 1990s*. Tokyo: Japan Echo, 2000.

Hendry, Joy. *Understanding Japanese Society*. 3rd ed. London and New York: Routledge Curzon, 2003.

Hollerman, Leon, ed. *Japan and the United States: Economic and Political Adversaries*. Boulder, CO: Westview Press, 1979.

Hunter, Janet. *Concise Dictionary of Modern Japanese History*. Berkeley: University of California Press, 1984.

The International Society for Educational Information, Inc. *The Japan of Today,* 3rd. ed. Tokyo: The International Society for Educational Information, 1996.

Jansen, Marius B., ed. *Changing Japanese Attitudes Towards Modernization*. Princeton, NJ: Princeton University Press, 1965.

Kawai, Hayao. "The Message from Japan's Schoolgirl Prostitutes," in Masuzoe Yoichi. *Years of Trial: Japan in the 1990s*. Tokyo: Japan Echo, 2000.

Keene, Donald. *Anthology of Japanese Literature from the Earliest Era to the Mid-nineteenth Century*. New York: Grove Press, 1955.

Keene, Donald. *Modern Japanese Literature*. New York: Grove Press, 1956.

Keene, Donald. *Emperor of Japan: Meiji and His World*. New York: Columbia University Press, 2002.

Kitagawa, Joseph M. *Religion in Japanese History*. New York: Columbia University Press, 1966.

Kusaka, Kimindo. "The Demise of the Japanese Salaryman," in Masuzoe Yoichi. *Years of Trial: Japan in the 1990s*. Tokyo: Japan Echo, 2000.

Lockwood, William W., ed. *The State and Economic Enterprise in Modern Japan*. Princeton, NJ: Princeton University Press, 1965.

Masuzoe, Yoichi. *Japan in the 1990s*. Tokyo: Japan Echo, 2000.

McClain, James L. *Japan: A Modern History*. New York and London: W. W. Norton, 2002.

Morita, Akio. "A Critical Moment for Japanese Management," in Masuzoe Yoichi. *Years of Trial: Japan in the 1990s*. Tokyo: Japan Echo, 2000.

Nakane, Chie. *Japanese Society*. Berkeley and Los Angeles: University of California Press, 1970.

Ozawa, Terutomo. "Putting the Pieces in Place for Japan's Economic Recovery," *Asian Pacific Issues*, 57, Honolulu: East West Center, December 2001.

---

[1] It is significant that a change of attitude in Japan led to the publication of a Japanese translation of this book in 1993.

Reischauer, Edwin O. *Japan—The Story of a Nation*, rev. ed. New York: Alfred A. Knopf, 1974, formerly titled *Japan: Past and Present*.

Reischauer, Edwin O. *The Japanese*. Cambridge, MA: Belknap-Harvard University Press, 1978.

Sansom, G.B. *Japan—A Short Cultural History*, rev. ed. New York: Appleton-Century, 1944.

Seidensticker, Edward G., trans., Murasaki. *Tale of Genji*. New York: Alfred A. Knopf, 1976. See also translation by Arthur Waley, Boston: Houghton Mifflin, 1925–1933.

Shimada, Haruo. "Asset Inflation and the Strained Social Fabric," in Masuzoe Yoichi. *Years of Trial: Japan in the 1990s*. Tokyo: Japan Echo, 2000.

Shirokauer, Conrad. *A Brief History of Japanese Civilization*. New York: Harcourt, Brace Jovanovich, 1993.

Storry, Richard. *A History of Modern Japan*, rev. ed. Baltimore: Pelican, 1965.

Tiedemann, Arthur E., ed. *An Introduction to Japanese Civilization*. New York and London: Columbia University Press, 1974.

Totman, Conrad. *A History of Japan*. Malden, MA: Blackwell Publishers, 2000.

Tsunoda, Ryusaku, William Theodore de Bary, and Donald Keene. *Sources of the Japanese Tradition*. New York: Columbia University Press, 1958.

Tsurumi, S. *A Cultural History of Postwar Japan*, 1945–1980. London: Methuen, 1987.

Ushio, Jiro and Ronald Dore. "Constancy and Change in Japanese Management," in Masuzoe Yoichi. *Years of Trial: Japan in the 1990s*. Tokyo: Japan Echo, 2000.

Van Vranken Hickey, Denis. *The Armies of East Asia: China, Taiwan, Japan, and the Koreas*. Boulder, CO: Lynn Rienner, 2001.

Varley, H. Paul. *Japanese Culture—A Short History*, 3rd expanded ed. New York: Praeger, 1984.

Vogel, Ezra. *Japan as Number One: Lessons for America*. Cambridge, MA: Harvard University Press, 1979.

Waley, Arthur. No *Plays of Japan*. New York: Alfred A. Knopf, 1922, and Grove Press.

Walthall, Anne. *The Human Tradition in Modern Japan*. Wilmington, DE: SR Books, 2002.

Ward, Robert E., ed. *Political Development in Modern Japan*. Princeton, NJ: Princeton University Press, 1968.

Warner, Langdon. *The Enduring Art of Japan*. New York: Grove Press, 1952.

INDEX

About the Authors

W. Scott Morton is professor emeritus of Chinese and Japanese history and culture and of ancient history at Seton Hall University in New Jersey.

J. Kenneth Olenik is professor of history at Montclair State University in New Jersey.